The
Last Lords of Palenque

The Last Lords of Palenque

The Lacandon Mayas of the Mexican Rain Forest

by
Victor Perera
and
Robert D. Bruce

UNIVERSITY OF CALIFORNIA PRESS
Berkeley   Los Angeles   London

University of California Press
Berkeley and Los Angeles, California
University of California Press, Ltd., London, England

Originally published by Little, Brown, Boston
First California Paperback Edition 1985

Special thanks are due Yaddo, MacDowell and the Virginia Center for the Creative Arts, where portions of this book were written. Portions of this book have appeared in *Center*, *Parabola*,
East West Journal, and *Quarry West*.

Library of Congress Cataloging in Publication Data

Perera, Victor, 1934–
    The last lords of Palenque.

    Reprint. Originally published: 1st ed. Boston:
Little, Brown, ©1982. With new postscript.
    Bibliography: p.
    1. Lacandon Indians.   I. Bruce S., Roberto D.
II. Title.
F1221.L2P47   1985   972'.00497   84-28056
ISBN 0-520-05309-5

Designed by Janis Capone

Printed in the United States of America
        3   4   5   6   7   8   9

The paper used in this publication meets the minimum requirements
of American National Standard for Information Sciences—Permanence
of Paper for Printed Library Materials, ANSI Z39.48-1984. ∞

For Chan K'in

The archetype of the old man who has seen enough is eternally with us.

— C. G. Jung

And to me the men in Mexico are like trees, forests that the white men felled in their coming. But the roots of the trees are deep and alive and forever sending up new shoots.

— D. H. Lawrence

The
Last Lords of Palenque

Introduction

I first met Chan K'in of Nahá* in 1957, when I was twenty-three and on leave from my studies at the University of Oklahoma. To my surprise, he already seemed to know all about me, possibly because of my introduction the year before to the Lacandon Maya community of Monte Líbano in Chiapas, Mexico. There I had administered medicines for the familiar symptoms of malaria, internal parasites, infections and snake-bite. Most of the questions I had asked José Güero, the leader of the community, regarding the gods and the cult I was seeing were met with the evasive "I don't remember . . . but maybe Chan K'in of Nahá does . . ." I had not realized that what he was really telling me, in his own way, was that no one was going to instruct me in the Lacandon religion without the approval of their highest traditional authority. I hadn't even known that they recognized such an authority, although I should have been able to interpret their affirmation that "he knows more than anyone else."

When I first saw Chan K'in I felt at once that I must never tell him the smallest lie, but I was not aware of anything that I would then have called "supernatural" about him. It simply seemed obvious that, just as I can see from a person's eyes and expression whether he is happy or sad, worried or amused, Old Chan K'in could see a bit more of the same; he could also see if a person was lying or telling the truth, if he was hiding something, and if so, make a pretty good guess at what it might be. (All my observations since then tend to bear out my first impression, except for those instances in which he revealed capacities that could be called parapsychological, for lack of a better understanding of them.)

When I told him that I hoped to learn of his traditions and write them

* Technically, Nahá should carry an apostrophe (Naha'), but for typographical convenience we are using an acute accent, as in Spanish (Najá).

2

down so they would never be lost, his answer was instantaneous: "Yes, I already know of your interest in our ways. Come to my house and I will teach you what you want to know."

After only a few days of Chan K'in's instruction, listening to the stories of the creation of the earth and the exploits of the gods, I had virtually the same information as the recognized authorities on Lacandon mythology had, only more of it. And there were significant differences in the sequence and structure of the narratives. On these points of difference, I began imagining how their informants must have said it in pidgin Spanish, and how my predecessors must have committed their errors in translation. But then I asked myself, "Or am I the one who has made the error in translation? Or to what degree are we all mistaken?"

Chan K'in would dictate to me something clumsy, unwieldy, which didn't make much sense no matter how hard he struggled for the words in his limited Spanish. Finally, he himself would become impatient and break over into Lacandon Maya, no longer telling the story to me but to any other Lacandon who might be present. The change was dramatic: His voice became smooth and fluid, full of changing inflections, and when I looked at the face of any Lacandon listener, I could see that the old man's words had picked him up and carried him away to some other world. This was not what I had been getting, nor had any of the other investigators gotten it.

There was only one solution to the problem: I must do my study in the original Lacandon Maya and expand my limited vocabulary from a few useful phrases to a proper and fluent command of the language. With Chan K'in's patient coaching and three- and four-hour-long daily drills in grammar and vocabulary, I soon made some progress. Besides the paradigms I made from short phrases with their rough and free translation into Spanish, my principal texts consisted of the recitations I had transcribed (without ever fully understanding their content), in which Old Chan K'in told of the creation of the earth and how the gods established their respective dominions over the various aspects of reality. I found that these stories often paralleled Genesis or the Quiché Mayas' *Popol Vuh* (Book of Counsel); corrected and somewhat expanded they still form the basis of what I now call *The Book of Chan K'in.*

I dedicated myself not only to studying the Lacandon language and culture full time, but to living as a Lacandon as well. I wore the cotton tunic (*xikul*), went barefoot and let my hair grow halfway down my back, and I carried a machete and a deerskin pouch over my shoulders. Besides cartridges and fishhooks, a file and a pocketknife, I also carried a notebook and pen, the only significant variation on the customary contents of a Lacandon man's *pooxah* (leather pouch). I also preferred a .22 caliber target revolver to a rifle or shotgun, the longer barrel of which would hang up on the brush and vines.

Except when I took out my pen and notebook and became engrossed in my work as an anthropologist and linguist, I began to look and act as much like a Lacandon as my physical and racial type would permit. Months of isolation completed my familiarity with the jungle environment to which the Lacandon culture was so admirably adapted. After three or four months my own adaptation was so complete that even now, years later, one or another professional colleague will say of me, "Bruce is no linguist. He is a Lacandon informant."

I

H is name is Chan K'in. Chan means "little" and K'in is "sun, prophecy, prophet." He lives at a place called Nahá (Great Water) on the lake of the same name. Chan K'in ti' Nahá could be translated Little Prophet of the Great Water. He is the firstborn son of the previous "great one," Bol Kasyaho'.

The "great one" — *t'o'ohil* in his own Maya language — is the religious and civic leader of the northern Lacandon Indians, a small ethnic group in the jungles of the state of Chiapas in southern Mexico. Chan K'in's community has no written traditions, so his genealogy becomes lost after a very few generations, but where it comes to an end it points directly back to the throne of Palenque, one of the most important archaeological sites of the so-called Old Empire of the ancient Maya civilization, which flourished in the seventh and eighth centuries A.D.

There is disagreement among the specialists, but every day it becomes a bit more clearly substantiated that the Maya civilization was a direct continuation or evolution of the ancient Olmec culture, whose origins are as yet lost in antiquity, some three millennia ago. The Olmec civilization rose from 1260 to 1200 B.C., although its formative stages reach back centuries earlier. By 1000 B.C., La Venta, one of its major cities, was built on

the Isthmus of Tehuantepec. Gigantic megalithic stone heads remind us
of the Olmecs' presence in the remote past, but no one really knows who
they were or where they came from. The remains of all the ancient civilizations of Mexico and Central America — those of the Toltecs, the
Aztecs, the Zapotecs, the Otomí and the Mayas — indicate that the
Olmec culture was their point of origin. The pantheon of Lacandon gods,
and the manner in which they are worshipped in Nahá today, also come,
directly and without Christian or any other known influence, from the
ancient Mayas.

Chan K'in of Nahá is in his eighties. He is the oldest and the most respected of the Lacandon elders, and the highest authority and spokesman
for the religion and cultural traditions of his people. Other Lacandon men
a generation younger have lost their vitality and are drifting into senility,
while he still has not a single gray hair in his thick, black mane. His eyes,
his mind and his voice are still clear and firm, and the youngest of his
three wives still bears his children.

He speaks familiarly of the Maya gods, of their individual personalities
and functions, and of the details of their proper cult and the manner of
addressing them. These are part of the living tradition of Lacandon culture, which came down to them without interruption from antiquity.
Chan K'in recites the stories, sings the songs, and dictates the ceremonial
formulae of his ancestors just as he learned them from his father.

Sometimes he says things which seem childish and innocent, as when a
rainbow arcs across the rainy sky: "It is the road of the Luumkab [rain-
bow spirits]. See! They were caught in the rain, and the water makes the
colors of their clothes fade and run."

Sometimes he pronounces simple truths with dazzling clarity: "How
can the missionaries say men shouldn't drink liquor if the gods had liquor
first and showed men how to make and drink it? They say liquor makes a
man loud and mean, but it isn't true. Liquor only makes a man show how
he really is. It is being loud and mean that the gods despise, whether one
drinks or not."

Sometimes he overlaps physical and metaphysical realities: "They are
only stones, but they are not only stones. Long ago the Chukuch
Nok' " — the Long Tunics, as he calls the southern Lacandones — "used
to behave correctly in the homes of the gods. They would say, 'If a person
breaks a stone, he dies,' and they knew that it was true. But now the
young Chukuch Nok' break the stones and shout, 'It is not true! See! I
break the stones in the house of the gods and I do not die.' But they do not
see that they die each time they break a stone."

The term "Lacandon"* is used indiscriminately to refer to both the
northern and the southern Lacandones, two of the groups that comprise
the Peninsular Mayas — the Mayas that live on the Yucatán Peninsula
and in the adjacent lowlands. Only the Lacandones escaped assimilation

* The stress is on the last syllable — La-can-DON; custom omits the acute accent.

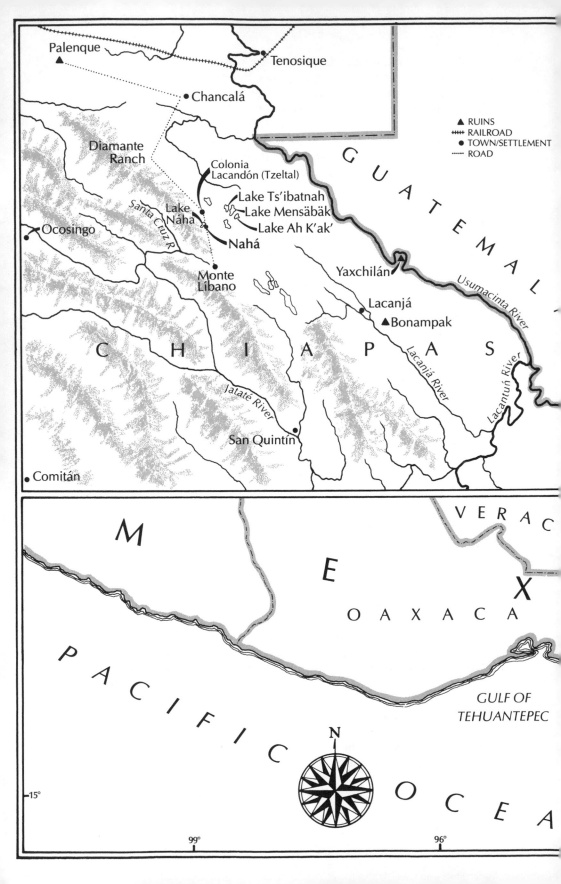

Palenque ▲

Tenosique

Chancalá

Diamante
Ranch

Colonia
Lacandón (Tzeltal)

Lake Ts'ibatnah
Lake Mensäbäk
Lake Ah K'ak'

Santa Cruz R.

Lake
Náha

Nahá

Ocosingo

Monte
Líbano

Yaxchilán

Lacanjá
▲ Bonampak

Usumacinta River

Lacanjá River

Lacantuá River

C H I A P A S

Jataté River

San Quintín

Comitán

▲ RUINS
╫╫╫ RAILROAD
● TOWN/SETTLEMENT
⋯⋯ ROAD

G U A T E M A L

V E R A C

M

E

X

O A X A C A

P

A

C

I

F

I

C

GULF OF
TEHUANTEPEC

O C E A

N

–15°

99°

96°

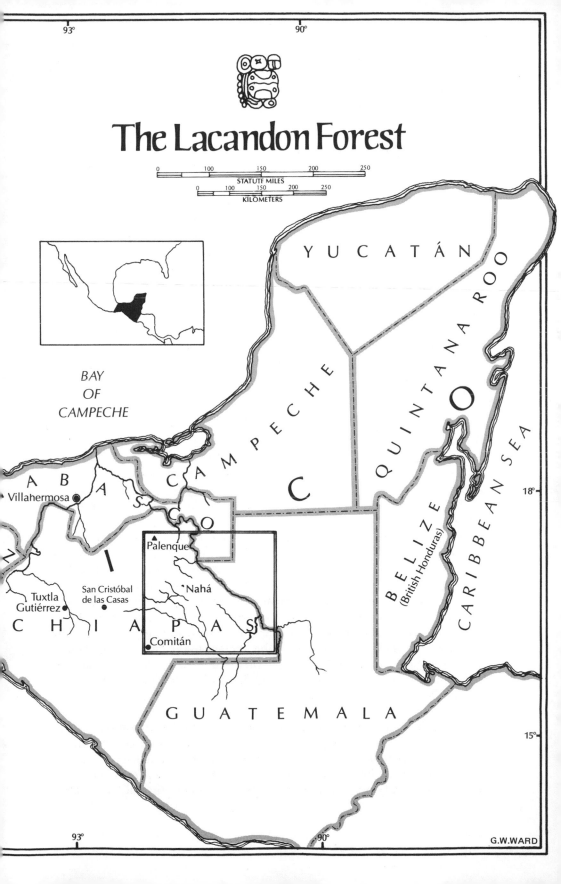

The Lacandon Forest

STATUTE MILES
0   100   150   200   250

KILOMETERS
0   100   150   200   250

YUCATÁN

QUINTANA ROO

BAY
OF
CAMPECHE

CAMPECHE

CARIBBEAN SEA

BELIZE
(British Honduras)

TABASCO

C

Villahermosa

Palenque

Nahá

San Cristóbal
de las Casas

Tuxtla
Gutiérrez

CHIAPAS

Comitán

GUATEMALA

93°   90°   18°   15°

G.W.WARD

or extermination during the Spanish Conquest and the nationalizing influences that came later. The southern group remained culturally intact on the Lacanjá (or Chan Sayab) river, not far from the ruins of their ceremonial center, Yaxchilán; the northern group lived not far from the ruins of Palenque. Each speaks its own dialect of Peninsular Maya, the language of the region. Culturally and linguistically, the degree of difference between them might be compared to that between a New Yorker and a Texan. The two belong to the same culture and they speak the same language. Just as the natives of New York and Dallas all speak English and can converse, so can northern Lacandones and southern Lacandones speak and converse in Peninsular Maya, though they often misunderstand local terms and always despair of each other's "atrocious pronunciation." Inevitably, when members of the two groups converse, there will be one who has no immediate wish to understand the speaker of the other dialect, and will categorically declare it "totally unintelligible."

The origin of "Lacandon" is the Maya plural form *äh akan-tun-oob,* which derives from the agentive *äh,* meaning "the" or "they"; *akan,* "standing" or "set up"; and *tun,* "precious stone" or "stone idol(s)." Thus the *äh akantunoob* were "those who set up (and worship) stone idols." This name was simply a term by which their Christianized Maya neighbors called them the "stone worshippers" or the "pagans." The term also may — or may not — have implied or alluded to "masons" or "builders of temples." Early Spaniards wrote of the Acantunes (the "Pagans" or "Maya wild Indians") and referred to their jungle habitat as El Acantún. Then at one time or another, some early author heard this form as El Lacantún (one of the major rivers in the area still bears this name). Finally, El Lacantún became further deformed to El Lacandón and its inhabitants became the Lacandones.

In the beginning, at the time of the Conquest, the Lacandones were simply the Mayas. Eventually, however, the Spaniards began to distinguish between already dominated and Christianized Maya groups and others — among them the ancestors of the present-day Lacandones — who continued the practice of their traditional, "pagan" religion. Just how many independent groups of Peninsular Mayas may have at one time or another been known as Lacandones we may never know, but they were all Peninsular Mayas. Each group had regional peculiarities of custom and dialect characteristic of their individual city-states or communities, which centered about one of the ancient Maya ceremonial centers. It is probably quite valid to compare them with the ancient Greeks, who didn't consider themselves Greek at all, but rather Spartans or Athenians or members of whatever city-state.

When there is agricultural work to be done, the Lacandon day begins with the first light of dawn. Thick white mist rises and gently billows above the mirror surface of Lake Nahá, and the myriad leaves of the exuberant vegetation hang low and heavy with the cold dew over the jungle trails. Any shady place near Nahá is always cool because of its elevation (twenty-seven hundred feet above sea level). At this altitude the banana plants and similar tropical vegetation meet the pine forests, which thrive on the surrounding hilltops. But the sun of latitude 15°1'20" N becomes uncomfortably hot in the open clearings when it reaches zenith, so work in the fields needs to be done by noon, or not long after.

Chan K'in's house has a two-sided roof some thirty feet long, thatched with leaves of the thorn palm (*kun*). Its rounded ends add another ten feet or so to its length. Rough planks of light balsa wood form the walls, which are without windows or other openings except for the several doors, but the cracks between the planks provide ventilation and, to the practiced eye, vision to the outside.

Apart from his three wives and their eight unmarried children, Chan K'in has three married sons and five sons-in-law living nearby, all willing to do for him any work that is required. But he takes pride in working his own land, his *milpa*. *Milpa* is a Nahuatl word which it is really only ninety percent correct to translate as "cornfield." The remaining ten percent of the *milpa* produces beans, squash, chili peppers, cassava, sweet potatoes, tomatoes, and an ample variety of other fruits and vegetables. Chan K'in also raises tobacco, the traditional commercial crop, which is planted between corn crops.

With the help of his wives and unmarried children, Chan K'in lives a life made up of one yearly *milpa* cycle after another. An area of forest is cleared. When the cut trees and brush have dried they are burned, and seeds are planted in the bare ground among the blackened remains of the charred tree trunks. The *milpa* is then periodically weeded, and is visited almost daily to protect it from the depredations of deer and boar, parrots, squirrels, gophers and anything else that might eat the growing crops. Though the Lacandon traditionally lives from his *milpa,* he must also be a good hunter. A deer that discovers a Lacandon *milpa* must be killed. Either the family eats venison, or later it will eat no beans, as only a few nightly visits of a gluttonous deer will cost the Lacandon his entire bean crop, and then the squash and corn.

When Chan K'in returns from his work in the *milpa,* he sits in his short traditional hammock woven of *majaua* bark. It is slung near one of the fires that burn between three hearthstones on the dirt floor at either end of the house. A calabash plate hangs from a thin fiber cord run through three holes in the edge and suspended from one of the roof beams near his hammock. It is full of *hach k'uuts* (real tobacco; original tobacco), as they call their traditional homemade and homegrown cigars. He is almost always smoking one of them, and generously offers them to the visitor who may come and sit in one of the nearby hammocks to chat and joke with him.

The visitor may often have a pressing motive for coming, but the traditional norms of Lacandon conduct demand that all things — especially the vitally important ones — be treated with calm and poise. Old Chan K'in has a well-earned fame among his people for his powers of *k'inyah* (divination). In the Lacandon view, he has the ability to sound those realities that are not yet manifest (what any occidental language calls fore-telling the future).

When asked if he is the *t'o'ohil,* Old Chan K'in of Nahá usually denies it. He will say, "No. Today no one is the *t'o'ohil.* In my grandfather's time, and even in my father's, there were *t'o'ohil* who were clairvoyant and could speak with the gods." But should one ask any other Lacandon of Nahá or the other northern Lacandon community of Mensäbäk, "Who is the *t'o'ohil?*" the answer is unhesitating: "Old Chan K'in of Nahá!"

Old Chan K'in's manner is much like the simplicity and unpretentious-ness of his house: He makes no display of his noble birth nor of the great respect in which his people hold him.

The clear air, the uncontaminated environment and the privileged cli-mate of Nahá, with the innumerable greens of its surrounding hills and the ever-changing blues of its lake, give it a unique place in the memory of the visitor. But the cultural and human atmosphere of the commu-nity — to the visitor who is sensitive to such things — is even more strik-ing. One usually becomes aware that these people are somehow different from any others he has ever known, but to define and evaluate the differ-ences is another matter.

The Spaniards were not unaware of the Lacandon community, but it was too small and too poor to provide a proper incentive for repeated ex-peditions into the inhospitable, malaria-infested area. Unlike the Yucatán Peninsula, Lacandon was plagued with marshes, flooding rivers, rough outcroppings of rock and impenetrable vegetation. These conditions made the forest impassable for horses and extremely difficult for mules; gunpowder quickly became damp, and Spanish cannons and armor were more of a handicap than an advantage. The few incursions attempted were, no matter how brilliant the apologies and excuses, either partial or total failures.

If the Spanish conquistadores deserve our admiration for their courage, this admiration should not be confused with justification of their deeds. Their derring-do was so spectacular, and is so often recognized, that at times we tend to forget that the Conquest was one of the most immoral and criminal offenses that man ever perpetrated against man.

Fray Diego de Landa, bishop of Mérida, was perhaps the occidental who came the closest to the Mayas' extraordinary knowledge and to the grandeur of their civilization. He was even given some instruction by the Maya nobles in their hieroglyphic writing, and in their sacred calendar, which combined astronomy, astrology and all major physical and meta-physical phenomena into a single, harmonious system. He collected the greatest possible number of these native books, representing one of the most profound bodies of scientific, philosophical and aesthetic knowl-edge the world has ever known — and burned them in the Plaza de Maní when he became aware that they contained "lies of the devil."

In place of the extraordinary library he burned, Landa left us his book, *Relación de las cosas de Yucatán* (An account of the things of Yucatán).

In this book we find, besides constant reiteration of farfetched apologies for the atrocities committed by the Spaniards, numerous data on the Maya culture at the moment it was being destroyed. Occasionally there will be lucid descriptions of ceremonies, rites, customs and beliefs, but they are inevitably followed by passages of ranting in which all the previously mentioned deities are called devils indiscriminately.

Once the Conquest had begun, the Spaniards were clearly in no position to expend too much admiration or sympathy on Maya culture; they had to destroy the Mayas' functional social organization before it would destroy them. Soon the deed was done: The great teachers and leaders were murdered, the books burned, the schools and temples razed, and from the fine limestone blocks of their rubble, new Catholic churches, chapels, monasteries and cathedrals were built. The traditional arts, sciences and ethnic values were lost. The people were confused, leaderless and enslaved.

Maya culture survived intact only in the most remote communities, and in ones small and economically unimportant enough to escape notice. These were cut off from traditional Maya commerce, and as the peasant population dwindled, the nobles had to lower their standard of living. From a leisured, esoteric elite, the astronomers, mathematicians and warriors became proletarians: *milpa* farmers, fishermen and hunters.

How long did their calendar, mathematics and hieroglyphic writing survive? Did they disappear in the first generation after the remaining Mayas lost contact with the Classic Maya city-states, which had been destroyed by the Spaniards? Or were they only slowly and gradually worn down, to become totally lost only a generation or two before the present? However the reduction of their cultural inventory may have occurred, it is clear that they clung to their religion and gave the metaphysical preference over the physical. Their hieroglyphic writing was reduced to a few abstract paintings on the backs of their incense burners. Their mathematics were reduced to the most basic elements. Their astronomy became only the recognition of the major planets and constellations — and an occasional declaration of awed admiration that their grandparents could look at the sky just after dark on the day a child was born and there read the child's destiny. Their vast calendrical lore survives only in a few lunar formulae for planting, and the few ceremonies that are determined by the solar year are not corrected by astronomical observation (with one or two exceptions), but by the time of flowering of one or another tree. Even so, the cultural fragments and incomplete formulae one finds fossilized in Lacandon culture are such that they could only have had their origins in a great civilization like that of the Classic Mayas. And the ancient Olmec civilization from which it derived could only have had its beginnings in some exaltation of human genius so radically different from our own that we are incapable of understanding it.

The Olmec–Maya calendar was an incredibly complex and sophisticated system of knowledge that tied together astronomy, astrology, climatology, meteorology and tellurological activity, together with the collective and individual destinies of men, in a single complex of interrelated, recurring cycles. It integrated the physical and the metaphysical, the natural and supernatural phenomena, in a single system that was the slide rule and computer of each and every Mesoamerican civilization. The same calendrical system was expressed in distinctive forms in the central Mexican plateau, among the Zapotecs, among the lowland or Peninsular Mayas, and among various groups of the southern Maya highlands.

This highly sophisticated system of knowledge is only conceivable (to the occidental thinker, at least) as the product of a long and cumulative tradition of methodical, scientific observation and analysis of the highest order. It would seem logical to assume that this occurred during the thousand years that elapsed from the laying of the foundations of La Venta on the Isthmus of Tehuantepec (about 1000 B.C.) to the carving, in Veracruz, of the two oldest Mayan objects with inscribed dates: a stela at Tres Zapotes carved in the Mayan year corresponding to 31 B.C., and the "Tuxtla statuette," a jadeite figure that bears a date only a few decades later. Both bear the Classic Maya style of writing, and both are Olmec. They can be thought of as the "missing links" between the Olmec and Maya manifestations of a single cultural tradition. It also seems reasonable to assume that any inscribed dates earlier than these were made on wood, paper, parchment, or other perishable materials — or on stones still awaiting the archaeologist. But we don't really know.

Current anthropological knowledge and methodology suggest that the present-day Lacandones of Nahá are in fact the direct descendants of the ancient Mayas of Palenque. Their language is the same Peninsular Maya, which is recognizable in some portions of the ancient Maya codices and in the inscriptions at Palenque. Their numerical system is also the same, down to the numerical classifiers and syntactic use. In addition, the Lacandones have no migration myth, and each group considers the nearest major ancient Maya ceremonial center (Palenque in the north and Yaxchilán in the south) to be the center of the earth and the place where the gods created man.

When Old Chan K'in of Nahá visited Palenque, he listed the gods who were the "owners of the houses." Each of the ruined temples was the house of a Lacandon god. Until the generation before that of Old Chan K'in, Palenque was the major site for pilgrimages. Pilgrimages are now made to secondary ruins and natural rock faces because Palenque is occupied by the tourists and guarded by the Mexican government.

Tourists in Palenque frequently ask: "But how could people *live* in such small, cramped rooms?" Of course, no one did. On the auspicious days indicated by the Olmec–Maya calendar — the Tzolkin and the Haab — religious theocrats donned the indumentary and the emblems, took their seats in the "houses," and there received offerings, and answered in the names of the gods they represented — or *became* — during the ceremony. Then they returned to their homes (probably much like

Old Chan K'in's), where they actually lived, swung their hammocks, roasted venison and wild boar, and smoked their cigars, as their women ground the corn and patted out and baked tortillas on clay griddles.

The names, titles and functions of the Lacandon gods may frequently be recognized in the inscriptions of the codices and monuments, and in the chronicles of the "pagan beliefs" of New Spain at the time of the Spanish Conquest. Some of the present-day Lacandon ceremonies survive directly from their Classic Maya counterparts. Fray Diego de Landa's description of the "renewal of the idols in the month of Pop" may be considered a very nearly accurate description of the renewal of the Lacandon incense burners in Nahá in 1970. The differences are characteristic of all the differences between the Lacandones and the ancient Mayas: Landa's description of the ceramic incense burners and their ceremonial treatment would be quite applicable to the Lacandon "god-pots"; but Landa describes wooden idols, which the Lacandones no longer make. The Classic Mayas' temple was also larger and more sophisticated than the palm-thatched "god-house" of Nahá. The Lacandon variation constitutes a reduction of elements and quantities, and in this respect it is not unlike the modifications of the Christian church after Martin Luther's Protestant Reform. A religion exiled by that of a dominant culture can neither afford nor defend great cathedrals or monasteries or extensive collections of sacred relics.

For the preceding reasons, we consider Old Chan K'in of Nahá to be the direct descendant of the rulers of Palenque at the time of its Classic splendor, or of the rulers of some other ceremonial center very much like it. This view is not shared by all authorities.

At present, several hypotheses of the origin of the Lacandones exist besides the one accepted in this book. To enumerate, discuss and argue their many and varied contentions would require our becoming far more technical than we care to here. It is beyond doubt, however, that the northern Lacandones today are the last people to practice the ancient Maya religion, which was once common to all of the Yucatán Peninsula and the adjoining lowlands, in anything like its original form and content. There are no more unknown, unexplored jungles to yield any other Maya ethnic group that might compete with the Lacandones' conservatism. The Lacandones are the last and the only direct cultural heirs of the Maya civilization. As the *t'o'ohil,* whose authority is recognized by all other Lacandon *t'o'ohil,* Old Chan K'in is by virtue of this position, not only Lord of Palenque, but the last of the *halach winik* (great lords) of the Olmec–Maya tradition. And as such, he is also Lord of Yaxchilán, of Copán, of Tikal, and though millions of Yucatec Maya voices may be raised in protest, he is Lord of Chichén Itzá and Mayapán as well.

In years to come, archaeologists and ethnohistorians may discover much more data and detail about the ancient Maya civilization, the shifts of power, migrations, wars and alliances, ends and beginnings of lineages, et cetera, and this will enrich our knowledge of Maya culture. But if Old Chan K'in is not, as we assume, descended by a direct line of primogeniture from one of the ruling families of Palenque, he is still the last traditional ruling lord of the Peninsular Mayas.

II

The northern Lacandones today number slightly over two hundred fifty — men, women and children. Even the greater number of a "total Lacandon population," arrived at by lumping northerners and southerners together, is still less than four hundred. Counting the number of scholarly and popular books, monographs and magazines and newspaper articles about the Lacandones brings one to the somewhat surprising discovery that there are more Lacandon publications than there are Lacandones.

What accounts for the worldwide fame of this small group of people, and for the passionate interest in them? Most of the ready answers must be recognized as rationalizations; for even persons who have dedicated years of their lives to studying the Lacandones are usually not sure what first sparked their curiosity and then grasped part of their being, never allowing them to lose interest in the *hach winik* — the true, or real, people, as the Lacandones call themselves. There are probably few places on earth where one finds more "seekers" than in the Lacandon jungle. Perhaps we sense that by studying the Lacandones we can discover where our sophisticated, occidental civilization went wrong.

Naturalists contend that "six square miles of land is an adequate basis for knowing nature and reality." The trouble with this contention is that most of us require contrast in order to appreciate and understand the vital truths we have right before us all the time. Even the greatest possible extremes of geographic separation between Old World cultures, such as those of the Celts, Africans and Chinese, cannot provide the contrast possible between any of these and Mesoamerican culture, which is to say, the descendants of the various high cultures of Central America and of southern North America, all of which have their points of origin in the enigmatic Olmec civilization.

As of the 1950's the formal contact between the Lacandon and occidental cultures had not changed significantly since its inception several decades before. Shortly after the tobacco was harvested, offered to the gods, and available for everyday use, traders would come from Tenosique, San Cristóbal and other surrounding towns. Usually it would be the same trader who had come for the tobacco the year before and who brought with him the ax heads, files, ammunition, salt, factory-woven cloth, needles and thread, and fishhooks that had been ordered on his last visit. Most of them also bought liquor. Some of the Lacandon men who acquired a lasting taste for the cheap rotgut or rum refused to do business unless the trader brought them a gift bottle to initiate the proceedings.

Others learned to accept the gift bottle, but to refuse to taste it until after the business had been conducted and the trader was gone.

The attitude of the young Lacandones whom I saw watching their elders deal with the bearers of a strange new culture is difficult for the occidental to describe. Indeed, the Lacandones themselves are a challenge to the capacity to describe and categorize in the occidental languages in which we think. One is tempted to call their watchfulness from a cool and proper distance "shy," but the word has connotations of fear that are simply not applicable. We cannot even call the Lacandones "respectful" without feeling that the term is somehow insufficient. For while the Lacandon's culture provides an automatic respect for each person and each thing in its proper place, his respect for the rights of others comes with no withdrawal — or even temporary suspension — of his own rights. Moreover, something in his attitude and bearing evokes the occidental's classifications of "haughty" or "proud," or even "insolent" or "arrogant" — though once again, the terms aren't totally satisfying.

The occidental term that comes closest to being fully applicable is "poised." The Lacandon seems as much at ease and as confident among local muleteers in a small-town saloon, or with the Mexico City crowds on the subway, or at a presidential banquet, or at an international Jet Set garden party, as he is in his native rain forest. Something about his thought, language and habitual behavior seems to provide him with a basic certainty of being in his proper place and in his proper relation to all other entities he may encounter, a quality difficult for the member of an occidental culture to grasp.

This poise was built into their language. In occidental languages the basic principle is a relation between cause and effect. Noun subjects combine with verbal actions directed toward other nominal objects. People who speak in this manner, or see reality through this glass, act similarly. They impose their verbal will on the objects in nature, domesticating horses and making weapons. People, animals and inanimate objects are treated as grammatical objects, and recipients of the actions of verbs chosen by the grammatical subjects. In time, occidentals extended their verbal will over neighboring tribes, widening political control over ever greater geographic areas.

The basic principles of Maya grammar are possession and location. Each entity has its owner and its place in relation to all others, manifest or hypothetical. Instead of dynamic political empires, the Mayas built harmonious, well-balanced pyramids, with each stone in its proper place. Instead of a dynamic technology and utilitarian science, the Mayas excelled in astronomy and mathematics, which interrelate all the phenomena of the universe, defining where each thing belongs. While occidentals sought to extend their dominion and control over the universe, the Mayas sought to find their proper place in it in order to live in the greatest possible peace and harmony.

It is possible that the Lacandon's "poise" is at the root of all that occidentals find so enigmatic about his culture; that his traditional cosmology provides him with the ability to feel "in place" and in his proper relationship with reality no matter where he may be, and that this sense of orientation is so unique and incomprehensible to the occidental that the vapors of his own failure to understand would appear to shroud the Lacandon in a cloak of mystery. If the ancient Olmec–Maya civilization is a thing of the past, its great cities now lying in ruins, overgrown with jungle vegetation and inhabited by the dumb creatures of the first creation, it is also a thing of the present, for it still lives at Nahá.

A few years after a Lacandon forest house is abandoned, it returns totally to the humus of the jungle floor, and the only archaeological traces that remain are the hearthstones or a few scattered potsherds. Somewhere near where the family god-house stood, an archaeologist might also find an abundance of flint chips, together with cinders and the residue of half-burned incense in what had been the god-house refuse dump. The more permanent traces of the Lacandones would be found at their local shrines — on rock faces — and would consist of petroglyphs and the ritual objects (mostly old incense burners) deposited there or in the ancient Maya temples. The *Popol Vuh*, perhaps the best-known source of ancient Maya traditions, tells how the gods tried several times to create the present generation of men, but that each of the attempts fell short of their expectations. So they ended the cycle and began again. When the second creation came to an end the descendants of these "men," who had been made of wood, returned to the trees of the forest in the form of monkeys. When the Lacandones, who were (according to their traditions) made of clay by the Creator, Hachäkyum, live out their lives, they and all their material possessions return to the floor of the jungle. Only their ancient Maya ceremonial centers — the homes of their immortal gods — remain standing.

All of the Lacandones of Nahá are members of either the Ma'ax (Monkey) or the K'ek'en (Boar) *onen*, or lineage, and it is said that the one can be distinguished from the other by the characteristic form of the fingernails. The *onen* (also called the animal name) is sometimes termed the totem, but this is incorrect: The Lacandones do not consider themselves descended from the animal of their *onen*. Nor is it a nahual, since one cannot take the form of the animal by sorcery; nor is it a tona (or tonal), since one's life is not linked with that of a specific animal. Still, the Lacandon *onen* shows partial and incomplete similarities with all these other native beliefs.

The southern Lacandones of Lacanjá are of the K'ek'en (Boar), the Yuk (Deer) and the K'ambul (Curassow) *onen*. The two last are said to be fierce and aggressive people, and even the Boar People are considered a bit less peaceful than the Monkey People — at least according to Old Chan K'in, who belongs to the Monkey lineage. A compatibility of *onen* is very important in determining marriage partners, since babies of the Boar and Jaguar lineages are said to have very large heads and can be borne with ease only from a Boar or Jaguar (Balum) womb. Babies of the Monkey *onen* have the smallest heads of all and are borne easily and quickly by a Boar or Deer mother, but a Monkey lineage woman can bear only a Monkey lineage baby without extreme difficulty. The *onen* to which one belongs is also important in determining which gods may be well disposed to cure him when he is sick. The gods, like people, have their *onen* and these must be compatible.

Another important factor in determining the possible supernatural causes of illness, and the chances of its being cured, is the recollection and analysis of recent dreams, either of the sick person or anyone associated with him. In the dream world one is able to see tendencies, potentials and all that is hypothetical or not-yet-manifest reality. A dream, properly interpreted, may give the clue or the formula for escaping a potentially adverse destiny.

III

The American missionaries' efforts to Christianize the Lacandones have been under way for over a quarter of a century, and they began some time after the Catholics' failure. (At least, the Catholics failed with the Lacandones who are still Lacandones today. It is possible that they were responsible for the conversion and acculturation of the Jaguar People and the greater part of the Curassow People, who are now assimilated Mexican nationals.)

In the first stages of the attempted conversion, which began at Nahá, it became apparent to the American missionaries that they were face to face with a profound religious dedication that dwarfed even their own most intense moments of religious devotion. The Lacandon man who continued his prayers for the fifth or sixth night without sleep, his face and clothes blackened with incense smoke and his eyes about to close, might interrupt his prayers to speak courteously with the well-dressed, well-fed missionary who peered into the smoke-filled god-house. This he would do because the gods demand courtesy of the "real person." But since he was registering nothing of the conversation, he would return to his prayers and feed incense into the bowl, which was beginning to flicker . . . This was no poor, bewildered, weak-willed savage, to be taken in by a little sweet talk, a glass of cold lemonade or Coca-Cola, and the magic of a transistor radio. Before the Christian conversion could progress, the ancient Olmec-Maya tradition had to be discredited, broken down, and gotten out of the way by any expedient method.

Some of the first strategies of the missionary who had felt himself "called" to be the savior of Nahá were rather infantile. Old Chan K'in still loves to recount with a chuckle how Felipe (Philip Baer), a missionary with the Summer Institute of Linguistics, told him that the power of Jesus Christ to make miracles is limitless. If one needs money, and prays for it with true faith, the next morning it will appear on the table.

Old Mateo, the most respected elder of Nahá after Old Chan K'in, would add, when all the laughter had died down, "But do you remember that after we laughed in his face and asked him, 'Does Jesus Christ *create* things where there was nothing?' he told us that when he had been desperate and prayed for money, one of his companions must have overheard him and put the money there for him — but that it was the spirit of Jesus Christ that made his companion do it."

"That is true," Chan K'in answered. "But just think of it a little. If you need money, and your companion has it to give — say *I* have the money — why would you pray to the gods for it? Would you not just ask me for it? How else should people do?"

"That is true, *yumeh,*"* Mateo answered.

Old Chan K'in shook his head and added, "What kind of people are these who would tell us of the gods? Long ago Hachäkyum and Akinchob [the god of maize] told our people how men should behave with their companions."

"But perhaps Jesus Christ has not yet told the foreigners?" Mateo asked wryly. "Perhaps that is why he needs to make miracles for them — because they do not yet know how to do things for themselves."

"True enough, *yumeh!*" Old Chan K'in answered. "But I don't think any god will do for a man what he knows how to do for himself, not even the god of the foreigners." He did not join Mateo in his laughter, and his eyes took on a faraway look, as though he were about to change from his role as friend and neighbor to that of the ethnic spirit of his people. "Remember the lord of the leaf-cutter ants," he said. Then he began reciting:

> Long ago there was a man, an ancient Lacandon, who went to his *milpa* to find it stripped of corn, beans and squash. He saw the leaf-cutter ants carrying the last of the crops away, and he picked up corn husks — all that was left of his *milpa* — and began burning them, to kill the leaf-cutter ants. Then, what looked like a man but was really Yum Ah Say [the lord of the leaf-cutter ants] appeared before him and asked, "Why are you burning my children?"
>
> The man answered, "Because they have ruined my *milpa,* and now I have nothing to eat. Look! There goes one carrying the last of my grains of corn! What shall I eat? Am I not worthy of respect?"
>
> "You are worthy of respect," the lord of the leaf-cutter ants answered him. "Go away, and come back in three days."
>
> When the man returned after three days, he found his *milpa* better than it had ever been, with much corn, beans, squash and chilis. He was very happy, for he and his family had much to eat.
>
> But the next year, the man thought of all the work that was necessary to make his *milpa.* He made only a small one. Then, when it was nearly grown, he put corn, tortillas and corn broth right in the path of the leaf-cutter ants. When they picked up the food and carried it away, he began burning the ants, until Yum Ah Say appeared before him again, and the man told him, "Look! They are carrying away my food! What shall I eat? Am I not worthy of respect?"

* *Yumeh* (literally, "my lord") is a term of respect used by one elder to another.

"Yes, you are worthy of respect," the lesser god answered him. "Go away and come back in three days."

The man was happy, thinking that they would do all his work for him, and when he came back after three days, he found a big *milpa* with huge ears of corn. When he went to grab them, he discovered that they weren't ears of corn at all, but hornets' nests — all over, on each stalk of corn. *Hwuum!* The hornets swarmed out and stung him from head to foot. He had to run away, and then he was hungry, for he had no *milpa* and nothing to eat.

Old Chan K'in concluded: "No. The gods will not do for a man what he should do for himself. The gods do not like lazy people."

Old Chan K'in's stories, which he had learned from his father, who had learned them from his father, in a tradition apparently three millennia old, are at the disposition of any Lacandon of Nahá in search of guidance, or of anyone else who comes to visit him. He is the classic authority, like that of a dictionary to be consulted. This is, indeed, the traditional Lacandon view of authority: Only the person with enough interest to come in search of counsel will make good use of it anyway.

The Lacandon culture at Nahá could be described as consisting of a flexible and unbreakable core, represented by the authority of its *t'o'ohil*, Old Chan K'in. The rest of the society is an aggregate of independent family units, each one drawn by some invisible force around the core, but all kept movable and separate by the principle of nonconfrontation. Any attack on the Lacandon social organization meets with no tangible, visible resistance from the units of the aggregate, which simply slips blandly out of the way of the intrusive force; and even the core of the organization appears to bend easily whichever way and as far as it is pushed. But the moment the intrusive force is withdrawn, everything returns to its original place and position, leaving no sign of the intrusion.

In their first encounters with the Lacandones, the anthropologists and missionaries must have felt much like the skin diver who sees a school of fish moving or resting in the water before him, a closely integrated mass of life, apparently with some internal organization making the school function as a single organism. Swimming through it, however, he sees it open before him, the nearest fish keeping just out of his reach, and at no point does he find a tangible, central organization. Having passed completely through the school, and looking back from the other side, he sees it just as it was originally, and with no sign of his passing.

In the late 1950's and early 1960's, Philip Baer, the missionary at Nahá, discovered the differences in religious observance between the northern and southern Lacandones, and moved to Lacanjá Chan Sayab. The southern Lacandones there had dropped their active religious practices since the death of their last priest and *t'o'ohil*, Cerón. (Their traditions by then had dwindled to a few nostalgic memories, legends and taboos on behavior.) Their whole Peninsular Maya way of life presupposed a central religious core like that of the northern Lacandones, to give meaning and purpose to their existence. They lacked it, and felt — without understanding their feeling — an undefined sense of loss before their un-Maya, meaningless existence. Their past was out of reach and their future was out of sight. Their present was a comfortless spiritual void.

Probably without fully realizing what he was doing, the missionary simply became a temporary substitute *t'o'ohil*.

José Pepe Chan Bol was the Lacandon who, according to the traditional order of succession at Lacanjá, should have picked up, but for some reason didn't, the original functions of a Lacandon *t'o'ohil*. After a very short time he managed to take over the new, occidental values and to function as preacher and "municipal president" for his community. The form of his function under the "new order" was traditionally Lacandon; only the content had changed.

The abstinences imposed by the new set of moral values were limited to abstention from tobacco and alcoholic beverages — rather simple and poor demands compared with those of their own Maya tradition. The Maya demands had included (though only for limited periods during ritual activity) sexual abstinence, limitations on diet (principally chili pepper), long pilgrimages, and the observance of the rituals indicated by *k'inyah* (divinations), which often implied many days of hard work and nights of sleepless vigil. Still, the new restrictions filled the intensely felt need of the southern Lacandones. It would seem that a set of strange, alien values was better than no values at all.

There is no totally impartial and trustworthy account of how the conversion at Lacanjá occurred, but there is reason to believe that the southern Lacandones simply accepted all that the missionary suggested or asked of them in their already established practice of humoring tourists, anthropologists and other occidental visitors in order to obtain the greatest number of gifts and trade goods from them. And because the southern Lacandones' isolation from the outside world had been broken only in the previous quarter century, they proved more vulnerable to the missionary's enticements.

In his attempt to Christianize the obdurate northern Lacandones of Nahá, who had been exposed to foreign influences since before the turn of the century, Philip Baer first obtained Old Chan K'in's permission to build his house and live there as a member of the community. The permission was gladly given, on the assumption that he would continue to administer medicines and provide transportation facilities on the light planes of Alas de Socorro (Wings of Aid), the organization at the service of the Summer Institute of Linguistics, whenever a member of the community was ill. Once the bungalow, with its electric power plant and modern comforts (at the service of the missionary and his family — not the Lacandon community) was built atop the best ground on the hill overlooking Lake Nahá, the missionary's attitude changed. He would accept nothing in the way of food or gifts from his Lacandon neighbors. Medicines and emergency transportation services were still available to any Nahá Lacandon on request, but the traditional Lacandon values demand reciprocity for favors received. When a Lacandon asked for and received medicines for his sick child, his gifts were not accepted. He was asked only, *"He' wah a na'ksik a wol ti' Hesuklisto?"* ("Now will you lift up your spirit to Jesus Christ?")

The Lacandones are a proud and independent people, and they soon became aware that the "silver lining" of safety and benefit for a Lacandon man's family hid a dark cloud: automatic humiliation and a price tag on their souls.

There were no open complaints, no quarreling, no confrontations. Old Chan K'in suddenly began cutting and setting the posts for his new house across the lake, about a mile away. With very few exceptions, the others followed him. The Nahá Lacandon named Chan Bol was constantly quarreling with his neighbors and had only resentfully accepted Old Chan K'in's authority. He became a convert and abandoned the gods of his fathers. Jorge, who had been living at the periphery of the community, maintained his same location, but one of his sons, Enrique, also became a convert and the missionary's caretaker.

In 1970 the missionary brought José Pepe Chan Bol and his two wives from Lacanjá to Nahá and indicated where José Pepe could make his *milpa*, take up permanent residence, and be actively present in each religious ceremony to carry on the fight against the dominion of the ancient Maya gods. This was simply too much for the northern Lacandones' traditionally peaceful evasion of conflict. Only the *t'o'ohil* had the authority to distribute land for cultivation or building sites. By this time they had learned that the problems arising from the failure of others to respect their rights would often be heard sympathetically by the governor of the state of Chiapas or by his duly appointed officials. A group departed for the state capitol at Tuxtla to protest. Their complaint against the missionary declared, "He may be *t'o'ohil* at Lacanjá Chan Sayab, but at Nahá we have our own authority." Even before they could return with an answer, José Pepe was flown back to Lacanjá.

The proselytizing on the part of the southern Lacandon "evangelists," however, had by no means ceased. The exact details of their work at the Lake Mensäbäk community, some twenty miles north of Nahá, are not known, but the results are painfully visible.

Mensäbäk is the name of the Lacandon rain god, the same Maya deity known as Chaac in Yucatán. His name derives from *men* (make) and *säbäk* (soot; black powder), and could be translated as Powdermaker. (It is said that he makes a black powder of incense soot and smoke, and his assistants scatter it on the clouds, causing thunder, winds and the rain.) The lake named for Mensäbäk is the largest of three interconnected lakes, which also bear the names of Lacandon gods: Ts'ibatnah (Painter of Houses), the lord of the graphic arts; and Ah K'ak' (Fire Lord), the god of hunting, courage and formerly, it would appear, of war.

The northern Lacandon community inhabiting this region became known by the name of the largest of the three interconnected lakes, which is usually rendered, according to the Spanish alphabet and the traditional Mexican disregard for aboriginal names, Metzaboc.

In the early 1950's, the largest subgroup of northern Lacandones was that of Monte Líbano (the Spanish name for Chun K'uche' — Cedar Grove — in the original Lacandon), some twelve miles to the south of Nahá. Its local *t'o'ohil* — who in turn looked for guidance to Old Chan K'in of Nahá — was José Güero. Second in rank to José Güero was Pepe Castillo. (Both of these Lacandon elders had begun life with the name Chan K'in, but began using Spanish names out of respect for Chan K'in of Nahá). In the mid-1950's, the invasion of their lands by neighboring Tzeltal Indians and *ladinos* began.* By the end of the decade, the invader's livestock (pigs, cattle, horses and mules) were intentionally driven into the Lacandones' *milpas* to make life unbearable for them. Then, in the early 1960's, the Lacandones of Monte Líbano made a mass exodus to the Mensäbäk region.

José Güero — who now lives at Nahá and is the father of one of Old Chan K'in's three wives — had suffered progressive arthritis for years and had cultivated an equally progressive alcoholism, which provided him a few hours of occasional general anesthesia. His personal problems were viewed with sympathy and he was still consulted as *t'o'ohil* for advice and critical divination rites. But those who consulted him almost never found him sober enough to offer them more than a drink.

With the exodus to Mensäbäk and the establishment of new houses and new *milpa* sites, the Lacandones of Monte Líbano bypassed José Güero's traditional authority and accepted Pepe Castillo as their *t'o'ohil*.

On their arrival at Mensäbäk, the band led by Pepe Castillo found a smaller, established community of northern Lacandones which had their own *t'o'ohil*, Celestín. To avoid confrontation, Celestín moved with his followers to the shores of Lake Mensäbäk, while the newcomers resettled on Lake Ts'ibatnah.

When the need arose for a literate young Lacandon to represent the group before the Mexican government as "municipal president," Pepe Castillo followed Old Chan K'in's example and "suggested" his firstborn son, another Chan K'in who had taken the Spanish name Joaquín Trujillo.

In Mensäbäk the newcomers from Monte Líbano soon felt the presence nearby of the American missionary and his emissary José Pepe Chan Bol. The missionary extended them the same services he offered the Nahá group, and with the same condition: They must lift up their spirits to Jesus Christ.

The latest phase began when Pepe Castillo developed a painful ulcer. This correct and responsible elder had always been a heavy drinker, but he suddenly found that the effects of even light social drinking appeared

---

* *Ladino* (and the feminine form, *ladina*) is the term used for all non-Indians except foreigners (*ts'ul*).

to be some kind of divine punishment out of proportion to any sins he may have committed. Perhaps José Pepe's preaching against drinking and smoking was being confirmed. At the same time one of his son Joaquín's small children died of an intestinal infection, and Joaquín was heard to lament not having had the preferential medical treatment offered to converts and their families. For whatever reasons or combination of reasons the *t'o'ohil* Pepe Castillo and his son Joaquín suddenly proclaimed themselves *"evangelistas."*

Since the principal force of traditional Peninsula Maya social organization is the loyalty and respect for the *t'o'ohil*, Pepe Castillo's example paradoxically evoked the most compelling Maya tradition to demand abandoning Maya religion, thus causing a split in the community.

Pepe Castillo had never been anything like a match for Old Chan K'in in philosophical depth, but he surpassed him in artistic and aesthetic expression. His flute music, ceremonial drawings and incised designs on the ceremonial objects made those of Nahá seem crude by comparison. His conversion to evangelical Christianity would have been one of the greatest losses to Maya tradition even had it not rent and disoriented the largest of the northern Lacandon communities, that of Lake Mensäbäk.

Even Celestín, the *t'o'ohil* of the smaller group on Lake Mensäbäk, was torn and tormented by indecision, and as he himself often tells, he eventually decided to abandon his gods and become a Christian. He loaded the most sacred of his ritual objects into his canoe and headed across the lake. What he might have felt as he left the symbols of his lifelong dedication to the religious duty that gave meaning to the only way of life he knew, this he does not tell. It would surely have touched emotions too deep for a Lacandon to express openly without risking loss of dignity. What he does convey is that on his return across the lake in his empty canoe, he suddenly felt a heavy, oppressive presence bearing down on him, like the foot of an angry god, preparing to press him and his canoe into the mud and slime of the lake bottom. A wave of fear engulfed him, and his ears hummed with a dull roar, like that of the Nah Ts'ulu', the supernatural jaguars who devour the worthless and outmoded beings still alive when the gods decree the end of a cycle of the earth's existence.

With all his diminishing strength, he frantically turned the canoe about, returned for his god-pots and accessories, and began his race with approaching oblivion. Somehow, reality held out for him until he returned them to their altar and lit offerings of incense. As he squatted on his haunches behind the row of flaming incense burners, chanting as the *hach winik* (true people) always have and always must, the fever subsided, the roaring of the Nah Ts'ulu' died out in his ears, and the impending oblivion withdrew. He finally pronounced his oath: "When the day comes, I will die, like everyone else. But until then, I will keep my gods, like a True Person."

Anyone who values the conservation of Lacandon religion and culture, not only for their sake but for our own as well, may find Celestín's story gratifying. The sad truth is, however, that most of the partisans decided the question of "traditionalist vs. evangelist" on far less philosophical grounds. While the confusion of values was such as to cast good men either way, about all that can be categorically stated is that the confirmed alcoholics remained traditionalist.

Once the traditional Lacandon religion had been broken down at Lake Mensäbäk, Pepe Castillo and his followers were easy prey for any new ideas, no matter how incongruous. It was at this point that a Yucatec-speaking Seventh-Day Adventist arrived on the scene and converted the evangelist Mensäbäk Lacandones once again. The first of numerous restrictions was the declaration that approximately half of the Lacandones' traditional game and fish were unkosher. Liquor, beer, the ceremonial drink called *balché* or anything else alcoholic, together with tobacco in any form, were sinful. The polygamous households were broken up. A man could keep only his first wife. The others, though they may have been happily married and faithful to their husband for ten or twenty years, discovered that they had been living in sin; each was obliged to leave the husband and marry some bachelor.

If we have difficulty understanding how the Lacandones could permit and accept such restrictions on their lives, perhaps we tend to underestimate the characteristic Maya religious fervor, and the greater sacrifices they were prepared to make for the new religion after they had finally become convinced it was better than that of their fathers. The Olmec–Mayan–Lacandon ritual duties are hard and exacting, and their occidental counterparts are bland and easy by comparison.

By no means does this imply that the typical Lacandon is conscious of the benefits and functional interrelationship of all the aspects of his traditional culture and religion. Quite the contrary. Like every other human being, he receives the entire package — an organic whole — as part of his cultural heritage. Tampering with cultural complexes is every bit as dangerous as tampering with the mechanism of genetic transmission in living organisms, and can result in equally grotesque, dysfunctional mutations.

IV

If the Lacandon culture is endangered by the evangelist missionary's attacks against its traditional social institutions, an even greater threat rises ominously from the provoked disorder of the ecology of the Lacandon jungle — the destruction of the environment to which the culture adjusted long ago and which it requires for its continued existence.

Since the time of the Spanish Conquest, the greatest defender of the Lacandones' ethnic unity has been their isolation, which resulted from two principal factors: the difficulty of transportation for the occidental and the lack of material objects necessary for his accustomed way of life, and the unhealthful conditions of the tropical habitat. In the latter category, the terrible specter of malaria stood at the head of a host of illnesses and of physical discomforts that can wear a man down to a point where he is easy prey for even minor ailments.

In the 1940's, both of these obstacles were drastically reduced. The road-building technology is adequate to reach practically any part of the zone. What had been lacking was a motive, a means of making the road pay for itself. This came about with the rise in price of precious tropical hardwoods: mahogany, red and white cedar, bari, chicozapote (sapodilla), guayacán (a kind of lignum vitae) and others. After a campaign of several years, the Mexican Department of Health practically eradicated malaria from the zone. Then it became apparent that the Lacandones, a forest-dwelling people, had remained sole owners of their jungle habitat simply because no one else had wanted it. The eradication of malaria made the forest desirable to outsiders, and the lumber company's roads showed the way.

In innumerable dry, barren and impoverished regions of Mexico, one can find old men who still remember when the eroded and sterile hills of the region were rich oak or pine forests, teeming with game and wild fruits; the air was clear and the rains were generous. But now only hunger grows from the deforested and eroded earth. The peasant farmers' mass migration to deforest the remains of the Lacandon jungle, turning it into another dry and sterile desert, is one of the great tragedies of our time. It is rather difficult to blame people for fleeing from starvation — even though starvation will overtake them in the next desert of their own making decades later.

Thousands upon thousands of agraristas — homesteaders in accordance with the laws dictated during the Mexican Revolution — descend upon the Lacandon jungle to practice a subsistence economy based on slash-and-burn agriculture. Each family will clear an area of several thousand square meters and burn a fortune in fine tropical hardwoods in order to plant and harvest a small crop of corn, beans, squash and chili peppers. Then after two years (or three at most) they will move on to clear and burn more virgin jungle, abandoning the cleared areas to grassland. The cattle barons follow them, overpasturing the land, which in a few years more erodes away to bare limestone.

No aspect of the Lacandon's existence seems entirely free of paradox. The Lacandon jungle, one of the world's richest rain forests, grows on some of the world's poorest soil, most of which consists of a few inches of topsoil over sterile, white Cretaceous limestone. This thin topsoil is covered by a few more inches of extremely rich leaf mold. Immediately after the huge trees are cleared away, the seeds of corn, beans and squash produce abundantly, but after a second year of cultivation the soil is already near exhaustion. At this point the Lacandones, who follow a seven-year rotation cycle, will abandon their tired milpas and allow them to grow back in weeds and second-growth jungle twice as high as a tall man's head; only then will they clear and plant again.

The Lacandon population, which in its natural state is self-limiting, could have survived indefinitely in its traditional manner, had our occidental culture left them enough of their ecologically balanced environment. But the invasion of thousands upon thousands of *agraristas* has changed all of that permanently.

In the mid-1960's, the heavy road machinery moved in from Chancalá Chiapas to the Lake Mensäbäk (or Metzaboc) region, cutting the mahoganies and other tropical hardwoods. The neighboring Lacandones watched with mixed emotions. On the one hand, where each giant tree had fallen lay the splintered and tangled remains of the three or four smaller trees it had taken with it, and the corridors that had been cut through the forest so that the bulldozer could pull out the felled trees, quickly became a closed mass of second-growth jungle. This was composed mostly of thorns and vines that made traveling nearly impossible for the Lacandon hunter. It also provided cover for poisonous snakes, which reproduced out of proportion to the design of even the most vengeful of the Maya gods. But on the other hand, Joaquín Trujillo, the municipal president of Mensäbäk, opened a bank account in the nearest town. Even a tiny fraction of the total price of the fine hardwoods, which was paid as *derecho de monte* (forestry rights), constituted an unheard-of fortune for any Lacandon.

The roads and the logging enterprise continued toward Lacanjá Chan Sayab, where José Pepe Chan Bol bought a gas stove with an oven for each of his two wives. Of course, the women were afraid to use them. They continued to make their tortillas on the traditional clay griddle set on three stones over a wood fire; but each wife had her gas stove and her oven, and the neighbors were impressed. Then the headmen began buying automobiles and trucks, in the name of the Lacandon community. When the brakes failed on the Volkswagen Safari, making it unsafe to drive, rather than have the brakes repaired, the vehicle was pushed into a ditch and abandoned.

The funds which the logging company paid for forestry rights were subject to the strictest controls, and these assured (at least in theory) an honest and equitable payment to the concerned parties. The greater part of the money was put in a Lacandon community fund, which the duly elected representatives from north and south would direct toward things of real and lasting value for everyone: schools, clinics, workshops, power sources, pure drinking water systems, community transportation facilities, and so on. Unfortunately, there are radical differences between the theory and the practice of politics, and especially politics in Latin America. The Christianized and acculturated southern Lacandones were the first to learn the political realities of Mexico and to exploit them to their own advantage.

They began by electing themselves exclusive representatives of the entire Lacandon community, which put them in control of the bulk of the funds directed toward "things of real communal value" for "all the Lacandones" and made possible the potlatch spending at Lacanjá. The northern Lacandones sensed and resented the fact that "something was wrong," but no clear objection or solution occurred to any one of them until most of the funds had been squandered. The southern Lacandones had proved to be the more adept at playing occidental games.

While the younger Lacandones of Nahá were fascinated by Joaquín Trujillo's bank account and by the wealth of gadgets in vogue at Lacanjá Chan Sayab, Old Chan K'in was concerned about the cost to the environment necessary for their traditional way of life. Several times he refused the offers of the lumber company, which were backed by the Mexican government. Then a formal notice arrived in the summer of 1977 notifying Señor Chan K'in de Najá and his son Young Chan K'in that José Pepe Chan Bol, designated "Commissar of the Lacandon Zone," had given permission for an official count of the mahogany trees at Nahá. One year later, the local representatives of the Lacandon community at Nahá signed permission for the cutting of their mahogany. They had come to the conclusion that their trees were going to be cut one way or another, and decided to cooperate in order at least to receive payment for them.

In December of 1978 an advance crew from the lumber company arrived at Nahá and began felling the four hundred giant mahogany trees, some of which had been growing before Columbus discovered the New World. They worked with a speed and efficiency that are common in Mexico only among those who have good reason not to be caught at what they are doing. No doubt there were some among them who understood, however dimly, the vital importance of the mahogany for the stability of the rain forest and for the continuation of Lacandon culture. Not only are the dugouts Lacandon farmers use to reach their *milpas* across the lake made of mahogany, but so is most of their furniture and the ceremonial "canoe" in which they beat and ferment their ceremonial bark-liquor (*balché*). In rough terms, it may be said that the mahogany tree is as central to the Lacandones' existence as the bison was to the Plains Indians.

By February of 1979 the cutting was completed and the bulldozers had made an unsurfaced road which passed through Nahá and reached a point some fifteen or twenty kilometers beyond it. During clear weather it was a rutted but passable road. After a day or two of rain it turned into a stretch of muck that only the high and powerful logging trucks and the company's four-wheel-drive vehicles could grind and slosh their way over.

The road does have some undeniable short-term advantages. During a spell of benign weather, Yong Chan K'in borrowed Joaquín Trujillo's three-ton Ford truck, and brought in 30,000 pesos' worth (about $1,350) of merchandise for his store. The cost of gasoline was 300 pesos, extraordinarily cheap when compared with the cost of several chartered flights (over a thousand pesos each) with a load limit of less than 400 kilograms. Moreover, thanks to the road, a person who was seriously ill could obtain transportation on one of the company's pickups or jeeps and be treated in the hospital at Palenque (a hundred kilometers away) within two and a half hours.

The long-term consequences are another matter, as the Lacandones have begun to discover. The same kind of road had reached Lake

Mensäbäk several years before. A month or two after the last mahogany trunks there had been hauled out, the road was abandoned. After two rains, it became an ugly, muddy gash in the jungle, which the young vegetation of a single rainy season sealed over. Except for the parts of it that were kept cleared and open by the eternal Maya travelers on mule or afoot, the road was useless.

Young Chan K'in, as president of Nahá, disregarded his father's respect for their isolation and repeatedly requested of the lumber company that they put down gravel surfacing, ditches and culverts. He asked that the cost be charged to the (Lacanjá-controlled) "community fund," which would never reach Nahá anyway.

That spring I received a letter from K'ayum Ma'ax of Nahá, Young Chan K'in's younger brother and next in line of succession to the position of t'o'ohil of Nahá:

Ne suk in wilikech Roberto,	My friend Robert,
y yonen Chak Balum.	of the Puma *onen*.
Behe' tiyanech ich Mexico,	Now you are in Mexico [City],
a wuyik yab huum ich nah	
kahal.	hearing much noise in the great city.
Ten ti yanen yok'ol k'ax	I am here in the forest
chen in wuyik u huum trator.	hearing only the noise of the bulldozers.
Behe' tan u pulik-graba	Now they are putting down gravel
chan paytan u pulik tunich	but first they put down stone
ich Mensäbäk	at Mensäbäk
pachil u pulik ich Nahá.	later they will put it down at Nahá.
Tin t'an wa 25 de Abril	I would say that by the 25th of April
ty lah pula tunich to wolol.	they will have put down all the stone everywhere.
Behe' mex ha'.	Now it does not rain.
Hach tikin u beli carretera.	Very dry is the way of the highway....
[Some jokes and general gossip]	
Bay mas pachil ak tsikbal.	Well, later we will converse.
U tal avion. Tin walah tech.	The plane comes. I have told you all.
Ne chakal k'in behe'.	The sun is very hot now.
Ne b'ekach chal k'in.	The sun nears its greatest heat.
Bay, Asta mas pach(il).	Very well, until later.
Ak tsikbal. Känänta Bäh.	We will converse. Take care of yourself.
K'ayum Ma'ax.	K'ayum [of the] Monkey *onen*.

(Perhaps the only omission of occidental tradition in K'ayum's letter was the date, which — judging from the postmark — should have been about the beginning of April 1979.)

The isolation of the northern Lacandones at Lake Mensäbäk and Lake Nahá has come to an end. The way is open to the tourist trade.

Old Chan K'in and Old Mateo often go up to sit at the edge of the road — where it passes nearest to the center of the community — to watch the pasing of an occasional pickup or jeep. When a bulldozer comes growling its way up the road, they will often comment: "The tractor is very strong. I have seen one pull a log that, in the old days, it would have taken twenty yoke of oxen to move."

Old Chan K'in plans to move his house from its present location to one about a kilometer back from the shores of the lake: to high ground just above the head of the new airstrip. The hilltop he has chosen also overlooks the new road. Most of the community will move with him. Young K'ayum and his father-in-law, Antonio, have almost finished building their houses at the new location.

Chan K'in's new god-house could well be described as the nucleus of the community at Nahá. Its construction should be a great ceremonial event. The god-house will be a traditional, open-sided, palm-thatched structure with rounded ends, some thirty feet long and more than half as wide. The god-pots (incense burners) will sit on a hanging shelf of even poles. They will face east, looking across the god-house and the small patio where the sacred canoes for making balché — hollowed-out mahogany logs of about twenty-gallon capacity — sit on their stands. In a loft at the east side of the god-house will be kept gourds and bundles containing the greater part of the objects used in the rituals. Beside the smooth sandstone for sharpening ceremonial tools will sit a clay bowl of water in which one must rinse one's hands before entering the god-house.

Periodically, and especially after an eclipse of the sun or some large natural (or unnatural) calamity, the Lacandones make a new set of incense burners and abandon the old ones at some forest shrine. The incense-burner renewal ceremony is the longest and most complex of those realized within the present-day Lacandon religion, and for the month or two of its duration, all of the participants are subjected to ritual seclusion, and no nonparticipant may witness any of the ritual activity. The ceremony involves prolonged periods of abstinence and dietary fasts, the preparation of many special foods and other offerings, the decoration of tunics with the red achiote (annatto) dye, symbolic of sacrificial blood, and the consumption of large quantities of balché. Lacandon men can take such long periods of time from their milpas only when the yearly cycle on which their way of life is based permits it: from the latter part of June through July and August, "when the crops are laid by," as an Oklahoma farmer would put it; or from November through December and January, after the long harvest and before the next clearing and burning. This is something which has not changed (just as the milpa system of subsistence has not changed) since pre-Columbian times.

During the renewal of the incense burners, the participating Lacandon men and boys live in a strange world belonging to ancient Maya ritual. In some respects, they are as human and earthbound as ever, but the unusual and unique characteristics of their life in ritual seclusion — the physiological stresses, including intense concentration on things not of this world, lack of sleep and dietary limitations — eventually build up to form the experience of a strange dualism. On the one hand, the Lacandon continues in the same reality as ever, with the same natural laws and forces functioning and with everything in its proper, natural order; but on the other, he has the sense of participating in another, simultaneous reality, in which the same things are not as they had always appeared to be. It is in this mental condition that the men discard their old god-pots, perform the exacting ceremonies day and night, and finally create the new clay effigy incense burners which function as the gods of the community for the next eight years, five cycles of Venus, or in the Classic Maya times, for a Uaxactun, composed of eleven Tzolkins.

In 1970 I was allowed to participate in the incense-burner renewal ceremony in Nahá, which lasted forty-five days and consisted of the most complex and conservative body of ancient Maya ritual surviving today. To the best of my knowledge, I am the only person besides the Lacandones ever to witness the ceremony from start to finish.

During the ceremony all of the Lacandon men taking part slept isolated from the other members of the community. All benches, hammocks, clothing and other personal effects that were not made new for this period of ritual isolation, were conscientiously washed, scrubbed or refinished, and no nonparticipant could use or even touch them. The women of the community continued to prepare our food, but without chili pepper, and the receptacles of food were brought and left for us at some neutral ground between the ceremonial and the mundane territories.

We slept in the open-sided temple. It was not nearly so comfortable as the ordinary Lacandon house, as we were far more exposed to changes of temperature and to the abundant biting insects. In fact, sleeping was so uncomfortable and ritual duties so intense — day and night — that for the forty-five days we slept, I calculated, an average of two or three hours — never more than four — out of every twenty-four. What most surprised me, and appeared to contradict my understanding of natural and physiological laws, was that not only did no participant suffer the slightest physical ailment — not a cold or neuralgia, nor the slightest infection from the occasional minor cuts and abrasions that occurred during the ritual labors — but we all experienced an enhancement of consciousness and perception.

It would be all too easy for anyone who has not lived the experience to question this unique state, this awareness of other dimensions of one's accustomed physical reality, by saying that physiological stresses such as celibacy, lack of sleep and vitamin deficiency over such an extended period of time could produce hallucinogenic effects. While the mental state achieved by the Lacandon participants might be *comparable* to some drug experiences, there is one very significant difference: perception of the physical realities one has known all one's life in "normal" conditions remains throughout — but it is sharpened and intensified. Nothing from the accustomed reality is lost, except the comforts that must be left behind when entering the ritual domain of the ancient Maya gods.

Words become charged and loaded with meaning, as with "Acapulco gold" (a high-grade marijuana or cannabis), but without the accompanying slowness of thought and thickness of tongue. The colors of life suggest the effects of peyote, but without any nausea or depression. Sometimes one's awareness suggests hallucinogenic mushrooms, although one never feels that tightened-scalp vertigo that sometimes comes from the *"niños."* The only ingested stimulant is an occasional offering of *balché,* but the hangover is either minimal or totally absent. None of the feelings are excessive, and all that one is clearly aware of is that every experience, and indeed reality itself, seems expanded and extended.

Normally one is aware that a word, like *k'ulel,* has quite distinct and different meanings: *k'ulel* is "whirlwind"; it is also "male spider monkey," which is an emblem of the solar deities; and Ah K'ulel (the Whirlwind) is one of the assistant solar deities at the service of the Creator, Hachäkyum. Ah K'ulel is also called the Sweeper of Our Lord's House, probably the same Maya god referred to in Pre-Conquest Yucatán as Mistic Ahau, which means (among other things) Sweeping Lord. During the state of consciousness achieved in the ceremony, one is as aware as ever of the different meanings or usages, but he is also aware that the word *k'ulel* is a single reality, like a gemstone whose different facets may reflect red, blue, white, green or yellow light, according to the angle from which one looks at it. Differences in meaning are but the reflection of different perspectives, and the perspective does not alter, or even touch, much less subdivide, the phenomenon.

Old Chan K'in told us, on the morning that the new god-pots were fired, that K'ulel comes and takes the ashes to our Lord Hachäkyum, just as he does when the *milpas* are burned. Right on schedule, we all saw the leaves rising to outline the invisible presence of the whirlwind moving across the low brush of the open clearing. It swerved some twenty-five meters out of its path to hover for a moment directly over the pyre of the open kiln. It (or "He") suddenly became a visible being, a dark form of ashes, smoke and flashing sparks, before moving on and disappearing into the forest on the eastern side of the clearing. No Lacandon would object to a description of what happened in terms of natural, physical phenomena. But it is more likely that he would speak in terms of the supernatural persons who incorporate these "natural phenomena."

None of us had any doubt that, had any participant broken his ritual abstinence — let us say, by secretly eating a chili pepper or sleeping with a woman — K'ulel would have sucked the flames from the roaring fire and set the guilty man's clothing on fire. But this did not in fact happen because no one had committed an infraction.

The god-pots at Nahá were last renewed in 1970. As of 1979, the most frequently evoked of the god-pots contained huge heaps of cinders, the residue of incense rose high above the rim of the bowl, and the effigy faces were caked with the smoke-blackened residue of food and drink offerings. It was well past the time for another incense-renewal ceremony.

Old Chan K'in did not state clearly whether the delay beyond the eight-year period (which he formerly said was the longest that should elapse between renewal ceremonies) was to coincide with the instate-

31

ment of the new temple, or if he was hopefully waiting for the logging activity to run its course, for the road to be abandoned, and for visitors to arrive at less frequent intervals, as before. Or, is the cult to the ancient Maya gods weakening, even at Nahá?

The daily arrival of tourists during this period would have been bad enough, but there were even greater foreseeable distractions. Officials of the Mexican government could drive up at any moment to demand the immediate attention of the head of the community, with little regard for "some kind of ceremony that is going on: 'This will only take a minute.' " The interruption could break the long and painstakingly achieved continuum of abstinences, restraints and concentration that eventually enables the men to act as intermediaries between their people and their gods. And the road, or either of the two airstrips, could at any moment bring José Pepe Chan Bol or another southern Lacandon instrument of the American missionaries to intrude on the most critical rituals, criticizing and ridiculing them.

The Lacandones of Nahá are the heirs of the ancient Maya theocrats of Palenque, who, in turn, were either the first disciples of the Olmecs or simply a direct evolution of the Olmecs themselves. The Lacandones' may therefore be the oldest unbroken religious and cultural tradition on earth today. But when the last incense burner is extinguished, it will have died forever. Tourists will walk through the ancient ruins and look at the ancient sculptures and inscriptions, and wonder what they may have meant. The archaeologists will be able to cite enough technical data to confuse or silence their critics, but they won't really know, either.

The flame that was kindled over three millennia ago still burns in the temple of Nahá, but it burns low, and flickers.

V

The language in which one thinks, which is to say, categorizes and gives shape to one's experiences, is of the greatest importance. Most of the notes I took during the incense-burner renewal ceremony were in Lacandon Maya, which provides convenient categories and concepts for the experiences I found myself living. But when I began translating them into English, I often felt as though I were trying to eat consommé with a fork.

In order to preserve nonoccidental cultures such as that of the Lacandones, we have to take special pains to preserve the language in which they evolved. We occidentals not only can, but must, learn from other cultures, or the unique and extraordinary power which our technology has given us will soon render life on this planet impossible — except possibly for the viruses that are being evolved in Arizona and Siberia. But nonoccidental cultures are fast disappearing, drowning in the flood of occidental civilization. The missionaries are on the job, with the merchants and the politicians right on their heels, and then come the conscientious and long-suffering schoolteachers.

And yet, when I tell someone on the road between Palenque and Nahá, "Soy el maestro de Najá" (I am the schoolmaster of Nahá), I experience a sense of pride that I never imagined possible. With the enthusiastic help of K'ayum Ma'ax, the third son of Old Chan K'in of Nahá, the school of Nahá is now standing. It is only another palm-thatched roof, but it has electric lights from a small, water-driven turbine that we installed. The turbine, electric lights and pure drinking-water systems are the first lessons in occidental technology and culture at Nahá; Chan K'in and his sons have recognized them for what they are, the inevitable results of conformity to natural laws, and not the blessings of any religious denomination or any political party. Much remains to be done, and I am now preparing the curriculum for the first classes. If things go as planned, the Lacandones will learn many useful lessons in how to participate in the material and technological wealth of our occidental civilization — and that in order to do so, they must not necessarily cease to be Lacandones (hach winik) and join us in our spiritual poverty, confusion of human values and collective psychoses.

I divide my time between my office on the main floor of the National Anthropology Museum of cosmopolitan (and infernally contaminated) Mexico City, and Nahá, Chiapas, where the last flickers of light from the Olmec–Maya–Lacandon cultural tradition seem a bit brighter every day — if only because the surrounding night becomes darker and darker. Any morning, funding and official permissions permitting, I get up an hour or two before dawn, throw my pack and machete into my car, and after some sixteen hours of driving (at standard VW speeds), I am nearing home.

When I first met Victor Perera in 1977, our friendship was as immediate as it was inexplicable, considering our differences in character. He had just returned from his first short incursion into the Lacandon jungle, where he had acquired a few penetrating perspectives and a lot more questions. His sensitivity and powers of observation prevented my simply writing him off as another tourist. I think it was then that my interest began to take a turn which I foresaw could reap benefits for all participants.

My view of the Lacandones and their culture has developed through a quarter of a century, but does the obvious advantage my experience gives me also presuppose some equally considerable disadvantage? Could my familiarity with each and every tree possibly obstruct my view of the forest?

During my first trips to the Lacandon communities, it was impossible to arrive without gradually becoming immersed, over a period of several days, in the jungle habitat to which they are in such remarkable adjustment. But how different would the scenes of their way of life appear to someone who comes directly from our "civilized world" and is abruptly hit in the face with them?

In agreeing to collaborate on this project, Victor and I struck a feasible compromise between the familiar and the new viewpoints. The newly arrived visitor runs the obvious risk of committing significant blunders and misinterpretations — like some of my own stumblings during my early years in the Lacandon jungle. At the outset, by personally introducing Victor to old friends, I cut down the time required for the Lacandones to take him into their confidence and to talk openly with him about whatever he might ask them. On our first trip together, I took along a small trunk filled with my old diaries, journals and field notes for him to read and for both of us to discuss in our moments of leisure at Nahá.

I have also been over the manuscript of his section of this book, correcting anything that he clearly mistranslated or misinterpreted, and I familiarized him with the Lacandon religious traditions that I have come to accumulate and understand over the years. On some points we are still in disagreement, but in those instances suffice it to say that each of us has listened patiently to the opinions of the other.

In some respects, Victor's descriptions should perhaps be considered more "authoritative" than mine, in that he tends to see the Lacandones as they are, rather than as they were, and in that he gives consideration to some present realities which I prefer simply not to think about.

From here on, it is Victor Perera's turn to describe the Lacandon Indians of the present, as you would find them today after a two- or three-hour drive from the end of the pavement at Palenque, or after a forty-five-minute flight in a light plane from San Cristóbal de las Casas or Tuxtla Gutiérrez.

Part 1.

Initiation

In November 1938, when I was nearly five years old, the President of Guatemala, General Jorge Ubico, commemorated the seventh anniversary of his "belevolent" dictatorship with a national fair that was to rival in everything but size the World's Fair in New York.

I was taken to the fair by Emma, a pretty salesgirl in my father's department store, who had just turned sixteen and was wearing lipstick and silk stockings for the first time.

The most interesting place in all the fair was a large area encircled by a tall bamboo fence. At one end sat several women who wove on looms beautiful cloth with bands of bright colors. At the other end was an enormous tall pole with a small round platform at the top. Four Indians in red headdresses shinnied up to the swinging platform and tied ropes around their waists. Then they all jumped free of the platform, upside down. They swung around and around the pole without bumping one another, lower and lower until their heads grazed the ground. At the last moment they jerked upright and landed on their feet, running.

In the middle of this enclosure, behind a barbed-wire fence guarded by soldiers, a group of five Lacandon Indians was housed in a small hut of bamboo and palm thatch intended to duplicate their jungle home. They wore long white tunics and had shoulder-length matted hair, so it was difficult to tell if they were men or women. The Lacandones walked in a half crouch, as if the roofs of their huts were too low. They were the most beautiful, gentle-seeming people I had ever seen. One of the men came out of the hut and walked right to the fence where we stood. He made a noise in his throat and stuck his hand through the fence. Before I could overcome my bewilderment and decide whether to offer him a coin or the piece of chocolate I had in my pocket, a soldier pulled him away. The look of sadness and confusion in his eyes will stay with me forever.

JANUARY 1977

When I asked Emma who the Lacandones were she said they were as old as the Mayas who had lived in Guatemala long before the arrival of the Spaniards.

Many years later I was to learn that these five Lacandones had been abducted from their jungle home in Chiapas, in southern Mexico, and smuggled across the border to please the vanity of a dictator who wanted representatives of all the Mayan tribes exhibited at his fair.

After I began attending military school in Guatemala I heard occasional references to the Lacandones by my Spanish classmates and teachers. "You look like a Lacandon," our grammar teacher would say to a boy who had let his hair grow too long, "—one of those who live like a monkey, in the jungles of El Petén." To them the Lacandones were remote objects of derision, more primitive than the most primitive highland Quichés and Cakchiquels, whom they employed as servants.

To our Indian housemaids the Lacandon was a bogeyman, like El Pipo and La Llorona, to whom they would turn whenever my sister or I misbehaved. Chata, our seventeen-year-old Quiché nanny, would scold, "Eat all your beans or the Lacandon will get you." Always, behind the threat, I felt the force of mystery more than I felt a naked menace. And yet, when Chata was knifed to death by her jealous lover some weeks after my experience at the fair, I thought at first that the culprit had been a Lacandon who had "gotten" her for invoking his name once too often.

I did not suspect then the ancient, deep-lying enmities that still endure between the highland Mayas and the forest-dwelling Lacandones.

Thirty-eight years after that first encounter I arrived in Chiapas to gather material for a book about the northern Lacandones of Nahá and their spiritual headman, Chan K'in. In the intervening years my experience at the fair had come to occupy a luminous place in my childhood memories, unlike any other. As my interest in the Lacandones grew I read most of the literature on them, from the early works of Alfred Tozzer, the Harvard anthropologist who was the first to write of their ceremonies at the turn of the century, to Frans and Gertrude Blom's journals of exploration in the Lacandon forest in the forties and fifties. The net effect of my reading was to deepen rather than to clear up the mystery of these "primitive" Mayas, whose ceremonies and stories bear vivid imprints of one of the most sophisticated civilizations ever to flourish on our planet.

In the spring of 1976 I taught a course on Central American literature at the University of California, Santa Cruz, which included as one of its texts the remarkable *Popol Vuh* (Book of Counsel), a collection of the Quiché-Mayas' creation stories and legends gathered by a Spanish missionary priest in the eighteenth century. For her term paper a resourceful student had borrowed from one of my colleagues a copy of *El Libro de Chan K'in* (The Book of Chan K'in), now out of print and rare, which had been written by the Oklahoma ethnologist and linguist Robert D. Bruce. From it the student chose four stories about the world's origin and matched them, point by point, with their counterparts in the *Popol Vuh*. The parallels between the two accounts were no less breathtaking than their differences. *El Libro de Chan K'in* recast the story of man's creation by locating it in a jungle setting, where jaguars and parrots took the place of coyotes and eagles, and the roles of the pelota-playing lords of the underworld were played by forest demons and Kisin, the singular, fungus-eating devil. But most astonishing of all was my discovery that the old storyteller, Chan K'in, was still alive in the jungle fastnesses of Chiapas, and functioning as the respected *t'o'ohil* or guardian of the Lacandon tradition.

Nine months later, in January 1977, I was on my way to Chiapas to seek out the eighty-year-old patriarch in the hope he would grant me an interview. But first I planned to visit the southern Lacandon community of Lacanjá, which had been evangelized by an American Protestant missionary.

I stopped at San Cristóbal de las Casas, a colorful Spanish colonial city in the highlands of Chiapas that is the spiritual center and marketplace for a number of Indian tribes whose ancestors prospered in the waning centuries of the Mayan civilization. In small towns and villages within a twenty-mile radius of this former missionary capital are found representatives of the Chamula, Zinacantán, Tzeltal and other Christianized Mayan tribes which conserve sturdy customs, crafts and traditions from their past.

San Cristóbal is also the gateway to the extensive Lacandon rain forest, which stretches across eastern Chiapas into northern Guatemala. In this dense mahogany forest are found most of the jewel-cities of the Classic era of Mayan civilization: Palenque, Yaxchilán, Bonampak (site of the famous murals), and on the Guatemala side, Tikal and Uaxactún.

In San Cristóbal I visited Gertrude Duby Blom, the seventy-five-year-old widow of the Danish archaeologist Frans Blom, who was one of the pioneer Mayan explorers of his time. Gertrude, or Trudi as she is familiarly known, is a journalist/photographer of formidable energy and presence, and the self-appointed doyenne of the Lacandones. When I told her of my project she warned me that my intended journey to Nahá and Lacanjá on horseback would be a back-breaking, two-week-long adventure through rough and varied terrain. After reaching the forest my progress would be slowed to a snail's pace and I would find the trails fraught with perils, among them the deadly *nauyaca* or fer-de-lance, a large pit viper whose venomous bite was until recently the principal cause of mortality among mature northern Lacandones, ahead of respiratory diseases and old age. I was persuaded, this first time, to charter a small plane so I could visit both Lacandon settlements, which are about sixty miles from one another.

I flew into Lacanjá after brief stops at Yaxchilán and Bonampak. On landing, the tiny Cessna 180 threaded its way between two dense walls of forest greenery, which grazed the tips of both wings. The transition from the cool Spanish colonial atmosphere of San Cristóbal could not have been more abrupt.

I was greeted on arrival by several young villagers in cowboy hats, jeans and dark glasses who seemed to hang out by the landing strip with nothing to do. Arriving and departing airplanes provide most of the daily excitement in Lacanjá. The president of the settlement, José Pepe Chan Bol, approached me in a white Lacandon tunic, but he conspicuously flaunted his large wristwatch and loaded key chain and wore a thick pair of horn-rimmed glasses whose function appeared to be as much totemic as optometric. The women, who wore colorful bead necklaces, stared at me from a respectful distance, most of them in flower-print shifts shaped like Hawaiian muumuus.

I asked one of the men who had met the plane if the music ceremony would be performed today, a Sunday.

"We no longer play the music," he replied listlessly. "Since the old priest Cerón died we have become very lazy . . . Have you got a cigarette?"

I told him I didn't smoke.

"Just as well," he said, with a sigh. "The missionaries say tobacco can kill you."

An American Baptist mission had set up camp in Lacanjá, and it had succeeded in a few short years where the Spanish Catholic friars had failed over five centuries. All the Lacanjá Lacandones I spoke with called themselves Christians, and had given up the ancient rituals.

The village was filled with children, some with the long, glossy black hair I remembered, others with the drawn faces and the unmistakable swollen bellies of hookworm and ascaris.

Atop a nearby breadfruit tree was perched a mainly decorative television antenna. There were no television sets in Lacanjá as yet, but every hut had a battery-operated radio or phonograph.

I was approached by a sociable *mestizo* from Durango, a head taller than the tallest Lacandon, who told me he was a road builder and logger for the Mexican Forestry Department. The road had just been completed, and they had begun to denude the surrounding forest of giant mahogany trees. For years Trudi Blom and other friends of the Lacandones had kept up pressure on the Mexican government to grant the Lacandones full legal title to their forest lands, which cover 614,000 hectares. Under President Echeverría the government did just that, in an outwardly generous gesture; it now pays them a small yearly stipend to cut down and remove the trees. The government has thus assured itself of virtually permanent control over the forest's hardwood resources, at a relatively trifling cost.

The one villager to whom I was immediately drawn looked about sixty, had strong, aristocratic Mayan features, and wore an immaculate ankle-length tunic. Na Bor had been rechristened Pancho Villa, and the name was somehow appropriate to his proud military bearing. Na Bor Pancho Villa's stiff dignity was sadly vestigial, a throwback to a time when the Lacandones were regarded as a fierce, cannibalistic warrior tribe that had repulsed Cortez's army with their mighty bows. (In all likelihood, the conquistadores had been loath to pursue them into the forest with their horses and heavy armor.)

Na Bor Pancho Villa greeted me in the pidgin Spanish Lacandones speak with outsiders. Its staccato cadence is peculiarly suited to formal exchanges. He then led me to his home, where I duly admired his well-provisioned hut, his .22 caliber rifle, his two goats, his collection of animal skins and his three wives, two of whom lived in separate "kitchens" with their numerous offspring. Polygamy is practiced freely by Lacandon men, who generally purchase their wives with cash or with long-term contractual service to their fathers-in-law. A patriarch like Na Bor or a community president can usually afford three or four wives and well over a dozen children. Since the advent of the missionaries, however, the younger men are confining themselves to a single spouse.

When I told Na Bor that I was from Guatemala, he nodded gravely. "My father went to Guatemala many years ago. He was taken across the Usumacinta River with four others of the settlement, and then they flew in an airplane to Guatemala. They came back with .22 rifles and other gifts — but my father was sick, and would not talk of Guatemala. When I asked him about it, he would say he just went *de paseo* — for a stroll."

My heart thumped, and I explained to Na Bor that I had probably seen his father when I was a very small boy, at the Guatemala National Fair.

Na Bor's face went blank. "*Aa sí,*" he said mechanically, but I knew he had not understood me, so I explained slowly and in painstaking detail the strange circumstances in which I had seen his father and the other Lacandones. (I did not know then that they had all contracted pulmonary and gastric disorders in the home of one of their kidnappers, and that the youngest of them had died.)

Na Bor blinked and a faraway look came into his eyes, as if he were seeing the scene I described behind the barbed-wire fence. After a moment he smiled, grunted loudly, and nodded his head. "*Aa sí* — that must have been my father." He touched my shoulder, but we did not embrace. From that moment I would see his eyes whenever I recalled the Lacandon who thrust his hand through the fence.

On my return to San Cristóbal I stayed at Na-Bolom, a one time monastery converted into a guesthouse, museum and center of Mayan studies by Trudi Blom. In the evenings Na-Bolom becomes a stage on which she reenacts — often in four or five languages — the remarkable drama of her life among the Lacandones.

"I have learned through bitter experience that you cannot hope to protect the Lacandones without safeguarding their forest," she said at dinner, in a clarion voice that held every guest spellbound. "In the dreams of the Lacandones, which regulate their waking lives, each animal, each plant and each ritual object is an instrument of prophecy or protective magic. As the forest is burned and cut down through our stupidity and greed, the animals disappear one by one; the jaguar, the boar, the puma, the spider monkey — they all disappear, and soon the souls of the Lacandones will also disappear." She shook her head impatiently at a guest's importunate question, and slapped her hand on the table. "No no no, it makes no difference how many of them will be left — the fact is, their souls will wither and die as their magnificent forest is destroyed, and all of us will share part of the blame."

I began to tell Trudi of the sadness and disintegration I had witnessed in Lacanjá, but she cut me off with a grunt and a sigh.

"Of course. What you are seeing is the last whisper of a magnificent culture. The missionaries, the timber prospectors, the Tzeltal colonists and the seductions of occidental technology are merely accelerating an inevitable process. Lacanjá has already gone to the devil. They are spending all the money the government gives them on worthless gadgets and junk. They have gone mad with spending, like the Americans in the twenties. And when the mahogany is all gone, they will have nothing. Absolutely nothing. They will be worse off than the poorest Indians on U.S. reservations." She lowered her voice. "But in Nahá, if you gain the confidence of Chan K'in and the other elders, you can still get an idea of what the Lacandon culture was about. Chan K'in in particular is an extraordinary man. So far, he has not permitted the government to cut mahogany around Nahá. When he dies, there will be no stopping them." She shook her head. "In Nahá, a young Lacandon has even opened a hotel: the Maya Caribe. Accch —" she waved her hand in disgust. "It is a joke, this hotel, with crude beds, worm-eaten Styrofoam mattresses and an ice chest. And it is a sign of worse things to come."

Staying at Na-Bolom as Trudi's guest was K'ayum of Nahá, one of Chan K'in's seventeen children, who was there with his wife and year-old son while he visited a dentist.

After dinner I met with K'ayum — his name means god of song — in the well-stocked library, and we sat down by the fire for a chat. He was an appealing, supremely self-assured young man in his late teens, and was regarded by some Nahá elders as Chan K'in's heir apparent, ahead of his older brothers. He wore the white genderless Lacandon gown, made more incongruous by blue knee socks and leather shoes, and an enormous wristwatch, which he consulted frequently, with a magisterial air.

"I have five thousand pesos to spend," he bragged, "and tomorrow I will buy all of San Cristóbal."

He laughed, and I asked, "With only five thousand pesos? How will you manage?"

"I will make the money work," he said. "I will lend three thousand pesos to a *ladino* or a foreigner, and get back four thousand. Then I will buy a record player and many records. All Chiapas music. I like the Chiapas music. And also a pair of eyeglasses, so I look like a rich man."

"And what happens," I asked him, "if you spend all your money and fall into debt?"

"Then I will make more bows and arrows, and clay animals and drums, and I'll sell them in the stores. I am a good craftsman. I use my head, like our Lord Hachäkyum." He jabbed at his temple. "With his head Hachäkyum thinks how to make this world. And he makes man of clay. Before there are any stones or animals or snakes, he makes the Lacandon from clay, in Palenque. Then he wets the clay, and in five minutes the Lacandon gets up. I also have a good head, like our Lord Hachäkyum. I make clay animals to sell to the foreigners. When I have sold enough, I will go to Mexico [City] to buy everything there." Then he adds, after reflection, "But I will stay only one day. The noise makes me crazy. I shut my ears, but the noise still hurts. If I stay in Mexico, I am dead."

I asked K'ayum if his father, Chan K'in, approved of his financial ambitions.

K'ayum stared into space, abstracted, as if he were traveling to Nahá to consult his father.

"My father, Chan K'in, is a good man," K'ayum said, measuring his words. "He has a good head, and a good heart. But he is an old man." He sighed. "My father will not change but I, yes, I will change. I have a good head from my father, who has taught me what he knows, but my heart — my heart is not so good." He stared into space again, and a sadness clouded his eyes. "When my father is dead, everything will change in Nahá. We are not a good people . . ."

I asked K'ayum what happens when a Lacandon dies.

"The body rots," he said unhesitatingly, "but the heart is alive. If a good Lacandon dies — like my father — his heart remains, but not everyone can see him. One moment he is there, and then he is not. But if a Lacandon lies or steals or sleeps with his sister, or if he kills another Lacandon, then his heart goes to Kisin — the Devil. You —" he said, poking me in the chest "you are many. You can kill one another and it makes no difference. But we are very few. If one Lacandon kills another, his heart goes to the lower world, and it burns there forever. It is then that Hachäkyum destroys the world."

* * *

On landing in Nahá I am met by Chan K'in's oldest son by his first wife — he is also named Chan K'in — and by Young Mateo, the "manager" of the Hotel Maya Caribe, who smokes a homegrown cigar. Young Chan K'in, a lean, darkly handsome man of thirty with a dapper mustache, tells me that his father and most of the elders have gone to the *milpa* across Lake Nahá.

"They will not be back until dark," he says, "and they have taken all the *cayucos* [dugouts]."

Despite my acquaintance with Trudi Blom, which is the best possible credential, I sense Young Chan K'in's guardedness toward me, bordering on hostility. For my part I do not discern in him the expansive humor or inquiring mind of his younger brother K'ayum. What they do have in common is an air of patrician self-importance. When the elder Chan K'in dies, the deliberation over his successor should be a lively one, with overtones of Jacob and Esau.

Next door to the hotel Young Mateo's little boy is carving a wooden airplane, shaped like the Cessna that flies into Nahá from San Cristóbal two or three times a week. Nahá boys yearn to fly airplanes before they ever lay eyes on an automobile.

Fourteen-year old Chan K'in Chico, another of Chan K'in's sons, squats in a corner of his hut, fashioning bows and arrows for the tourists in San Cristóbal. He keeps a dead toucan and a blue jay at his side, for the feathers, and a pile of tiny flint chips for the arrowheads. Although barely in his teens Chan K'in Chico has a wife his own age, who is too shy to show herself.

"Don't you use these yourself?" I ask Chan K'in Chico, mindful of the Lacandones' legendary reputation as bowmen.

"Sometimes," he says. "But they don't shoot straight. When I am older I will have a rifle, like my older brother."

As in Lacanjá, several Nahá villagers are proud owners of .22's, but very few have ammunition, which is expensive and requires a license. In any case, there are few large animals left to kill in the surrounding forest.

I ask Chan K'in Chico to take me to the *milpa* across the lake, so I can meet his father. He agrees, but when we get to the lakeshore we find that the *cayucos* are all gone.

"You will have to wait until sunset, when they return," Chan K'in Chico says testily, as he fondles the Swiss army jackknife I carry on my belt. "That is a pretty knife," he says. "Will you sell it to me?"

I tell him I might give it to him as a present if he'll take me to Chan K'in's home, so I can wait there for his father to return.

The trail to the main settlement, about half a mile distant, takes us through mud and dense forest. As we get away from the landing strip and the Hotel Maya Caribe I feel as if I am crossing an invisible boundary. The towering mahogany and *chicozapote* trees festooned with liana, the thick shrubs choked with creepers and parasitic plants, the busy chatter of parrots and the calls of brilliantly plumaged song birds form a no-man's-land between the westernized section of Nahá and the main settlement, which has not yet conformed to the rhythm of wristwatches and arriving and departing airplanes. Unlike their Mayan forebears the Lacandones do not keep a calendar or record on stone the movements of the moon and the stars. Until the white man arrived they had no interest at all in dates or statistics. None of the Lacanjá or Nahá elders know their own ages for certain, although they are keenly aware of who is senior to whom. But they do share with their ancestors an implicit belief that the world is subject to continuous cycles of destruction and renewal, and one must order the business of one's life accordingly.

We arrive at the settlement, a tight cluster of huts near the south shore of the lake, and find them all empty. All the men and women, including Chan K'in's three wives, have gone to clear the *milpa* of its last corn and prepare it for planting tobacco, their second major crop. There is an atmosphere of charged expectancy in this group of empty huts that makes my heart race. The slant of the sunlight on the thatched palmetto roofs, the sound of the wind in the trees, are more distinct and intense than I am used to.

In the god-house close to Chan K'in's hut are set three rows of god-pots, whose smudged faces betray recent use. The beaten white bark for the *balché* has been freshly laid on top of a hollowed tree trunk and covered over with palm leaves. When the time comes the son or son-in-law of Chan K'in who has been elected to officiate at the ceremony will light the god-pots with the resin of the copal tree and offer prayers to the gods in a low, guttural chant. The rest of the men will sit on low mahogany benches to sing, smoke cigars, swap jokes, and gorge on the bitter *balché*, and by the following morning they will all feel purged of dark shadows and sadness for another few weeks.

As I walk around and peer through mahogany slats into the dark interiors of the huts it seems astonishing that Nahá has survived all the destructive influences of the past forty years. First came the rubber prospectors, the chicle gatherers and the alligator hunters, who brought greed, violence and disease to the forest; the missionaries and the government loggers arrived with their costly promises of salvation. Northern colonists and their slash-and-burn agriculture have wreaked their destruction on the Lacandon forest, as have the cattle ranchers who followed in their wake and are converting the exhausted *milpas* into grazing grassland. The oil drills cannot be too far behind. And yet scarcely seven years ago Robert Bruce partook of the Lacandones' sacred ceremonies, exchanged dreams with them, planted, harvested, played and hunted with them at a time when game was still abundant and encounters with jaguar, puma and wild boar were relatively commonplace. (Today, skilled Lacandon hunters have to forage for days to bring back monkey flesh for their sacred ceremonies.) And Chan K'in, the community's patriarch and *t'o'ohil*, had entrusted this young foreigner who had learned their language, with the ancient folk tales and legends of his people.

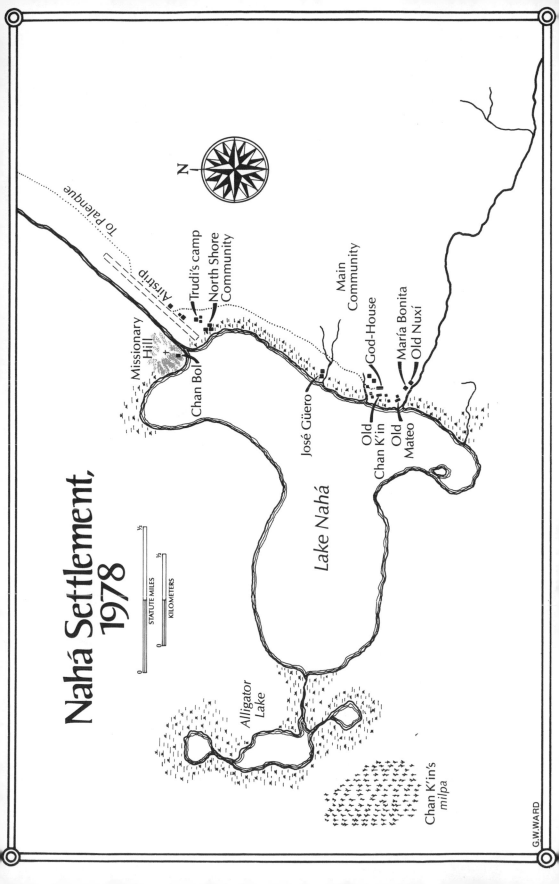

Nahá Settlement, 1978

STATUTE MILES
0 ½

KILOMETERS
½

N

To Palenque

Airstrip

Trudi's camp
North Shore Community

Main Community

Missionary Hill

God-House

María Bonita
Old Nuxí

Chan Bol

José Güero

Old Chan K'in
Old Mateo

Lake Nahá

Alligator Lake

Chan K'in's milpa

G.W.WARD

During this reverie Chan K'in Chico examines me closely. "Come," he says. "We will now visit José Güero."

He leads me back by a different route, along the shore of Lake Nahá, which not long ago abounded with alligators. But it is the deadly *nauyaca* I am concerned with as we trudge through the reeds and the brush. We cross a small corn patch and come to a clearing, in the middle of which sits the hut of José Güero, one of the respected elders of Nahá. As we approach he calls to Chan K'in Chico from within the hut in a sharp tone that makes me feel an unwelcome intruder, too large, pale, and clumsy of movement.

"What is he saying?" I ask Chan K'in Chico.

"He says everybody is at the *milpa*. There is no one to see."

Between the wooden supports of the hut I make out several pairs of eyes, scrutinizing me. At that moment I know that I will have to overcome my uneasiness and speak to José Güero face to face, for he is the key to my meeting Chan K'in. If I miss this opportunity, I may never meet Chan K'in at all.

"Chan K'in, leave me here," I say.

He stares at me, calculating, one wandering eye magnetized to my Swiss jackknife.

"Leave me here," I repeat firmly. "I will find my way back alone. And here, you can have the knife."

He grabs the jackknife with a triumphant whoop and ambles away, turning to grin at me before he disappears in the brush.

I sit down on a tree trunk about ten yards from the hut and take out my harmonica. I play rough approximations of Mayan highland songs I've heard in San Cristóbal. A small boy peers out the door. He is deformed in one eye, like Chan K'in Chico and other Nahá children. (Later I am told that the strabismus is the result of inbreeding.) Next a girl leans out the door and smiles. She is lighter-skinned than I am and has light blond hair — too light to be normal in this setting. Her older sister emerges, another albino. I am gathering an audience, but José Güero remains inside.

I play "On Top of Old Smokey," and then "Blowin' in the Wind." I bend to the melody, winging it to Chan K'in in the *milpa* across the lake.

On the third chorus a flute answers from within the hut. It picks up Dylan's phrases accurately, then goes off on its own melody — a delicate, bittersweet refrain repeated over and over, like a songbird's call. I attempt the harmony with my Marine Band harmonica. Somehow it works: the duet sounds plaintive but not too dirgelike.

"How much is your flute?" asks the hidden voice, in Spanish.

"It's yours," I reply.

"Come inside. Come inside."

The hut is dark and cluttered, yet large enough for a sizable family. José Güero, a dim, emaciated figure, sits on a raised pallet in the rear. He looks sixty, but I see no gray in his thick hair, which falls well below his shoulders. A half-empty bottle of cheap rum stands at his feet.

I hand him my harmonica and he shows me his flute, a blue and red plastic toy from a five-and-dime store.

"We do not make the old kind anymore," he says, grinning, obviously proud of his ability to coax such lovely music from a cheap toy. He blows on my harmonica and laughs, pleased with the sound.

"A good gift," he says. "It is a good gift for me because my legs are stiff." He slaps his withered arthritic knees. "Two years now, I cannot walk about. I cannot work. I stay home and listen to music." He points to a phonograph in one corner. "And I watch the women work."

José aske me where I'm from and why I've come. I tell him I'm a writer and a student of Lacandon culture. I add that I am interested in meeting Chan K'in.

"He is in the *milpa*. Chan K'in is an old man, older than me, but he works in the field from sunrise to sunet, while his strong sons loaf by the airstrip, smoking cigarettes and dreaming of San Cristóbal."

I tell José that I am expected back in San Cristóbal before sunset. "Today perhaps Chan K'in returns early," he says. "Or perhaps not." He laughs.

We lapse into silence. I am aware of the buzzing insects in the hut, the low hiss of the tortilla as it is placed on the grill, the shuffling of the children by the door, watching me. Once more I picture old Chan K'in in the *milpa*, bending over the dry corn, and I summon him from the depths of my being. I am entering a state in which images, dreams, symbols have a life apart from the words used to describe them.

When I look up, José Güero is gazing at me with glowing eyes, and the light in the room is several times brighter. I feel light-headed, nearer dreaming than awake.

"You go . . . you don't go," José Güero says in Spanish, several times. "*Te vas . . . no te vas.*" He uses the familiar *te*. The pauses between repetitions draw me deeper into the silence within the hut. And then it happens. A luminous picture of Chan K'in appears spontaneously in my inner eye; it is much sharper and more vibrant than the images I had conjured up on my own. Chan K'in is bending over, cutting a swath in a patch of weeds with a long machete. I can see the grass fly, and the yellowed cornstalks around him, which tower at least two feet above his head. Chan K'in's long black hair covers his face. He unbends and stands erect — still in my mind's eye — and looks all around him. I still cannot see his face, but I have an immediate sense of his receiving and acknowledging my signal. He bends down and resumes his cutting.

I turn to José Güero, who is grinning faintly. "*No te vas,*" he says, with a note of finality. "You do not go." I smile and nod my thanks to José for empowering me to have this televisual experience — if that is what it was. I am appreciative but also puzzled. I know I have experienced something most unusual, but cannot tell how much of it is purely subjective— born of my intense desire to communicate with Chan K'in — and how much of what I "saw" exists outside myself and can be put to an objective test. I am aware that José Güero is initiating me in some way, guiding me along planes of everyday Lacandon reality.

Young Chan K'in arrives with his wife, Koh, and their month-old daughter. He seems surprised to find me with his father-in-law.

"We made music," José tells him.

After gazing intently at me Young Chan K'in says he will write a letter to his brother K'ayum so that I can take it to him, with some money.

I agree at once, touched by this conciliatory gesture. I tell them I must go now, my time is running out.

As I get up to leave, one of José Güero's albino daughters brings me three small hen's eggs, which she places carefully in my shoulder bag.

I get back on the path to Chan K'in's house, one eye peeled for snakes. As I enter the village I am intercepted by a friendly young man who invites me to his hut.

I sit on a stool and he hands me an old, torn sheet of blue paper. "Write," he says, and dictates a letter to a professor friend in Mexico City who had given him a phonograph:

"I am K'in Bor. I am well. I received your letter. I have the phonograph. It is a good phonograph, but the batteries died. When do you come?" He signs the letter painstakingly and brings me his friend's address. I copy it on an old, crumpled envelope and promise to place a stamp on it and mail it myself.

"Good!" says K'in Bor, beaming proudly. "Now we are friends, you and I. What is your name?"

I tell him.

"You wish to meet my father-in-law, Chan K'in?"

I tell him that is the chief reason I have come.

K'in Bor signals me to come outside, and for a long minute we stand in silence as he listens to the wind in the trees. His eyes become abstracted, distant, as K'ayum's had in Na-Bolom when I first asked him about his father.

After what feels like an hour but cannot have been more than ten minutes, K'in Bor's ears perk up and his eyes suddenly spark, like an animal's. "My father-in-law is coming," he says.

I look toward the lake, but see nothing. After an endless two or three minutes a woman's head appears above the brush, about forty yards away. As she emerges into the clearing I see that she is preceded by a small boy, Chan K'in's youngest son, who carries an umbrella. The woman, wife number one, has a wide strap across her forehead and a large bale of maize and dried corn husk on her back. Wife number two and the youngest one walk directly behind, with loads that bend their small bodies almost double. Last is Chan K'in, walking erect in his gray tunic and carrying a blue Lufthansa shoulder bag stuffed with dried corn.

I start forward, but K'in Bor holds me back.

Chan K'in enters his hut and comes out almost at once. He looks about him, as if sniffing the air. When he sees us, he claps his hands.

"Now you may go," K'in Bor says, and gently pushes me forward. As I approach the Lacandon elder, he touches my shoulder lightly and asks me inside his hut. There is no doubt in my mind that he has anticipated my visit in some way, although he has never heard my name. He straddles a hammock, this small, extraordinarily vigorous man of seventy-nine or eighty, and I sit down on a stump. Black stalactites of palmetto hang from Chan K'in's roof. The entire ceiling is black from the smoke of wood fires.

The hut is as spacious as José Güero's, and less crowded. I see no plastic utensils anywhere, only the conventional gourd bowls, dried beans and sheafs of tobacco hanging from the rafters. As we talk the wives walk in and out, including the twenty-year-old, who carries Chan K'in's small son. She is the only one who avoids my gaze. None of the women speak Spanish; they smile and gesture to make me feel welcome.

I convey to Chan K'in warm greetings from Trudi Blom, and mention that she referred to him as "my father."

"But *she* is my mother," Chan K'in says, in the childlike Lacandon Spanish, and grins widely.

I am not in awe of this slight, jovial patriarch with the long, jet-black hair, sparse mustache and deep-set oriental eyes that sparkle with humor and vitality. I have waited long for this encounter, and now that I am here his physical presence is recompense enough. We exchange grins and I repeat his name several times, varying the stresses so it sounds less Chinese.

I tell him I have many questions to ask, but my heart is already full. He nods his head and points to his chest.

". . . And I also have an airplane to catch," I add lamely.

"Ah, you must not miss your airplane," he says, in a teasing voice. "If you do, you will have to stay in the Hotel Caribe." Tears of laughter fill his eyes as he shakes his head at the preposterous — and inevitable — reality of the Hotel Maya Caribe, the wave of the future.

I take out the harmonica I'd brought for him and place it in his hands. On opening the bright red box he says, "Ah, it is like before —" and I know he is recalling the flutes. He plays a few chords with gusto until wife number two gently snatches the harmonica from him and places it on a far shelf, with other gifts.

"Chan K'in," I say, turning serious, "what will happen to the Lacandones when they cut down the trees?"

His expression turns sober, but the sparkle remains in his eyes. "I know they will cut down the forest," he says. "They will cut it all down, not only the mahogany. I alone cannot stop them. There is too much cold. Our Lord Hachäkyum will make everything die, because of the cold. The grass wishes to die. The seed, the animals all wish to die. And the true people also — we all die. In thirty years Hachäkyum will destroy the world. . . . But I am not afraid." He shrugs one shoulder and falls silent.

I ask Chan K'in about the missionaries, who will be paying frequent visits to Nahá now that Lacanjá has been Christianized.

"They are very serious," he says, putting on a mock-somber face.

"They do not drink *balché* or beer, they do not smoke cigars or eat tamales or *posol* [the Indian corn broth]. Hachäkyum does not like serious
people who will not drink, smoke, or eat *posol*. I think perhaps their
hearts have something lacking, and they wish to complete themselves by
making others the same as they are."

Once more he laughs, and I ask, "What does Hachäkyum think of
Christ?"

"Christ is another," he says. "He is perhaps good, a good god, but he is
not Hachäkyum. Christ is the god of the *ts'ul* — the foreigners. My father
was a son of Hachäkyum, and his father also, and they were born here
and they died here. And I will too." Then he adds with a sigh, "Everyone
wants me to change but I do not change."

"Chan K'in," I ask, "can a white man become a *hach winik* [true per-
son]?"

He ponders a long time. "You are not one of us, but you can live like the
hach winik. You can plant maize and tobacco and give offerings to
Hachäkyum so he will be pleased, and accept you as his son." And now
the sadness enters Chan K'in's eyes, and he lowers his voice. "Now
everything changes. My sons also change. They no longer give the *posol*
to Hachäkyum. They do not take part in the incense-burning ceremonies.
Soon they will not even make the *balché*, as happened in Lacanjá after
the elders died. My sons make bows and arrows to trade for bullets and
batteries for their phonographs. They sell our sacred drums to the
foreigners. They are very interested in money. This is not at all pleasing
to Hachäkyum and that is why he destroys the world."

I tell Chan K'in about the earthquake in Guatemala, and about the
death and suffering I witnessed there among the Indians. He is so affected he does not speak for a long time.

"Hachäkyum makes the earthquake," he says at last.

"And what will happen," I ask him, "when the world is destroyed?"

"Hachäkyum will order his son-in-law, Akinchob, the god of maize, to
gather all the men and all the animals, and he will shut them inside a
boat — all the creatures, even the snake. Akinchob will keep the seeds of
all the trees in his house, and then the god of wind will come and knock
down all the trees. Then it will rain. The rains will fill everything. After
ten years the boat will descend slowly, slowly, to Palenque, where
Hachäkyum will make the world new. Then the true people and the *ts'ul*
will rise from the boat, and the animals also. Akinchob will then plant the
seeds and the trees and the flowers will rise, and the bush will be full of
life. Then we begin again to offer our prayers to Hachäkyum, and to drink
balché and make tamales and the *posol* in his honor, and to burn incense
in the god-pots. And he will be pleased with his children once more."

The five southern Lacandones who were exhibited at the Guatemalan
National Fair, November 1938
(PAUL ROYER)

Robert Bruce with K'ayum de la Laguna and his family, Lacanjá, 1954
(ROBERT BRUCE)

José Pepe Chan Bol (right) and his wife, mid-1950's
(TRUDI BLOM)

José Pepe Chan Bol, Lacanjá, 1977
(VICTOR PERERA)

Obregón and Vicente Bor,
mid-1950's
(TRUDI BLOM)

Old Mateo with freshly
killed game (curassow),
Nahá, 1959
(R. B.)

Pepe Castillo making ceremonial fire, 1958
(R. B.)

(Below):
Antonio with a ceremonial pot in which red dye is prepared for "god-hats," Nahá, 1959
(R. B.)

Opposite
(Above):
Lake Mensäbäk
(TRUDI BLOM)

(Below):
Chan K'in and his wife Koh II, 1976
(TRUDI BLOM)

Thatching a Lacandon house, Nahá, 1959
(R. B.)

Making new god-pots for the incense-renewal ceremony, Nahá, 1970

K'in Paniagua and Young Mateo knead the clay
(R. B.)

Old Mateo and K'in García mold and shape the new pots
(R. B.)

Young Mateo and Chan K'in apply the final lime coating after the firing
(R. B.)

A Lacandon boy with a toy bow and arrow, 1954
(R. B.)

José Güero making a fire with flint and steel,
1958

Part 2.

Chan K'in and His World

San Cristóbal

"Ki' iba a wilik," Robert Bruce said as we climbed into bed in our cozy, firelit room in Na-Bolom, exhausted from the sixteen-hour drive from Mexico City. "Be careful what you see [in your dreams]." This was the first Lacandon Maya phrase he had taught me, and it would prove to be good advice during our weeks together in Nahá.

"Laila tov," I replied in Hebrew. Good night.

On the road to San Cristóbal we had been swapping Maya and Hebrew phrases, and found the two languages astonishingly sympathetic, both phonetically and structurally. This affinity would be one of the foundation stones of our association, and of our friendship.

At breakfast the next morning in the spacious Na-Bolom dining room we chatted with Trudi Blom about the current state of the two Lacandon communities, Lacanjá and Nahá. Robert had not been to Nahá in three years, and it was several more since his last visit to Lacanjá. It had been almost a year since my own brief visits to Lacanjá and to Nahá, where I had interviewed Chan K'in. On my way home I had stopped in Mexico City and looked up Robert Bruce. At that first meeting the idea came up to collaborate on a book about Chan K'in and the northern Lacandones.

Robert and Trudi discussed the important differences between the two Lacandon communities, in language, temperament, and even in physical characteristics.

"The Lacanjá Lacandones look as if they had stepped out of a Classical Mayan frieze," Trudi pointed out. "The Nahá Lacandones look more like the Tzeltal Indians, who have mixed blood."

"And yet," Robert said, "it is the Nahá Lacandones who have stubbornly held onto their ancient traditions, while the Lacanjá ones have gone Baptist."

We shook our heads and grew silent. The cultural differences between the two communities had taken on a vital political importance, as the Mexican Department of Forestry was trying to set up the Lacanjá president, José Pepe Chan Bol, as spokesman and signatory for both groups. In this way they expected to bypass Chan K'in's authority and gain control of the mahogany around Nahá, which had thus far been denied them.

Even before arriving in Nahá, we were already embroiled in a life-or-death issue, for without the mahogany the ecological stability of the rain forest would be disrupted, and the Nahá Lacandon community would most likely wither and disperse. This process was already well advanced in Lacanjá. Mensäbäk, the other northern Lacandon settlement, was not far behind. Roughly half the families there were already evangelized, and most of their mahogany had been logged.

"Things are out of hand at Lacanjá," Trudi said, in her ringing voice. She was dressed in a bright-blue pantsuit, and had blue eye shadow under straight, plucked eyebrows; the effect was to make her craggy, handsomely chiseled features look even more monumental. "They are spending money there as if there is no end to it. They have four cars now, including an ambulance and a VW Safari. Next thing you know, they'll be wanting television sets and their own Cessna!" She waved her arms in disgust. "Ach — it's terrible there now. I've gotten reports that José Pepe Chan Bol is getting more money than is due him. He has been corrupted by the government. Too much money, too much money, and what have they got to show for it? They live in filth, just like before, and they have collected a lot of worthless junk!" She sighed, dropped her hand on the table. "But José Pepe is not a bad man at bottom. I know him. He can still be corrected."

"And how is it at Nahá?" I asked.

"Old Chan K'in had a bad scare when a tree branch fell on his head," she said. "But he seems to be all right." Again she sighed. "It will all be on his shoulders now. The good news from Nahá is that his son K'ayum has straightened out, after getting carried away for a while by money and ambition. Even Young Chan K'in, who is president, is becoming more responsible. The father's influence seems to have brought them around. And K'ayum's letters are getting better. He can now differentiate between the Spanish *v* and *b* — a remarkable achievement for an unschooled Lacandon. And he is painting."

Trudi asked Robert what he had thought of the film *Cascabel,* on which he had collaborated as a consultant. *Cascabel* (Rattler) is an antiestablishment commercial film, part documentary and part feature, which presents the Lacandones as Mexico's aboriginal conscience, exploited by demagogues and the government lumber interests. The lead role of "Chan K'in," a youngish Lacandon spokesman who is betrayed by the sympathetic liberals he has come to trust, is well played by a Mexican actor, but I felt that the film's rather heavy-handed polemics, aimed squarely at the Echeverría administration, damaged an otherwise effective portrayal of the Lacandones' predicament. *Cascabel,* which was playing to packed houses both in Mexico and in Europe, had provoked President López Portillo, Echeverría's successor, into issuing an official statement in support of the Lacandones' title to their forest resources.

"It was not as good as I had hoped," Robert said, "nor as bad as I had feared."

"They mixed up the southern and northern Lacandones," Trudi said, "as if they were one and the same. This is unpardonable. But the ones who appeared in the film were marvelous; they confirmed my belief that Lacandones are natural actors — all of them."

"Yes," Robert agreed, and smiled wryly. "They are superbly adaptable. They always sense what an outsider expects of them. I sometimes get the feeling they're showing me only the face I expect to find, and no other."

"Perhaps," I suggested, "that is one of the keys to their survival."

"Yes, and it can also become the key to their extinction," Trudi said pointedly. "The ancient Mayas were equally adaptable. They absorbed the Toltec invasion, the Aztec invasion, even the Spaniards. They Mayanized all the invaders until there was no Maya left."

Afterward Trudi took us up to her room and showed us a watercolor K'ayum had painted of the water-lily lake in Nahá. It was done in green and blue, with deft daubs of white and yellow for the water lilies. It reminded me of a crude work by an early Impressionist, with a keen sense of the play of light and shadow over water.

"You see?" Trudi said, with understandable pride. "K'ayum is a brilliant painter."

I remarked on K'ayum's audacity. He had skipped the classical, Byzantine and Renaissance periods and gone straight to early Monet.

"And it is the same with religion," Robert said. "They have skipped the Catholic Church, and gone straight to Protestant Technology."

"K'ayum is brilliant," Trudi insisted, returning to her favorite. "Old Chan K'in is intelligent, but K'ayum surpasses him. I will have to see he gets a proper education. After Chan K'in dies, Nahá is finished. The road will pass through the settlement, the mahogany will be cut down, and Phil Baer or his replacements will turn them all into Baptists and Adventists, as has already happened at Lacanjá and Mensäbäk."

In the afternoon, after lunch, Trudi saw us to our car. She had heard that Robert was carrying two cases of Scotch into the forest, and warned Robert against sharing it too liberally with the Lacandones.

"They have no defense against liquor," she said, "— and you should know better."

Somewhat sheepishly Robert promised to see to it that the Scotch drinking would be kept in moderation.

Trudi frowned skeptically. "Oh go to hell!" she said, and turned toward me. "Watch him!" she snapped, glowering severely, and turned away.

The two cases of George V Scotch in the back of the Safari had been a source of concern from the day we left Mexico City. Robert, an admitted heavy drinker, called it "evangelist retardant" because it prevents some Lacandones from converting and causes others to relapse. I need not have worried, however. The Lacandones were to teach us a lesson or two about excess and moderation.

Ocosingo

Robert had decided to fly to Nahá from Ocosingo, a town eighty-seven kilometers north of San Cristóbal, on the gravel road to Palenque. This would cut our flying time in half, as well as our fare, and as we were loaded down with equipment, the saving would be considerable.

We stopped in town to buy sausages and deviled ham to supplement our anticiapted diet of beans and tortillas. Robert had warned that I would have trouble digesting the forest diet in the first few days, and absorbing the necessary proteins. I already had fifteen pounds of trail mix, purchased on a panicky impulse in a Santa Cruz Integral Yoga store. As it turned out, none of our equipment was wasted. We used nearly all of it during our sojourn in Nahá, and afterward the camping gear, alkaline batteries, propane lighters, Swiss army jackknives made excellent parting gifts. Even the trail mix was happily shared with Lacandon children.

The road to Ocosingo had not been graded since the last heavy rains, and the drive was as jolting as we had been led to expect. Still, Robert's Safari negotiated the fifty miles in two and a half hours. We ate a tamal dinner at Ocosingo's only tourist restaurant, checked in at the only tourist hotel, and sat in the square to watch the sun set slowly behind the cathedral. Ocosingo had the air of a sleepy lowland town that is undergoing a gradual but perceptible transformation. About ten miles from Ocosingo we had passed two huge lumber mills and a number of new Tzeltal settlements — new, that is, since Robert last visited the area. In town there was new construction on both sides of the plaza, and a number of young, restless city Mexicans paced to and fro in the park, taking the evening *paseo*.

They looked as if they might be technicians from Pemex, the state-owned petroleum monopoly that is carrying out exploratory probes in the valleys and hills around Ocosingo. In four or five years Ocosingo may begin to look like another Villahermosa, the oil boomtown on the northern coast. The pace and atmosphere of the town will alter drastically, and the New Acquisitiveness will hone the slack faces of the young townies, who yearn to be oil drillers and engineers.

As the sun set behind the cathedral bell tower, I savored the doomed stillness in the plaza, and the twang of guitar strings from the soldiers sitting idly in the barracks. I reveled in the shrill cawing of the blackbirds roosting in the park trees, the pestering cries of gum hawkers and bootblacks, the glances of pretty girls strolling by in bright gingham dresses. Ocosingo would soon be the new frontier, and not far beyond lay the razing of the Lacandon forest by the lumber companies and the cattle ranchers, and the cancerous proliferation of the oil drills.

When we showed up at the tiny airstrip early next morning, the surrounding hills were concealed by a bank of clouds. The regular Ocosingo pilot, whose name was Chino, promised to take us in an hour or so, after the ground fog lifted.

At around eight-thirty he said, "Let's go."

We piled all the equipment into the Cessna 180 and flew over the first ridges. My heart raced. Would they be expecting us at Nahá? Always before, they had known the day of Robert's unannounced arrival, and more than once they had cleared trails for him that had been blocked for weeks, so certain were they of his coming.

As we approached the second ridge, I saw that it was covered with thick clouds. Chino shook his head. "Still blocked," he said. He banked the plane, and my heart sank to the floor.

"I hate to go back," Chino said, as the spire of the Ocosingo church came into view. "But it is too risky." Knowing the fatalistic bent of bush pilots, I seriously wondered if he would make another attempt today. The death in an air crash four months earlier of their best pilot, Pepe Martínez, had made all the local fliers skittish.

We waited at the airport café for two hours, while Chino made some routine flights to nearby ranches. At around ten-thirty he took off, and there was no sign of him for over an hour.

"Chino has gone and abandoned us," I said to Robert, half in jest. He sat grimly quiet, sipping at his third cold beer. I had become aware in the past week of the heavy toll Mexico City had taken of Robert's health. He drank heavily ("I am the last of the hard-drinking anthropologists," he had boasted in a letter) and smoked three packs of cigarettes a day.

He looked up at the clouds, still stalled above the hills.

"Could be a *norte* coming," he said flatly, and shot me a dark, hooded glance.

This was to be the low point of our expedition. I felt all the momentum that had accumulated since my visit to Nahá last January suddenly ebb away. A three-day storm now could well mean the end not only of our journey but of our entire collaboration, whose chief glue up to now was a shared but untested enthusiasm.

After I had returned from Nahá last January, it had taken me five days to locate Robert Bruce in Mexico City. He had moved from his apartment and left no telephone number or forwarding address. The staff at the Museum of Anthropology had been taciturn and distracted, and had led me repeatedly to the office of Alberto Ruz, the discoverer of the famous tomb of Palenque.

"No, no! *Bruce!*" I had shouted. "Roberto *Bruce!*" I did not know then that he was housed in the linguistics wing of the enormous museum complex, just down the stairs from the entrance and to the right. As a last resort, I had left messages for him at the Institute of Anthropology, and in the Anthropology Department of the University of Mexico.

When I finally got the call from Robert at the María Cristina Hotel, I had nearly stopped believing in his existence. I concluded that *The Book of Chan K'in* and *Lacandon Dream Symbolism* must have been written by one of the ghost aliases of B. Traven.

"Bruce speaking," he said, in his soft, Oklahoma drawl.

"So you exist."

"Of course. Is there a rumor to the contrary?"

"I've had more trouble locating you than I had finding Chan K'in."

"Of course," he said again. "Chan K'in lives in the forest. I inhabit the jungle."

I told Robert of my conversation with Chan K'in, and that night — my last in Mexico City — he had come over for drinks. He turned out to be a tall, heavily built and weathered-looking man of forty-three, my senior by a little less than three months. By the end of the evening we had discussed the possibility of doing a book together on the Lacandones.

After that it had been long, discursive letters, full of Lacandon lore and idiom, exchanges of books and manuscripts, erratic long-distance calls, the book contract and an advance, our meeting in Mexico City. When we started out for San Cristóbal we had known each other eleven months, but our time together added up to less than six hours.

Our partnership was an exercise in calculated risk, but the currents underneath ran deep. After a week in Nahá we would be calling each other *hermano* — brother — and speculating that we had known one another in past lives.

Arrival in Nahá

At eleven-thirty Chino returned in his red and white Cessna. The cloud bank had lifted slightly. "It looks good," he said. "Let's try it."

We were in the air in no time, and now the clouds thinned and parted before us. High ridges and green valleys opened up below. After fifteen minutes the first tall hardwoods came into view, on the high spurs.

Robert pointed to a cluster of houses in the center of a rolling meadow, and slowly shook his head. "That is El Real ranch. Ten years ago this was surrounded by forest. It used to take me two days to get here from Ocosingo, by mule."

"And in ten years more, all of it will be cattle-grazing land," Chino said. "Take a good long look at your forest, Don Roberto."

We flew over a colony of Tzeltal Indians, who have been moving into the Lacandon forest in growing numbers as the highland farmlands wear out. All around it were the familiar swatches of cleared forest, like ugly bald spots in the towering tree line, where cornfields had been blazed from the green forest, cultivated for three or four years, and then abandoned. As we approached Nahá we saw several more of these scarred areas, where banana and citrus trees grew unobstructed by the mahogany, Spanish cedar, ceiba, *chicozapote* giants; these would take many generations to recover, given a chance. The attrition was well advanced.

Lake Nahá came into view, with billowing nimbus clouds reflected on its mirror surface. A sudden squall battered the plane, and the lake disappeared from sight. The hard, pelting rain was accompanied by strong gusts that lurched us sickeningly from side to side.

"Let's hope the runway hasn't gotten too soaked," Chino said softly. "This will be my first landing in Nahá."

Once again my heart raced, and I held my breath. But then the clouds parted and I saw the runway below us, washed in brilliant sunlight. Already white-clad tiny figures had emerged from the huts and converged on the airstrip.

Chino circled the runway twice, to get a fix on its dimensions and condition. On the second turn we flew over the main settlement on the south shore of the lake — our final destination — and saw doll-sized Lacandones looking up and waving to us.

The landing was bumpy but well executed. We suffered nothing worse than a bone-rattling jolt as the plane skidded to a halt.

"Not a bad runway!" Chino said, grinning. "The ground is solid, and it is longer than I expected. Next time, it will be like coming home."

I wanted to hug the man for his skill and offhanded courage. So this was how bush pilots earned their hero status.

He turned at the far side and taxied toward the cluster of huts. A dozen villagers had gathered to welcome us. Although the cargo-cult stage was long past in Nahá, they looked at us with dazzled, wonder-struck faces.

Flights from San Cristóbal and Tuxtla are almost daily events now, but the moment of landing is still fraught with anticipation.

The dazed silence lasted until Robert stepped out of the plane, waved and shouted, "We have come."

"Eh, Roberto, did you bring the whisky?" Young Mateo calls out, and a ripple of laughter spreads among the men. Apparently, word has traveled ahead via one of the San Cristóbal pilots.

We take down the two cases and the rest of the luggage, as a Lacandon man approaches Chino and asks him about plane fares to Ocosingo.

Contact is established, but Chino does not step off the plane. He starts up the engine and looks quizzically at us as we are engulfed by the long-haired, white-gowned Lacandones.

"See you on the thirteenth!" he calls, as he takes off.

We gather all our equipment in one pile, and then an awkward silence descends. How will we get across the lake?

K'in Bor steps forward, thanks me for the photos I had sent him, and says he will take us to the south shore. He says his father-in-law, Chan K'in, is expecting us. There are no handshakes or *abrazos*. "So you have arrived?" "So you have returned?" Acquaintance is reopened with obvious comments, which are followed by more intimate queries: "How is your spirit?" The response becomes long-drawn and meticulously graphic. Like Old World Jews, Lacandones punctuate reunions by swapping calamities.

At the canoe landing Robert pauses to distribute cigarettes and to toast our safe arrival with a pint of whisky. Jorge, the elder of the north-shore community, a morose-looking man of about sixty, hangs back cautiously until the whisky bottle is passed around. "So you have arrived, Robert," he says with a flushed grin, after quaffing a double ration. "Later on you will come drink *balché* with us — you and your companion."

"*Ne tsoy* [very good]," Robert says. "Now I go."

"Go," Jorge says, waving ceremonially as we board the *cayuco*.

The lake crossing takes about fifteen minutes, but it feels much longer. Huge silver-gray clouds drift across our bow. The tensions of the past days begin to recede, borne away on our wake as we skim between banks of cattails and water-lily pads. What a contrast to the hour-long trek through the deep mud and liana-choked trails of my first visit! Last January I had come to Nahá as a stranger and neophyte who had to cross buffer zones and submit to interrogation before meeting with Chan K'in. Now, thanks to Robert, I am approaching him as a privileged guest; perhaps, I fear, a little too privileged.

"How is the game?" Robert asks K'in Bor, who is reputed to be the most skilled hunter of Nahá, at least on the "traditionalist" side of the lake.

"So-so," he says, in laconic Lacandon Spanish. "Not much pheasant or boar, but there are pacas and small deer. We are eating meat — when there is ammunition." He paddles with firm, powerful strokes. Although only about five feet four, which is tall for a Lacandon, K'in Bor has the forearms and shoulders of a much larger man.

"Good," Robert says. "Then we shall have meat." I know he has brought along several dozen boxes of .22 and .38 caliber shells, which, along with the propane lighters, will be our most valued gifts.

"And your wife, Nuk?" Robert asks.

"So-so as well. She wakes up at night, screaming. She is afraid of the dark."

"Afraid, or jealous?" Robert teases. "Does she know about the Dutch girl?"

K'in Bor laughs. "Lies, Robert, lies. There is no Dutch girl."

"Well, Marianne told me she likes you, when I saw her in Mexico."

"She exaggerates," K'in Bor says, a little nervously. This man-talk is part of a ritual, a way of reestablishing social parity after a long absence.

"So you brought much whisky," K'in Bor retaliates, paddling steadily. "Robert requires his whisky." He laughs. "Whisky is Robert's girlfriend."

Stung, Robert laughs good-naturedly. "The blonde everyone loves," he says, parodying a popular light-beer commercial.

"Tomorrow," K'in Bor says, "we will have *balché*. We shall see if you can still drink with the men."

"Very nice," Robert says, in Maya. "I am always ready for a good *balché*."

Two of Chan K'in's small sons, K'in and little Chan K'in, wait at the landing and help us unload. The path from the lake is flooded and laddered with crossties, and I stumble and slide with my navy duffel bag and heavy suitcase.

Old Chan K'in awaits us by his hut, looking small and dark and bright-eyed in his white cotton tunic. Dogs bark menacingly at my approach and are silenced by Chan K'in's eldest wife, Koh I, who throws a stick at them.

"I have come to see you," Robert says in Maya.

"Come in, come in, Roberto," Chan K'in answers. "It is good that you have come."

Robert introduces me formally, as if we hadn't met before. Chan K'in's relaxed, beaming countenance puts me at ease at once. I extend my hand, and he takes it limply, retracting his smile momentarily. I would not make that mistake again. No need for physical greetings, among Lacandon.

He shows us into the hut next to his. It had been cleared out and the dirt floor swept clean. Corn is stacked neatly in one corner, and bunches of tobacco hang from the thatched roof. Three of Chan K'in's small sons follow us inside, chattering excitedly, touching us and our equipment as if to verify our solidity.

"Here is your bed, Roberto," Chan K'in says, pointing to a striped canvas hammock neatly suspended between roof beams.

"Ah yes. That's the Tenosique one I left here three years ago."

"And your companion?" Chan K'in asks. "How will he sleep?"

"He brought his own," Robert assures him.

"I will leave you now, so you can rest. We will eat in a little while.

Chichin, chichin," he repeats, to indicate how soon, and walks out the door.

I string up my jungle hammock with the aid of the two older boys, K'in and little Chan K'in, nine and ten respectively, who are expert knot tiers. They have taken turns setting up tents and stringing hammocks for Trudi, whose permanent camp is located near the airstrip.

They watch avidly as we unload our flashlights, my water canteen, toilet articles, notebooks and tape recorders. When I take out the fifteen-pound bag of trail mix from the bottom of the duffel, Chan K'in's littlest son sticks out his hand. "For me."

He takes some in his mouth, chews tentatively, smiles approval. "Tastes good," he says. I give some nuts, raisins and dried fruit to the two older boys.

K'in, the nine-year-old, keeps spinning a carved wooden propeller, which he calls his *avión* — airplane.

"I have one too," I tell him in Spanish. "But mine flies." I make a helicopter spinning motion with my hand.

He looks at me, skeptical but eager, and I pull out a wooden puddle jumper from my duffel bag.

"Outside," I say.

I twirl the stem of the puddle jumper between my palms, and it soars up above the palm roofs of the huts.

The two boys squeal with delight.

I hand it to the younger brother, K'in, who is larger and more aggressive. With one deft twirl he sends it aloft, nearly as high as my toss. He had watched me carefully, and had mastered the spinning motion on his very first attempt. We spend the next half hour flying the puddle jumper, which keeps landing on the palm roofs and has to be rescued with a pole. The mothers come out to watch, in silence, and I spy the elder Chan K'in peering at us from inside the hut.

"*Avión! Avión!"* They yell, as they spin and hurl the propeller into the sky, and their bodies lift off the ground with the yearning to fly. I too am a small boy playing with the wooden toy — the five-year-old who saw Lacandones at the fair and thought them beautiful and sad.

Although I was not aware of it then, a circle was being closed.

Chan K'in's Kitchen

A tiny boy calls us to lunch. We move into the kitchen, a large hut directly across from ours. In the center sits a large wooden table, covered with an old flowered oilcloth. The kitchen is well outfitted with enamel pots and kettles, a gas lamp, assorted silverware and a shelf of bottled conserves, but the primitive clay oven in the rear burns small firewood, corn husks and cobs. On the upper beams are stacks of unfinished arrows, and two old .22's are propped in one corner.

Chan K'in tells us there is fresh pork for dinner, which is a rare treat as the Lacandones have been reluctant to keep domestic animals other than dogs, chickens and an occasional pet. The pig had been one of the last survivors of an aborted hog-raising experiment on the airstrip side of the lake. They had proved too adept at breaking out of their frail pole-fenced enclosures and rooting up the sweet potatoes. Our arrival had provided a good enough pretext for Jorge to slaughter one of his last hogs and send a generous portion to Chan K'in's household.

Koh II, Chan K'in's beautiful second wife, who is also the strongest and most talented, serves us black beans, rice and large tortillas on metal soup plates. The pork is tasty, although it will take me several days to become accustomed to the half-cooked beans, just as Robert had predicted. Koh smiles, but does not look at me as I return the soup plate with half the beans intact. It will be two more weeks before she addresses a word to me directly.

We bring in our first gifts — pork sausages, canned deviled ham, and a rich Ocosingo cheese, which is immediately opened. We also contribute a quart of honey and some brewers' yeast, which they eye suspiciously. There will be frequent jokes about the yeast, which tastes like dirt to them.

"Many vitamins," I reassure them, and they probe in it with their knives, seeking the evidence.

"Vitamina," the kids say, liking the sound, and laugh aloud. "Mucha vitamina. Vitamina tastes like dirt." I try to teach them to sprinkle it on their beans, or stir it into their coffee, but the taste is still disagreeable to them.

They also make fun of the sausages, which they call "dog's turds." But they eat them heartily all the same.

After lunch we smoke a leisurely cigar, my first taste of Nahá tobacco, which I find full-bodied but slightly sour. Chan K'in is in fine spirits, relaxed and garrulous. He laughs frequently at Robert's witticisms, and at his own. He still does not have a gray hair on his head, although I detect new lines around his eyes and some white stubble on his chin.

Chan K'in tells us of his mishap with the fallen tree branch. He points to the center of his forehead, where the branch hit him as he was clearing underbrush in the milpa with his machete. The branch apparently belonged to a charred tree that had survived the previous burn. "It knocked me to sleep," Chan K'in says. "If it had been bigger, I would be dead. But Hachäkyum does not want me dead yet."

Young Chan K'in leans in the door and greets us both without breaking a formal distance. As president of Nahá and the eldest son of Chan K'in's number one wife, Young Chan K'in is mindful of his dignity. He recalls my first visit last January, and remarks on its brevity. "Much airfare for such a short visit," he says. "This time you stay longer."

I feel that an official welcome has now been extended. Robert fetches some .22 shells and a propane lighter, and I give Young Chan K'in some alkaline batteries. He nods approvingly. "Ah, these are the good ones," he says in acknowledgment. He sells the ordinary kind in his store.

Robert then speaks of his own accident two years earlier, when he totaled his car against a horse, in Tehuantepec, and received a severe gash on his forehead. He shows us the scar.

"Hachäkyum wants you alive also, Roberto," Chan K'in says almost motheringly, and goes into a peroration about cars and snakes. "In Mexico the cars kill," he says. "In Nahá, it is the snakes." We make a reckoning of the number of people Chan K'in has known over the years who died of snakebite, while Robert and I add up the number of our acquaintances killed in car accidents. Chan K'in, whose life span is roughly the sum of ours, knows a dozen people who have died of snake venom. Between us, Robert and I have over twenty acquaintances who were killed in automobile accidents. Chan K'in judges that snakes are more beautiful killers than cars. All things considered, it is better to die in the forest.

At this juncture in the conversation Chan K'in's son K'ayum pokes his head in the door, an instant after an image of his face had flashed through my mind. I nearly jump from my seat as he exclaims, "I was asking myself when that Victor would come back —"

In Na-Bolom, ten months earlier, K'ayum and I had exchanged dreams, and then interpreted them for one another using Lacandon and Jungian principles. It had been an exhilarating experience.

"And I was asking myself what had become of you," I say. "Were you painting?"

"No. I was pounding sugarcane for tomorrow's balché."

"Aha!" I tease him. "So the straying lamb has returned to the fold."

"K'ayum is a good son," Chan K'in says. "Tomorrow, he will preside over the ceremonies and perform the prayers."

We return to cars and snakes, as K'ayum tells of his experience with a small nauyaca that bit him when he was a small boy. "I fainted, and was carried back to my hut. When I awoke, I thought I was dead. Now I am afraid of snakes, and I don't go to the milpa much anymore because it is full of nauyacas."

"When the road comes," Robert says, "you can drive to the milpa in a Safari, as they do in Lacanjá."

Everyone laughs. Automobiles fascinate Lacandones almost as much as airplanes, although few of the younger ones have ever seen a car. The drawings given to us by Lacandon children are full of fanciful winged automobiles and tanklike buses with eight or nine wheels.

"Did you know," says Young Chan K'in, "that Young Mateo wants the logging road to come through Nahá, so he can drive his own car?"

"How will he get one?" I ask.

"He borrows money from everyone, and makes secret deals in San Cristóbal. They say he has much money in a San Cristóbal bank."

The notion of a Nahá Lacandon banker who drives his own car seems as incongruous as it is sad. The laughter loses its merriment, and we disperse to our huts.

A Swim

An hour later K'in Bor comes by with his small son, K'ayum, and takes Robert and me for a swim in the lake. As we walk to the landing, K'in Bor whispers, "You will see — an alligator will bite you and take away your leg."

We all swim naked except for K'in Bor, who has a pair of yellow trunks given him by a visitor. We are joined by little Chan K'in and K'in, who paddle their own canoe and are excellent swimmers. The "alligator" never appears. All the large crocodiles of Lake Nahá had been hunted out years before, although small ones can still be found in a small connecting lake. When they grow over two feet long, K'in Bor shoots them and turns them into shoulder bags.

We bathe and then shave, sitting on the oars of the *cayucos* under the intensely curious gaze of little K'ayum, K'in and Chan K'in, who laugh out loud when I fall trying to pull on my trousers while balancing on one leg. Tunics are so much easier to slip on and off. Little K'ayum rubs my smooth cheek with his hand, then traces with one finger his father's sparse mustache and chin hair. Like all American Indians of the Mongolian type, Lacandon Mayas grow very scant facial hair and rarely if ever shave.

Old Chan K'in visits us in the afternoon, with a guitar and a brand-new Sony tape recorder that a generous visitor had left with him. He places the tape recorder in front of Robert, hands him the guitar, and commands, "Sing, Roberto," with a mock-solemn expression.

After wetting his whistle with a swig of Scotch, Robert picks up the guitar and sings "Rancho Grande," "Cielito Lindo," and some *corridos.** He plays well, and has a soft, surprisingly rich baritone.

"More singing," Chan K'in says, and Robert sings the Falangist hymn from the Spanish Civil War era, "Los Luceros." I then accompany him in "La Quinze Brigada" and other Lincoln Brigade songs as well as in "Hava Nagila," which we had rehearsed together on the way down, never suspecting we would have to sing it in a "command performance" for Chan K'in.

Chan K'in plays us back and declares, *"Uts* [acceptable]." We all laugh at the aboriginal anthropologist passing judgment on the musical talents of his western informants.

For three days running the tape is played back at dawn, full blast, and I can overhear the Lacandones laughing and passing comments on Robert's performance. "His guitar is good, but his singing has been better," I hear someone shout before I am fully awake.

"Imagine what they'll say two hundred years from now," says Robert, "when they find that tape among the rubble of Nahá village. Some legacy we are leaving them: the Loyalist and Nationalist hymns of the Spanish Civil War."

* Mexican ballads and narrative songs.

K'in García

After dinner Old Chan K'in and K'ayum come to our hut to share a cigar with us, and a nightcap of Robert's whisky. They are joined by K'in García, Chan K'in's eldest son by Koh II. K'in is the handsomest of Chan K'in's fifteen living children; he has light-hazel eyes, a dashing mustache and long curly black hair that has earned him the nickname Louis XIV in Na-Bolom. K'in sits silently in one corner, eyeing us intently and giggling at the humorous turns in the conversation, but seldom taking part. I get no sense of the weight of responsibility that must sit on his shoulders as Chan K'in's firstborn son. He seems abstracted and somehow soft, although he has his mother's strong physique and thickly muscled forearms. He stays behind after the others leave, and has two more drinks with Robert. When he departs at last, Robert tells me K'in is the only Nahá Lacandon he has ever known to get mean drunk on bottled liquor.

"He has a lot of complexes," Robert adds, "but he is neither so simpleminded nor as shallow as he has chosen to appear."

As the firstborn son by Chan K'in's eldest wife, Young Chan K'in's claim to the title of t'o'ohil has precedence over K'in García's, though K'in is a year or two older. And Old Chan K'in has passed over K'in and settled on K'ayum as the next heir apparent after Young Chan K'in. Robert predicts that K'in García will eventually move across the lake, to the airstrip side, where he can develop his own personality away from his father's presence. One other son, fifteen-year-old Chan K'in Chico, who had been my guide on the first visit, had already moved there after marrying one of Jorge's daughters, and is performing son-in-law service to fulfill his contract. (In Nahá at present, a healthy bride fetches her father the equivalent of two to three hundred dollars.) Robert says Chan K'in Chico has grown lax in his ways since he moved to the north shore, and is made fun of by his pretty, spoiled wife, who is a year or two older.

At around nine, after writing in my journal, I spray myself thoroughly with Cutter's and climb into my jungle hammock. The zippered mosquito netting keeps out the cockroaches, fleas, spiders, no-see-ums and other rainy-season pests.

Rocking gently, I fall asleep, and have rich sensual dreams.

Onen

"That means you will eat meat," Chan K'in prognosticates at breakfast when I mention my erotic dreams.

"Is that all?" I ask Robert, disappointed. I had hoped to describe some of the more evocative scenes, which I felt had redeeming symbolic value.

"Erotic dreams always mean good hunting," Robert explains patiently. "The Lacandon are not interested in the aesthetic qualities or the psychological content of dreams. They are used chiefly for purposes of prophecy and to ward off potential calamities. One exception is a dream involving the *hach pixan* (real soul), which could mean a direct communication between two persons, living or dead. Now, if you dream of forest animals, for instance, Chan K'in's interest will almost certainly be aroused, for this could have a specific meaning. And if you or someone close to you dreams of the same animal repeatedly, this could be a way of discovering your *onen.*"

For the next several nights I concentrate on dreaming of dolphins, which I secretly wish to have as my *onen.* Instead, I have more erotic dreams, which interest neither Chan K'in nor Robert, although they strike me as especially good ones. "You will eat meat" is tantamount to saying, "You will arise in the morning," for there would be plenty of game and delicatessen on Chan K'in's table for the duration of our stay.

On the fourth night I dream of a blue-green hummingbird that hovers just above my head. Robert says, "Ah, now we are getting somewhere." He reports the dream to Chan K'in, who nods and says, "Let us wait and see."

From that day on I have one encounter after another with blue birds and hummingbirds. The second time I dream of a long, crested, blue bird Chan K'in brings out a Peterson's bird guide someone had left him and Robert points to a blue grosbeak. "Your *onen,*" he says.

I am disappointed. Finding my *onen* was becoming as important as tracing my Sephardic ancestry back to Spain, and a blue grosbeak seems lacking in grandeur.

Robert says, "You have to remember that your *onen* is passed down from father to son. You cannot have an animal of your own choosing — not in Nahá, at any rate."

Balché

After breakfast we bring out the remainder of our gifts, and present most of them to Chan K'in to distribute as he sees fit. Robert gives him snake serum and assorted medicines. The .22 rifle shells are especially prized, as Lacandones cannot buy ammunition in town without a license, except at prohibitive black market prices. Chan K'in gives two of the boxes of precious shells to K'in Bor, who seems deeply moved. "My father-in-law is a good man," he says afterward. But K'in Bor knows he will be expected to put meat on the table.

I give Koh II some scissors, safety pins, needles and thread, which make her smile and nod appreciatively. She is the most accomplished weaver and seamstress in the community. For Chan K'in I have brought a Swiss army knife, flashlights and disposable lighters. He barely nods his thanks at the more expensive gifts, which are whisked away for safe-keeping by Koh II. But he seems positively overjoyed by the ninety-five-cent Bic lighter.

"In the name of Hachäkyum!" he shouts, then laughs at himself for using the archaic expression.

The red Bic lighter never leaves his side while we are there. He uses it to light his cigars and incense pots during the minor ceremonies.

"Yes, the Americans know how to make things well," he said once, rubbing the lighter in his hand as if it were an amulet. "Almost as well as the Japanese." (A Japanese scientist had visited Nahá several months earlier, and had left some lighters and the Sony tape recorder. Chan K'in, it seems, has been conducting a comparative market analysis of Japanese and American gadgets.)

Chan K'in leads us back of the god-house to check on the fermentation of the *balché*. He lifts the palm-leaf cover from the ceremonial canoe in which the *balché* bark and the sugarcane had been mashed the day before, and then left to soak in gallons of water. The *balché* had already frothed and had turned the color and approximate texture of Guinness ale.

"It will be ready by noon," Chan K'in says.

We sit down to chat under the eaves of the god-house, a long, rectangular thatched structure with no walls or mahogany siding, so that the god-pots, drinking gourds, bark-cloth tunics and other ceremonial items are exposed to the air and the sunlight. About twenty low mahogany stools are arranged around a banana-leaf mat, and the gourds are stacked in the middle. The fifteen god-pots — each representing a major Lacandon deity — are lined up in two rows in the rear. Their protruding faces are black with countless layers of burned incense, an indication that a renewal ceremony is not too far distant.

Chan K'in had invited Robert to be a participant observer — the first occidental ever to be extended this privilege — in the previous incense-burner renewal ceremony, during the summer of 1970. The time is fast approaching to discard the old god-pots and make new ones: Chan K'in has warned Robert that eight years, or five cycles of Venus, is the maximum allowable interval between renewal ceremonies; otherwise, there will be dire and unforeseeable consequences for the world that Hachäkyum has made, and for all the creatures in it.

Our event, by comparison, is a lighthearted social gathering to celebrate the return of Nahá's adopted foreign son, Robert. But it has a more solemn significance as well. The end of the rains in December is nearly upon us, and with it a new cycle of razing, burning and planting will commence in the *milpas*. While the last of the corn is being harvested, the first quarter of the August moon — three weeks before the drenching September rains — will signal the time to plant tobacco on the cleared soil.

As we sit chatting, Old Mateo appears with a stave and a large bowl of fresh pine resin, which he intends to mash into *pom*, the ceremonial incense. Copal resin, from which the traditional incense is made, has grown scarce around Nahá in recent years.

"Eh, Roberto, where have you been so long?" Mateo calls in a hearty, high-pitched voice. "We thought Mexico City had swallowed you up." After Chan K'in, Mateo is the most respected elder in Nahá, and his association with Robert is as old and nearly as strong as Robert's with Chan K'in. The encounter proves unexpectedly dramatic when Mateo pulls out his dentures to show Robert a scar in his cheek, where a stake had pierced it while he was working in the *milpa*. Mateo's face had been severely burned when he was a small boy, and his toothless, gaping mouth gives him a ghoulish appearance reminiscent of a Goya etching.

I snap a picture before I know what I am recording.

The Balché Ceremony, I

The men arrive in the god-house one by one, with fistfuls of home-grown cigars and the new lighters Chan K'in has distributed among them. The younger ones stroll in with the jocose swagger of gladiators about to participate in a tourney, and plump down on the low stools. The air soon crackles with jokes and taunts, hurled seemingly at random.

K'ayum fills the huge *balché* pot and sways under its weight as he carries it to the god-house. The sight triggers a memory of the first time I had borne a heavily ornamented Torah through the hallowed aisles of my father's synagogue in Guatemala City. K'ayum looks pale, and his ankles have turned to rubber; it is exactly how I remember myself, quaking in my boots for fear of dropping the holy scroll. This mnemonic link with K'ayum will remain a constant source of wonder.

K'ayum pours *balché* for each of us, placing the bowls on wooden coasters so they will not be polluted by the ground, which is the vault of Kisin's realm. Before settling down to drink, we each wash our hands outside the god-house, and sprinkle *balché* over one shoulder as an offering to the gods. We sit down facing the east, with our backs to the fifteen god-pots.

The coversation begins haltingly, with Robert teasing several of the older men about a long-remembered sexual mishap or some revealing idiosyncrasy. Mateo parries by recalling one of Robert's notorious drunks (he holds the Nahá record: eighteen bowls at one sitting), and making sport of his run-ins with the American missionaries. The pairing of "*evangelista*" with Kisin — the lord of the underworld — never fails to raise a good laugh.

The *balché* tastes less bitter than I had expected — rather like fermented coconut water. It gets easier with each bowl. Robert dispatches two gourdfuls before I make a dent in my first one. I am struck by how quickly his features relax. After a pint of whisky he will often turn sarcastic, and his eyes will become hooded with suspicion, particularly when in the company of Mexicans. After two more bowls of *balché* his cheeks start to glow, and his voice becomes firm and cheery. Even his teasing is more robust.

Chan K'in passes me a cigar, and accompanies it with a little homily on smoking and drinking. "After you smoke a cigar, you get dizzy and have to lie down," he says. "After you drink balché, you are contented, and can still walk around. If you smoke a cigar and drink balché at the same time, you are contented and a little dizzy, and you can sit or walk around, as you wish. It is perfection."

Young Chan K'in adds pointedly, "And balché does not give you a headache and a hangover, like whisky."

I ask, "And what if you drink too much balché and smoke too many cigars?"

"Ah, then you get sick and vomit and piss all night until you pass out," Chan K'in replies. "The next day you feel like one newly born."

I would soon discover the beneficial effects of the "balché cure" on Robert's drinking, and on my indigestion.

Young Chan K'in sits down next to the elder Mateo, and they discuss watches and rifles with considerable animation. Young Chan K'in hopes to travel to Mexico City soon to purchase a new Springfield .22, but he complains that the air of the city makes him vomit blood. After two bowls of balché he too becomes more relaxed than I have seen him, although he does not shed his presidential hauteur until Robert begins to twit him about his former occidental "wife," a fortyish Canadian-Italian painter and weaver who had lived with him for nearly two years.

Graciela had come to Nahá to help the Lacandon women establish a profitable cottage industry from their weaving. Upon arrival she had developed an immediate and reciprocated interest in Young Chan K'in, who was a handsome, intelligent and highly eligible bachelor of twenty-two. Like his father before him, Young Chan K'in had put off marriage in his twenties for lack of a suitable father-in-law, one to whom he could render service without lowering his standing in the community.

Old Chan K'in gave his blessings when the couple decided on a Lacandon/occidental union, which meant, essentially, that they exchanged gifts and resolved to live together as long as it pleased them. Social mores in Nahá are flexible and allow for almost any kind of arrangement between consenting parties — short of filial or sibling incest — so long as they cause no inconvenience to anyone else.

Graciela wore a shift that her mother-in-law, Koh I, had made for her and learned to make tortillas (a Lacandon marriage is consummated when a woman first cooks for her husband). She also acquired the Lacandon knack of playful laughter and wifely gossip; and she was soon settling marital squabbles with Young Chan K'in in the accepted Lacandon manner, by throwing loose objects at him. But she did not succeed, by her own account, in giving up her occidental habits of self-assertiveness and independence.

Her marriage to Young Chan K'in gave her a position of authority in Nahá second only to Trudi's, and she did nothing to discourage visitors from regarding her as a "rival queen" who was challenging Trudi's supremacy. In any event her influence over Young Chan K'in continues to have repercussions for the Nahá community that have long outlived their stormy two-year marriage. After she left, Young Chan K'in had married the fairest of the daughters of José Güero, whose father is reputed to have been a Spanish rancher.

"Why has Koh grown so thin?" Robert asks him.

"I don't know," young Chan K'in answers, truthfully, for this was a matter of growing concern with him since the birth of their first child the year before.

"Have you been talking in your sleep?"

Young Chan K'in smiles ruefully. "No, it isn't that. She is not the jealous type. I think it must be worms."

"Or perhaps a snake named Graciela?" Robert insinuates, causing young Chan K'in to flinch. During our stay it was often discussed whether Young Chan K'in's marriage to Graciela and their traumatic separation had marked him permanently, or if Koh was already helping to bind up his wounds.

The laughter that ensues is tense but infectious. Crude and pointed as many of the exchanges are, there is no malice behind them, and I soon recognize that they serve a purpose by relaxing stiffness and closing formal distances. The *balché* drinking acts as a social as well as a visceral purgative.

K'in Bor shows up late, with a dazed expression on his face. I wonder if he might have been doing some solitary drinking, but he says he has been "reading." Since I know him to be illiterate, I express some surprise. He grins like a fox and takes out of his alligator bag a paperback book on whales and dolphins.

"My American friend gave me this," he explains. "He said they live in the sea, beyond Mexico, and they are very large, but they are not fish. After looking at the pictures I see that they do not look like fish, so I want you to tell me what they are."

I attempt to explain to K'in Bor the differences between fish and marine mammals, which are warm-blooded as we are. Our discussion attracts Chan K'in's attention. He points to a dolphin and nods his head vigorously. "This is the *onen* of Robert's friend Janet Nordyke. It lives in the sea, a place of great water."

Robert had told me that dolphins are acceptable as family symbols in Nahá, although none of the Lacandones has ever seen one. His grandfather knew about them, Chan K'in says, and that is good enough for him.

I point to a blue whale, which dwarfs all the other whales in the illustration.

"That," I say, "is the largest animal in all creation."

K'in Bor stares at me. Everyone has fallen silent. I am the center of attention. With the spur of the *balché*, I rise to the challenge. Whales are my favorite subject in all the world.

"They are the largest living creatures," I repeat, "but they are very gentle. They do not kill men or other large animals to survive, as we do. They live from eating many, many tiny creatures the size of my little finger, which are called krill."

"How long are the blue whales?" K'in Bor asks, disbelieving.

"They are as long as this god-house," I say, extending my arms, "and then another god-house, and part of another god-house. They are at least two and a half god-houses long."

I see that Chan K'in's jaw has dropped, literally, and his dentures are hanging out. It is a sweet moment.

I point to a black-and-white killer whale. "These are called orcas. They are hunters, just like men. They hunt in large packs, and kill many creatures with their sharp teeth. Sometimes they will attack a blue whale that is sick or wounded; after they kill it, they will eat only the tongue."

Loud murmurs and exclamations. Old Mateo asks Robert if what I say is true. When Robert confirms my story all shake their heads and click their tongues.

K'in Bor snatches up a large praying mantis that has flown in under the eaves. "Now we shall see if Victor tells the truth," he says, and places the mantis in front of me. "Bite him if he lies," K'in Bor commands. The mantis makes no move.

Bold with balché, I say, "Did you know that the female mantis devours its mate in the act of lovemaking? In the same instant she becomes pregnant, she starts chewing on her mate's head."

"Xämän." K'in Bor addresses the mantis by its Mayan name, which means north. "Xämän: Is what he says true? If not, bite him."

The mantis still does not move.

"Now I will show you something," K'in Bor says, and picks up the mantis from the back with two fingers. "Xämän, xämän, which way is north?" The mantis's long tapered neck and praying forelegs turn to the right, which is due north.

"The xämän says a north wind is coming," K'in Bor says. "That means heavy rains."

We scan the sky for clouds, but none are visible. Instead, little Chan K'in shouts, "Avión!"

Minutes later I hear the drone. Young Chan K'in and K'ayum rise to squint at the airplane as it comes over the mountain ridge.

"It is from San Cristóbal," K'ayum announces.

"Turista," Young Chan K'in says.

The gaiety goes out of the balché ceremony, all at once, as we wait for the visitors to land and cross the lake.

Half an hour later the pilot Antonio approaches with three tall westerners, two men and a blond woman.

The mantis had it wrong. The ill wind is blowing from the south.

"May we come in?" Antonio asks, attentive to protocol.

"Come in," Chan K'in says. "You can drink balché with us, but the woman will have to sit outside."

The three camera-laden visitors approach the balché-canoe area, whispering in German. The two males gaze in at us after taking light-meter readings inside the hut, and fiddle guardedly with their camera dials.

Chan K'in regains his seat, and goes on drinking *balché* and smoking his cigar with admirable unconcern for the intruders, who begin clicking away.

In this moment I know what it feels like to be a "native," subjected to callous foreigners who come to snatch a piece of your soul for their slide collections. But a part of me feels scruffily romantic: Robinson Crusoe striking postures for the greenhorns. I feel a surge of shame for my race that no amount of *balché* can wash away. Looking around me at the transformed expressions of the revelers as the German tourists take their pictures, I remember Robert's words about the Lacandones' inclination to turn whatever face a visitor expects of them. He had added, "The truth is, Chan K'in regards most occidentals who come here with a bemused disdain."

The two tourists finish their rolls of film. Someone gives the woman a sip of *balché,* which she gulps down without flinching. Antonio then thanks Chan K'in formally for allowing them to take part in the ceremony. Chan K'in shakes the visitors' hands tepidly, and they all go away. But the spirit of revelry has been shattered, and soon afterward we break for lunch.

As we step out of the god-house little K'in calls me over with a wink. His older brother is hiding something behind his back. They both grin impishly, daring me to guess. I reach behind little Chan K'in, but he backs away, laughing. In the next instant he twirls the puddle jumper and it flies high up above the huts, higher than it had flown before.

When I retrieve it I see that it is a different color and weight from the one I'd given them. The Katzenjammer Kids, as we have named them, had carved their own replica. I twirl it between my hands, and it bounces off my chest. Twice more I twirl it, but again it hits me in the chest instead of flying up. I am thoroughly perplexed. When I pick it up for the fourth time I see that the blades of the propeller are carved in reverse. I then twirl the stem in the opposite direction and it spins up into the sky.

The children howl in triumph. They had carved a mirror image of my puddle jumper, and it flies higher than the store-bought original.

"Two dollars," Young Chan K'in calls, from the door of his store. "It costs two dollars. Do you want to buy it?"

His younger brothers go into gales of laughter, and begin spinning one another with arms extended, like dervishes.

This was my second lesson in what Robert has named "Lacandon reversal"; the first was when Chan K'in placed the tape recorder in front of us and commanded us to sing. Lacandon reversal, or mirror imaging, is an integral feature of their storytelling and interpretation of dreams; and it can also serve to keep an obtuse or importunate foreigner in his place, as I would have occasion to discover again and again.

Having mastered the puddle jumper, "Hans" and "Fritz" soon lose their enthusiasm for it, and I have to draw deeper into my bag of tricks to keep them interested. After lunch I bring out my Duncan yo-yo and turn some fancy tricks for them. As an adolescent I had been a district champion in Bensonhurst, Brooklyn, and I've kept up my skills with occasional practice. The yo-yo does the trick. It will take them several days to get past the beginner's "sleeper" toss.

During lunch, Chan K'in lapses into a somber soliloquy about José Pepe Chan Bol and the coming decimation of the forest around Nahá.

"José Pepe sent me a message that we should all move to Lacanjá, and live under him as president. He says we are all brothers, and should live together."

"And what did you reply?" Robert asks, barely containing his anger.

"As president, my son Chan K'in wrote him a letter to say we are content here; this is our home, and we intend to remain until we die."

Young Chan K'in speaks up. "José Pepe wants us out of Nahá, so the government loggers can come in and cut down our mahogany. It appears that José Pepe collects from the government for all the mahogany that is cut in the forest — not only in Lacanjá — and he will collect for each of the trees that are cut around here."

"The government put him up to it," Robert says. "I've known José Pepe for twenty years, and I know he is not capable of this kind of scheming by himself. The government has set him up as head of the whole Lacandon forest by feeding his pride and greed."

"I think José Pepe has become sick," Chan K'in says, with a heavy sadness. "When he was younger he often visited Nahá, and he was always courteous. Now, I hardly recognize him. He is much younger than I am, but his hair and even his skin are turning white."

"He has been corrupted," Robert says. "I knew him as a young man, soon after he led Carlos Frey and Giles Healey to the Lacandones' sacred shrine in Bonampak. He was a trusting, very idealistic person who wished to believe the best of his occidental friends. The desecration of Bonampak by outsiders after Healey received all the credit for its discovery proved to be a painful awakening for José Pepe. Now, with everything that has happened in the forest, he has turned cynical and greedy." Robert shakes his head sadly. "And to think he could have been a decent *t'o'ohil*."

"José Pepe has become another person," Chan K'in says, "ever since Don Felipe Baer turned him into an *evangelista*."

"It seems," Robert says wryly, "that he discovered Christianity and the Devil — Kisin — at the same time."

A ripple of laughter lightens the melancholy. But later, in the godhouse, Young Chan K'in confides that the money paid them for taking part in the film *Cascabel* had been sent directly to José Pepe as part of the Lacandon communal funds apportioned by the government. None of it had filtered down to Nahá. The irony of this had not escaped Young Chan K'in's notice, for the movie is an indictment of the government's greed and duplicity in exploiting the Lacandones.

Koh II listens to all of this in silence, a hovering guardian presence. She gazes solicitously at each of us as she serves us rice and beans, spiced with some of our "dog's turd." I find Koh exceptionally beautiful. She has fine, strong features and the high cheekbones of the Classical Maya. Although she must be approaching fifty, she looks much younger, a sturdy, supple woman who has borne Chan K'in ten fine sons and daughters, the oldest of whom (K'in) is over thirty. I long to ask her how she feels about her husband's drinking and reveling while she has to stay behind and attend to her daily chores. But Koh speaks no Spanish, and my Mayan is in the rudimentary stage. I resolve to converse with her before my departure, even if it has to be with deaf-mute gestures.

After lunch most of the men take a siesta, and the afternoon session is slow in starting. Robert brings his tape recorder to the god-house, with the intention of capturing the changing moods of the ceremony. But he cannot get the mechanism to work. Chan K'in's son-in-law Antonio — who is the father of K'ayum's wife, Margarita — a strikingly handsome man with wild curly hair, offers to fix the recorder with a special tool. He repairs to his hut and comes back with an ax, which he lifts high above the damaged tape recorder.

"This will fix it like new," he says. Robert jumps in the air as the ax comes down centimeters from the recorder, to wild peals of laughter from the revelers. This is exactly the right catalyst, and the serious drinking gets under way once more.

As the afternoon wears on, the sky clouds over menacingly, and it begins to drizzle. "*Xämän,*" Chan K'in says, looking up at the leaden sky. Just as the mantis predicted, it will rain for three nights and two days; the lake will flood, and the forest trails will turn thick with mud.

Robert picks up the borrowed guitar and plucks some chords. I finish my bowl of *balché* and smoke another cigar. K'ayum checks with Robert before refilling my gourd. I have begun to feel logy and a touch nauseated, but the intense scrutiny of the men stiffens my determination to pass this initiation.

Shortly after, K'ayum rises from his stool and begins molding nodules of *pom* incense for the ceremonial offering to the gods. He fills with *balché* the two rows of gourds in front of the god-pots. He then dips a folded palm leaf into the bowls and dribbles *balché* on each pot. The formal part of the ceremony has begun, but it does not cramp in the least the drinking and conversation. Quite the contrary: Robert's guitar and K'ayum's sotto-voce chanting in the rear seem to loosen everybody up. The laughter becomes shriller as the gossip intensifies. When Antonio tells a ribald joke about the Chamula Indians, Chan K'in delivers himself of a laugh such as I have never heard in my life. It begins as a childlike squeal, drops to a lower register, ripples like cascading water and ends with a fulsome, wonderfully resonant "eeee-hah." It is a laugh from deep within the loins and belly: the exuberant outburst of a vernal soul.

As the rains come down, our walks to the bushes become more frequent. I finish my fourth bowl and coast on a smooth, level high by urinating as often as I drink. Robert had alerted me to watch the color of the urine; white to light yellow is healthy. Brown piss is an index of the body's accumulated poisons. I did not see anyone vomit that afternoon. The heavy drinking and the roughhousing would come the following week, across the lake in Jorge's camp.

One of the boys sitting at the edge of the god-house cries out and jumps when he is stung by an ant. A double column of army ants is advancing on the god-house. Within seconds the other boys are up and sprinkling ashes on the advancing legions, talking aloud to reroute them away from us. The inch-long ants are light brown in color, and they move incredibly fast. But Robert assures me these are the middling size of army ant, not the true *sak'al*.

"The big ones come out when the camp gets overrun by large insects," he says. "They help control the cockroach population by killing them and carting away thousands of corpses at a time. It is best to stay out of their way. Once they're on the march, they will attack any slow-moving organism, and strip it to the bone in an impressively short time."

The ashes work. The middling-sized army ants circle the god-house and move back into the forest without breaking rank.

Suddenly, without warning, Chan K'in begins to sing. Robert puts away his guitar and turns on the recorder. I recognize the word *balum* and realize he is singing "The Song of the Jaguar," which I had read in Robert's collection of Nahá songs and stories. But this is another version.

A jaguar, who is really a minor god in disguise, follows a mother and her small son, with the intention of devouring the child. The boy is one of the elect of the gods and the mother, who has magical powers, turns him into a sweet potato and hides it in her *milpa*. The jaguar climbs a tree and looks over the field, trying to guess which is the sweet potato with the boy inside.

The song is an exercise in paradox and metamorphosis, and we are all transfigured watching Chan K'in describe the movements of the jaguar with his hands as his eyes range from side to side, taking in our eyes and carving out the storyteller's space in front of him. The timbre and inflection of his voice alter dramatically as he becomes each of the personages in the story: the jaguar, the mother, the boy.

At the peak of our enthrallment, as we sit high on the crest of the tree with the jaguar, looking over the field, Chan K'in stops — and turns to little K'in, who has been sitting on the edge of the circle, watching the grownups at play. "And you — " he says, fixing the boy with his eyes — "what will *you* do to get across the lake when they have cut down the trees, and there is no mahogany to make canoes from? How will you get to the *milpa*?"

Little K'in's mouth drops, and his round eyes fill with images. He will not forget that question as long as he lives. And neither will any of us. I picture Chan K'in turning to K'ayum in the middle of the creation story and nailing him with that piercing gaze: "And you — what will you say to Don Felipe when he comes to you bearing gifts and speaking soft words, and tells you Jesus Christ is the true god? What will you answer him?"

Chan K'in finishes the song, which culminates with the little boy's deliverance and ascension to his rightful place in the upper heavens, thanks in part to the prayers of the Lacandones, who alert the gods to his jeopardy. He then explains its meaning at considerable length, giving us the logic behind each of the transformations. In the end he comes back, inevitably, to the despoiling of the forest.

"What the people of the city do not realize," he says in a heavy voice, "is that the roots of all living things are tied together. When a mighty tree is felled, a star falls from the sky. Before one chops down a mahogany, one should ask permission of the guardian of the forest, and one should ask permission of the guardian of the stars. Hachäkyum made the trees, and he also made the stars, and he made them from the same sand and clay, ashes and lime. When the great trees are cut down, the rain ends, and the forest turns to weed and grass. In El Real, six hours from here, which used to be forest before the trees were felled, the top soil erodes and disappears, the streams have dried up, and the corn that grows there is stunted and dry. All becomes dry, not only here but in the highland as well — not only in this heaven, but in the higher heavens above. Such is the punishment of Hachäkyum. I know that soon we must all die — all of us, not only the *hach winik*. There is too much cold in the world now, and it has worked its way into the hearts of all living creatures and down into the roots of the grass and the trees. But I am not afraid. What saddens me is that I must live to see the felling of the trees and the drying up of the forest, so that all the animals die, one after the other, and only the snakes live and thrive in the thickets.

"My father was born here and he died here, and so did his father, and they saw many hard things. They saw the shutting out of the sun, and the ravages of many jaguars. They saw the terrible Yum K'ax and other lords and demons of the forest who devour men. My father saw many companions die from the white man's diseases; they suffered many calamities and they saw the work of Kisin in all his malevolence. But they did not have to see the end of the forest, as I do, and the dispersal of our companions. This task has fallen to me, and it is hard, very hard . . ."

All of this he has spoken in a soft, halting Spanish. We sit in silence, smoking, drinking the last of the *balché,* as K'ayum goes on chanting in the rear. He has given the *balché* offering, and now he is anointing each god-pot with the *pom,* alternating one male with one female nodule. His voice rises to a fluted pitch as he addresses each individual god in its own voice.

"Next time you come," Chan K'in says to me, "I would like us to converse in Maya. I have told you all that I can in your language."

I promise that it shall be so.

"That will make me content," he says, smiling.

Most of the revelers have wandered off to their huts to sleep off the *balché.* K'ayum lights the god-pots one by one, and recites prayers over them: "I light your incensory, O my Lord, so that you will be contented. I offer you this *pom* and this *balché* so you will be contented with us, and so you will look after my son, and so there will be no illness and we have enough to eat. These offerings are for you, O my Lord . . ."

Night has fallen, and the red light flickers over K'ayum's features as he squats down before the incensories, chanting and swaying. He is barely out of adolescence, and yet the red flames playing on his solemn face make him look ageless.

We eat a light dinner and retire to our huts to light a fire. It is raining hard and a cold wind is blowing in, but the hut remains dry and snug. Tonight there are no visitors to share Robert's whisky.

My head spins and my stomach is swollen, and I cannot go to sleep. The day's events dance before my eyes. These have been the fullest thirty-six hours of my life, and I need to digest at least part of the experience before I surrender the bulk to the unconscious. I ask Robert to translate snatches of conversation and the parts of Chan K'in's explanation that had sounded particularly interesting. To my surprise, I find that I have absorbed much of it already. I had understood Chan K'in's stories partly because he had wished me to, and I in turn had opened myself up and tuned my senses to his frequency, as José Güero had taught me to. I seemed to be taking in Chan K'in's teaching by a kind of osmosis. In three weeks, with Chan K'in's and Robert's patient coaching, I would learn enough Maya to carry on a simple conversation.

I lie down on my hammock, pick up Robert's diary, and read of his first encounter with Chan K'in, in 1958. He had lived in Lacanjá for several years, and already spoke some Maya when he came here. Robert wrote of finding Chan K'in, but it became clearer with each diary entry that it was Chan K'in who had chosen *him* as his spokesman and interpreter to the outside world. ("Robert knows everything," Chan K'in had said to me, the first time we met.) Robert would retell the fabulous old songs and stories faithfully, and in the process he would become part Lacandon.

I listen to the steady drumming of the rain on our roof, and to Chan K'in's muffled, drunken singing from next door. It is a soft, contented sound. Just before falling asleep I am struck by the absurdity of our pretending to "study" an aboriginal whose understanding encompasses our own.

Dreams

In the morning I trudge through the mud in my plastic poncho to the sugarcane field. I feel as if I'd been given a purgative. Among its other uses, *balché* acts as a natural enema. There is no hangover, and when we sit down to breakfast, we both devour the Ocosingo cheese, tortillas and scrambled eggs. I feel newly minted.

There is a sound of pounding outside, and Chan K'in explains that Antonio is preparing the bark for another *balché* session, to be held the next day.

"I hope it pleases you, Roberto," Chan K'in says, with a grin. "It is good to drink with companions after such a long absence."

"This could become too much of a good thing," Robert whispers to me, as Chan K'in goes on smiling and singing. He is in excellent spirits.

As the heavy rains continue, our breakfast chat stretches into an hour, and then two. There is no *milpa* today, for Chan K'in or anyone else, although the corn harvest is not yet completed.

"When the rains stop, and the *balché* is finished, then I will go back to the *milpa*," Chan K'in says.

Robert tells him he dreamed of stone birds, and Chan K'in predicts he will see a puma, which is Robert's *onen*.

Shortly afterward K'ayum walks in, looking none the worse for wear, and asks me if I have dreamed. I say that I had sensual dreams and did not bother to repeat them because I knew they only meant I would eat meat.

"But dreams are for companionship also," K'ayum says.

Robert explains that in Lacandon Maya the word *bäho* — companion — is the plural of *bäh* — oneself. When Chan K'in says he dreams for companionship, he is speaking of persons who are extensions of himself — both the dead and the living. I recall that on my first visit, when I asked Chan K'in about his dreams, he said, "I dream pretty. It is a good way to see your companions." He meant, I now realize, both *bäh* and *bäho*.

Robert switches to English, and lowers his voice: "Remember that the Lacandon does not set up artificial barriers between his self and others — or between his unconscious life and his conscious one. That is one reason why he feels equally at ease with presidents and Tzeltal mule drivers. To him, life is one continuous stream of experience, just as it is in dreams. He does not distinguish between 'seeing' a companion in a dream and seeing him in the flesh."

K'ayum tells us he dreamed he saw his older brother K'in García carrying someone with a nosebleed who keeps falling down. Afterward K'in sees blood on his arms. The person he carried is unknown but could be a tourist.

Chan K'in tells him, "You or K'in will kill a wild pig."

Robert and I exchange rueful smiles, recognizing that the dream-prophecy formula had originated in a time when game was abundant in the forest. No wild pig had been seen around Nahá in years.

"Perhaps," Robert says, "it really means that K'in will shoot a piggish tourist."

We laugh, but two days later K'in does in fact hunt and kill a small deer, which he shares with us. It is the first game he has killed in several weeks.

All through our conversation Koh II has once again listened attentively, and I surmise she understands more Spanish than she lets on. Koh wears several strands of red beads around her neck and has bright toucan and parrot feathers tied to the end of her braid. In contrast to Chan K'in's two other wives, Koh II's white shift and red-bordered underskirt are immaculately clean. She is only about four feet ten, but she projects a disproportionate size, strength and dignity. Her arms are more thickly muscled than those of many of the Lacandon men, and her shoulders are broad and round. I recall Alfred Tozzer's remark in his 1905 *Comparative Study of Mayas and Lacandons,* that Lacandon women are bigger and stronger than their Yucatecan counterparts and are expected to do heavy manual labor alongside their men.

Koh meets my admiring gazes, but will not address me directly except to ask if I want more coffee or if I have finished my food.

"*Ts'oki* — I have finished," I say. She examines critically the small mound of half-cooked beans that I have pushed to one side. She never urges me to finish any of her cooking, but quietly registers my preferences and dislikes. (There is no waste in any case. The kids wolf down all the leftovers in a twinkling.) And she manifests her approval or disapproval by a suggestive gesture, a quick glance of appraisal and, on occasion, with a dazzling smile. We gradually build a silent language.

José Güero

After lunch the rains let up for a spell, and I set out for the house of José Güero. I want to record his flute playing, and to present him with some gifts. On my way out I drop off a poncho and my U.S. army surplus Vietnam jungle boots for K'in Bor, who had expressed admiration for them.

K'in Bor is sitting on his hammock, carving arrowheads from chips of flint. A stack of completed bows and arrows accumulates against the wall. His face lights up when I give him the boots.

"These are good for the forest," he says. "When the rain stops, I will take you on a hunt — but don't tell anybody."

I promise I won't. Telling others bad dreams is a way to make the prophecy "take shame" and reverse itself. Divulging good prospects is a way to dispel their power. I tell K'in Bor I plan to visit José Güero, and he says, "A snake is going to bite you on the trail — and you will never leave Nahá."

I nod and smile, accepting K'in Bor's dire prediction as a Lacandon equivalent of the theater actor's "Break a leg"; but there is more mischief than solicitousness in K'in Bor's grin.

K'in Bor's wife, Nuk, looks in at the new boots, and quickly disappears. I have yet to see her face up close.

"Is she all right?" I ask.

"She is nervous," K'in Bor says. "Last night she dreamed I was going to kill her, and she woke up screaming. She is afraid. She has not been well since K'ayum was born."

I promise to bring her an extra poncho I have with me, and he says that would please her.

"Watch out for the snake," he says, as I step out.

The trail to José Güero's house is even more difficult than I'd expected, and I nearly turn back more than once. The heavy rains have roiled up the mud into a soupy morass that threatens to suck the boots from my feet. It seems odd to be approaching José Güero's home from the opposite direction. On my previous visit his house had been the first important milestone, the open sesame to the riches of Nahá and a prelude to my meeting Chan K'in. It was José Güero who had first instructed me in the charged silences of the forest, so that I could "send" messages to Chan K'in across the lake and summon him.

That encounter with José Güero has sat within me for a year, as a lump of unassimilated magic. I wanted to test myself in his presence, and to see how his powers as well as mine have held up. I still did not know exactly what had happened in his hut on that January afternoon, but my telepathic and other so-called extrasensory abilities have sharpened appreciably since then. I had almost come to take for granted the frequent coincidences and synchronous events in my everyday life; in past months I'd begun having dovetailing and tandem dreams with several close friends, and even with students. Still, a part of me has remained skeptical. The enhanced sense of connectedness provided by these experiences was offset by my suspicion that they are the small change of the psyche's true business, and bear only incidentally on the exacting discipline of personal growth.

And now there was a new element as well. I had found that José Güero's father had been a Spanish rancher (güero is Mexican for "fair" or "light-skinned"). José Güero is the second-oldest patriarch of Nahá, after Chan K'in, and one of the most respected despite his mixed parentage. In all, José has sired about twenty children with at least four wives, two of whom have left him and married other men. Among his offspring are some of the most remarkable members of the Nahá community, including Koh II, Chan K'in's fair and beautiful second wife. Young Chan K'in had married another fair and much younger daughter of José Güero's after Graciela left him. The four youngest children of José all suffer from some visible deformity: albinism, strabismus, twisted limbs — and at least one of his sons is epileptic.

José's fair Spanish genes have introduced a divisive and potentially explosive element into the community, whose impact is only starting to be appreciated. With the arrival in Nahá of attractive foreign women from all over the world, light-skinned wives have become premium among young Lacandon men, to whom they represent symbols of power as well as modernity. The Lacandones believe that Hachäkyum had originally created them fair-skinned and curly-haired, with red or blue beards. It was Kisin who had spitefully darkened their complexions and spoiled their hair with a little round stick while Hachäkyum's back was turned. José Güero's daughters are regarded as aristocrats by virtue of their light pigmentation, and are highly favored as wives and daughters. Only his two young albino daughters remain unmarried.

I cross the stream and come to José's small *milpa*. His youngest son, who is about eleven or twelve, comes out to meet me, after the barking dogs announce my arrival.

"I've come to see your father," I say in formal Lacandon Maya.

"Come in — *oken*," he says, tilting his face to regard me with his good eye as the other strays to one side. A loud squawking draws my attention to the chicken yard, where a large white rooster is mounting a hen. I am startled by the intensity of the spectacle, and its effect on the compound: all the animals start yowling and howling and squawking at once. When I look back, José's son is regarding me with a twisted grin.

I am caught in the web of José's peculiar province even before I set foot in his hut.

"*Oken*," a voice repeats from within the hut, and I walk inside. José sits exactly where I had left him last January, on a raised pallet, with his arthritic leg crossed under his good one.

He does not recognize me at first, and waits for his son to identify me. "Oh yes, the harmonica player. You were born in Guatemala, is that right?"

"Yes," I say, pleased that he remembers. But there is a change in him, which I sense at once. His voice is shaky and his Spanish is so badly slurred I can barely understand it. In the dim light of the hut, his body looks more emaciated than ever. In less than a year, José Güero's health has visibly deteriorated.

He seems to guess my thoughts. "My knee is bad," he says in Spanish. "It is worse than before. See?" He taps his left knee. "Come and touch it." I step up to touch his withered leg, which is cold and hard, like stone. A shiver goes up my spine. José's eyes are red and thick with rheum, and his tongue lolls over his lips like a very old man's. "You see?" he asks, with perverse triumph. "Stone-cold. I cannot feel a thing." He scans my shoulder bag, and weighs it in his hand. "What have you brought me? Whisky? I hear Robert brought whisky."

I tell him Robert will bring him whisky the following day.

"Do you have earrings for my wife?"

A rustle from the rear, as his wife rises up from a corner, expectantly.

"No," I say. "I'll bring those next time. I brought you batteries."

"I have batteries," he says, and points to his record player in the corner. "I can get those in my son-in-law's store."

"But these are alkaline," I say, taking out a pair. "They are special. These last much longer than the ordinary ones."

He studies one of the "special" batteries closely, then raises it to his mouth and bites it, as if to test its voltage.

"M'm," he says, still skeptical. "Anything else?"

I hand him a propane lighter.

"Good — *ne tsoy*," he says. I adjust it for him, and he flicks it several times. "Yes, a good gift. For my cigars. Now I can smoke all day as I listen to the music. You want to hear my records? I have good *rancheras* — from Mexico."

"I would rather hear your flute," I say, "so I can record it."

"Good," he says again, and digs into a pouch for a reed flute. "But to-morrow you bring me whisky, and earrings for my wife."

"Yes," I say. "Whisky tomorrow. Earrings next visit." His wife drops back into her corner, like a shadow.

I turn on the tape recorder as he raises the flute to his lips and plays a simple melody. It consists of two short, undistinctive phrases, of the kind a schoolboy could master after a month's practice on a recorder.

"Good?" he asks, like a schoolboy eager for approval.

"Good," I say, hiding my disappointment. Has José Güero gone senile or is my memory faulty? With the red-and-blue, store-bought plastic flute he had played intricate, haunting melodies, and had improvised the har-mony to "Blowin' in the Wind" masterfully. This is a far cry from the old flute players, like Celestín of Mensäbäk, who reputedly can still heal ill-nesses with his rich flute songs. Is José Güero putting me on?

"Could you play something else?" I ask softly. "I would like to play your music to my friends."

"All right. But first you must hear some rancheras,* and record them in your machine." He gestures to his son, who turns on the record player. I pretend to record "La Rosa de Mi Rancho," ground out on a scratchy record.

"Good, yes? And I have others like it, by Mexican charros." He rises proudly in his pallet, a man of property. He then takes out a larger flute from his pouch and plays another melody. This one is longer and more ambitious, but it has nothing to distinguish it as Mayan. It sounds more like a primitive, northern Mexican ranchera. The magic of our musical duet has evaporated. That moment has passed forever, and I let it go. Nei-ther of us is the same person he was then.

I thank him and rise to leave.

"Before you go, take a picture of my wife and children," he says, point-ing to my camera.

The younger wife and her son and one albino daughter pose for me, stiffly, in front of the hut. I notice again as I focus the lens that the boy's head is disproportionately large, and his left foot is splayed, with two middle digits glued together. And José's wife is wall-eyed, as well.

I walk around the chicken yard, through the corn patch, and start across the bridge when an unearthly humming sound stops me on my tracks. I turn to see a huge top spinning above the churned-up mud, as though it were on a parquet floor. I blink my eyes. José's son stands with the string dangling from his finger and the sly, twisted smile on his out-size face.

"Ne tsoy," I say, and ford the stream, as the humming goes on in my ears.

---

* Songs that are analogous to "country-western" songs in the United States.

Witchery

In the next twenty-four hours I feel as if I have fallen under a spell. I sense that I am being watched, tested, evaluated. My relationship with Robert is under constant scrutiny. The Lacandones seem to sense what each of us is looking for, and they are so elastic and intuitive they anticipate friction between us and adapt to it even before tensions break into the open. K'in Bor is also watching me. When I surprise him chipping arrowheads he says, "I am preparing a poisoned arrow for you, because the alligator and the xämän and the snake did not get you."

"Why do you want to poison me?" I ask.

"So you will stay in Nahá."

"But then I'll be dead."

"Yes," he says, laughing.

José Güero's witchery seems to have affected our electronic equipment, which develops odd bugs. Whole snatches of conversation disappear from my tape recorder, my watch enters into an alternating pattern with the clock in Chan K'in's kitchen, so that only one can function at a given time. Robert's brand-new Nikkormat camera jams continually, and my dreams take on a surrealistic turn. I sense José Güero's hand in all of this. During his enforced idleness he has developed unusual mental agility in spite of his drinking problem, and he employs his young sons to carry out his pranks. His youngest son appears in our hut at dawn the following day, and Robert is so unnerved on waking to find him peering down at him, with his roving eye and a fistful of coins, that he gives away a bottle of his best Scotch.

When I discuss these sensations with Robert, he advises me to write down anything unusual just as it happens. He is noncommittal, and a bit skeptical of my speculations about José Güero's brujería (sorcery).

Journal

December 5, 1977. "I feel bewitched." This is what I wrote last night, and it still holds. It's the forest. This morning I taped morning sounds, including running water in the brook by the spring that feeds Nahá village. I then read into the tape recorder the inscription on the cement cover of the spring, which is dedicated to the engineer Francisco Espinoza. Right after that I slipped on the wet wooden plank, and the recorder fell in the mud. When I played back the tape, the entire section had self-erased. Later, Chan K'in told me Francisco Espinoza, an old friend of Nahá, had died in Pepe Martínez's plane crash. . . .

2 P.M.: After lunch I start out again to José Güero's house, with some scissors for his wife. I carry my tape recorder, machete, camera and binoculars. I get on the road, and after a hundred meters or so my boots are steeped in black, oozy muck and I decide to turn back. "The road says

no" goes through my mind. I am still spooked by the self-erasing tape when I fell this morning. I return to the hut and suddenly feel drowsy. I am shaking on my "jungle legs." My sense of time has slipped, and I have no idea what part of the day it is. I lean against the hut door, with my arms dangling out, and try to focus on what is happening to me. One of Chan K'in's small sons, little Chan K'in — "Fritz" — watches me closely, grinning and twirling an imaginary puddle jumper.... Perhaps this mood began when I touched José Güero's cold leg. Just thinking about it gives me the shivers. The copulating rooster and the whirring top must also have something to do with it. It was like entering another dimension, and now I feel as if I am sleepwalking. I can only think one thought at a time, feel one sensation at a time. Is José a brujo? Robert is still noncommittal, but interested. "You and I have a lot in common," he says, "but your receptivity to this place is on a different wavelength from mine. I wonder just what you are picking up?"

In any event, I am now experiencing the dark side of Nahá . . .

My dreams are part of it. In my first dream last night there was a performance of some sort I wished to attend. (A movie, I think.) But nothing goes right. The obstacles keep shifting. Nothing remains constant. I cannot get to the theater. When I told Chan K'in about it this morning, he interpreted it as a direct reversal. (Of course.) It means I will not be enthusiastic about seeing something, but I'll be taken anyway. Despite its vagueness, this is the first of my dreams that Chan K'in has shown a moderate interest in.

December 6.   At dinner, Robert and I continue our exploration of the Lacandon's peculiar time sense. He explains that their language has no formal future tense, only a hypothetical one. "When a Lacandon says, 'I come to your house tomorrow,' he usually follows it with 'I think,' or 'if it does not rain.' This is a statement of present intention, not a firm commitment projected into the future. What he is really saying is, 'I will come tomorrow if conditions at the time are suitable for my coming.' "

I point out that this sounds remarkably close to the Santa Cruz hippies' "See you tomorow, baby — if it feels good."

Robert agrees, in principle, and then adds, "But I prefer to think that the Lacandon's philosophy is a bit less self-indulgent."

Koh I

Koh I, Chan K'in's oldest wife, who is about seventy-five, walks in and out of the kitchen during lunch, with a half-smoked cheroot in her mouth. She carries a thin strip of ocote (pitch pine) with which to relight her cigar. Koh I, the mother of Young Chan K'in and two married daughters, is in charge of curing the tobacco and rolling cigars, and she has her own separate kitchen for that purpose in back of the common one. None of the three wives (they are all named Koh, which means tooth) ever eats with us, although Koh II occasionally sits down to sip tea or coffee beside her husband.

Koh I is particularly amused by the persistent growling of the dogs when I am near. If one of them barks at me she picks up a stick or a piece of firewood and throws it with unerring accuracy, cussing out the dog at great length, itemizing all his transgressions and warning him about further reprisals if he persists. But an indulgent smile always plays on her face. The dog will whine and slink away, and then will growl again with renewed menace when I walk past the hut.

This, I discover, is part of the village theater. The dogs are expected to growl and bark — that is their role — as they are trained to be vicious hunters and watchdogs; and the women can work off some of their aggressions by throwing sticks at the dogs and berating them. What sort of jokes do they tell on their men, I wonder, when they are alone by themselves?

Two nights after my meeting with José Güero I have jumbled, surrealistic dreams that have no sense or logical progression — rather like episodes in everyday city life. In the morning, on opening my eyes, I hear the rain, and see the gray misty light filter between the slats. I hear cocks crowing and turkeys gobbling in the yard, the fitful coughs of small children, and the ritual *"Aah ech?" "Aah en"* (Are you awake? I am awake) of early risers greeting one another. The smell of woodsmoke and toasting maize wafts into the hut, and the grinding sound of pestle against mortar, as Koh II prepares tortillas for breakfast.

I awake into dream.

The Balché Ceremony, II

The second *balché* ceremony begins earlier than the first, but I tarry in my hut to catch up on my reading of Robert's diaries. "Hans and Fritz" and other small boys come in and out of the hut to play with the yo-yos and marbles I brought for them, and to ask me to make Guatemala-style paper airplanes, which they fly outdoors during the brief lulls between downpours.

When I join the men in the god-house, the *balché* drinking is in full swing. Antonio's *balché* is considerably stronger than K'ayum's — possibly because he used refined sugar instead of cane — and I get quite high on my very first bowl. This one tastes more pungent but also sweeter, like a blend of Guinness ale, sugared coconut water and Mexican pulque.

Everyone is in lively spirits, and Antonio has no difficulty in persuading Robert to play his guitar and sing. This time he sings "La Llorona," "Benito Canales" and two other *corridos.* He is in fine voice, relaxed and genial. He ends the set with a Lacandon version of "La Cucaracha" that plays on the words *turista* and *evangelista;* a slight stress and a glottal stop turn the last syllable into *ta',* meaning "shit" — which pitches the revelers into hysterical fits.

When I extend my bowl for more *balché,* Chan K'in gives me a graphic illustration of the differences between *p'enkach yaab* (full to brimming), *tibil* (halfway full, or enough), and *tibil chichin* (just barely enough) — by scratching marks on the bowl with his index fingernail.

I assure him I am in good health and roundly disposed to a *p'enkach yaab* of *balché.*

"Good," Antonio says, and passes me a brimming gourdful, as Robert approvingly lights my cigar. "You are becoming a *hach winik,*" he says.

K'in Bor walks in late, looking troubled and morose. As he sits down on his stool I sense in him the tensions of divided loyalties. His brother Enrique is one of the three converts in Nahá, a Baptist who has lived in Phil Baer's camp on Missionary Hill for the past eight years. His father, Jorge, is the patriarch of the secessionist enclave on the north shore — and we are to hear rumors later that day that Jorge "disapproves" of our drinking *balché* with the elders and of our sitting in on the prayer ceremonies. But K'in Bor owes son-in-law loyalty and service to Chan K'in, whom he greatly admires. I recall the intensity in his voice when Chan K'in gave him the two boxes of .22 shells and he said, "My father-in-law is a good man."

When I get up to urinate I trip on my low stool and nearly fall on my face. This reminds Chan K'in of another jaguar song, which he proceeds to chant. It concerns a man who gets drunk on *balché,* and on his way home from the god-house is attacked and eaten by a jaguar. The jaguar becomes drunk from the *balché* in his victim's blood and slips into his tunic. He goes to the man's house, sits down to dinner, and the man's wife serves him tamales made with the remains of her husband, which the jaguar has presented to her as monkey flesh from the day's hunt. After the meal the jaguar, who is really a minor god, falls asleep in his chair, and the wife spies his tail under her husband's gown. She then deduces what happened, fetches an axe, and chops off the jaguar-god's head.

At this point in the story Chan K'in is interrupted by the arrival of an airplane from San Cristóbal. The pilot, Jaime Cuello, has risked the rains and flown in with two Mexican tourists, who appear to be film actors. Chan K'in invites them in, seemingly unperturbed by having the thread of his story broken, but requests that they not take any pictures. Antonio offers Jaime some *balché,* which he shares with the tourists.

The two Mexicans ask Chan K'in if he has seen the film *Cascabel.* He shakes his head. Did he know, they ask, that he and two of his sons had appeared in it?

"Yes, I have been told," Chan K'in says.

One of the young actors tries to open a discussion of the moral issues raised in the film, in regard to the Lacandones and their forest land. Are they aware that the government will despoil their land for its mahogany?

I can tell that neither Chan K'in nor the other elders feel like discussing the film or the plunder of their forest. They have taken the measure of this brash young visitor and they do not trust him.

"And did you know," the young Mexican persists, "that President

López Portillo in a recent interview has vowed to respect the Lacandones' title to their forest lands?"

"*Ahh sí,*" Chan K'in nods vaguely with glazed eyes. Behind him Mateo and Antonio mumble and cluck their tongues, like village idiots.

"Well, do you believe him?" the young man asks, in exasperation.

"Why not?" Chan K'in says and shrugs.

Mateo feigns a sudden, intense interest in the visitor's watch. "That is a pretty watch," he says. "Will you sell it to me?"

"It is broken," the visitor says. "It stopped running two days ago."

"Ah certainly." Mateo nods sagely, and asks him to remove it. "I fix for you," he says, in a childlike, pidgin Spanish, although he is one of the most articulate in the community. He returns with an ax, and the young man watches in fascinated disbelief as Mateo raises the ax above his head and brings it down no more than an inch from the watch, burying it in flying mud and grass. An outburst of laughter as Mateo digs out the watch and holds it to his ear, like a limp mole.

"It died — ahh, poor thing," Mateo says, returning it to its owner.

The visitors laugh and nod their heads, and the pilot, who is in convulsions, appears to enjoy the joke most of all. But they do not tarry too long, and this time the high spirits continue after the tourists' departure.

One by one we all get up to urinate, wash our hands, and resume drinking *balché.* But neither Robert nor I can persuade Chan K'in to go on with his story. "Later," he says, and casts a pointed glance at my tape recorder. Too late, I realize that he does not like to be taped when he has been drinking.

The watch-fixing joke gets everyone off on a gadget-testing session, one of the favorite pastimes in Nahá. K'in complains that his watch does not run on time, and K'in Bor offers to open it and clean it. In no time we are all tinkering with our watches and propane lighters, cracking them open like eggs to look for the yolk. When Koh II appears to call us to lunch, we are sitting with our watches and lighters open on our laps and assorted pieces of mismatched machinery in our hands, giggling cretinously.

At the kitchen table, after I have put away my tape recorder, Chan K'in continues the jaguar song. His eyes flit from one to another, looking at us, beyond us; his ancestors are in his eyes and in his voice. Not until his storytelling magic has raised a flush to my cheeks does he rest his gaze on mine and regale me with a smile. Chan K'in sets the tone and the rhythm for our contacts with him, for our entire stay, for that too is a story and must proceed in a measured, just cadence.

"... The jaguar, who is really a minor god, does not die when the woman chops off his head. In the middle of the night he rises, places his head back on, and hunts for the woman's small son. But the woman has hidden the boy in a pot of chilis, so that the jaguar cannot get his scent. The mother climbs a zapote tree, and throws unripe fruit at the jaguar. . . . The jaguar then devours the woman."

Koh II, who has been listening attentively, reminds Chan K'in that he left out a part in which the wife chops off the jaguar's front claws.

Little K'in says, "But the jaguar already ate the woman."

"No, he does not eat her," Koh corrects him. "This happens before he can eat her."

Chan K'in grins slyly. "She is right. I left out that part. Well, now I lost the drift. We shall continue the story later." And all at once he reaches into Robert's plate for a piece of discarded pork fat. He drops it in his mouth and licks off his fingers with a flourish, grinning from ear to ear.

Koh follows this spontaneous gesture by sitting down and rubbing her back against his, like a cat. He pours some of Robert's whisky into her cup and she sips at it, laughing softly. It is the first physical intimacy they have permitted themselves in our presence.

Later in the evening, sitting in our hut, he will tell us a slightly different version of the story, and Robert will fret about getting it on tape, because it is one he has not heard before.

". . . The woman had not *really* been eaten by the jaguar, only stunned. She is an expert weaver, and when the jaguar climbs the zapote tree after her, she chops off his front claws with her loom shuttle. The jaguar falls to the ground to heal his wounds, and to wait for morning. . . . Akinchob, Hachäkyum's son-in-law, who is man's protector, gets wind of the situation, and is sent by his father-in-law to straighten matters out. He helps the woman descend from the tree and orders the jaguar not to eat people anymore because they are Hachäkyum's favored creations."

Chan K'in interprets the song for Robert, who records it on his tape. The woman who defends herself with the shuttle is the moon goddess, Akna', during an eclipse. The gods — Hachäkyum, Akinchob and T'uup (keeper of the sun) — don't know of her plight because her face is hidden. It is the Lacandones' duty to pray to them and give offerings as soon as the eclipse begins, so that the three gods will heed their summons and defend Akna' from the jaguars. If the Lacandones neglect to pray and alert the gods to her peril, Akna' will not be very sympathetic when she is asked to come to the aid of a woman suffering a difficult childbirth.

After he finishes the story Chan K'in drinks a small glass of Robert's whisky and picks at the trail mix I offer him, examining each ingredient critically before placing it in his mouth. "Ah, certainly, a dried grape — yes, we have these at Nahá — and peanuts." He knows each of the fruits and nuts, and names them all, including the cashew, the dried apple and the coconut.

It strikes me that Chan K'in will never run out of jaguar stories. No matter how many more times Robert or I come, he will always have a new song. He is filling us with the legacy of his ancestors, and there is no bottom to it. Chan K'in tells stories for the joy of it, and he tells them from an old, old obligation.

As he gets up to leave our hut he turns outside the door and laughs aloud. "You will sleep well tonight, Roberto," he calls through the slats. "You won't be drunk and alone in the hut. Victor is there to make certain that the jaguar does not eat you."

It is the first time he has spoken my name.

After the rains I wake to a dazzling sunrise: mist rising above the lake, blue skies overhead. As the spaces open up above and around me, I have the illusion that I have gained time during my three days in Nahá. I can get married again, raise a family, and write all the books that are in my head. Somehow, the world will go on. This expansiveness will last throughout my stay, and for a good stretch beyond it. Here, it does not seem farfetched to suppose that one can "borrow" time and stay the host of calamities that are bearing down upon our beleaguered planet. Each time I swim in the lake or chat with Chan K'in or take a deep breath under a star-filled sky I store up uncontaminated experience against my return to the postindustrial world.

II

Geneviève

In the afternoon two travelers arrive from Mensäbäk: Geneviève Buot, a young French doctor who is working in the Lacandon forest and has set up a well-stocked clinic next to the airstrip; and her companion, Frédéric, a young Parisian cartographer who is mapping the Lacandon forest for his graduate degree from the University of Paris.

Geneviève and Robert greet one another in Maya, which she has nearly mastered during her first year in the forest. She and Frédéric, who is slight and wiry with shoulder-length black hair, have walked eight hours on the heavily muddied trails from Mensäbäk, the other northern Lacandon community, and are grateful for a shot of Robert's whisky and some of our trail mix. ("Small, agreeable tidbits," is how Frédéric describes it.)

Geneviève is from the northwest of France, and radiates a Norman farm girl's robust common sense. She is too sturdily built to be conventionally pretty, but her green eyes are lucidly intelligent and a gentle, mothering quality lurks behind her masculine determination. I can understand why the northern Lacandones have grown so fond of her and call her *la doctora,* a title of considerable respect for a woman of twenty-five or twenty-six. Geneviève has an especially close bond with Koh II, which is based on mutual admiration.

Frédéric looks rather peaked, and retires to our hut for a nap, but Geneviéve seems as fresh after her eight-hour ordeal as if she had been on a picnic. Robert asks her about the situation at Mensäbäk, and she says that seven families have now been converted by the Seventh-Day Adventist from Yucatán, and most of the remaining ten families have moved across the lake. She adds that the Adventist has forbidden the Mensäbäk converts to eat pork or paca, fish without scales, parrots, and all other game birds.

Geneviéve sighs. "You know, Robert, that their diet was already poor in animal protein because of the growing scarcity of game, but now they've had to give up most of the still available ones, including the delicious and plentiful catfish of Lake Mensäbäk."

Robert fumes and turns sarcastic. "And hasn't the Adventist supplied the converts with the Lord's manna? Surely the vitamin and mineral content of an omer of manna would amply compensate them for the forbidden meat?"

"Well, I'm afraid not. In fact, I've diagnosed the first case of pellagra."

Geneviève adds that the missionary had also broken up several polygamous households by remarrying the younger wives to single men. The Adventist had recently married himself, to a *ladina* from Yucatán, and they had built a spacious concrete house around which the converts had gathered.

"There is much sadness there," she says. "The road to Mensäbäk was completed years ago, the tractors came in to clear the forest, and the mahogany has all been cut and taken out. I heard rumors that the government will soon build a new airstrip there, large enough to accommodate jet planes."

"And the elders?" Robert asks, in a low voice.

"Most of them are holding on, after some wavering. They are northerners after all, and they remain traditionalists at heart. Celestín is still playing the flute, and it is said that he has healed many illnesses with his marvelous melodies. After listening to him play, I can believe it." Her cheeks color, and she laughs. "Of course, I speak strictly off the record."

Geneviève also tells us of José Valenzuela, one of the elders who has become more conservative than ever. He has regular *balché* ceremonies in his god-house and still blows the conch shell to call the celebrants. This practice had been abandoned at Nahá several years ago, when Chan K'in's mother died shortly after he dreamed of a conch. To dream of a conch is considered a death omen, and they no longer wanted one around to tempt fate.*

We next speak of the effects of inbreeding in the three Lacandon communities. Geneviève plans to do an in-depth genetic study in Nahá when her work is completed. She is as intrigued as I am by José Güero and intends to begin her interviews with him and his extensive family. I bring up the curious fact that none of the Nahá elders, including José Güero and Chan K'in, have any gray hair, whereas at Lacanjá I had seen several men in their fifties and sixties — Pancho Villa, Vicente Bor, José Pepe — whose hair was heavily streaked with gray.

Geneviève shrugs and purses her lips in Gallic fashion. "Well, I am not sure. The Mongolian races generally do not develop gray hair until very late in life. José Güero, of course, is a special case, but it could still be that the Nahá Lacandones are a purer strain than the Lacanjá ones."

"It is evangelism," Robert says. "If I had been converted by Phil Baer, my hair would turn white overnight."

* In 1980 they resumed use of the conch in Nahá.

Geneviève says that she has discovered among young Nahá women a pattern of multiple miscarriages after bearing a first child. "You will notice that few couples under thirty have more than one or two children."

I had noticed, and wondered if it was a response to changing conditions in the forest and to uncertainty about the future.

"It is probably genetic," she says, "and due to the amount of inbreeding. My feeling is that most of the spontaneously aborted children would have been born with genetic anomalies, so the miscarriages are an effective means of natural control."

I ask, "And what of K'in Bor's wife? He says she has been waking up screaming at night ever since the birth of her son K'ayum."

"Yes," Geneviève says, "Nuk's anxiety attacks and her miscarriages are part of the pattern I've mentioned. Of course, K'in Bor's erratic temperament also plays a part. He has a lot of violence in him, most of which he works out on his hunts and in the *milpa*. When game is scarce, or during a *norte* when he can't leave his hut, Nuk often has to bear the brunt of his pent-up emotions."

Geneviève goes off to complete her medical rounds of the village, giving tetanus shots to everyone and cough medicine to the children. During the rains, many small children have come down with influenza. She gives Robert alkaline tablets for a sour stomach — the result of too many cigars and the cheap Scotch — and then leaves us to pay a visit to Domingo, an elderly Lacandon of sixty or so who lives with his young wife in deep forest about a kilometer from the settlement. He is so infirm he has to walk with the aid of two crutches, Geneviève says, but they still cultivate their *milpa* and Domingo prays regularly in his god-house. When I ask why he chose to isolate himself, she says, "Perhaps because he is childless, and can afford only one wife because of his infirmity. Perhaps he is shamed by his contemporaries Mateo and Chan K'in, who are healthy and have several wives and children. But he is hypochondriac as well, and deathly afraid of contagious diseases."

I am curious to meet this sensitive hermit and his wife, but Robert persuades me to respect his chosen isolation, as the sight of strangers causes him acute embarrassment.

"And he doesn't mind Geneviève?" I ask.

"Geneviève is — well, *la doctora.*"

This redoubtable Frenchwoman has converted the whole of the Lacandon forest — the Tzeltal and Chol settlements included — into her medical "beat," and walks from one end of it to the other, healing and administering medicines as offhandedly as if she were back in her Norman village.

Journal

December 7, 1977. Chan K'in and Koh II are two wholes, and they are evenly matched. Each would have been just as remarkable if he or she had mated with someone else. Together, they are far more than the sum of their gifts and strengths.

There are mango, orange, lemon, banana, grapefruit, avocado trees in Nahá. The Lacandones grow squash, onions, tomatoes, mint, sweet potato and cabbage. But we eat, mostly, tortillas, black beans and fresh meat — day after day after day. My body craves chlorophyll, solid greens. At night, lying awake in my hammock, my stomach rumbling from the half-cooked beans, I have visions of a huge Caesar salad.

Since the balché ceremony I cannot fix events by day of the week or month. I seem to float through time, so that each experience has its own rounded fullness, untainted by the hurrying, dividing minutes and hours.

There is community here. Without community there is no real life for Homo sapiens. Sitting in Chan K'in's kitchen, I think often of Sheik Sharif of Hebron, the centenarian Sufi holy man and spiritual head of Hebron's Moslem community. There was so much light in the dark, subterranean cellar of his mosque. It is the same here.

Chan K'in and his children, like the whales and dolphins, have an intelligence no Stanford–Binet IQ test can measure. So much the worse for Stanford–Binet.

The Lacandones have a highly developed sense of private property. I noticed that each of the kids kept the toys I gave him for himself, and does not share spontaneously with his brothers and cousins. Similarly, the functions of each of Chan K'in's wives seem fairly clearly divided. Each has her own separate kitchen, and looks after her own set of utensils. As the t'o'ohil, Chan K'in is not only the spiritual leader and guardian of Nahá traditions, he is also responsible for the equitable distribution of all property, gifts and land holdings. In Nahá, property is inherited through the father's line, as in one's onen. But women have their own sphere of influence, as I'm just beginning to discover, and have a number of resources for exerting influence on their men.

The hygienic standards of the average Lacandon family are certainly primitive, and the interiors of most huts in Nahá resemble pigpens; but they are still several cuts above conditions in the typical state-run Pemex gasoline station.

December 8. Chan K'in now says Kisin, not Hachäkyum, caused the earthquake in Guatemala.

Since the arrival of the white man in the forest, Kisin's role has been upgraded to that of a full-fledged devil. At the time of Tozzer's visits, just after the turn of the century, Kisin's role was well defined, and he was not considered especially malevolent. He was known as the earthshaker and the lord of death. Kisin fell to the underworld when Hachäkyum caused an earthquake that swallowed him up. He gets back at Hachäkyum's fa-

vored creations by periodically kicking the pillars of his kingdom —
Metlán — and causing devastating earthquakes.

Today, Kisin is associated with criminal violence, theft, lying and all
kinds of ill tidings, among them the arrival of the missionaries.

There is a mystery surrounding the Haawo' onen, or Raccoon People,
who became extinct years ago. According to Chan K'in they could talk
with the gods face to face. One of them wore a gold disk around his neck
when officiating at the rites.

Chan K'in said his grandfather once came in, speaking strangely and
using the rare second person plural, and confessed to them he was not of
the Spider Monkey onen but of the Haawo' or Raccoon. You were not
supposed to mention this onen aloud, ever, or many enemies would come
and despoil your cornfield. Must explore further.

None of the Lacandones in Nahá have abused Robert's Scotch, not
even K'in. They only take balché in excess, for there the effect is calculated. They are moderate in nature. How long will it last?

December 9. 11 A.M. Reading Robert's 1956 diaries, I realize how
much he always strains to his physical and mental limits. He seems to do
his best work on the edge of the greatest tension. Now he has heartburn
again from too many cigars, and cannot enjoy his own whisky. But he is
writing well and steadily.

Coming to the Lacandon forest is like discovering the part of Guatemala that had been missing from my childhood. The five Lacandones at
the fair provided a glimpse. After thirty-eight years and two trips around
the world, I have come back to the starting place and begun anew, immeasurably the richer. I feel like an amputee who is growing a new limb
from an old stump.

As I look over my notes of the balché ceremony, I am struck once more
by Chan K'in's phrase about the mahogany and the star: "What the men
of the city do not realize is that the roots of all living things are tied together." This is the key to Chan K'in's philosophy, and is worth repeating
again and again, like a catechism, until one understands it the way Chan
K'in does, with the heart and the loins as well as the head:
The roots of all living things are tied together. When a mighty tree is
felled, a star falls from the sky; before you cut down a mahogany you
should ask permission of the keeper of the forest, and you should ask
permission of the keeper of the star.... When a mighty tree is felled, a
star falls from the sky; before you cut down a mahogany you should ask
permission of the keeper of the forest, and you should ask permission of
the keeper of the star.... A star falls from the sky; before you cut down a
mahogany you should ask permission of the keeper of the forest, and you
should ask permission of the keeper of the star.... Before you cut down a
mahogany you should ask permission of the keeper of the forest, and you

should ask permission of the keeper of the star.... You should ask per-
mission of the keeper of the forest, and you should ask permission of the
keeper of the star.... You should ask permission of the keeper of the
star.... Ask ... permission ... star.... Permission ... star. Star.

Simios

K'ayum comes to our hut carrying an old typewriter Robert had left
behind three years ago. It is covered with jungle rust, and half the keys
stick together when you press any one of them.

"If we could dip it in kerosene, it would come out good as new," Robert
says. But there is no kerosene, so Robert cleans the keys with rubbing alcohol instead, puts in a new ribbon, and soon after, K'ayum is typing out
his name, pressing down on each key with great concentration.

"K-A..Y--um** M=AA#X..!!!!" he writes, calling out each letter at the
top of his voice. "Next time, a full line!" he brags, grinning, and punches
out two rows of asterisks and exclamation marks. And then he types out
the Spanish word for "ape" but mispells it: *simo*.

"With an *i*," Robert corrects him, as K'ayum imitates a convincing sim-
ian snarl and jumps up and down, thumping his chest.

When K'ayum was in Mexico City for the filming of *Cascabel*, in which
he had one spoken line, now ironic — "Here Lacanjá" — he had seen
Conquest of the Planet of the Apes. K'ayum, whose lineage animal is the
spider monkey, had a strong reaction to the film, which he refers to simply as *Simios* because he has no grasp of the word "planet" and "conquest" means nothing to him. In Lacandon Maya there is no word for
"conquest" — nor, for that matter, for "war." There is "soldier" (*solaw*)
and "quarrel" (*ts'iktal*). (When pressed by Robert, Chan K'in gave a pro-
visional definition of war as *"kinsik u bäh solaw"* [soldiers killing one
another.])

The men with apes faces had seened to K'ayum incarnations of his
Monkey *onen*, and he dreams of them constantly. He has become obsessed with the subject, and pesters Robert and me with questions about
the film: How was it made, how was the makeup applied, who were the
actors in real life?

"*Simios!*" he shouts as he pounces from behind a tree with a hideous
gorilla face, his arms dangling at his sides.

Kisin

A torrential downpour in the middle of the night. Chill north winds
rattle the slats and penetrate my sleeping bag so that I have to twist and
curl up with my legs under me to keep warm. I have gruesome dreams of
cancerous fungi blooming on the flesh of women I embrace. When I start
awake from one of these nightmares there is a sickening lurch and my

hammock flips over, trapping me inside. The zippered mosquito netting holds me like a winding-sheet, with my butt against the cold, damp ground.

"Robert," I hiss, as the winds howl outside and the rain pelts the roof. Earlier that evening we had killed a huge spider, and the cockroaches infiltrated the trail mix. My imagination teems with tarantulas, scorpions, hordes of army ants, all about to stick their pincers into my vulnerable ass.

"Robert, wake up, I'm stuck inside this thing!" I yell at last above the wind and the driving rain.

Finally Robert snorts, rolls over, and emerges from under a pile of blankets. He turns on his flashlight.

"Good Lord. You look like a disaster area."

"Did I tear the hammock?" I asked, suddenly nervous about my sixty-dollar investment.

"No," he says. "The knot slipped, is all. You must have given it quite a kick."

"Nightmares," I say. "Horrible. I haven't dreamed like that in years."

He unzips the mosquito net and boosts me up and out. We retie the hammock and I climb back in, cautiously, after Robert returns to his. The first time I twist I flip over again. My sense of equilibrium has abandoned me entirely.

"This is the last time tonight, pal," Robert says, after getting up and unzipping me once more. "Next time you stay on the ground."

Robert and Chan K'in have a good laugh the next morning, at my expense.

"And so," Chan K'in says, "it seems you were paid a visit by Kisin last night."

"So it seems," I agree, still shaken. Although we stabilize the hammock with extra ropes, I was not to sleep restfully in it again.

The North Shore

In the afternoon the *norte* stops blowing and the sun shines brightly. Robert suggests we pay a visit to the north shore and "have a taste of Jorge's *balché*." After protesting our participation in the village festivities, Jorge has done an about-face and invited us to his *balché* ceremony. Robert says this is typical of Jorge and an indication of the intense rivalry between the two camps.

"Jorge is keeping up with the Joneses," Robert says. "And I am sure he knows about the propane lighters and other gifts we gave Chan K'in."

We get to the landing and find that all the dugouts are flooded and the lake water has risen above the laddered path. Another prophecy fulfilled: Two nights before, Robert had dreamed of cheese, which Chan K'in interpreted as a forecast of heavy flooding. The *norte* has caused the lake to rise to its highest level in three years.

We decide to hike across on the forest trails, and find ourselves up to our ankles at once in mud that has the color and consistency of cold lentil soup. We stop by K'ayum's house on the way and he agrees to join us as he has a business matter to take up with Young Mateo, manager of the Maya Caribe, who had borrowed five hundred pesos from him and neglected to pay them back.

"Mateo always wants me to accompany him to San Cristóbal," K'ayum says, as we slog along with our eyes to the ground. Icy dollops of rainwater drip down my neck from the overweighted trees. "He has friends there who lend him money and give me marijuana. I smoke with him, sometimes, but — I don't know. It is not as good as my father's *balché* and cigars. Marijuana grows well here, and the hippies come down and want us to cultivate it and sell it. They say we get a better price for marijuana than for our tobacco. But I don't like the way they look, and the way they talk. They seem like crazies to me — *locos.*" He does a wild, stoned-hippie impersonation, which more closely resembles a *simio* running amok.

"And Young Mateo?" I ask him. "What does he think?"

"Mateo likes them. He likes to smoke and get drunk with the crazies. Mateo also wants the logging road to be completed, so he can buy a car and drive it to San Cristóbal and to Mexico [City]. He is very jealous of the people in Lacanjá who already own a car."

"Does his father know this?" I ask K'ayum.

"Perhaps yes," he replies hesitantly. "But he doesn't say anything. He doesn't like it, but he doesn't say anything."

I am puzzled by the apparent abdication of parental authority, and turn my question over to Robert.

"To the elders Young Mateo is a grown man," he says. "What he does with his time and money is a matter between himself and Hachäkyum on the one hand, and Kisin on the other. The elders will intervene only if Mateo's actions pose a direct danger to the community."

"But how is that decided?" I ask impatiently. "And at what point?"

Robert shrugs. "Usually after a *balché* ceremony, and often after it is too late. You have to realize, with all these new developments Chan K'in's and the elder Mateo's moral authority is not what it once was. They are deeply fatalistic, like all Indians, and see the workings of the gods in everything." He stops and turns to me. "And can you blame them, really? Young Mateo's father is forty years older than he is, and Chan K'in is almost three full generations older than K'ayum. Young Mateo is keenly aware that it is he and not his father who will have to coexist with the white man's realities; it is he who will have to put up with a denuded forest, and with the invasion of the *ladinos* and foreigners. In contemporary terms, you could say Young Mateo is simply 'going along with the flow.' He is a survivor."

I study K'ayum's sensitive, troubled expression, and ask Robert in English, "And are you saying K'ayum is not?"

"K'ayum will survive," Robert replies, after a moment. "But it remains to be seen if his soul will. Like Trudi says, he is an artist, and potentially a brilliant one. There's no question that his father's teachings go very deep, even when he rebels against them. K'ayum's struggle is bound to be more intense and complicated than that of the others."

We trudge on in silence, concentrating on each footstep. K'ayum walks ahead to clear the trail of overhanging vines, and to warn us of hidden hazards. I reflect that I have made a commitment to the Lacandon, and that I am being drawn into their struggle for survival, just as Trudi and Robert have been.

We come to a stream and stop to drink, smoke a cigarette, and wash the stubborn muck from our boots and trousers. K'ayum, in his white cotton gown and black plastic shoes, is the least soiled, although even he has slipped and skidded more than once and his knees are caked with mud.

A little farther on Robert stops to point to an overgrown trail. "About a hundred meters from here is the Nahá cemetery," he says. "Up until recently a Lacandon was buried inside his hammock in line with the north star; with him were buried a dog made of palm leaf, a lock of hair, a bone, a bowlful of corn, and various tools to aid him in his journey into the underworld. A little hut was erected above his grave, in a precise geometric design believed to be auspicious to the soul's journey."

I ask Robert what is the significance of the palm-leaf dog and the other objects.

"The bone is tossed to the vicious dogs of Metlán, so the dead person's soul can pass unharmed. The hair is thrown to the swarms of lice, and the corn is fed to the bands of chickens that stand in the way. Then the soul comes to a wide river teeming with alligators, and here the palm-leaf dog is most important, for it represents the most loyal among his hunting dogs, who takes pity on his former master and swims him across the river. The good soul then comes to the house of Sukunkyum, older brother to Hachäkyum, who will feed him and look after him until he makes his home in Sukunkyum's underworld or ascends to one of the five heavens, according to the kind of person he was or the manner in which he died. Sukunkyum will tell the soul that the dogs, the lice and the chickens were all illusory. They were there to frighten and discourage those who might return to earth. The alligators are illusions as well, and the river is simply the torrent of tears wept for him by his wives, his friends, and his brethren. . . . It is a lovely story, and Chan K'in among others still believes in it, just as they believe in the fiery place of Metlán, where the bad souls are alternately roasted and frozen by Kisin for their sins on earth. Still, the huts and the graves have been allowed to decay and many of the old burial practices have fallen into disuse since the missionaries arrived . . ." He sighs. "When Chan K'in dies, he may well be the last Lacandon in Nahá to receive a traditional burial. Isn't that so, K'ayum?"

"It is so." K'ayum bows his head. "My father is a good man," he says. "His heart will not remain in Metlán after he dies. But it is different with the rest of us."

As we approach the airstrip settlement towering mahogany trees appear on either side of the trail. K'ayum tells us that one of the smaller ones nearby had been cut down before our arrival, and they had begun to hollow it out for a new *cayuco*. It will not be completed for several weeks because of the rains.

A little farther on we come to Trudi's camp. It is bare and silent, but a stand of brilliant poinsettias blooms all around the empty wooden frames: the perfect Trudi touch.

We pay a visit to Geneviève, so Robert can get more alkaline tablets for his upset stomach. We also intend to ask her if she will consent to interview Koh II for us, since she has gained Koh's confidence.

Geneviève and Frédéric are staying in the small medical clinic she shared with a Mexican intern, Mario, who had just completed his tour of duty and left the forest, probably for good. The clinic is constructed of mahogany siding and corrugated tin, but is deficient in amenities like hospital beds and oxygen tanks. It is supplied with antibiotics, vaccines and snake serum, and various kinds of respiratory and gastrointestinal medicines. Pulmonary diseases, worms and dysentery are the commonest complaints in Nahá, particularly in the rainy season. I've been in the forest less than a week, but the clinic already looks to me like an outpost of occidental civilization.

Geneviève treats us to herb tea with wild honey, which tastes delightfully like Grand Marnier.

"You can get drunk on this honey," I say.

"That's because it's unrefined," says Geneviève, "and it's made deep in the forest, by a variety of stingless bees."

"Of course," I say, lightheaded. My threshold for paradox has been so often stretched in the past days, I accept unquestioningly that this viper- and scorpion-ridden forest should be home to bees that don't sting.

Robert asks Geneviève about her last census of Mensäbäk and Nahá. "With Young Mateo's newborn son, there are now one hundred eight in Nahá," she replies. "And I counted one hundred four in Mensäbäk altogether, including the new converts."

"Trudi's last count at Lacanjá was one hundred sixteen," says Robert. "Taking into account the family that recently fled to San Quintín, the remnants in El Petén, Guatemala, and in a few other scattered *caribales,** that adds up to about four hundred."

"That means," Geneviève says, "that they have more than doubled their numbers in less than fifteen years."

I ask her, "How much of that is due to better hygiene and modern medicine?"

"Quite a bit, I suppose. Infant mortality has dropped off rather dramatically, and the vaccines and anti-viper serum have cut down on the number of adult deaths."

"Four hundred is the highest population they've had in decades," Rob-

---

* Small Lacandon settlements.

ert says, and shakes his head. "How sad that over half of them should be evangelists. It is an old story. The numbers increase, and the culture goes down the drain." He starts to say, "I saw it happen before, as a child in Oklahoma . . ."

Frédéric takes me aside to show me his detailed map of the Lacandon zone he has covered thus far. He points out small settlements and *ejidos* (cooperatives) of homesteading Tzeltal, Tojolabal and Chol Mayans, many of them as inaccessible in winter as Nahá itself. In every case, he says, the most remote and ill-equipped settlements were the most hospitable and shared their scant supplies with him.

"But you know, all of them have sold their mahogany to the Department of Forestry or to private loggers — every single one, except for Nahá. And here, it is only a matter of time." He asks, "Have you seen the prospector's markers outside?" I shake my head, and he leads me to a tree by the airstrip with a wooden marker that reads ZONA LACANDONA: 267 CAOBA (Lacandon zone: 267 mahogany). It is signed by the Department of Forestry and Fauna.

"And there is another farther up, on the opposite side of the runway. In all, they have counted 376 mahoganies."

I remind him, "But Chan K'in has not given them permission to cut down the mahoganies."

"So, they will wait until he dies," Frédéric says, sucking on his pipe. "Or they will set up someone to overrule Chan K'in's authority; perhaps they will pick one of the three converts who live up on Missionary Hill." He points up toward Philip Baer's large bungalow, which is screened by dense foliage. "And the worst thing is that they'll get almost nothing for them. Do you know how much they pay the Lacandones in Mensäbäk, for each mahogany tree? Between two and three hundred pesos. After they cut up and process a good-sized mahogany it is worth about ten thousand pesos, or nearly fifty times what they paid for it. It is tragic, an absolute scandal."

Angry and dispirited I return to the clinic and tell Robert about the two markers.

"That figure is deceptive," he says in a controlled voice; but his face has turned gray. "They don't count the tropical cedar, *chicozapote*, *guayacán*, logwood and the other trees they cut down and haul out at the same time. It doesn't say that when a four-hundred-year-old giant mahogany is felled, it takes four or five smaller trees with it, including other centenarian mahoganies. What that number means, in simplest terms, is that this whole damn forest will go. All that remains, when they are done, is a tangle of splintered and broken tree trunks in which only the poisonous snakes can thrive and pass at will."

"That is true, Roberto," K'ayum says solemnly. "It will be the end of Nahá, and we will have to go to another place. My father says it has happened before, because of the chicle gatherers. But this time it will be much worse. My father says he will not go this time. He will stay here in Nahá. The other elders also, they will stay and die in Nahá. But the rest of us, I don't know . . ." His voice breaks, and he falls silent. "We will see," he says at last.

K'ayum leads us to the god-house and Jorge rather coolly invites us to sit around the *balché* pot, which is in the care of one of his four sons-in-law, Vicente. I find the *balché* insipid, even though Jorge has spiked it with cheap brandy from a pint bottle he keeps by his side. He is about fifty-five, a widower with one surviving wife, and has deep lines on either side of his eyes. Jorge is an epileptic, and his periodic violent fits have left him with jerky, nervous movements and a curdling laugh. He wears a red cowboy bandana around his neck, as if to protect his infirmity.

There is an aura of corruption and primitive guile about Jorge that puts me on my guard. When Robert finishes his first bowl of *balché*, Jorge hints crudely that he would like a disposable lighter like the one we gave Chan K'in. We promise to bring him one on our next visit. "And a bottle of whisky," he quickly adds. Jorge is the father of seven children by two wives: K'in Bor, a Baptist convert named Enrique, and five other stalwarts and young wives of the Nahá community, on both sides of the lake. Among his sons-in-law is fifteen-year-old Chan K'in Chico, who had asked for Jorge's pretty but sullen daughter Margarita without consulting his parents, Chan K'in and Koh II. Vicente, Chan K'in Chico and Pancho, who live nearby, all render son-in-law service, and this makes Jorge a powerful figure in the community.

Robert and Jorge seem to get along well. Their friendship dates from an incident fifteen years earlier, when Jorge fell into a particularly violent fit and Robert held him and gave him a sedative to calm him down. Jorge felt afterward that he had betrayed his infirmity to Robert and Robert had not taken advantage, a magnanimity that Jorge has repaid with a rough sort of loyalty.

Young Mateo sits with a Sony tape recorder at his feet so he can record Robert's singing. His moist round eyes droop as his head rests against one of the beams. A cigarette sticks out of his mouth. He has polished off several bowlfuls of *balché* already. His future son-in-law, fifteen-year-old Juan José, son of the Nahá evangelist Chan Bol, is raucously drunk on his very first bowl, and sings broken *corridos* in a high, weepy voice. Jorge's oldest son-in-law sits cross-legged in the rear, staring at the ground with glazed eyes, his arms draped over his knees.

The incense burners in the rear of the hut will not be lighted until the *balché* is finished, and the prayers to the gods will be perfunctory. The red *achiote* dye and the ceremonial bark-cloth tunics are there only for show. This — as Robert says — is the crumbling edge of the Nahá community.

I do not enjoy this ragged occasion, not even after Robert starts to sing Spanish Civil War songs and urges me to join in. It is not so much the religious element that I find sorely lacking, as the sense of a living tradition that retains an inherent dignity even at its most boisterous. These north-shore Lacandones speak almost as much Spanish as Mayan, and call each other by Christian kinship terms, like *compadre*. I now have a better sense of what becomes of the *balché* ceremony after the elders die off, as in Lacanjá.

Young Mateo goads K'ayum and me into drinking heavily, but my heart isn't in it and I escape into the bushes as often as I can. Each time I return, however, I find my *balché* bowl filled to the brim. During one of these rushes I trip over Chan K'in Chico, who has passed out on the ground after vomiting his *balché*.

Young Mateo senses my unease, and gazes into my eyes. *"Ki' iba a wilik,"* he says, although I am not yet ready to take my leave — "Be careful what you see." His brown shining eyes hold mine a long time. His father is the most disfigured Lacandon, but Young Mateo resembles a Raphael angel.

"I will," I say. "I will."

When I finish my bowl Young Mateo rises and takes my arm. "You must come see my house and the hotel. Come. You will like them."

Mateo leads me inside his large cabin, which has outer walls of laminated tin and mahogany plank, and a tar-paper roof — the only one of its kind in Nahá. He also has the only gas oven in the settlement, and the shelves above it are stacked high with supermarket provisions, including canned meats and cocoa. But the oven seems little used and out of place, and there is a cool sterility about the dark, empty corners of the house. He takes me to a storage room in back, where he stores the clay drums and the sets of bows and arrows for the tourist trade. At least once a week one of the Lacandones takes a drum-and-arrow shuttle flight to San Cristóbal. The economy of bow-and-arrow manufacture requires a fully loaded plane in order to meet expenses and turn a modest profit. There have never been so many bows and arrows in Nahá, none of which are used in the forest; and there have never been more ceremonial drums, all of which are silent. Formerly a symbol of cultural cohesion, the arrows and drums have become symptoms of Nahá's disintegration.

Next door, the Hotel Maya Caribe, which Mateo owns and manages, has new walls of mahogany, two cots, three pillows and a sleeping bag. The rates, he boasts proudly, are twenty pesos a night (less than a dollar), including meals, which are cooked by his wife, Margarita. She sits on one of the unused cots in a blue cotton dress and nurses their infant son, who was delivered in San Cristóbal two weeks before.

"My son has influenza," Mateo says, in a suddenly anxious tone of voice that does not match his drunken expression. "I will have to take him back to San Cristóbal, to see a doctor."

"Didn't you take him to see Geneviève? She has medicines."

"Yes, I took him, but the medicine she gave him is no good. It did not stop his coughing. My son needs the hospital doctor in San Cristóbal because he is very small and frail." His face is now a contorted mask of grief, and his round, Raphael eyes are brimming. *"Pobrecito* — poor little thing. If I don't take him soon, he will die." He then adds, "I will have to pay Enrique two hundred pesos to use Don Felipe's radio to call an airplane. It is too much money." Mateo smiles through his tears. "When I am an *evangelista* like Enrique, I can make the calls for nothing."

I approach the infant, who is suckling contentedly at his mother's breast. His eyes are dry and half closed.

"Come," Mateo says, "I will show you my chicken yard." He takes me to see his two pigs and the scrawny chickens in the hen coop, and then points out the frame of a small new hut that is under construction. His voice is buoyant with ownership, and the tears have vanished from his face. "This will be for my son-in-law Juan José and my daughter," he says. "He is erecting the hut by himself."

At that moment the daughter — she is only five years old — appears, leading her soon-to-be husband by the hand. He toddles drunkenly, singing bawdy songs in a cracked voice. Juan José is not yet fifteen.

"Juan José will be a good son-in-law," Mateo says. "He is a hard worker and takes good care of my daughter, like an older brother. But he is still young and cannot hold his *balché.*"

"*Hola, suegro* (father-in-law)," Juan José calls in Spanish, and waves his hand as he is led to his hammock by little Nuk, who barely comes up to his waist.

Mateo waves back, and laughs as Juan José stumbles and falls on his face. "In two years," he says, "I can leave Juan José in charge of the hotel when I travel to Mexico."

I stop to see Geneviève, and she tells me that she had indeed seen Mateo's newborn, and had given him medicines for a slight chill.

"Mateo has done this before, with the older son and daughter," she says. "The little ones get sick, and he won't give them the medicines I prescribe. This leaves him an excuse to fly to San Cristóbal with the sick child, stay at Na-Bolom for free, and tend to his little business deals. If you're here for a while you'll notice that one of Mateo's children is at death's door on the average of once a month. The curious thing is, he really believes it himself, every single time, and he nearly makes you believe it too, and take pity on him. That is how he borrows money from everybody. He looks at you with those melting, soulful eyes, and you feel absolutely terrible for doubting his sincerity.

"Mateo," she adds, "is an original. He is like a fallen angel. He is more ambitious than Jorge, and is already starting his little dynasty of sons-in-law. And he has begun with the son of an evangelist! But you know, his innocence is as real and as wholehearted as his corruption. I was a little in love with him myself, until I understood what was going on behind those beautiful eyes."

I return to the god-house to find the *balché* ceremony in its last gasps. The canoe is tilted on a stick and bone-dry. Jorge has retired to his hammock, and Vicente and the oldest son-in-law sit in a stupefied trance while Robert and K'ayum play guitar and sing off key. Juan José has returned from his hut and wrestles on the ground with Chan K'in Chico, beside a large stain of fresh vomit. Behind a nearby bush, Jorge's and Chan K'in Chico's wives comment on the scene and snicker with arms crossed.

I have little difficulty persuading Robert and K'ayum that it is time to leave, although they wait to quaff their bowls before rising.

When Robert goes off into the bushes, K'ayum confesses, "Mateo made me drink and drink, saying I am not a man if I refuse. So I have to throw up and begin again, so he will not laugh at me and say I am not a man. I do not like to vomit. It makes me feel cold and empty inside, and not contented." He turns to me. "Did you like his new house?"

"It is big," I say, "and it seems safe against storms. But it is not very sunny or friendly."

"I do not like the tin walls or the tar paper," K'ayum says. "I like a palm roof better. It is fresher on hot days, and it looks prettier. But I will not say that to Mateo's face. He is older than I am. I say it only behind his back."

I ask, "Did he pay you back the money he borrowed?"

"No." He shakes his head. "He said he did not remember borrowing it from me." He adds, crestfallen, "I will never lend him money again."

We pass the cemetery trail, cross the stream, and take a deep breath.

Debriefing

I stop by K'in Bor's on my return, and he promises to take me on a hunt the following day. He is fletching arrows with colorful parrot, toucan, and hawk feathers that hang in plastic bags from the eaves of his hut. For years, Trudi has been after the Lacandones to use chicken feathers for their arrows, and spare the scarce wild-bird population around Nahá from further depletion. To no avail.

On reentering our hut, I find Chan K'in talking with Robert in a quiet, intense voice.

"What was the *balché* like?" he is asking.

"It was . . . *ma' tsoy* — not good," Robert says, and trails off.

"Why? Was it sour? Or bitter?"

"The brandy . . . Jorge put in brandy."

"*Eh hah*, the brandy. Presidente brandy?"

"Yes."

"*Ma' tsoy*," Chan K'in says disapproving. "Did Jorge say anything?"

"Well . . ."

"Did he ask you for anything?"

"Well, yes. He asked for a lighter, like yours."

"*Eh hah*, a lighter. Anything else?"

"Whisky. He asked for whisky."

"I see. Whisky. And Young Mateo? Did he try to borrow money?"

"Well . . . yes."

"How much?"

"Five hundred pesos. His baby boy is ill, and he needs it for plane fare."

"Did you give it to him?"

"Well . . . yes. He promised to return it next month."

"We shall see." Long pause. "Did he get drunk?"

"*Chichin* — a little."

"And Chan K'in Chico?"

"Yes."

"Did he vomit?"

"Yes. Juan José also. They both vomited."

"I see. And Jorge?"

"No, he did not. He retired early."

"*Eh hah.* How did K'ayum behave?"

"Very well. Young Mateo tried to get him sick-drunk, but he held up."

"*Ne tsoy* — very good. How many bowls did you have? Did you keep count?"

"Eight or nine. Not as many as I had here. It was bad *balché* . . ."

"*Ehhh hah.*"

It dawns on me that Chan K'in is interrogating Robert not only to satisfy his curiosity — he is readmitting him to his protection. It is a kind of drill, reminiscent of the five-hour-long daily sessions in Mayan grammar. Robert's answers become gradually more coherent and forthright, and after a half hour he seems almost completely sober.

Eclipse

After nightfall the stars are out bright and clear, and K'in Bor and I sit on a log talking until our pine torches burn out.

"My father-in-law knows the names of the stars," he says, "but the rest of us have forgotten."

A shooting star blazes across the Milky Way, and K'in Bor wonders if it came from Mexico or the United States.

"It came from much farther away," I say. "It is the piece of a star which falls from the sky and burns up before it hits the earth."

After a moment, he says, "But I have seen stars that move across the sky from one end to the other, and they do not burn up."

I slap his shoulder. "You win, K'in Bor. Those are man-made stars, called satellites, and they come from the United States and a distant country called Russia."

We fall silent as we gaze up into the vaulted sky. "I am afraid," he says at last. "I am afraid when the sun hides during the day. If the sun is completely covered, as happened once before, then the jaguars come out of the ground and eat us — all of us — and then the world comes to an end."

"But it is only the moon that covers the sun," I explain. "Your ancients knew of the eclipse, and were able to predict the exact day and hour when it would happen. Your ancestors did not fear the eclipse."

K'in Bor shakes his head, unconvinced. "But they also said that some day, together with the eclipse, will come an earthquake. When the world comes to an end," he continues, "it is because the eclipse lasts too long, and Kisin awakes. He kicks the pillars of the earth and it shakes and shakes until the ground splits open. Then the jaguars come out — the great jaguars, the Nah Ts'ulu'. They eat most of the people. Then it is cold — very cold. The trees all dry up and die with the cold, because there is no sun. Then Hachäkyum gathers the people — those the Nah Ts'ulu' have not eaten — at his house in Yaxchilán. Then he will chop my head off. If my blood is good, he will use it to paint his house. If my blood is not good, he will just throw it on the ground, with the others'; but he will chop my head off just the same, and the jaguars and eagles will eat my body.

"But my heart will not go to Sukunkyum for his judgment. It will go far up to the heaven of the lesser gods, the *chembel k'uh*. There is no sun there — no stars. The good and the bad all go there together in the dark. Maybe I will find pine for torches to see a little, I don't know, but I will never see the sun or the moon or the stars again. And neither will my wife, Nuk, or my son K'ayum."

"Then you are afraid of dying?"

"No." Again he shakes his head. "No, it is not dying I am afraid of. I am afraid of what will happen to my son K'ayum, if I die and my heart goes to the dark place."

"And what about your wife, Nuk?" I ask. "Will Chan K'in take her back if you should die?"

"Oh, she will marry again," he says, matter-of-factly. "And I too will marry if she dies first. A year after one of us dies, the other will remarry. But I am afraid of what will happen to K'ayum."

Another silence. "My brother Enrique asks me to speak with Don Felipe Baer, and he tells me that if I am Christian my heart will go to his heaven when I die. He says the Christian heaven is a good place high in the sky, where there is sunlight always and no one goes hungry. If I remain Lacandon, he says my heart will go to the dark place and remain lost forever. Sometimes, I do not know what to believe."

In the bright crisp moonless night as we sit in silence, I realize with sadness that the missionaries may yet get to this brave hunter because of his fears. I wonder how many others in Nahá are beset by similar forebodings.

K'in Bor visits our hut after dinner. His mood has changed for the better, and his fears are all but forgotten. He teases Robert about his drinking, and insists I share his glass of Scotch. "You will see," he says. "Tomorrow in the forest a *nauyaca* will bite you, and you will die."

"Do you want me to die?" I ask, half seriously.

"Yes," he says. "If you die you will have to stay in Nahá — and then we will eat you."

"K'in Bor, why do you want to eat me?"

"Because," he says, laughing, "you are a good man."

The Stars

I am lying in my hammock, reading, nearly dozing, when a loud shout rouses me alert. I pull on my pants, grab a flashlight, and step outside.

Chan K'in's eldest son, K'in García, is pointing to a group of stars that hang low in the horizon, half hidden by tree branches. Chan K'in comes out of his hut and K'in continues to point to the stars, jabbering excitedly.

"What is it?" I ask in Spanish and Maya, but neither of them answers me. I think K'in might have seen a huge fireball behind the trees, or a UFO.

Speaking in a calm, soothing voice Chan K'in explains the problem to him. K'in calms down at last, and returns to his hut. After a lingering look at the sky Chan K'in also returns to his hammock.

"What was that about?" I ask Robert, nervously. "I thought the sky might be falling."

"Oh, it's nothing. K'in had a little too much to drink and got the galaxies mixed up. He confused the Pleiades with Gemini, and he became agitated. Chan K'in straightened it all out. Come on. Let's get to bed; it's cold out here."

The Hunt

K'in Bor comes for me at dawn. I am up picking the night's fleas out of my underwear — quietly, so as not to rouse Robert, who stayed up late with his diary. I brush off the cockroaches from two oranges and a banana that little K'in had picked for me, and stick them into my shoulder bag, along with my camera and binoculars and a small ration of trail mix. As I remove the door posts I hear Robert mumble, more asleep than awake: "Break a leg, chum! May a tree fall on you, and a *nauyaca* bite your ankle." A perfect Lacandon send-off.

We set out through the back entrance of the village and cut across Antonio's corn patch, which is shrouded in slowly rising mist. We ford a creek and begin the long ascent up the first of three thickly forested hills. Our progress is slowed at once. The trail is all chewed up by the *norte*, and every stride requires a heel-wrenching effort to break the mud's grip. K'in Bor, who left his new Vietnam jungle boots behind, seems to skim above the mud in his plastic shoes. He has brought all five of his hunting dogs, and they yap at my heels, excited and eager. Before reaching the first hilltop I have fallen three times, and K'in Bor has been forced to wait. He seems as impatient as his dogs, and I do my best to cover up my exhaustion. But his faintly scornful smile each time he stops lets me know that my stamina is being tested.

"At the top of the next hill we will rest," he says. Another interminable quarter hour of uphill slogging, with the squishy slushy mire determined to pry the boots off my feet. How does he do it? He springs up the slope like a goat, carrying a heavier load than mine plus his rifle and machete.

At last we sit down on palm fronds to breakfast on oranges and bananas. For the first time, I look up at the forest around me. The crests of mahogany, cedar and *chicozapote* filter out the early-morning light. The smaller trees, thorn palms, lianas and low shrubs form a vegetal wall that spills onto the trail so that it has to be reopened anew after each heavy rain. K'in Bor points to a *chicozapote* tree that has crow's-feet slashes along the full length of its trunk.

"I bled that tree myself, two years ago," he says. "It gave good chicle, but the price of raw gum is so low now, it no longer pays."

"How did you climb it?" I ask admiringly.

"Like this!" He jumps up and imitates a monkey scurrying up a tree, chattering its teeth.

His mimicry of my astonished expression likens him even more starkly to a spider monkey. K'in Bor is in his element.

As I get up I hear a thrumming sound behind me; a large emerald and blue hummingbird hovers directly in front of us, looking from one to the other with tiny little eyes before it zips away into the forest. It is the first wildlife we encounter, and it gives my flagging energies an instant charge.

"Perhaps that is your *onen*," K'in Bor says. "He is looking for you." I assume he is joking again, but his expression has turned serious. Before he can take off I laugh and call out, "K'in Bor, this is impossible. I can keep up neither with your stride nor with your changes of mood."

"You will learn," he calls back, without breaking step.

I fall twice more as we negotiate the third hill, and feel so badly at delaying the hunt I compound my shame by confessing to a debilitating touch of diarrhea. Already loaded down, K'in Bor insists on carrying my shoulder bag as well. After another fifteen minutes he announces, "We have reached the top," and hands back my *morral*. "Now we can travel faster."

On the level trail I catch my second wind and can finally keep up with his hunter's pace. The last time I fell I brushed against a thorn palm, and my hand is covered with spines. Although concerned that they might fester, I decide not to tell K'in Bor until our next rest stop.

Now at the summit, a little more milky light filters through; as my breathing falls into an even rhythm I am able to appreciate the ghostly wonderland around me, without falling behind. The trunks of the giant trees are covered with nests of thick moss which accommodate brilliant scarlet and pink bromeliads. Clusters of red and black berries and a cassavalike fruit droop from low and high branches. There are small spreading palms everywhere, and elephant ears fit for mastodons. I soon become accustomed to the rancid odor of rotting vegetation.

Suddenly K'in Bor stops to tear a leaf into narrow strips. He raises a thin sliver to his lips and blows on it to make a piercing wounded-animal sound. He tosses back his head, with his eyes, mouth and ears agape. He blows again, and waits for the echoes to subside before going on at a quickened pace. We are now jogging along so rapidly I have no time to think of my burning palm, or to look out for snakes or the weeping tree, whose sap can blind you if you brush its leaves.

One of the dogs starts to yowl, and they all leave the trail and bolt into the thick of the forest. I dash in after them, but get instantly fouled in low-hanging vines and fall on my face. All five dogs are now in full cry, and K'in Bor has vanished behind them. I think, "He must see better than I do," as everything before my 20/20 vision is a dark, impenetrable mesh of leaves, vines and branches, and all else underfoot is an impediment designed to make me stumble. Somehow I claw my way through the brush until I come to the tree where their prey is cornered.

"He's in there!" K'in Bor shouts, pointing to a tangle of roots at the foot of the giant ceiba. His cry flushes the animal from its hole, and it takes off across my path. I see a flash of brown followed by five howling mottled blurs, then a deafening detonation makes me shut my eyes. When I open them, the six shapes are gone, and K'in Bor is regarding me with a wild look of ecstasy.

"*Tepeiscuinte!* Did you see him?" he shouts, with the stock of his smoking rifle jammed against his hip.

"It's big," I say, although I have no idea of the paca's actual size, it all happened so fast. "Did you hit him?"

"I don't know," he says, and melts into the trees like a ghost.

I stumble and pitch downhill through the shrubbery in the direction of the barking dogs. And I pick up another fistful of thorns. I find K'in Bor and the dogs all gathered at the foot of the hill.

"We have him now!" K'in Bor calls, breathless with excitement. "He is in his cave."

The five dogs are jammed around the mouth of the paca's burrow, growling and poking at the edges. K'in Bor unslings his rifle and lays it on the ground. He then uproots a small tree and shoves it into the opening, to cut off the paca's escape. "You can relax now," he says. He chops off a palmetto frond with a single blow of his machete, and places it above the burrow.

I sit down on the frond and take out the tweezers from my jackknife to remove the thorns.

K'in Bor spies me, and smiles. "So the thorn palm got you," he says. "Now your hand will rot and fall off." I ignore him, but he interrupts his labor to snap off a spine from a nearby palm. "You need a spine to remove a spine," he says. "That thing is good for plucking eyebrows." And with the spine he picks out the thorns from both hands before I can protest.

K'in Bor sets to work digging a hole with his machete, about two feet above the cave entrance. When he reaches the tunnel he sticks in his machete and gets an immediate tug. "He's in there," he says excitedly. But when he sticks the machete in a second time, there is no response. I hear tiny squeaking noises under the ground, just below me.

"It seems to be heading toward me," I say. I feel a slight quiver beneath the ground.

"Yes, the burrow is a long one." With a loud grunt, K'in Bor uproots another small tree and slams it into the hole he has just dug. "I will have to move you," he says, and places the palmetto frond a few feet to the left of where I've been sitting. With swift, furious energy he digs a second hole with his machete, and does not pause until he reaches the tunnel. Again he sticks in the machete, and again the paca swipes at it . . . then nothing. Astonishingly, I hear the tiny squeaking noises again, as the paca turns the corner and burrows toward me.

"K'in Bor . . ."

"I will have to move you again," K'in Bor says, and does not pause to seat me; he stops up the second hole and digs a new one with his bare hands. This time the paca swipes at the tip of the machete twice in a row, and K'in Bor looks up in triumph. "No more tunnel — we have him."

And now at last he takes a deep breath, as his shoulder and neck muscles momentarily relax. He picks up the rifle, slips the muzzle into the hole. An explosion, smoke, the sharp scent of gunpowder. And he is grinning at me.

"Did you get him?"

"Yes."

K'in Bor puts down the rifle, delicately. He sinks his hands into the burrow and begins to yank, evenly, with intense concentration. The tension and violence in his movements have turned into something else, exultant yet almost tender. The *tepeiscuinte* comes out slowly, head-first. It is covered with sweat and a thin layer of black dirt. I see the red puncture on its forehead first, then the two rodent front teeth, pathetically useless. It is a hefty specimen, and has a dappled, dark-brown coat like a spotted fawn's. It had rolled itself up into a ball at the extreme end of its burrow. When it is all out, lying in a shroud of black dirt, K'in Bor has to kick the dogs to keep them from tearing at the large red gash on its side, where one of them had ripped it.

"I missed him the first time," K'in Bor says, after examining it on both sides. "I am a bad hunter."

"I think perhaps I distracted you," I say, to salve his pride.

"It is no matter. Tonight, we eat fresh meat."

K'in Bor slings the paca into his *morral*, and we stop by a nearby tree to rest and eat our lunches. He mashes five oranges into his mouth, one after the other, then crushes a sixth in his palm to wash the dirt off his hands with its juice.

"I eat like a pig," he says, and laughs as I am still peeling my one remaining orange. After dividing up my trail mix we have a cup of coffee each, from his canteen.

"How is your diarrhea?" he asks.

"Better," I say, and blush. Although true, it had been a lame excuse.

"If it comes back, I will slash open your stomach with my machete, and stuff you with the guts of the *tepeiscuinte*. Then you will be cured."

He is relaxed now and expansive, and asks if I want to see a quetzal.

"Quetzal! Where?" The very sound of the word jolts fresh adrenalin into my veins.

"Up on that hill. I saw several there last month."

My head spins. I have wanted to see one of these legendary birds of Mayan royalty since I was a small boy. But the quetzal, Guatemala's national bird and a symbol of freedom, has virtually disappeared from the highlands, although the penalty for shooting one is severe. The long green tail of this majestic red-breasted trogon had adorned the headdresses of the great Mayan lords, the *halach winik*. In Classical times, the quetzal feather had been the highest unit of currency in the whole Mayan realm.

We scale the hill, and now I am the impatient one, trudging ahead as K'in Bor pauses to pick handfuls of delicious red berries, and to scrape honey from a hive of stingless bees which he splits open with his machete. "Very good for making *balché*," he says.

As we approach the summit, K'in Bor tears off a leaf, slivers it, and repeats the wounded-animal call. But there is no response.

"I saw a flight of five quetzal here," he says. "But it was closer to midday. At this hour of the morning they are still near the treetops, feeding on berries."

As we climb, I tell K'in Bor about Quetzalcoatl, the Toltec god-king of the feathered serpent. He is only mildly interested.

"What did he do?" he asks.

"Well, he founded the Nahuatl Empire, and brought in laws and the priests. He was an artist, and it is said that he taught your ancestors to illustrate their books, which the Spaniards later burned."

"What else?"

"After he died, they say he went into the underworld for four days, and came back as a god. Your ancients knew him as Kukulcán."

"Then he was a good man," K'in Bor says. "Like my father-in-law."

We reach the hilltop and he gives two sharp consecutive whistles. I look up, but the crests of the trees are screened off by foliage. He whistles two or three times more, and then I join in. I hear the sounds of bark rubbing against bark as trees sway and creak softly in the wind; the primordial hum of flying insects; the crack of a distant branch falling to the forest floor. Assorted chirps and twitters. No quetzal.

We walk along the ridge, stopping frequently to cup our lips and emit the two short whistles. And then — unmistakably — I hear two clear, rounded notes, the blend of a peacock's call and a jay's whistle. My heart stops with a thump, then races wildly. But there is no repetition. The quetzal is high up in the trees and is not fooled by our mimicry.

We walk a mile or so through dense forest, and K'in Bor stops to point out edible fruits and plants, so many that a lost wayfarer could subsist on them for weeks. He shows me five or six different shrubs whose leaves or roots are medicinal, another used for bathing newborn infants, to prevent rash; the thorn palm frond serves as a broom and its heart is considered a delicacy. The taller, thicker palmetto along with the thorn palm provide the thatching for the roofs of the Lacandon huts, and a flowering wild cane, *caña brava,* over ten feet tall, is used to make arrow shafts. There seems to be no part of the forest, no tree or shrub or lowly weed, that does not yield some primary service to the Lacandones.

Periodically the dogs yelp and take off after a fresh scent, and K'in Bor drops his load and takes off after them. But they turn out to be false alarms. Once we glimpse the flash of black and white wings, but the curassow is gone before K'in Bor can take aim.

I have grown almost nimble at sidestepping the thorns and lianas, and my depth perception has improved enough so that I can anticipate hazards more than a foot or two in front of my nose. But the worst of the morning's hike is by no means over.

Back on the trail, K'in Bor stops to show me the infamous *chechem* (weeping tree), whose elm-shaped leaves exude a noxious liquid that blisters the skin horribly on the lightest contact. Very carefully he slits open the leaf's veins, and the milky sap oozes out. "If I touch your eyes with this, you will be blinded, and I will have to lead you back by the hand like an old, old man."

"K'in Bor, you are a gentleman and a scholar," I say, and we both laugh at the alien sound of my English.

We start down the highest hill, and I slide on my butt at once. If the ascent had been tortuous, the descent is to be an unmitigated horror, as the mud has been roiled and churned even further by our boots, and there is no firm footing anywhere. The thorn palms and the weeping trees discourage me from attempting the sides, so I slip and slide and occasionally tumble down each of the three hills, and my boots and jean bottoms become layered with black ooze. K'in Bor's jungle legs betray him once or twice, but this does not slow him down.

We wash ourselves off in the creek. As we emerge into Antonio's cornfield the bright sun blinds me momentarily. My weary legs buckle over every small hummock or anthill.

"Now you know how I feel in Mexico [City]," K'in Bor says, with a chuckle. "I fall down on the hard street and I hurt all day in my knees. After a day of walking there I cannot stand up."

It is a good hour before lunch, and I join K'in Bor and little K'ayum for a reviving swim in the lake. On our way back, K'in Bor says gravely, "Next time, come in the dry season, and I will take you to the cave where the winds are born. It is only a half day's walk from here — three hills beyond the quetzal place." His eyes grow round. "You come near the cave and the air is warm and very still. But inside it is cold, and you hear the screaming of the winds being born." He drops his voice. "But you must not tell anyone, until we go."

Quetzal

After lunch, we linger around the kitchen table to chat, and to tell of our successful expedition. Chan K'in jokes that I have brought "hunter's luck" to K'in Bor, and he will have to look for another mascot after my departure.

We are visited by Antonio Ruiz, a tall Tzeltal Indian of about sixty-five in cowboy hat and boots, who for years has been Trudi's "camp boy" during her periodic safaris to Nahá. He remembers Robert fondly, and recounts colorful anecdotes from his early visits to Nahá in the sixties. Ruiz is a converted evangelist, and Robert used to take pleasure in coaxing him to drink whisky until he denounced the missionaries at the top of his voice.

Koh II remembers that the unmarried girls used to tease Robert and pester him in his hut while he was writing. One day he grabbed the most forward one by her long rope of hair and twisted it around his wrist, so she could not run away.

"*Malo Roberto,*" she reproaches him, as if it had all happened just the day before.

"It did no good," Robert protests, flushing. "They were back at it the following day."

I tell them of the quetzal we had heard, and Antonio Ruiz says it is just as well I hadn't seen him, for this is their molting season and they look short-tailed and scrawny.

"In April their tails are at their longest and brightest, and then there is no sight to compare with a flight of eight or ten quetzals, gliding above the trees." Ruiz adds that in Zaragoza, a nearby settlement, there are so many quetzals in the spring that the settlers shoot them for food and sell their tail feathers.

I remind Ruiz pointedly that across the border in Guatemala the quetzal is rigorously protected, and the penalty for shooting one is lifelong imprisonment.

"Is that so?" Antonio nods, but his face has gone blank.

A little later K'in García (Louis XIV) comes by for his afternoon drink, looking more sullen and distracted than usual. I ask him if he has ever seen a quetzal, and he answers in a flat voice: "A quetzal? Yes, it is a very pretty bird, but there's not much meat on them."

The Interview with Koh II

In the afternoon Geneviève visited Koh II while Chan K'in was praying in the god-house for the recovery of his smallest son, who has pneumonia. They chatted for awhile, and she was able to work in some of the questions Robert and I had outlined to her. Geneviève reported Koh's replies to us in the evening. Koh confirmed that she was one of José Güero's twenty or so living offspring, but would not admit that her grandfather had been a *ts'ul* (foreigner) — a Spanish rancher from Ocosingo. Her mother, María, had left José after bearing several of his children, and was now living in Mensäbäk with Pepe Castillo, half brother of Old Chan K'in and an Adventist convert. Koh assured Geneviève that she got along well with the other two wives, each of whom has her own separate functions and her pride of place. She had gladly consented to his acquiring a young third wife, for he was the *t'o'ohil,* and it was altogether right that he should have many children. She said the elder Koh had accepted *her* in just the same way.

When asked about the *balché* drinking she had laughed and insisted that she does not mind it at all, as she has a great deal of work to do and the ceremony keeps the men out of her way. Her only concern was that one of them might drink too much and fall into the lake and drown.

One of the other wives had walked in just then, and Koh immediately got up and left. But Geneviève promises to try again.

That night we find that one of the dogs has eaten our Ocosingo cheese, and the black beans Koh serves us are even less cooked than usual. Chan K'in does not tarry to chat with us after dinner, but returns to the god-house to pray for his sick child. I have no way of knowing if all this is coincidence or if we are being penalized for interviewing Koh without first asking Chan K'in's permission. Robert and I retire to our hammocks feeling chastened and not a little like the Bibical snake after offering the apple to Eve. Is there no reconciliation possible between our professional obligations and the trust we owe Chan K'in and Koh as privileged guests?

I again have bad dreams of looking for my younger sister and not being able to locate her. It is the third night in a row I dream of Becky, who has been in a state of despondency for years. When I tell Chan K'in these dreams at breakfast he asks for details, and I mention the hotel in which I look for my sister by pressing all the buttons on the elevator and knocking at every door. For the first time, Chan K'in seems genuinely interested, and tells me through Robert that this may be a dream in which my *hach pixan* (real soul) is manifesting itself. He says the obstacles might be a sign of a breakthrough and that, through dreams, I may be reaching her at last and alleviating her despondency. Chan K'in's eyes hold mine steadily as he interprets my dream, and I am grateful, not the least for this evidence that he harbors no ill feelings about our interviewing Koh.

Meek'chäl

Geneviève described the rites of adulthood (*meek'chäl*) that Lacandon girls undergo when they reach puberty. Whereas a boy has arrows and axes offered to the gods in his name by his appointed godfather, a girl's godmother will give spindles of spun cotton, net bags, wooden combs and other feminine accessories. The loom, which was basic equipment for a Lacandon woman, is now offered ceremonially, since most women no longer weave.

The initiate wears a new tunic for the ceremony, and her godmother instructs her in the proper way to cook and use various household utensils.

"This is how you sweep the floor of the hut — but I am lazy, don't learn from me," the godmother will say.

"Take the bowl to your husband and place it above the fire this way — but don't learn from me, I am clumsy and spill it on the ground."

"You take the shuttle and move it like this — but don't follow my example. I no longer spin."

The instructions are performed with a show of modesty by the godparent, and are repeated over and over with consummate courtesy and patience.

In daily life, the young girls and boys learn to perform all these functions by imitating their parents.

Journal

December 10, 1977. One of K'in García's large pigs wandered away from its pen and drowned in the lake, so that it had to be butchered at once. We had it for dinner tonight, along with fresh paca and the remains of the cabrito (a small deer) K'in shot two days ago. The paca, whose flesh is tender and juicy, tasted even better than the venison or the pork. Robert quipped: "A twenty-pound rat, two-day-old venison and a drowned pig, all in one meal. How unkosher can you get?"

We did not stop laughing for several minutes, although the Jewish dietary laws would have meant very little to Chan K'in. For me, the triumph was in proving to myself that I can now digest just about anything and suffer no ill effects the next day. My rabbinical ancestors must be spinning in their graves.

Chan K'in's littlest son is still sick, which is why Chan K'in hasn't gone to the milpa. He spends much of the day praying and lighting incensories in the god-house. In the evening his spirits had improved, and he told a story about a supernatural bird that makes people blind if anyone keeps it or eats it. Is this an indirect reference to the taboo on killing quetzal? It would make sense.

Chan K'in remembers his father as having a thick white beard and a very loud voice. Chan K'in thinks he has lots of gray hairs himself, although I can only detect some white stubble on his chin. "Oh, not like the ts'ul," he says, with a touch of derision.

The role of t'o'ohil is hereditary, subject to competence. Should all of Chan K'in's sons die or prove incompetent, Old Mateo and his sons would be next in line.

December 11. Robert says puma prey on deer, jaguar on jabalí (wild boar). The jabalí are gone from Nahá, and so are the jaguar. There are still some puma around.

Robert described how Lacandon parents deal with preadolescents who get carried away with their petting and attempt to make love. "So you want to make love like a grownup?" the father will say to the boy. "Well then, you can work in the fields as I do"; and he will put him to work clearing the milpa, while the girl's mother will set her to grinding corn and sweeping the hut. If they still desire each other at the end of a hard day's work, then they are considered old enough to fend for themselves.

December 12. I caught a glimpse of Koh III, Chan K'in's reticent twenty-two-year-old third wife, when I entered the hut to give Koh II some needles and thread. She was curled up on her pallet with her three small children, like a bitch with her litter. Ever since her littlest one took sick, Koh III has spent most of her time nursing him, with her full, rounded breast poking out of her soiled cotton shift. The little boy's own shift is black with filth, and none of the three children (or their mother) look or smell as if they've had a bath in several months. Unlike the older two wives, Koh III's features are coarse-grained, and her movements are lacking in natural grace. But she has a sturdy, compact body, slender legs, and can look sexily alluring when she wants to. And how fondly old Chan K'in dotes on her and their five little ones! I fantasize her making love with Chan K'in in the milpa, gratifying his every erotic whim. She must know how to keep him happy, and she is certainly a prolific breeder. But what about her progeny? What will become of these coarse, sturdy children, who so obviously lack the breeding and poise of a K'ayum or little K'in? What is Chan K'in's design for them?

This evening Koh III's little boy is better. For the first time in several days, he did not cough all night. Chan K'in's prayers and Geneviève's medicines seem to be taking effect. Feeling expansive, Chan K'in had some whisky after dinner and sang three new songs that Robert had not heard before. In the first one, Kisin visits one of the ancients, who, in the spirit of hospitality, invites him to dinner. Kisin eats corn broth and tortillas. The next day, all of the ancient's seed corn has turned into little stones. The maize of his companions, who had offered only to the friendly gods, ripens in five days. The moral is, one should protect one's crops from Kisin, even at the cost of appearing inhospitable.

In the second song Tu'up, keeper of the sun and youngest son of Hachäkyum, uses clay to make a rooster — the first — to keep watch over his father and protect him from Kisin.

The third song tells of a god who asks one of the ancients to come with him into the underworld because he had committed incest with a non-permissible relative. The ancient pleads that he cannot leave because he is harvesting his sweet potatoes. The god picks up a sweet-potato vine, draws three circles above the ancient's head and creates an android surrogate to stay behind and fulfill his functions.

In the evening the ancient's double asks his wife to bake sweet potatoes for supper. After eating them he gets a terrible fever and dies, for the vine was part of his being.

In the middle of the last song Robert's tape recorder broke down and he had to borrow my microphone. He was determined but patient, considering how frequently our electronic equipment keeps going on the blink. And he must know by now that there is no end to Chan K'in's stories.

December 13. The "Haawo'," it seems, may not refer to the Raccoon clan at all, as Robert first thought. It is a form of reference for some of the minor gods. If so, when Chan K'in's grandfather said in a strange voice, "Ten Haawo'," he may have been intimating he was one of the gods. Is Chan K'in suggesting that he has inherited divinity?

Robert's linguistic facility is extraordinary. In the ten days we've been together he has learned almost as much Hebrew as I have Maya, although I have both him and Chan K'in as teachers. Robert's retention is almost a hundred percent. Today I taught him the conjugation of lëechol, to eat.

Robert tells me that in Maya, the terms for "good man" and "good spirit" are the same (tsoy y-ol). And the word for money (ta'k'in) means shit of the sun. It figures.

Robert has brought his old .38 pistol to Nahá, and carries it on our hikes to the north shore. He says he brought it for the snakes, and for target practice.

There is an episode in Robert's diaries that recurs again and again. He writes of shooting at a spider monkey on a tree. He hits the monkey, but it doesn't fall to the ground. Instead, it curls its long tail around a tree branch and hangs by it, stone dead, until a harpy eagle or other predator gets to it. I have read of this incident in at least three or four separate entries, and suspect it must return to haunt him now that the spider monkey population is almost entirely depleted. Robert is one of the very few occidentals who regularly ate monkey flesh, and enjoyed it.

The spider monkey is the onen of Chan K'in and most other Nahá Lacandones, and yet they too have contributed to its disappearance since they began using .22 rifles. Spider and howler monkey flesh is used in preparing tamal offerings to Hachäkyum. What effect can the disappearance of his lineage animal have on Chan K'in and his heirs? It is as if they have killed and sacrificed to the gods their own alter egos. Is it a prelude to their own hecatomb, or a last symbolic vestige of the human sacrifices practiced by their ancestors?

When magic retreats from a community, all that remains are individual people, good, bad, and somewhere in between — just like everywhere else.

Bol

Early in the morning I go swimming with Chan K'in's thirteen-year-old son Bol, who has his father's reflective nature and his mother Koh II's muscular physique and light skin. After K'ayum, he is the most intelligent and appealing of their seven sons. More than any of his brothers Bol loves to swim, and he never fails to soap down afterward and wash his hair. I have yet to see adult villagers, male or female, swim in the lake or take a soap bath. Hygiene still has a very low priority in Nahá. Chan K'in's hands are so sooty from lighting his incense pots every evening that Geneviève will not let him vaccinate his ailing child. And the same applies to Koh I and Koh III, whose faces are always smudged with dirt or cigar smoke. Only Koh II is immaculately clean, in her red and white apron.

After our swim I ask Bol if he knows the famous alligator lake, and he nods and offers to take me there. We start across the lake in his father's large *cayuco* and skim past the reeds and water-lily banks. The white clouds and blue sky are mirrored flawlessly in the dark-green water, which has never known the taint of motor oil. The dugout's rough mahogany floor chafes my knees sore and I soon tire of paddling, but Bol keeps us on even keel with his smooth powerful strokes.

He confesses that he has never been to Ocosingo or San Cristóbal. In fact, he has never been outside of the forest; but he knows a good deal about airplanes and asks me if I own a car.

"Would you like to visit San Cristóbal?" I ask.

"Perhaps one time I will go with my brother K'ayum or Young Chan K'in, to sell my arrows. But I will not stay long. I don't like what happens to my brothers in San Cristóbal."

My ears perk up, but I do not press. We paddle in silence, and then Bol says, "I think K'ayum is much influenced by Young Mateo, who likes to drink whisky in town, smoke marijuana, and sleep with foreign women. Whenever K'ayum goes to San Cristóbal without Margarita, I see her face become sad and worried. She knows what he does. . . . I like Old Mateo," he adds, squinting one eye, "and Antonio is a good man, like my father. But Young Mateo? I don't know, I think it is not good what goes on at the other side of the lake. They turn evangelist and go to live with Don Felipe, like Enrique and Atanasio, or they become crazy like Jorge, or they learn to steal like Young Mateo, who never returns what he borrows."

"Do you like to drink and smoke?" I ask Bol, as I have seen him do both, although not in the god-house. Nahá children learn to smoke and snatch swigs of *balché* in their infancy.

"Yes, I like to drink *balché* and smoke cigars, but my father has not yet

127

given me *meek'chäl* (the rites of adulthood). Next year he will give bows and arrows and other offerings in my name, and then I will drink and smoke with the elders, and I will have the protection of the gods." He laughs. "Until then, I can sample Robert's whisky."

We reach the far shore. Bol eases the *cayuco* into the reeds and ties it to an overhanging branch.

"Come. You can see the lake from the top of the ridge."

We climb quickly to the top, although my calves are still sore from yesterday's expedition. We look over a round muddy pond no bigger than a swimming hole. The brown water is absolutely still, so that every movement causes a visible disturbance on the surface. Bol spies a large turtle sunning itself on a submerged log — but no alligator.

"They are hiding now because it is daylight," Bol says. "Not long ago K'in Bor killed a big alligator here, and now they are afraid to show themselves."

A stinging in my ankle makes me jump to one side. When I look down I see a small hawk or falcon carcass that is crawling with small black ants. Its body is all but eaten away, but its beautiful silver and gray feathers are intact.

"That is the one my brother K'in shot two days ago," Bol says, "when he was hunting deer. He does not like hawks because they kill his chickens. He will not even use their feathers for arrows."

I add up the score: two strikes against K'in García. A quetzal, and now an immature hawk. At what cost will he wrest his independence at last from his father's authority? To all intents and purposes, K'in is already a north-shore Lacandon, like his brother Chan K'in Chico.

The wasteful shooting of the hawk has spoiled my afternoon, and we head back to the *cayuco* without waiting to sight an alligator.

As we paddle back, I ask Bol if he would take me to the *milpa* the next day. He points to the sky, which is growing overcast with scudding gray clouds from the north.

"If it does not rain," he says. "Perhaps," he adds after some moments, "it is better if you wait and go with my father."

The mood of the lake changes abruptly. A stiff breeze arises, riffling the surface and fracturing the sky's reflection.

"My father has not been to the *milpa* since my little brother became sick. But next week, when he gets better, you can go and help him gather the last of the corn."

"But I won't be here next week," I say. "We leave this Sunday."

"Then when you return," Bol says gravely.

The stubborn investigator rises up in me. Bol's reticence redoubles my interest in seeing the *milpa*. "Perhaps I will accompany K'ayum instead. Doesn't he have his own *milpa*?"

"K'ayum has a *milpa* but he does not always work it himself," Bol says. "He is afraid of snakes, and so he pays Tzeltales to harvest his maize and tobacco."

Astounded, I ask, "Where does K'ayum get the money?"

Bol shrugs. "From selling drums and arrows in San Cristóbal, I think. Young Mateo also hires Tzeltales."

After docking the canoe I walk ahead to reflect on our conversation. I bridle at the notion of Lacandones becoming wealthy landowners and hiring Tzeltal laborers to work their fields. A few yards beyond the laddered path I am stopped by a snake lying across the trail. When I see it, my right foot is only inches from its tail, but it makes no attempt to get away or coil itself up to strike. The snake is mottled green and yellow, with a diamond pattern on its back; its girth is approximately that of a common garden hose, and it is at least four feet long. We stare at each other unmoving for a minute or so, and then it slides slowly into the underbrush with an undulation of its tail. I am more surprised than alarmed by its calmness; I am used to snakes that slither away at my approach. It is as if he had stopped deliberately in the middle of the trail, to be seen and admired.

Bol comes up just as its tail disappears in the brush.

"*Nauyaca*," he says, softly. "A small one."

That night a second *norte* strikes Nahá, overturning my plans to visit the cornfield the following day. I discuss with Robert Bol's shocking disclosure that K'ayum and Young Mateo have been paying Tzeltal laborers to work their *milpas*.

"Oh, that's been going on for some time," he says. "Old Mateo is doing it too, on a seasonal basis. It's a classic instance of reverse peonage, like the wealthy Japanese factory owners who now import Italian coolies. Before long, Chan K'in and Antonio and one or two others will be the only ones in Nahá who still till their own fields."

Cousin Jaime

In spite of the wind and the heavy rains I wake up next morning feeling better than at any time since my arrival. The fleas have not kept me awake, and I have no borderline-diarrhea shakiness. I dreamed about my cousin Jaime. We are together in the store, in Guatemala City, chatting casually. In the dream I know he is dead (he died in a boating accident in '71) but I keep seeing him appear, talk to me, and go on about his business as if he were alive.

Chan K'in says that as he is the son of my father's brother, Jaime and I share the same *onen*. The dream means that my *onen* is nearby, although I may not have seen it.

I saw a hummingbird two days ago in the hut with K'in Bor, and one yesterday — a large blue one with a curved beak — when I was relieving myself in the sugarcane break. He hovered and looked directly at me, just like the one in the forest.

Robert reminds me that the hummingbird is one of the accepted *onen*. He thinks that there may be some connection between my Mayan birth date, 13 Ahau, and the hummingbird in the *Chilam Balam*.

Of course, I am disappointed that I did not dream of a dolphin, which is my preferred *onen*. In Lacanjá they believe that everyone has two *onen*: an inherited one and a personal one. That makes sense to me. I tell Robert that it is hard for me to imagine my father or any of my rabbinical ancestors as hummingbirds, whereas Robert seems a perfect *chäk balum* (mountain lion).

Don Alfredo

After breakfast I ask Chan K'in if he has ever killed a tiger with bow and arrow, and he says yes, he has killed about twenty of all kinds and sizes, with the aid of hunting dogs. Besides jaguar, he mentions puma, ocelot, lynx and *bolay* or *tigrillo*, a spotted wild cat smaller than the ocelot. He adds that José Güero's father had been the first to use a rifle in Nahá — an old muzzle-loading shotgun.

I ask Chan K'in, "Who was the first white man you met?"

"Ehh so many . . ." He waves his hand wearily. "Too many white men. My father and his father had met many chicle gatherers, alligator hunters, soldiers, tradesmen and anthropologists." He sighs, strokes his stubbled chin with his bent hand. "The first white man I remember was Don Alfredo [Tozzer]. I was a small boy when he came to our village and lived with us. A very nice man, Don Alfredo. He gave us gifts and was always respectful, unlike the *kah* [*ladinos*] and some of the *ts'ul* who came after him. My father treated him with much courtesy, but he did not always tell him the whole truth. He told him exactly what he asked for, nothing more and nothing less." He laughs. "And sometimes not even that. Don Alfredo was very interested in our ceremonies and in our way of life, and he wrote everything down in a little book. If one of our companions told Don Alfredo a lie, he would write it down in his little book, and then it became true."

I feel my cheeks redden at Chan K'in's muted laughter, as my pen is poised above my yellow pad. I slip it quietly under my seat, and Chan K'in goes on:

"My father never knew the airplane. He walked to Tenosique to sell wax, tobacco, bows and arrows, and he bought salt, a metate and machetes. He never saw the airplane or the car."

"What about missionaries?" I asked.

"No, my father did not know the missionaries. The first evangelist I knew was Don Felipe, and he is still here after many years. But now, it may be that Don Felipe is changing. Before he always said that Hachäkyum is no good, only Jesus Christ is good. Now, Don Felipe tells me, 'Chan K'in, when the road is built, men will come who want to steal your gods. You must hide your incensories, so the men will not steal them.' So yes, I think perhaps that Don Felipe is changing."

Robert asks Chan K'in how he would react if one of his sons-in-law —

K'in Bor for instance — were to turn evangelist, and still want to go on living in the village. "Would you throw him out?" Robert asks.

Chan K'in shakes his head. "If K'in Bor wants to be an evangelist then I think he will move to the other side and live with Don Felipe, and my daughter will go with him if she wishes. But I do not command him to do anything. That is not for true men to do. But if he stays on and drinks *balché* with us when his heart is no longer here, then after a time I will say to him, 'K'in Bor, don't you think you would be more contented with your own kind?' "

Two Women

Bol visits us in the afternoon, and I offer him some trail mix. He accepts a cigarette, but politely declines Robert's whisky. (Good for him.) He is more relaxed and outgoing when his older brothers are not around. He is softer, more compassionate than either K'in García or K'ayum, and very sensitive to our moods. I am tempted to attribute this sweet temper to his never having been out of the forest, but I recall that some of his younger kin can be quite pesky and inconsiderate. Bol is always watching us, like the other villagers, but he does not laugh at my clumsiness when I fall in the mud or look secretly amused when a dog barks and snaps at my heels, as happens at least once a day. When I lost my balance yesterday and nearly fell into the water, Bol blamed the narrowness of the *cayuco*. Hans and Fritz would have rocked with merriment and giggled and joked about it for two days, with the appropriate slapstick.

Bol is an excellent informant. He knows what we are after, and freely volunteers information before we ask for it. Today he tells me of María Bonita, a middle-aged woman living nearby with two young husbands. Apparently theirs is the first instance of polyandry in Nahá in several generations. When I mention her to Robert his eyes light up, and he recalls María Bonita from fifteen years ago as the most beautiful young woman in Nahá. After her husband died she had fallen in with a *ladino* liquor dealer and became a "loose woman." She has had a child or two by one or another of her Tzeltal lovers and by unattached Lacandones.

"Quite a story," Robert says. "Her first son was paralyzed from the waist down and mentally retarded. She used to carry him around on her back, until he was bigger than she. At fifteen he died, and soon after, her husband died as well. After living in Monte Líbano for many years she moved back to Nahá, and has led an unconventional life. Most unusual for a Lacandon woman."

Bol also gives me some background on his sister Nuk of the twisted jaw. She is a daughter of Chan K'in and Koh II who has been married three times, and is one of the few Nahá women who speak Spanish. Nuk's story is that her intended husband, Vicente, shot her in the face because her complexion was too dark, and he then ran away to Mensäbäk and married another woman. Nuk recovered after an operation that left her with a deformed jaw, and she has turned into something of a feminist. When the rain stops, we will try to speak with both of these women.

Journal

December 15. *I learned today that after the birth of a Lacandon, his parents place the placenta and cord on a palm leaf and bury it beside a tree, deep down so the dogs won't dig them up. After his death, the Lacandon's soul will come looking for the placenta before it can proceed on its journey into the underworld. If the soul cannot find the afterbirth, calamity will befall his living relatives — and it will not go well for the soul in its passage through Metlán.*

One of the repeated rituals in Chan K'in's kitchen: He absentmindedly rolls a tortilla in one hand while telling a story. His spotted black and white dog reaches up between his legs and bites off the end of the tortilla. Chan K'in goes on telling his story, without batting an eye.

Little K'in burned a large spider with candle wax, in our hut. "That is how Kisin burns people," he says, "when they don't pray to the gods." Chan K'in has taught him well.

December 16. *K'ayum makes money selling photographs to Tzeltales. He uses the latest-model Polaroid, which a foreigner left behind.*

Bol tells me that Mateo senior will eat many animals none of the others will touch, including opossum, mico de noche, snake and coatimundi. He seems none the worse for it.

K'in Bor carried 100 kilos of corn from his milpa today, in one single load. And yesterday I saw Antonio, his wife and small son and smaller daughter returning from their milpa, each with a large bale. Antonio's own load looked to be about 75 kilos.

K'in Bor and the kids and I went fishing. He caught a small crappie, or sunfish, which is the largest you can catch in this lake.

Chan K'in and Young Chan K'in speak frequently of presidents Echeverría and López Portillo, in the same casual tone with which they refer to Trudi or José Pepe. Chan K'in is fond of Echeverría because it was under his presidency that the Lacandones were given full title to their lands. (Still, when he tells me I look a little like Echeverría, I am hard put to take it as a compliment.) They ply Robert and me with questions: Where did Echeverría retire? Is it true that he amassed many millions? What is López Portillo up to now? Is he a trustworthy man? They also *ask me about Guatemalan presidents, in the same familiar tone. It is clear that they regard presidents as their equals.*

December 17. *Nahá has survived nicely Robert's two cases of Scotch whisky. But Robert has a sour stomach and a bad cold.*

Young Chan K'in

I stop by Young Chan K'in's store to buy chewing gum and cookies for the children. His pretty wife, Koh, is swaying their small daughter on a hammock in the back room. I go to fetch a color print I had taken last January of Koh and her newborn daughter, and present it formally to Young Chan K'in.

He is pleased with the photo, but then he sighs and shakes his head, and his eyes darken. "She is so much thinner now — I don't know why." He takes the photo to Koh, and I hear a cry of delighted recognition. She is nursing and cannot come out to thank me. Instead, Young Chan K'in and I have our first real conversation.

He begins by filling in some genealogical background and points out that both K'in Bor's and Antonio's wives are his sisters, daughters of Koh I. We speak of his father's two other wives, and their many children. I am tempted to ask him how he feels about his elderly father having an infant son who is younger than his own daughter.

Divining my thoughts, Chan K'in smiles and says, "My father is a special case. He is a wise man who knows how to treat his wives. With us now, it would only lead to quarrels. We will not have many wives and children as he has. Those times are passing."

I tell Chan K'in of the snake I'd seen that morning, and remark that I had admired its serenity.

"*Nauyacas* never run away, like other snakes," he says. "They know the power of their poison."

Young Chan K'in is the most worldly and practical of Chan K'in's sons. During his two-year common-law marriage to Graciela he visited her in Oaxaca and Guanajuato, where he stayed for weeks at a time. Away from Nahá he polished his conversational Spanish, and he also acquired a fundamental grasp of occidental politics and economics. Young Chan K'in is not only community president, but as Chan K'in's firstborn son by his first wife, he is in direct line of inheritance to the title of *t'o'ohil*. Through dream and divination old Chan K'in has determined that one of his sons will be the last *t'o'ohil*, or Lord of Palenque. The prophecy specifies that his sons will live to see the next *xu'tan* or End of the World, which is due to occur around the year A.D 2008.

Should Young Chan K'in falter in his spiritual and moral obligations K'ayum will succeed his father as *t'o'ohil*, and his preparation for this eventuality by Old Chan K'in has been as thoroughgoing as the elder son's.

133

It still remains to be seen whether Young Chan K'in's marriage to Graciela and his exposure to the civilized world have done irreparable harm — as Trudi fears — or if he is making a successful readjustment to the Lacandon way, as Old Chan K'in and Robert believe.

As we chat, Young Chan K'in leans against the counter of his store, toying with a can of insect spray. On impulse, I ask him if he is afraid to die. He replies that he does fear death, a little, but that it is a matter for God to decide whether he dies or goes on living. I am not immediately certain if by *el Dios* he means Hachäkyum or possibly Graciela's Biblical God.

I find myself telling him of the ozone layer in the earth's atmosphere and of some scientists' speculation that aerosol spray cans may damage the ozone cover so that the sun's ultraviolet radiation will intensify and cause skin cancer. He nods his head gravely, but I have no idea how much he has understood.

I tell him of hydrogen bombs, and of the insane stockpiling of nuclear weapons by the Soviet Union and the United States.

He nods again. "Graciela told me," he says.

I then mention the fears in the West that fossil fuels are running out, and tell him of the desperate scramble by rich nations to find substitute sources of energy.

His eyebrows shoot up. "You mean mahogany?"

"That too," I say. "And coal. And nuclear plants. And perhaps — in the future — energy from the sun."

For the first time he looks perplexed. "But that is a matter for Hachäkyum and T'uup, the keeper of the sun. People can only give offerings to the sun and ask its permission."

"Yes," I agree. "In the future — very soon — we will all have to ask permission of the sun to go on living."

We talk of hunting and of ocean fishing, which used to be my passion. I try to explain the change in my ecological perspective that has led me to give up fishing, but I do not feel he understands. "In the north," I tell him, "people do not hunt and fish from the need to eat. Most of them do it for sport."

"You mean, like soccer?" he asks, and smiles for the first time. He apparently has watched soccer matches in San Cristóbal or Oaxaca.

"Something like that. In some places they give a prize for the one who catches the biggest fish, or kills the deer with the biggest antlers."

Chan K'in shakes his head, still smiling. "In that case, when they die, the hearts of those people will go straight to vulture heaven. Yum Ch'om — lord of the vultures — will turn them into carrion birds, and they will eat only the flesh of animals that have been killed needlessly and have been left to rot."

I immediately think of K'in García and the immature hawk, but do not tell Young Chan K'in. Instead I ask myself, "And on what authority can I judge K'in for killing a quetzal to feed his family?"

"The moon will change tonight," Young Chan K'in says, ending our conversation. "It will bring good weather tomorrow."

At dinner he shows Robert and me a letter from the Mexican Subsecretariat of Forestry and Fauna, which addresses José Pepe Chan Bol as "president of communal assets" of the Lacandon zone. It lists four hundred forty-four mahoganies in the Nahá area that have been counted and marked, and solicits Chan K'in's permission to make the count official:

> By means of the present we beg that you bring to the consideration of Sr. Chan K'in of Nahá the permission we solicit from you to mark or quantify the trees in said community in order to determine the volume for the '77/'78 season, making it clear that this is solely for the quantification of the existing volume in the zone.

After a lengthy, heated discussion, Young Chan K'in agrees to address a letter to President López Portillo denying that José Pepe has the legal authority to sign such an order and requesting that the mahoganies not be molested. By now Robert has seen the markers by the airstrip, which meant that the Forestry Department had gone ahead and marked the trees without bothering to solicit Young Chan K'in's or his father's signature. Robert promises to present the letter to the proper authorities in Mexico City, and he and I will publicize the matter there and in the United States.

At one point in the conversation I throw my pen down in frustration and bury my head in my hands. There is a shocked silence in the kitchen, as my unseemly show of emotion embarrasses Chan K'in and his son. Robert explains later that it is acceptable to abuse one's enemies verbally, but a physical outburst of emotion offends the stoical sensibilities of the Lacandones.

Journal

December 18. *A new moon! Lovely.*

Chan K'in says he dreamed of flood waters up to his chest. That means there should be a lot of visitors in the next few days: Tzeltales and/or foreigners. Later this afternoon we learned that K'ayum's milpa did actually flood from the heavy rains, and he will lose a lot of his corn.

Dirty Laundry

The next morning is clear and bright, just as Young Chan K'in predicted. The *norte* had been a brief one — "*chichin xämän,*" Chan K'in called it — and the rain had been lighter than last week's. The dry season is approaching. On our return visit there will be almost no rain, and a good deal less mud and standing water. Chino, the Ocosingo pilot, had agreed to pick us up on Tuesday, and Robert had decided to drive back to Mexico City to pick up his salary checks and bring back his eleven-year-old daughter, Diana Lynn, during her Christmas break. I plan to drive back with Robert, and then stay a week in San Cristóbal before rejoining him in Nahá right after the New Year.

After breakfast we present our dirty laundry to Koh II, who had offered to wash it. To my surprise, Chan K'in insists on supervising the transfer of dirty clothes, which he marks off item by item with a resonant *"bay"* (The Lacandon equivalent of "Okay"). In Nahá, with its low hygienic standards, washing a guest's clothes is a consequential affair which requires the headman's official witness. In a sense, this little ceremony reminds me of Mahatma Gandhi's solicitude for the condition of his guests' stools when he had visitors to his ashram.

K'ayum's House

We visit K'ayum's house to look at some of his drawings and to play music. He has cleaned the typewriter, and types out several sentences for Robert to show him that the keys no longer stick. We teach him the Spanish counterpart of "The quick brown fox jumps over the lazy dog": *Extiendo vale por mil kilos de haba, garbanzo y frijol.*

The hut is spacious, with stout *chicozapote* cross-beams, well-crafted mahogany siding and a wide reed cot with a mosquito net. There are the usual enamel pots, plastic cups and saucers, a hammock and clothesline, a plastic laundry hamper, and the omnipresent stack of bows and arrows in the rear. In one corner there is a plastic bathtub for little Mario, K'ayum's eighteen-month-old son, which has a drawing of Popeye. Color photographs of K'ayum and his family hang on the wall, and also a pop poster that shows a group of lounging university students. K'ayum is one of the few villagers who owns no radio or record player.

Little Mario plays on the ground with plastic cars and trucks, which he deftly pushes from one end of the hut to the other. He imitates their engine sounds and siren wails as accurately as any city child. When I offer him a cookie he gazes a long time in my eyes, then forms a pistol with his right index finger and says, *"Pooj."* In the next instant he snatches the bag of cookies from my hand. Where did he learn cowboys and Indians? Mario is my favorite among the small children of Nahá. He has his grandfather's innate self-possession, a fearless manner in addressing strange adults, and his father's playful imagination. When he grows up, I expect he will ask K'ayum some hard, forthright questions.

K'ayum shows us some watercolors he's done around Nahá, and a portrait of K'in Bor. None are nearly as good as the drawing of the water lilies he gave Trudi. He promises to make more drawings of the lake and send them to Robert. He offers me the sketch of K'in Bor, which shows him perplexed and glowering, with his mouth typically agape. Although it is more a rough sketch than a finished portrait, I recognize K'in Bor's intensity, and accept it as a gift. K'ayum signs it ceremoniously, as if it were a Klee or a Miró. I fear that he may develop an exaggerated idea of the material value of his work before it has a chance to mature. Even as a "primitive" impressionist he has a good deal to learn about technique.

K'ayum then brings out an old accordion that he insists was given to him by B. Traven, the expatriate German writer who lived and wrote under a number of aliases, and who died when K'ayum was a very small boy. Robert and I accompany him with guitar and harmonica as he plays and sings "El Rancho Grande," "Cielito Lindo" and other Mexican songs in a flat voice. "I am a *charro*," he brags. In Nahá singing *charros* rank next to pilots and presidents in popularity.

Margarita and Mario go out for a walk and return with her father, Antonio, who peers in at us through a square peephole in the wall. I am struck once more by his wild youthful curls and his rugged, handsome face. He is Nahá's third elder, although he is only about forty-five. And Antonio is the only one who does not travel to San Cristóbal.

"It is too noisy in the city," Antonio says. "The smoke makes my eyes tear, and I vomit blood. I am afraid of the cars in Mexico, and of the Chamulas in San Cristóbal."

"Why the Chamulas?" I ask him, well aware of the ancient enmity between the Lacandones and this highland community of Mayan tradesmen.

"Because they are bad people. They invite you to drink with them, and after you get drunk they rob you of your money. If you refuse to drink with them, then they kill you to get your money. It is bad either way. I prefer to stay here in the forest, with the jaguars and the snakes." He laughs. "They also kill you, but they do not tell lies or steal your money." He is in a jovial mood, but I feel the weight of sadness in him, as heavy as in Chan K'in. Antonio seems the least likely of the elders to survive the decimation of the forest. He is the forest.

We all drink some of Robert's whisky and talk about women. Robert speculates about Young Mateo's affairs in San Cristóbal, and hints at K'ayum's complicity in some of his adventures with foreign women. K'ayum smiles and lowers his eyes; he is reluctant to speak in his father-in-law's presence.

After Antonio's departure he admits to Robert that he has had an affair or two, but not like Mateo. "But Margarita always knows," K'ayum says. "When I return from San Cristóbal, she will not make tortillas for me. If she asks me, I cannot lie. So she won't prepare food for me. After four or five days, she cooks for me again."

I ask him, "Would you like to have another wife, like your father?"

He shrugs. "One is enough. My father can have a young wife because he is the *t'o'ohil,* and he knows how to keep her contented. But now, the women want more than in my father's time. They want earrings and record players and many expensive things. And if you cheat on them, they go back to their father's house and you have to live alone. That is no good. When Margarita goes, I feel lonely and sad, and I don't like to cook for myself."

Margarita returns with little Mario, and a silence descends on the room. She is a pretty woman of about eighteen or nineteen, with clear resolute features and a no-nonsense, efficient manner. Margarita is six months pregnant with her second child, and is not shy about it or self-effacing, like Nuk, K'in Bor's wife. But she will not speak Spanish, and her *hax t'an* (Lacandon Maya) is barely intelligible. Even Robert has difficulty understanding the vernacular of Nahá women and children.

K'ayum and I go for a walk by the spring, and I ask him what he intends to do after his father dies.

"I will be very sad," he says. "When my father dies I will be too sad to stay here, so I will go away for a time. But I will come back. I will come back after a time, and remain in the forest all my life."

"Trudi said it would be good for you to attend art school and get an education. Would you like that?"

He tilts his head. "Yes." He picks up a stone and rubs it slowly. "Yes, I would like to be educated."

"Even in Mexico City?"

He drops the stone carefully in the center of the pool. "Yes, even in Mexico City. My wife and son and I could live there for a time, while I get my education. But I don't like the noise, and the crowds. It is bad for little Mario. Afterward, I will come back and teach my companions to read and write. I will learn medicine also, so I can heal my son when he gets sick, and I will teach others. That way it will be all right." He smiles. "Oh, and I will learn to play the accordion also, and the guitar, and I will be the best singer in Nahá."

"You have a good head, K'ayum," I say. "I know you'll survive."

"Yes, it's good, but not all that good," he says. His face clouds. "My father teaches me what he knows, all of it, but I forget too much. I always forget. That is why at the *balché* ceremony, I pray to Hachäkyum that he will look after the health of my son Mario, and of my wife Margarita, and also that he will help me not to forget what my father teaches me.

"My father took care of me well," K'ayum says, in a thoughtful voice. "He was good to me and my older brothers. If I was lazy and did not want to work in the *milpa,* he beat me with a vine, and the same with K'in García and Young Chan K'in. He did well by us. But after me he became too old. When Chan K'in Chico disobeyed him and my father tried to beat him, Chan K'in Chico hit him back and they both fell on the ground. After that my father was afraid and he did not try to hit Chan K'in Chico, or Bol, or any of my younger brothers. That is not good, I think, and that is why Chan K'in Chico was the first of us to disobey my father and move to the other side."

"You have changed, K'ayum. Remember last year you told me you had a good head like your father and you would use it to make money and buy up all of San Cristóbal? Do you remember?"

"*Ah sí.*" He laughs and nods his head. "Yes, I remember. I was different then. My heart is better now. I wanted everything, like Young Mateo. I wanted a recorder and a record player and even a car, like he does. But now I think, they are not such good things. They make you change so that you want more, always more, and you are not content with what you have. My dreams tell me that. When I wanted to buy a car I had night- mares of crashing and dying, and I screamed in my sleep so that Mar- garita had to slap my face and wake me up. And then I dream of the quiet of the forest and I am sitting under a tree playing with Mario and the sun is shining and I am happy again."

The next morning K'ayum appears at the breakfast table looking som- ber, and asks me if I dreamed during the night.

I tell him I dreamed of an elephant in San Francisco Bay, which takes me for a ride.

"It means you will take a long journey," K'ayum says, "in an airplane, with many friends." He interprets the elephant as a tapir, which prophe- sies wind.

I ask him if he dreamed, and at first he says no, he had no dreams. After a moment he describes a dream in which Mario is snatched away by a pretty white woman with long white hair. He is very sad and goes looking for his son. When he finds the white-haired woman he snatches Mario from her arms, but then she turns into Margarita, who rebukes him: "Why are you snatching our son from me?"

"I have this dream many times," he says, dejectedly. "Always it ends the same way."

Drawing on intuition I say to K'ayum that there will be many changes in his life and in the life of Mario that will create distances between them, and draw them apart. "But in the end," I say, "you will know what you must do to win him back."

"That's right!" K'ayum slaps his hand on the table, his good humor in- stantly restored. "Now you and I are like this," he says, joining the index fingers of both hands.

The Invention of Money

At dinner Chan K'in is in a light mood, and tells another story Robert has not heard before. Akyantho, the white man's protector, creator of the machete, of illnesses and medicines, was also the inventor of money. It happened like this: When he first made the machete, Akyantho gave it to the white man as well as the Lacandon. The Lacandon soon learned to handle the machete with dexterity, and used it to blaze trails in the forest and to clear out his *milpa*. But the white man, who lives in towns and cities, has soft hands, and the machete raised painful blisters on his palms and fingers. Akyantho took pity on the white man. He invented money and gave it to him so he would not have to use the machete and suffer from blisters.

Robert says, "But then the white man came to the forest and gave back the money to José Pepe Chan Bol, and to Young Mateo."

"That's right," Chan K'in says. "And if José Pepe and Young Mateo go to Mexico to spend their money, they will have blisters like the white man, and their hair will turn white."

"José Pepe already has gray hairs," I point out.

"So he does," Chan K'in nods.

"And also Na-Bor Pancho Villa," I added. "And yet Pancho Villa is a better man than José Pepe."

"That is true," Chan K'in says, unhesitant. "When we were in Mexico for the filming of *Cascabel,* Pancho Villa would always share his food with us. If he bought watermelon or mangoes, and we did not have any, he would give us half. Pancho Villa is a proper man, even if he has turned evangelist."

Robert and I agree that Pancho Villa is one of the Lacanjá *hach winik* still worthy of respect. Once again I realize what pains Chan K'in takes to avoid polarizing the two communities, and to confine his quarrel to José Pepe.

Chan K'in pays us a visit after dinner for a nightcap of Robert's whisky, and continues the story of Akyantho and the invention of money.

As protector of the white man, Akyantho also gave them cattle and barnyard stock, which they domesticated successfully and have used ever since as a source of food and other benefits. The Lacandones were also given cattle, but they were negligent and the animals kept running away into the forest.

"The *hach winik* have never known how to tame animals," Chan K'in says with a smile. "That is why we had to become good hunters. When the animals Akyantho gave us ran away, they turned wild. The cattle became deer, the horses turned into tapirs, and the pigs into wild boar. Because we were so neglectful in the past, we now have to hunt and chase them all over the forest. Even today, our pigs keep breaking out of their pens, and our chickens do not know how to lay eggs."

The Letter

Young Chan K'in comes in with the freshly written letter, which he has addressed to "Sr. José López Portillo." Robert reads it aloud:

> I do not want them to cut the mahogany, here in Nahá. They have already marked the mahogany, but we do not want the trees to be cut in Nahá. If they cut the trees there will be no jungle, it will be the end of the forest and the end of the woodland and the soil will become very poor. José Pepe Chan Bol has given the Subsecretary of Forestry and Fauna permission to count the mahoganies but we do not wish him to give permission for the trees here in Nahá to be cut. I do not want José Pepe Chan Bol to give permission for the mahogany to be cut. Here in Nahá, it is an-

other community. In Lacanjá they speak differently, here in Nahá pure Maya is spoken.

The letter is signed, "Chan K'in of Nahá, President of Nahá Commune, Chiapas." In a postscript, Young Chan K'in adds that the mahogany is necessary for making *cayucos* and "other things," and that José Pepe has no authority to sell the mahogany cheap, at three hundred pesos per tree. The postscript ends, "But I do not want them to cut the trees in Nahá."

Despite obvious lapses in grammar and a number of misspellings, we concur that the letter is an eloquent statement of the situation in Nahá and a true reflection of the community's sentiment. Robert and I again pledge to publicize the plight of Nahá in Mexico and in the United States.

"Why haven't you shown me the government document before?" Robert asks Young Chan K'in.

He shrugs. "Because I was afraid they would make trouble for you, since you are a foreigner here."

Robert nods and falls silent. He is clearly moved by Young Chan K'in's sensitivity to his position, and by his instinct to shield him from a hazardous confrontation with the government.

"In this case we are all foreigners," he says at last.

"I think it will have an impact," Robert says later of Young Chan K'in's letter. "Mexican presidents like to identify themselves with the Lacandones. Echeverría had photographs taken of himself with Chan K'in on a number of occasions. He felt it invested him with the aura of being a president of all the people, even the most remote and 'primitive' tribes, such as the Lacandones. López Portillo has also shown sensitivity to the Lacandon issue, particularly since *Rattler* came out, and he has been photographed with José Pepe Chan Bol at least once. Perhaps Chan K'in's letter will rectify the imbalance, somewhat."

"Let's hope so," I say, wanting to believe. But I've had enough experience with Latin American governments to harbor serious doubts.

"We'll wait and see what Trudi has to say," says Robert, who has misgivings of his own.

Eve of Departure

Our last night in Nahá, December 18, is cool and dry. A bare sliver of a new moon hangs in the clean-swept night sky, above the lake: a good omen, and a sign that airplanes will fly the next day.

I feel sad about leaving the forest, particularly now that the rains are abating. But after our two weeks in the wild the comforts of civilization exert an undeniable allure. It has rained on all but two days since we've been here, and Robert and I are both fighting colds. The steady bean, tortilla and fresh-meat diet has also left its mark on my metabolism, which is in full revolt. I long for salad greens and ice cream, a soothing pint of yogurt.

But it is not only my stomach and sinuses that cry aloud for respite. My mental circuits are overloaded, and I need time to sort out and absorb all the new information.

Robert is out of both cigarettes and whisky — we had consumed the last bottle with Chan K'in at dinner. K'in García, K'ayum and K'in Bor pay brief visits, and we hand out the last of our lighters, batteries and assorted equipment. I give K'ayum my tennis shoes for wading in the marshes, and tell him he can use the jungle hammock and the sleeping bag while I'm gone.

"I will take good care of them," he says, looking pleased.

During the night, Chan K'in's smallest son suffered a relapse and coughed all night long. We offer to take the child with us to see a doctor in San Cristóbal, as Geneviève has left for Mensäbäk and will not be back for several days. Chan K'in thanks us, but says he prefers to treat the boy at home. We leave with him the last of our medicines, as well as the snake serum. Robert tells Chan K'in he plans to be gone a few days at the most, and will then stay in Nahá with his daughter through the holidays. I will join them a week later.

"When you return, the rains will be over, and I will take you to the *milpa*," Chan K'in promises.

"I would like that," I say. I do not mention several other of our projects that were disrupted by the rains, among them a talk with María Bonita and the elder Mateo, a visit to the evangelists on the north shore, and Geneviève's interview with Koh II.

Leave-Taking

After packing our gear I leave with Koh all our household utensils, for which she thanks me without meeting my eyes. "*Ne tsoy*," she says.

Chan K'in sees us to the lake trail. "Be careful!" he shouts, and turns quickly on his heel. Bol, K'ayum, Hans and Fritz all help us with our equipment.

"Bring us slingshots!" Hans and Fritz yell from the landing, waving and jumping up and down. That morning they had brought me several new drawings of houses and tigers, and they gave Robert a large clay alligator that makes an unwieldy lump at the bottom of his knapsack.

"Aha!" Robert grins. "That explains their sudden largesse, the little mercenaries — Katzenjammer Kids to the hilt."

The sun sparkles on the water as our *cayuco*'s bow slices through the reeds. The reflections of clouds and hills are so dazzling they hurt my eyes.

Our oarsman, K'ayum, makes jokes about the good times awaiting us in San Cristóbal, but Robert and I are subdued.

"By tomorrow morning," Robert says, squinting in the sun, "all this will seem nothing more than a dream."

"And nothing less," I add, in a whisper.

III

Again Na-Bolom

"It is hopeless," Trudi said, wearily, "but you have to at least try."

We were sitting at the dining table after all the guests had retired; Robert had just shown her the document from the Forestry Department, and Young Chan K'in's reply.

"The only thing to do," she went on, "is to form a delegation, march to Mexico City, and present the community's grievances directly to the government. Young Chan K'in, as president, should represent Nahá, and an articulate young man who is not under José Pepe's thumb should go for Lacanjá." She proposed K'in Yuk Bats', a son of Vicente Bor who was staying in Na-Bolom. "K'in is bright, he can read and write better than Young Chan K'in, and he is fed up with José Pepe's dirty tricks." She sighed gustily, and poured herself and us more tea. "But I'll tell you frankly, I think it's a hopeless situation. The government has fixed on José Pepe as the representative of all the Lacandones, for its own convenience, and López Portillo has given his sanction by having himself photographed with José Pepe."

"And the elder Chan K'in?" I asked Trudi.

"He is an old man!" she shouted. "Of course, he is the one who should go to Mexico City. His sons will never have his authority — but he is too old, and cannot even sign his own name. Old Chan K'in is not a fighter. In the capital, he would just be swallowed up! You have to fight occidentals with occidental methods."

She rose and paced the floor in her jungle fatigues. "Oh, it's enough to tear your hair out. How can you persuade the government of your determination to save the forest when there is all this greed and stupidity. I am not speaking only of Lacanjá. In Nahá itself there is Young Mateo, who opens a hotel and comes to San Cristóbal twice a month to wheel and deal with God knows who — and this young idiot wants a road built to Nahá so he can drive a Safari, just like yours! If you ask me, he is a worse crook than José Pepe Chan Bol!" She pounded her hand on the table.

"And you!" — she shouted at Robert — "Why don't you talk to Mateo? You damn anthropologists, you write your goddamned books, and you never tell them anything!"

Trudi was at the top of her form: a fury of indignation and despair, with a core of indomitable resolve. At dinner she had unceremoniously slapped the wrist of a grown Belgian guest who had reached for the teapot out of turn. "Look here!" she had shouted, with no sense of incongruity. "I know damn well they award me all these prizes to get me out of the way!" Only minutes before she had been courting praise for the gold medal recently conferred on her by a journalism group.

"I am glad I am old!" she shouted now, in a belling voice. "I am glad I am old so I won't have to see what happens to that magnificient forest — and so I won't have to see all the young Lacandones turn into a bunch of goddamn consumers!" She ran her hand through her short-cropped silver hair.

"About the letter —" Robert interjected.

She swept around. "It's not enough! Why, he does not even mention that mahogany is necessary for houses and furniture, as well as for the *cayucos*. And it is full of grammatical errors." She lifted her arms to the heavens. "His spelling, my God, it's like a fifth-grade schoolboy's! You'd think that bitch would at least have seen to it that he learned some correct grammar while she was leading him by the nose all over Mexico!"

"But that is what makes the letter effective," Robert calmly insisted. "I have written correct, official-sounding letters for them in the past, and they have fallen on deaf ears."

Trudi calmed down, as suddenly as she had exploded. "Yes, all right, take the letter to Mexico City and see what you can do. At least, it's a start. But now go talk with K'in. He is waiting for you in the library."

K'in Yuk of Lacanjá

She shepherded us to the library and shut the door behind her. A slight, dark figure, dressed in a bright flowery blue shirt and slacks, sat alone next to a roaring fire.

"Roberto!" He rose and shook Robert's hand, western-style, before they lapsed into Lacandon formality. K'in Yuk recalled the old days when he was a small boy and Robert would take him fishing on the Jataté River with his father, Vicente Bor.

"I am sorry about your father," Robert said, stiffly. "He was a very good friend."

K'in shrugged and said, "With a good doctor, he would still be alive today. He died of an embolism, almost a year ago."

"Yes, I'd heard that." He offered K'in a cigarette. "And you?" he said, in his teasing inflection. "Do you still smoke?"

"Oh yes." He grinned and lit his own and Robert's cigarettes with a propane lighter. "And I also eat meat, and I even, on occasion, drink a little whisky."

"*Mal evangelista*," Robert laughed, and relaxed immediately.

K'in Yuk is the schoolteacher of Lacanjá, and speaks the best Spanish of any Lacandon I've met, northern or southern. As a boy he had been adopted by Trudi, and was educated in San Cristóbal schools. K'in is already learning English so he can teach it in the village. His younger brother, K'ayum, had been a medical aide there.

They spoke of the situation in Lacanjá, and K'in confirmed all that we had heard of José Pepe's machinations. He added details to a story we had heard about a village mother, rumored to be one of José Pepe's lovers, who had killed her own child and been put in jail. José Pepe had interceded with local officials and managed to get her out. Speculation was rife in Lacanjá on what favors José Pepe may have extended the officials in return. K'in added that José Pepe's secretiveness and his abuses of authority had turned most of the community elders against him, including Pancho Villa and Obregón.

"*Ma' tsoy,* Roberto," K'in said, over and over, as he poked at the fire and puffed on Robert's cigarette. His gestures were emphatic but oddly refined, in keeping with his snug western clothes and carefully groomed short hair. "It is no good, no good at all. José Pepe keeps all the money to himself, and doesn't talk to anyone. He is turning into a dictator."

K'in agreed to act as representative in any future delegation sent to Mexico City, and Robert and I retired to our beds exhausted. We were to leave for the capital at dawn.

I woke up sweaty and feverish, with a case of diarrhea that was traceable to a greasy goat broth we'd had on the road from Ocosingo. Robert's cold had returned, in the highland chill.

Alicia

The following afternoon we arrived in Robert's modest suburban home outside Mexico City. We were greeted at the door by a brash but friendly Dalmatian and by an impatient Diana Lynn, who had already packed her belongings for the return journey to Nahá.

Robert's wife, Alicia, had just come home from her last day of teaching English before the holidays. She is a striking, olive-skinned brunette in her late thirties, descended of high-born Chichimec warriors. She is as easy with English as Robert is with Spanish, and switched from one to the other to impart a calculated tone or nuance to her conversation. My immediate impression was of a mercurial, highly sensitive woman governed by intuition. Alicia had been trained as a Freudian psychologist.

She took my hand and shook it warmly, and asked how everyone was at Nahá.

I told her Chan K'in was well, and she smiled and nodded her head. "I feel I am a friend of Chan K'in's, although I have never met him."

Alicia declined to return to the forest with us because of her acute fear of spiders and scorpions, which she referred to proprietarily as "my arachniphobia." Instead, she entrusted to us gifts of tobacco and assorted condiments for Chan K'in and his wives.

We stayed a day in Mexico City while Robert put his affairs in order and presented Young Chan K'in's letter. I holed up in the Hotel Polanco with Lomotil and Enterovioform and by next morning, when Robert and

Diana Lynn came by, I was on the mend. By the following afternoon I had recovered enough to enjoy a nude swim in the Chorreadero, a natural-spring pool about thirty miles north of San Cristóbal. The chief excitement of our journey came when Robert found a large mantis near the spring. He picked it up behind its abdomen and recited "Xämän, Xämän, which way is xämän [north]?" in proper Lacandon Maya, but the mantis twisted its long neck right around and tried to bite his thumb.

"Perhaps," I suggested, after Robert released the creature unharmed, "that trick only works before a storm."

In Mexico City Robert had given a copy of Young Chan K'in's letter to a woman friend of his and Trudi's who has strong connections in the Forestry Department. For the present, it was all that he could do. On his return from Nahá he would bring more documents and show them to journalist friends. To write of the Lacandones' plight directly, over his own signature, would risk expulsion from Mexico as an undesirable alien. I myself could do nothing until my return to the States.

We stayed at Na-Bolom that night, free of charge, as Robert enjoys full Lacandon privileges with Trudi. The following morning Robert and Diana left for Ocosingo and their flight to Nahá. I planned to stay in San Cristóbal a week or so to catch up on research in the Na-Bolom library.

It felt good to be on my own again. In the last days, after reading through several volumes of Robert's diaries, I had begun filtering my impressions through his eyes and through his extensive experience in the bush. This was a good time to split up for a while and reassess our separate perspectives.

In the next three days I alternated several hours of daily reading in the library with visits to Chamula, Zinacantán and other highland villages. I reread Tozzer, and Frans and Trudi Blom's journals of their travels in the Lacandon forest beginning in the early forties.

Trudi

Of the six or seven explorers and anthropologists who have shaped our present understanding of the Lacandones — I include Tozzer, Soustelle, Frans Blom and the American adventurer Charles "Carlos" Frey, who actually lived like a Lacandon with the Lacanjá group until he drowned in the Jataté River in 1949 — three are still active in the field: Robert, Philip Baer and Gertrude Duby Blom. Trudi, who is seventy-seven, has been at it the longest, since 1940, soon after she read of the Lacandones in Jacques Soustelle's book and knew that she would have to spend years exploring their culture in their forest home. Today she is the uncontested Queen of the Lacandon, a title she earned in the fifties and early sixties as the consort of the Danish archaeologist Frans Blom. In those years she and Frans established Na-Bolom and she fought tooth and nail for the Lacandones' title to their forest preserve. In the past years, as the govern-

ment has undercut her efforts by "buying" the mahogany from the Lacandones at nominal prices — and corrupting most of them in the process — Trudi has at times borne her queenly title more like an albatross
than a crown. And she has taken on the mantle of the prophetess, in-
veighing against the monstrous waste of our planet's natural resources
and the desolation of its forests.

Trudi began life as a pastor's daughter in a Swiss village high in the
Alps, which had no electricity or running water. The beginnings were
appropriately austere; there followed the activist antifascist period in the
thirties, clouded with rumor and hearsay, during which she spent time in
a Mussolini jail and was married to a socialist member of the Swiss par-
liament, Kurt Duby, whose name she still bears, together with the name of
her second husband. The factual details recede in importance; the legend
is already substantial, and Trudi adds to it every day of her life. I have
dealt before with self-made legends, but none that were so immediately
accessible, and whose stature continues to grow at an age when most
others acquiesce to a graceful decline. By outliving her time, Trudi has
been stranded in our own as a nineteenth-century figure, a tragic one, too
large and cranky and intractable to be fairly appraised by the grudging
prescriptions of the seventies and eighties. "When people leave food on
their plates," she said on our return from Mitontic, on New Year's Day, "I
want to pick it up and crush it into their faces. I simply cannot tolerate
waste."

Along the way Trudi has made enemies, and at times they seem more
numerous than her admirers. She is accused by some of exploiting the
Lacandones for her aggrandizement. She is accused of having used Frans
Blom's name and reputation to forge her own. She is charged with having
been a Communist and a Nazi sympathizer—and of being self-indul-
gently romantic and ruthlessly calculating. There are grains of truth in
many of these charges, for Trudi is large enough to contain an abundance
of passionate contradictions. She not only thrives on controversy, she is
regenerated by it. In my own observation I have seen her seek adulation in
almost the same breath that she scorns it; she can be insufferably patronizing, and loves to play mother-hen to dependent, immature aborig-
ines. There is more than a touch of Albert Schweitzer's paternalism in her
attitudes toward the Lacandones, and she has made some serious errors
of judgment: at one time Frans and Trudi had tried to encourage intermarriage between Lacanjá and Nahá Lacandones in order to increase their
numbers, and they even suggested intermarriage with Christian Tzeltales,
whom the Lacandones despise. It was Robert who raised Trudi's awareness of the deep fissures between southern and northern Lacandones,
and who convinced her that intermarriage would prove a cultural disaster. Today, Trudi tends to espouse these opinions as her own.

In a sense, Trudi's contradictions have become those of the Lacandones, as representatives of a culture that has outlived its time, and her
destiny has become inextricably wedded to theirs. If Chan K'in may be

seen as a kind of forest Lear, silently sorrowing over the destruction of his kingdom, then Trudi is Hecuba, keening over her adopted children, whose tragic end she is powerless to prevent.

The Library

While browsing through Trudi's early books I uncovered some curious biographical details about Chan K'in and other Nahá elders in their younger days. Among these were the bizarre circumstance that Old Mateo had been married briefly to Chan K'in's mother, after she became widowed. While she lived, Chan K'in had referred to Mateo as *in yumeh* — my father, my lord — although Mateo is his junior by more than a decade.

And Mateo, I learned, had a predilection for hair cologne, and was a mechanical wizard who repaired Philip Baer's rifle by manufacturing spare parts from scrap metal. Chan K'in's sister Petrona had been married to a Christian *ladino,* and later on to a Mensäbäk Lacandon named Quintín, a notorious tyrant who had killed his own brother. This same Quintín had been the first husband of Koh II, who lived with him as a young girl. After old Quintín died, Koh returned to Nahá, married Chan K'in, and bore him ten children. Trudi described vividly Quintín's cruel treatment of both Petrona and Koh, who had been a very pretty and vivacious teenager. It also turns out that Chan K'in's third wife, Koh III, is a niece by marriage of Jorge, who is Chan K'in's nephew by another sister and his former son-in-law as well. So the rifts between Chan K'in's Spider Monkey *onen* and Jorge's Wild Boar lineage are exacerbated by complicated blood ties, as has been true of clans since long before the pharaohs.

What was I to do with this welter of information? Where did it fit in? The more I read about the interbreeding among blood relatives in Nahá, the more labyrinthine the family trees became. Short of filial and sibling incest, and marriages between parallel cousins, it is open season in Nahá. There is an almost Sadie Hawkins Day casualness to the way northern Lacandones marry, unmarry, and remarry cousins, nieces, aunts and nephews. In theory, Lacandones are encouraged to marry across *onen,* as a check on excessive inbreeding. Chan K'in's three wives are all of the *k'ek'en* (Wild Boar) lineage, whereas he is a Spider Monkey. But the community is so small that the distinctions between these two remaining *onen* of Nahá are blurred by constant cross-marriages, even if the old clan rivalries persist. More ominously, Trudi mentioned more than one instance of fratricide and uxoricide in Nahá, within her own time. My idyllic picture of Nahá as a kind of Athens to Lacanjá's Sparta had begun to sprout warts.

I also learned that both the southern and northern groups have practiced various forms of infanticide. James Nations, a student of Lacandon culture, learned that until recently, deformed or feeble infants in both communities were starved or smothered at birth as a matter of course, on the assumption that they would not survive the rigors of the forest. In Mensäbäk, which has traditionally favored the sons, daughters were often starved slowly, and mothers with twins of different sexes will still favor the boy and withdraw their breasts from the female twin. In Lacanjá, where daughters are prized for their ability to attract future sons-in-law-in-service, the reverse is true, and the daughters will be favored over the boys. In all cases, one twin is customarily allowed to die because Lacandon mothers normally do not have enough milk to sustain both twins. Of the three communities, Nahá is the most balanced, with a proportionate number of male and female survivors.

I examined a study by Philip Baer, written with his wife, in which he traces the history of tribal violence in Lacanjá from the late nineteenth century to the early days of his evangelical campaign, beginning in 1957. Baer records forty cases of homicide, nearly all of which involved clan feuds or quarrels over women, and innumerable rapes, abductions and incestuous marriages. (In the forties, when young marriageable women were scarce in Lacanjá, the men formed raiding parties to abduct single women from Nahá.)

Baer's extensive research has undoubted historical value since it portrays a tribal culture disintegrating from within, following the death of its religious elders. But there are glaring omissions and inconsistencies. In his chronicle of recent events in Lacanjá, Baer conveniently glosses over the murder of K'ayum Carranza by Obregón, who is today a deacon of the settlement — and he claims, against mounting contrary evidence, that there have been no acts of violence there since he introduced Protestant Christianity in 1957.

Long before reaching the end of this seriously compromised "history" I recalled Robert's assessment of it: Bishop Diego de Landa also gave us invaluable data on Mayan customs in the seventeenth century, but only after he had burned nearly all the codices as "the work of the devil." After he destroyed the evidence, how much value can one place on his interpretations?

I did garner from Baer's book the important information that until the nineteen forties, southern Lacandones for the most part lived in scattered family groups (caribales) because of their inherent distrust and suspicion of one another. The arrival in the forest of alligator hunters, chicle gatherers and northern colonists had compelled them to gather in larger settlements as one caribal after another was overtaken or set afire by the callous invaders. The dispossessed southern Lacandon families and clans had had no choice but to bury the hatchet and attempt — very much against their natures — to get along with each other in an expanded community at Lacanjá.

The same had been true of the northern Lacandones, most of whom had lived in small groups in scattered sites such as Monte Líbano, El Censo, Ocotal Chico, El Granizo and Ts'ibatnah, until the encroaching loggers and Tzeltal settlers forced them to evacuate and band together at Mensäbäk and Nahá. Chan K'in, as the t'o'ohil, has had to assume responsibility for a far larger number of dependents than either his father or his grandfather had known, and this had added immeasurably to his burdens. The stresses and strains of enforced communal life made it easier to understand the aberrant behavior of some of the young wives of Nahá, and the intense personal conflicts of K'in Bor, K'in García and Young Chan K'in, among many other younger males.

The Chilam Balam

I pushed aside Baer's book and looked up my Mayan birth date, 13 Ahau, in the *Chilam Balam,* a collection of Yucatec–Mayan prophetic writings recorded after the Conquest. It turned out that 13 Ahau, which Robert had computed for me, is the last date in the Mayan calendar round, and its prophecy reads as follows:

> The bouquet of the rulers of the world shall be displayed. There is the universal judgment of our Lord God. Blood shall descend from the tree and stone. Heaven and Earth shall burn. It is the word of God the Father, God the Son and God the Holy Spirit. It is the holy judgment of our Lord God. There shall be no strength in Heaven and Earth. Great cities shall enter into Christianity, any settlements of people whatever, the great towns, all over our land of Maya Cuzamil Mayapan.* [It shall be] for our two-day men, because of lewdness ... the sons of malevolence. At the end of our blindness and shame our sons shall be regenerated from carnal sin. There is no lucky day for us. It is the cause of death from bad blood, when the moon rises, when the moon sets, the entire moon [this was] its power; [it was] all blood. So it was with the good planets which were looked upon as good. It is the end of the word of God. The waters of baptism shall come over them, the Holy Spirit. They receive the holy oil without compulsion; it comes from God. There are too many Christians who go to those who deny the holy faith ... to the *Itzá* and the *balams.* There is an end to our losing ...

> (Page 101 is left blank in the *Chilam Balam of Chumayel.* It contains a note in a modern hand stating that a page of the book is missing here.)

Historically, 13 Ahau corresponds to the middle years of the sixteenth century, when Spanish friars spread Christianity throughout the conquered Mayan lands. But Chan K'in would appreciate the resonance of this plaintive, agonized prophecy to the Lacandones' predicament. No wonder Robert expressed astonishment when he computed my date! When I came to the phrase "a page of the book is missing here" a shiver went up my spine. Is it the Lacandones' final drama that is meant to fill that missing page? If there is any foundation to these calendrical correlations, and Robert believes there is, then it made sense that I should have

* In the margin next to this line "(unclear)" was written.

150

come upon the Lacandones now, as a witness to the decline of their ancient culture and their entrance into the new.

K'in Yuk's Story

In the evenings, after dinner, I conversed with K'in Yuk, Margarita and their two boys, next to a roaring fire. He patiently taught me some of the differences between southern and northern Lacandon dialects, which boil down to colloquial variations and forms of address. With no t'o'ohil to preserve their "true" language and to support their millennial ethnic pride, Lacanjá had adopted far more Spanish usages than Nahá. K'in also recalled stories and songs his father had taught him as a boy, when they lived in the small community of San Quintín.

"My father was a clever man who remembered many of the ancient stories," K'in said. "He was very dramatic, and was the last to sing the old songs and to wear nose ornaments in his nostrils. But our house was too isolated, and in danger of raids from chicle gatherers and alligator hunters. One day my father's older wife left with her three sons for Las Margaritas, and then my mother died. Only my younger brother K'ayum and I were left. Frans and Trudi Blom took my father and us into Na-Bolom, and we stayed here until my father recovered from his grief and craziness. After we settled in Lacanjá, he lost interest in the old stories and became an evangelist."

I recalled that the only time I had met Vicente, his chief concern had been to obtain a tin roof for his house, like José Pepe's. "The old songs are no good," he had said. "Christian hymns are better."

K'in nodded somberly. "Yes, he was a changed man by then. When I was a boy, he would tell me about the pelota game his ancestors had played with a rubber ball; he knew a great deal about the lords of the underworld, and he said that a true house is to be built during a lunar eclipse because it confers supernatural powers. When you have finished building, the moon comes out of hiding, and the house will stand forever. Of course"— K'in smiled — "in my father's time men were terrifically strong and could build houses much faster than today."

"Did he have an *onen?*" I asked.

"Yes, he was Yuk — Deer — as I am, but his personal *onen* was the armadillo. My personal *onen* is the howler monkey."

At the dinner table Trudi showed me a fine salad fork and spoon K'in Yuk had made from dark, polished *jobillo* wood.

"This is what they should be doing in Lacanjá, and planting vegetable gardens, instead of squandering their money on junk."

Trudi remembered her famous, hour-long verbal battles with Vicente Bor, in the old days. "He was a shrewd, intelligent man with a very ironic twist of mind. K'in is much more sensitive, and he is adapting to present-day conditions better than anyone else. I will never have to worry about K'in."

She told of how one day he had disappeared from Na-Bolom and walked all by himself to Lacanjá to find himself a bride. "He chose one of Obregón's daughters," she said, "and the marriage has worked out very well."

K'in's wife, Margarita, is a robust, moon-faced woman who wears occidental dress, but she does not speak Spanish in public. Still, she asked me pointed personal questions through K'in, and laughed openly at his humor, and at her own. Their bright ten-year-old son, K'ayum, wears city jeans and sweaters, but his glossy black hair hangs nearly to his waist, like that of a Chicano flower child.

"When will you come to Lacanjá again?" K'in asked one afternoon.

"Perhaps I will come with Robert, on our next trip."

"Your next trip!" He laughed. "Who knows what Lacanjá will be like then?"

"A boomtown?" I suggested.

"A tourist trap for gringos," he said, with a caustic smile.

"The José Pepe Hilton!" I shouted.

"Color television in every room," he countered. "Free mushrooms and cheap marijuana for the hippies."

"And you?" I asked, when our laughter subsided. "What role will you play?"

"I?" he said. "Why, I'll be the president of the chamber of commerce."

"Of course." We raised our teacups across the table, and toasted the future president of the Lacanjá chamber of commerce.

Late that night three Lacanjá men arrived in a garishly decorated ambulance, with a little boy who was running a high fever.

"My God!" Trudi shouted through the hallways. "They have bought their own ambulance and painted it all up. Did you see it? It is the size of a hearse! Did you see it?" She bellowed to anyone within earshot, stamping her boots from one corridor to the next. "And they drove it themselves, all the way from Lacanjá. Where will it all end?"

The three arrivals stayed all of the next day, after the sick child was taken to the hospital. K'in disappeared from view. When he reappeared at dinner he looked sullen and remote, and stayed in his room until they left San Cristóbal.

"They are José Pepe's people," he explained.

Chan K'in Missionary

In Na-Bolom I dreamed of Chan K'in in a U.S. city street, passing out leaflets that read, "Hachäkyum lives!"

This dream image spawned a rash of exquisite reveries in which Chan K'in sets up a missionary camp on the courthouse steps in Dayton, Ohio.

The conversion drive starts with children, who are drawn to his jaguar stories and to little K'in's bow and arrows. Next come the skid-row vagrants, the recently unemployed and the city's poor, who flock to Koh's soup line and her wholesomely exotic tortillas and half-cooked beans. Divorcées, business executives and politicians are transfixed by the devilish schemes of Kisin, forever on the alert to sabotage the gods' master plan and destroy their favored creations. Defrocked Jesuits, alcoholics, revivalists and Masons plead for counsel in how to escape the cauldrons and the ice chambers of Metlán. As word spreads, blacks line up behind Chan K'in's thatched-palm tabernacle, jiving and chanting hallelujahs as they seek rebirth in Hachäkyum . . .

Chamula

I visited Chamula and Zinacantán with Walter ("Chip") Morris, a young American who collects highland textiles, and who has become an expert in the Tzotzil language and culture. We rode a truck to the home of the Lacandones' traditional enemies, the Chamulas, on a day of pre-Nativity *posadas*, when delegations gather from small mountain villages to give offerings and perform rituals before the peppermint-colored town church. I found it difficult to see in these festively dressed pilgrims the brigands who regard the Lacandones as stone-eating brutes, and who will rob and kill them at the first opportunity. Robert, who loyally shares the Lacandones' prejudice, regards Chamulas as Coca-Cola–addicted cultural degenerates.

In the bustling San Cristóbal marketplace, where the hill tribesmen gather in bright regional costumes to sell their produce, Chip Morris introduced me to an articulate Chamula friend and informant. In the course of the conversation I brought up the old antagonisms. At the mention of the Lacandones his face tensed, but then he smiled genially. "Ah, those old stories. That was before. Long before. Today it is different. The Chamulas have more money, and the Lacandones also. There is no need to steal." He laughed and rolled his narrow, shrewd Chamula eyes. I believed him, but I still would have hesitated to conduct business with him if we had been drinking together after dark, Christmas spirit or no.

I like much better picturesque Zinacantán, where the elders were preparing a beautiful Nativity flower crèche inside the roofless town church, which had been burned in a recent fire. Zinacantán has its own tradition of dream interpretation, as attested by Robert Laughlin's excellent study, *Of Wonders Wild and New: Dreams from Zinacantán*. It also has a wise, elderly shaman, Xun Vaskis, who uses methods of dream prophecy that compare with Chan K'in's in various and interesting ways. Zinacantecans have their own ancestral animus toward the Lacandones. During the carnival celebrations in February they parade through the narrow streets a burlesque effigy of a Lacandon, who is jeered and pelted with trash.

I tried to picture how a Lacandon would look through the eyes of a rugged, evangelized Chamula or Zinacantecan: a dirty, long-haired, androgynous apparition, absurd in his white gown and plastic shoes, who carries more spending money in his *morral* than the average Chamula earns in a month of menial labor for despised white bosses. Viewed from this vantage, the grudges were not so difficult to understand.

Piñata

On Christmas Eve, Chan K'in Chico flew in from Nahá with his wife and a planeload of clay drums. Trudi gave a *piñata* party for all the children of the community, including K'in's son, K'ayum, who took wild, mighty swats at the papier-mâché Donald Duck. When I suggested to Trudi it might be fun to enhance a Nahá celebration with a *piñata*, she winced and shook her head.

"I've thought of it on occasion, but look what happens to these kids as soon as the *piñata* is broken. They all pounce on the candy like animals, without considering the smaller children. In Nahá this spirit of 'grab-what-you-can' has not yet become established, and I do not wish to encourage it."

She was right, of course, but I could not forget the joyous *piñata* parties of my Guatemalan childhood. It was hilarious to watch Chan K'in Chico following the drama with eyes and mouth agape, sitting on his hands to keep from grabbing the broomstick and swiping at the colorful swinging animal pot. I could almost gauge the resentments he would work off by smashing the fat feathered duck to little pieces and eating out its heart. Chan K'in Chico had been the first of Old Chan K'in's sons to rebel against his authority by marrying without permission.

When I teased him about it, he snapped, "I will get the stick and I will break your head with it; and then I will put your head on a stake and charge two hundred pesos to look at it."

"Two hundred pesos? Is that all I'm worth?"

"Two hundred fifty," Margarita murmured, giggling behind her red rebozo.

"No, two hundred only," Chan K'in insisted, "because he talks with Chamulas and goes to their village."

"How do you know?" I asked astonished.

He pointed to his right eye. "It is known."

In the months to come my fidelity would be tested again and again. And I would discover that when a Lacandon leaves the forest, two realities predominate: the Chamulas and the *hach winik*. They are the two poles of their universe. Compared with these, the white man's is a passing intrusion.

José Pepe's Resignation

Geneviève appeared in Na-Bolom that evening, fresh from her tour of Mensäbäk and Nahá. With her was young Atanasio and his wife Koh, the daughter of Chan Bol, who had been the first northern Lacandon to be converted by Philip Baer, over fifteen years ago. After his conversion Chan Bol moved his house to Missionary Hill, and he is so fearful of Chan K'in's opprobrium that he has become a hermit; to this day he will run away and hide at the sight of a traditionalist across a field.

Geneviève, who looked sunburned and fit, said Robert and Diana seemed in excellent spirits and awaited my arrival the following day.

"There is more news — prepare yourself: Young Mateo visited Lacanjá, for God knows what subterranean purpose, and José Pepe Chan Bol told him that he intends to resign the presidency in two weeks, because he is sick of the pressures."

This was stunning news. Things were moving too fast. "Who will replace him?"

"A man named Carmelo; not too bright, apparently, but bound to be an improvement, at least in the short term."

At dinner I checked with K'in, who said he'd heard the news that morning.

"What about Carmelo?" I asked him.

He shrugged. "We'll wait and see. Personally, I do not trust him. He is one of José Pepe's men."

Atanasio and Koh

Geneviève, Atanasio and Koh came to visit in our room after dinner. Speaking in French, Geneviève confided that she had spoken again, but only briefly, with Koh II, and she had confirmed the story of her first marriage to the old fratricidal tyrant Quintín, among whose numerous other wives had been Chan K'in's sister Petrona. Koh verified that he had been harsh with her, and very demanding, and she had been happy to return home to her parents after his death. Chan K'in had then spoken to José Güero and arranged to take Koh as his second wife.

But it had not been easy. Koh confessed to Geneviève that she had not liked Chan K'in when he had first come to court her because he was already forty and rather ugly. But Chan K'in had persisted doggedly, journeying frequently to Monte Líbano, where they lived, to obtain José Güero's consent. José had also been reluctant to give Chan K'in his prettiest daughter for Chan K'in was already supporting one wife, and he was not then a man of means despite his reputation as a sage. The protocol of bride-requesting calls for wit and perseverance on the suitor's part, and the father is expected to put off the suitor until he has shown unswerving determination and the ability to support his daughter adequately. Chan K'in had literally hung out on José's doorstep, day after day, pleading and wearing down José's objections until he gave in. After the agreement was formalized with an exchange of cigars and other gifts, Koh carried no regrets into the marriage, for she too had come to respect the elder's nimble wit and determined persistence.

Geneviève added as a footnote that when Young Chan K'in went to José Güero for a bride the tables were reversed, for he was a most eligible bachelor. José went through the denials in a perfunctory way, and in fact invited Young Chan K'in to taste his daughter's cooking and to lie down beside her after he had too much to drink. By then, Old Chan K'in was the established *t'o'ohil,* and his eldest son by his first wife was first in line of succession.

"You could say that Koh has known the two extremes of marital experience in Nahá," Geneviève said, "from marriage to a murderous old bully, to raising a family and finding fulfillment with a saintly *t'o'ohil."* On the practical side, Koh told her she makes tortillas every third day, and would like to have more food for her children — especially sugar, oil and rice. She would also like more cotton for weaving clothes.

"I still do not dare ask her the intimate questions," Geneviève confessed. "One of the other wives is always nearby, and Chan K'in seems a little bit suspicious." She smiled and shrugged one shoulder.

I thanked her for her valuable assistance, and she said, "Now I have a favor to ask you. I took Atanasio with me to Mensäbäk, and he met with his father, José López, who is one of the strongest traditionalists remaining there. José does not seem to know that Atanasio has become a Christian by virtue of his marriage to Koh. Koh herself is an evangelist, like her father, but I am curious about Atanasio. I have the feeling that it is a marriage of convenience, so to speak, and that his conversion is only skin-deep; but he is too shy to speak of this with me because I am a woman. Perhaps you can get something out of him. I'd be curious to know."

I agreed to try, and she left me with Atanasio and Koh, who cleaved to his side like a barnacle, with both hands clasped firmly around his forearm. They turned down the white wine I offered them and readily accepted some apple juice. They are a strikingly handsome couple, trim, smooth-skinned and clean of dress, and they look better fed than the majority of Nahá villagers — not altogether surprising since they have access to the Baers' vegetable garden and a pantry stocked with conserves. Because Atanasio shares with K'in Bor the reputation of being Nahá's most successful hunter, there is always fresh meat on the table.

I understood at once Geneviève's problem in speaking with Atanasio. Koh is such a jealous guardian that she answered for him any question she considered prying or out of place. She was continually giggling and making jokes, which Atanasio deferentially translated into Spanish. He is not henpecked like Chan K'in Chico — he is too sturdy for that — but Koh used her sharp wit to censor or modify his remarks.

I attempted to get around this barrier by engaging in casual male banter, and by telling Atanasio of my hunting expedition with K'in Bor.

"K'in Bor is a good hunter," Atanasio agreed, respectfully.

Koh burst out with a wholly unintelligible remark, and laughed shrilly. "My wife is bad," Atanasio explained, after giggling himself. "She says K'in Bor is crazy, and she is afraid of him. She says she feels sorry for his wife."

"But K'in Bor is a good provider," I said. "He is very strong, even if he is not as good-looking as Atanasio." Which is true. Even in his unflattering white sack-shirt, Atanasio exudes a youthful grace that contrasts with K'in Bor's bullish, melancholy tread. I envisioned Atanasio gliding noiselessly through the forest, like Arjuna the bowman, leaving no trace of his passage. I do not blame Koh for hanging on to Atanasio for dear life.

"I too am strong," Atanasio said, rising to the bait. "I kill tiger and deer, and I skin them with my own hands. And soon, soon Don Felipe will take me to Lacanjá, to hunt wild boar."

"Philip Baer is taking you to Lacanjá?"

"Yes — he promised. In Nahá there is no boar left, but in the hills behind Lacanjá, there still are many." Pretty Koh squeezed his forearm, and he fell silent.

I decided on a direct approach, since there was nothing to lose. "Geneviève tells me you accompanied her to Mensäbäk and met with your father."

"That is right," he said, lowering his eyes.

"Did you tell him your father-in-law is an *evangelista?*"

Atanasio flushed as consternation spread over his face. "No, he does not know," he admitted at last.

I held my breath. "And did he not wish you to bring back your incense pots from Mensäbäk and pray to them?"

"If he tries," Koh blurted out in Spanish, with a wild look in her eyes, "Atanasio will crash on the ground and burn in the flames, like Pepe Martínez." She filled the room with shrill laughter.

IV

Arrival

Late the following morning Jaime Cuello flew me to Nahá. The settlement looks deserted and unnaturally still, as it was the first time I set foot in it a year ago. All the men are in the forest or working their fields, except for K'ayum, who greets me at the airstrip and takes me across the lake.

Robert appears on the path from the sugarcane break, where he had gone to relieve himself. He wears an orange Nehru jacket, and looks exceptionally fit and relaxed.

"So you have come!" he exclaims, parroting the laconic Lacandon greeting. He leads K'ayum and me inside Chan K'in's kitchen and pours each of us a drink.

Some minutes later twelve-year-old Diana Lynn walks in, with Koh III's oldest daughter. They had been down near the boat landing, picking oranges.

"Oh dadd-y!" she scolds him. "Drinking and smoking already? It's not even afternoon."

Robert stammers a word or two in embarrassment, and puts out his cigarette.

"Oh, hello, Uncle!" She brightens suddenly, as if she'd just discovered me, and gives me a tight hug. "How was your week?"

"Good," I say. "We toured the highland towns for the Christmas *posadas,* and I got a lot of reading done. And you?"

"Well," she says, reverting to a small-girl voice, "I learned to fly the puddle jumper, and did a lot of drawings with little Nuk here, but I've hardly done any mathematics at all."

"Tell them about your cooking lessons," Robert urges.

"Oh yes. My godmother Koh taught me how to make tortillas, and she promised to teach me to weave on her loom."

"Terrific," I say. "You'll make a proper *hach winik* in no time."

"Oh not yet, Uncle," she says, exposing two winning buck teeth. "But I'm thinking of teaching little Nuk here some karate and Hawaiian dance."

"Great." I'd forgotten that Diana Lynn is a brown-belt hula dancer, in one of her other lives. She has a strong psychic bent, and can be almost frighteningly precocious one instant and childishly querulous the next. She is ambidextrous, bilingual, a cultural amphibian. With Diana Lynn I have to be constantly on my toes.

After a second drink Robert relaxes and plays guitar for us. The ruddy glow on his face owes more to the sun than to whisky, and even his smoker's cough has loosened, as "Chan Puk" strictly limits him to a pack of cigarettes a day.

Chan K'in and his wives return from the *milpa* in the middle of our singing. Even before I see him I sense an airy brightening in the room, which reflects in everyone's eyes. Chan K'in sits down quietly and pours himself some whisky. He does look decidedly lighter and more clear-eyed than he had the day we left Nahá. The reasons are soon forthcoming: His little boy has recovered from the fever and cough, the rains have stopped, and he has been going to the *milpa* every day for the past week.

Conversation

Young Chan K'in appears at the door, and we settle down to some serious talk.

They have heard of José Pepe's intentions to resign, but are skeptical of his motives; and they share K'in Yuk of Lacanjá's misgivings about Carmelo.

"I like his father, he is a serious man," Chan K'in says. "But I fear Carmelo is under José Pepe's influence."

"He is greedy," Young Chan K'in says. "He is one of those who likes cars and gas ovens and tin roofs. Years ago he took ten thousand pesos from us to buy provisions for our store. He has never returned the money."

Robert says, "I am sure he and Young Mateo had a good deal to talk about."

Chan K'in is amused by the story of the painted ambulance. He laughs softly and shakes his head. "Even with their cars and all their money, I do not think the men of Lacanjá are very content."

I say that K'in Yuk must be the exception, as he seems to be adjusting very well to the outside world.

"K'in Yuk is from San Quintín, not Lacanjá," Chan K'in reminds me. "He is more self-reliant and has a strong sense of his past, like his father, Vicente." Young Chan K'in recalls K'in's marching off to Lacanjá to fetch himself a bride, after he'd lived much of his childhood and adolescence in Na-Bolom.

"I can talk with K'in," Young Chan K'in says. "If it is necessary, I will go with him to Mexico City, and talk to the President about the road. K'in and I understand each other."

"We will have to wait and see what Carmelo does," Robert says.

"That is so." Chan K'in and his eldest son agree.

But I fear that time is running out.

The Katzenjammer Kids enter the kitchen and sit next to their father. They roll their eyes at me and make slingshot motions with their hands. I roll my eyes back at them and gesture to them to have patience. ·

I then present Chan K'in with a new Bic lighter, and this puts him in such a good humor he bursts into song. I quickly put away my notebook, and Robert turns on his tape recorder.

The Xtabay

Once more I am in the spell of the storyteller, as Chan K'in's eyes range over ours, drawing us in. Freed of my note-taking compulsion, at least for now, I become absorbed in the puppet-play of his hands, in the rising and falling of his voice as his tale unwinds between heaven and earth. I catch only a few of the words, but his voice carries me back to the beginning, to the dawn of jaguars and men:

A Lacandon farmer becomes so enraged at the animals that keep raiding his *milpa* he finally lights incense to Akinchob, the god of maize and protector of farmers, and asks to be changed into a jaguar, so he can chase the animals off. But when Akinchob accedes to his request, the farmer/jaguar sees the animals as his kin, and instead of eating or chasing them off, he takes pity on them. "You poor people," he says. "You must all be hungry. Come in, come in, I have plenty to eat in my *milpa*. I am just lying in wait for some damn animals that have been stealing my corn, so I can eat them."

"Of course," explains Chan K'in, "the farmer did not realize that he was now an animal himself, and that other animals looked like his companions, whereas humans would now look like animals and he would have eaten them."

When my head stops spinning, I am filled with the sense of well-being that Chan K'in's stories invariably instill in me. My senses register that the parameters of the room have expanded, the sunlight filtering through the east window is several times brighter, and another dimension has crept into the space we occupy, causing everything to pulsate in rhythm with my heart. My mind is lucid, the taste of my breath is sweet, and I feel revitalized and whole, as if some vestigial enzyme had been triggered that enables the life-force to flow directly into my bloodstream. I cannot tell how much it is the form, how much the content of Chan K'in's story that has produced this enhancement, or if it is a power issuing directly from him, for which the story is a convenient vehicle.

Still vibrating to Chan K'in's voice, I dare his silence to ask what has become of the red-haired nymphs of the forest, and of the trolls and demons I had read about in *The Book of Chan K'in*. The Xtabay, beautiful sirens with red skin and red pubises, had been consorts of the minor gods. Chan K'in claimed that some of the ancients had seen them as they wandered in the forest, and that they would call out to the ancients, "Stay with me. Stay with me. I will bear your children." The lucky ones so chosen were not to tarry too long with the Xtabay, however, but were well advised to make their way to the home of the keeper of the forest, Kanank'ax. If they spent the night with Kanank'ax they would have his blessing, and would always be able to see the Xtabay by lighting incense to him. Those who stayed with the wood nymphs without paying respects to the forest god would find themselves on the trail back to their village, and would pay for their heedless pleasures by never laying eyes on the Xtabay again. In the place where they had once made love, they would find only barren rock. It is one of the loveliest of Lacandon legends; I like to think of Chan K'in as one who has lain with the Xtabay.

"Ah, my grandfather knew the Xtabay," Chan K'in says, in answer to my question. "He said they made him very contented. In his time the Xtabay and the minor gods walked freely in the forest. I myself saw some *lo'k'in* (cannibals) when I was a small boy, and they tried to carry me away. They are huge ugly people with green warts, and they cover their bodies with jaguar skins. My father and his father had many encounters with the *lo'k'in,* and several of their companions were carried off by them and never returned. If a female *lo'k'in* caught you, she would force you to cut wood all day long and make love to her at night until you died of exhaustion. Then they cooked you and ate you whole. The ones I saw were running away from soldiers who had shot one of their women. They were frightened of the white men and their rifles; my father talked them out of carrying me away by lying and saying he was a friend of the soldiers. When my father and my uncle returned with their machetes, the *lo'k'in* had vanished." He puffs on his cigar, and shrugs. "Today, with so many foreigners and *ladinos* in the forest, the *lo'k'in* have gone into hiding. And the same is true of the red-skinned maidens. The Xtabay and the *lo'k'in* are hiding in their caves." He lifts one shoulder. "Who can say when they will come out again?"

Finding the Enemy

In our hut that evening Robert and I fill one another in on the week's events. He had inquired about María Bonita, and found she is living nearby, on the other side of Old Mateo's house. He proposes we visit Old Mateo the following afternoon, and talk with María Bonita the day after. He also suggests we accompany Chan K'in to his *milpa* toward the end of the week.

I tell Robert of my conversation with Atanasio and Koh, and get upset all over again at the idea of Phil Baer flying Atanasio off to Lacanjá and mixing up his allegiances.

"I am convinced, as is Geneviève, that he remains a traditionalist at heart," I say, "but that damn Baer is luring him to Lacanjá with promises of wild boar and God knows what else. It's obscene."

"Take it easy, little brother," Robert says, sipping on his Scotch. "Phil Baer is not the enemy. He has saved many Lacandon lives with his medicines and his transportation facilities over the years, and he did me a good turn once when I was young and foolish. It may well be, as Chan K'in says, that he has come to his senses and turned a new leaf. If you met him, you'd probably find him a personable guy." He sets down his cup, and refills it. "Of course, he can still go to hell, for all the harm he's done in Nahá, Mensäbäk and Lacanjá."

"Look," I say, growing heated, "I know damn well Phil Baer is not the enemy. The Mexican government is not the enemy. The road builders and the loggers are not the enemy. So who the hell *is?*" I am shouting now, as the anger dammed up over the past weeks explodes in my head. "Who the hell *is* the enemy, Robert? We feel so damn superior to Bishop Landa because he had the incredible gall to write about the Mayas after he had burned all their codices. But we are burning the evidence too; we burn it every day, just by the way we live. Here is this old man Chan K'in, who should be honored as a great Mayan chieftain in all the cities of the world; for his stories alone he deserves a Nobel Prize — and instead, we are breaking his heart. All of us, we are all doing it!" I clench my fists as tears scald my eyes. "Dammit, Robert, we are the enemy — all of us. All we do is take, and what do we give in return? You know damn well that all the air in our lungs could not make up a single breath of the oxygen

Chan K'in will need to go on living, once his forest is gone. And yet a single story of his gives us enough substance to survive a whole year in Mexico City or New York."

"That's right!" Robert raises his plastic cup. "To survival," he toasts, in his ironic, mock-stoical, older-brother "I've-been-there-many-times" voice that makes me want to sock him right on the jaw.

But when I look into his eyes again I can hardly bear to see the pain.

"To survival," I mutter, swallowing my bile, and I tip up my cup. The dam is intact, but my unseemly outburst has let off steam, and the whisky does help.

I lie awake in the hammock, listening to Chan K'in's low chanting, and soothe myself by envisioning him on a midwestern crusade: As the campaign gathers momentum, Old Mateo sets up a *balché* canoe in Toledo, Antonio and Young Chan K'in light god-pots in Cincinnati and Cleveland, K'ayum and little Mario heal the lame and the blind with their magic flutes in Ann Arbor, Michigan. Everywhere Chan K'in goes, multitudes gather to hear and touch this slight, cigar-smoking saintly figure as he carries Hachäkyum's message into rural Indiana, Kansas, Iowa, the small towns of Minnesota and Wisconsin . . .

At around midnight I fall asleep and dream that Robert is approached by a young tough in jeans and cowboy shirt who questions him aggressively about his ideas, political and otherwise, in specific reference to the Lacandones. Robert passes the young rebel's interrogation and is made leader of a revolutionary guerrilla band.

When I report the dream at breakfast Robert smiles obliquely and says nothing. Chan K'in's interpretation is that someone will have occasion to speak ill of Robert. I feel as if I had dislodged a deeply imbedded thorn.

Nuk of the Twisted Jaw

K'ayum and young Bol visit us in the evening. K'ayum has brought some fresh samples of his typing. He can now turn out long declarative sentences in Spanish: "My name is K'ayum Ma'ax and I am an ape." I can picture him recording for posterity his father's stories and legends, in his own inimitable voice. He has also brought his accordion, which he plays with spirit, resolutely off key. There is no limit to K'ayum's curiosity and versatility. In public he can be curt and rude, and his bragging at times gets downright insolent. As Robert says, "K'ayum has little patience with those less intelligent than himself, and that includes just about everybody."

And yet he is a model of patient attentiveness with those few people he respects, or with those who can teach him something he wants to learn. This evening he has brought with him his brand-new savings-deposit book from a San Cristóbal bank, and he asks Robert to explain to him the mechanics of deposit and withdrawal. It was Young Mateo who persuaded him to open a bank account; Mateo himself has shady friends who manage his financial affairs.

K'ayum is fascinated by the idea of "interest": money that is born from the capital that sits in the bank, idle and unused. He wants to know if the interest that accrues from his original deposit is the same kind of money or if it is worth less than the capital.

"Yes, it is all the same 'shit of the sun,' " Robert says, using the Lacandon vernacular, *ta'k'in*.

"Then, I will use it to buy another wife," K'ayum jokes. "With the interest I will buy a gringa wife. She will be made entirely of money. She will not be a real person, like Margarita, because the money is not real money. It is shit that gives birth to more shit." He laughs at his joke, louder than anybody.

Later, when he and I are alone, I tell K'ayum of our intention to visit the elder Mateo the following day.

"He is a good man, Mateo," K'ayum says, echoing his father's and his brothers' sentiments. "He has a good head. He knows how to make things and fix rifles, and his heart is also good, but not as good as my father's. And also, Mateo is not so good with his wives."

He confirms the story I had from Trudi and Robert, that after Mateo's first wife — Chan K'in's mother — died, he had lived alone for a long time, forlorn and celibate; he eventually married a very young girl and her elder sister, who was sterile. The pretty girl became the mother of Young Mateo and his younger brother Bol, the two scamps of Nahá, who are always getting into mischief of one kind or another.

"Young Mateo was married before to my sister Nuk," K'ayum says, "But she left him."

"You mean Paco's wife, the one with the deformed jaw?" I had seen her leaning out her hut door and haranguing the children who played outside. She is the only Nahá woman to respond to my greeting in Spanish. Geneviève enlisted Nuk's aid when she wanted medical information from a reticent Nahá matron. Nuk would tease the women about their shyness, telling them that times had changed and they should also. Geneviève referred to Nuk as "Nahá's first feminist."

"Why did Nuk leave Young Mateo?" I ask K'ayum.

"Because of her ugly face; he would not make love to her, and she was very sad. Also, she did not get along with Mateo's first wife, my sister Margarita. Young Mateo had to pay my father fifteen hundred pesos to take Nuk back, because she cried every night.'Young Mateo is like his father. They both like pretty women."

I point out, "But the elder Mateo's face is deformed worse than Nuk's."

"Yes, but he still likes pretty women. When he was younger, he always put perfume in his hair, to smell pretty for his wives. He is a vain man, Mateo."

"Kayum, how did Nuk's jaw get broken?"

"Roberto did not tell you?" K'ayum asks, suddenly cautious.

"Only a little," I say. Both Robert and Geneviève had told me a part of the story, but the two versions conflicted in important details.

K'ayum finishes the last of the whisky, crosses his legs, and puts on his storytelling voice. Like his father, he gesticulates vividly, and his eyes range from one side to the other, as if the hut were crammed with listeners. "Long ago Nuk almost married Vicente, son of Nuxi', who lives in Nahá. Vicente is not happy with my sister Nuk because her skin is too dark. He wants a woman with a fair skin, like José Güero's daughters. So one day he shoots Nuk in the face and he runs to the *milpa* to tell my father that Jorge has killed Nuk. My father and Jorge always quarrel with each other, so Vicente lies to put the blame on Jorge. But Nuk is not dead, and so Vicente has to run away, to El Censo. Trudi takes Nuk to Mexico, and she has an operation. They fix Nuk's face, but she is not pretty anymore, and Nuk learns to speak Spanish with Mexican women in the hospital.

"While she is in Mexico my father and my mother find a new husband for Nuk, Maximiliano, but a snake bites him and he dies before she comes back. After she returns, Nuk marries Paco, and now she is content; but she talks, talks all the time, she asks Paco to buy her many things she saw in Mexico, and she teaches other women — my wife also — to talk, talk all the time and to ask their men for many things."

"What does she ask for?"

"She wants earrings and dresses and expensive things. Also Nuk asks Geneviève about pills and a hook that she puts below, and this means she does not have children if she does not want them. So Geneviève gives her the pills, and now she can make love without children until she wants children. And she tells other women to use the pills and the hooks when they do not feel strong enough to have children or when they are sick — and so now some of them do it also."

"And your wife, Margarita?"

"She is pregnant now, so she doesn't take the pills. But after she has the baby, she will probably take them again."

I ask, "And how do you feel about it, K'ayum?"

He frowns, then shrugs. "I think perhaps it's good. It's too expensive to have children now. Before, the women had children in the birth hut, and it did not cost anything. Now it costs too much to fly them to San Cristóbal, and sometimes there are complications. K'in Bor also feels this way. It's better to have only two or three children." He grins. "But if Margarita takes the pills, then I can also make love to a gringa who takes them, and everybody will be happy without having to have children." He bursts out laughing.

"K'ayum, what happened to Vicente?"

"Oh, he went to Mensäbäk and found another wife, an Adventist. He is happy now, also. Young Mateo is also contented with Margarita. Everybody is contented."

Mateo Senior

In the afternoon we arrive at the elder Mateo's house near the southern edge of the village, and are greeted by his older wife, Nuk, who is stirring *posol* in a huge pot with a wooden paddle.

A very pretty young woman sits by a window in the rear, and I think at first she is the younger wife, but it turns out to be his oldest daughter, Chan Nuk. Two young boys of eight or nine, who are also exceptionally good-looking, stare at us with huge black eyes before resuming their play. The mother of Young Mateo comes in from the kitchen and smiles invitingly at us, then vanishes into the shadows. She is about forty now and thick-waisted, but still strikingly handsome, with her son's large almond eyes and a youthful pertness in her manner.

"Come in, come in, Roberto," Old Mateo calls out warmly, and rises from his hammock. He accents the last syllable — Rober-tó — as though to invest the name with a distinguishing intimacy. He invites us to sit on low mahogany stools, next to the door. Robert's stool is covered with a paca hide, and mine is newly polished.

Mateo's expert handiwork is in evidence everywhere in the hut. Hanging on the walls are two .22 rifles with finely carved stocks, several sturdy leather bags, and the finest saw I've seen in Nahá. I recall Robert's and Trudi's stories of Mateo's legendary prowess with metal tools of all kinds. "In Mexico City," she has said, "Mateo would have been a first-class engineer."

We give Mateo a Bic lighter, alkaline batteries and the .22 ammunition we had brought for him, and he repays us immediately with half a dozen tightly rolled cigars.

We light up and smoke, with a nip or two of Robert's whisky. In addition to his mechanical skills and his talents as a craftsman, Mateo owns the greenest thumb in Nahá. He sends out his boys to the orchard, and they return with armloads of squash, lemons and six enormous grapefruit that fill our shoulder bags to bursting.

I puff cheerfully on my cigar, which is tasty and mild, and listen to the cadence of Mateo's anecdotes. He is about sixty, slim and strongly built, with no gray hair. His forehead and left temple are badly scarred, and he has no eyebrows or eyelashes; he is missing one ear and most of the second, has no nostrils to speak of and no upper lip, and yet he speaks in a firm, commanding voice, accompanied with broad gestures. I have grown accustomed to his disfigurement, and am bowled over by the sheer energy of the man. I remember the vigor with which he pounded the pine resin the day I first saw him, and his titanic, spread-legged stance when he bent to wash his hands before entering the god-house. Although nearly a generation younger, Mateo is Chan K'in's closest peer in prestige and influence. What Mateo lacks as a storyteller he makes up in physical presence and his own religious intensity. He too is a man of seeds and roots, a bulwark of continuity with the ancestral past. As he gesticulates and waves his arms, I notice he is missing the little finger of his left hand, another casualty of the hot coals that scarred his face when he was an infant.

The second and older wife, Nuk, who looks about forty-five, sits quietly by the pot, stirring the corn broth with a smooth, even rhythm. She seems at peace with herself, although it is well known in the village that she is barren and that she suffers from acutely painful menstruations that cause her to moan aloud in the night.

Her pretty younger sister, also named Nuk, remains half in the shadows as her hair is braided by her daughter Chan Nuk. As the mother of Mateo's children she claims the privilege of being spoiled, and seems to give more attention to her appearance than to daily chores. Occasionally she pouts and gives us a provocative glance from her moist brown eyes. I detect in her look an implicit rebuke — almost petulant — that we have not brought her any gifts. I kick myself for this oversight and make a note to bring her some scissors, safety pins and soap the next day.

I find it hard to keep my eyes from the beautiful Chan Nuk and the two boys, either of whom will soon threaten Young Mateo's standing as the village Adonis.

Old Mateo's face is so badly scarred I cannot reconstruct what it might have looked like had it never been burned. I imagine he would have been a handsome man, as the younger Nuk cannot be solely responsible for their beautiful offspring. His sunken eyes are lively and restless. I feel I am in the home of a master craftsman and an aesthete whose soul is devoted to physical beauty. Mateo is both the Daedalus and the Pygmalion of Nahá.

We rise as Mateo offers to record for Robert a chant to the soul of a departed relative.

"It is too noisy here, Roberto," he says. "We will do it outside, under the trees."

On the way out, I spy on a shelf above one of Mateo's rifles a half-empty bottle of Brut Fabergé.

The song Mateo records turns into a haunting litany, an admonition to the departed soul to go and rest with Sukunkyum — and to watch no longer the going and doing of those of this world:

> Do not count my steps where I walk.
> Do not watch my coming and going,
> For I have given you all you need for your journey to Metlán —
> Your dog, your candles, your parched corn, your posol offerings . . .

As a practical measure, Mateo mentions Robert's name at the start and at the end of the chant. Mateo also knows something about the copyright laws.

As we walk back under the citrus trees, Robert reveals another aspect of their relationship:

"When I first came to Nahá, I was adopted at once by both Chan K'in and Mateo. If Chan K'in became my second father, then Mateo was a guardian uncle. He escorted me personally to the cliff temples of Mensäbäk, and stood by as I underwent an initiation of sorts with the rain god and his servants. I climbed the rock face that is said to be their house and recorded the petroglyphs painted on the walls. It was an eerie and powerful experience, climbing up that sheer cliff face and tracing the ancient paintings while Mateo waited below. He was sitting in his *cayuco,* and I half think he expected to have to fish up my body from the lake. But I did not fall, and apparently I passed muster, for on my return I found I was now fully accepted in Nahá. Trudi had passed a similar trial some years earlier. You may have to go there or some place like it one day, if you intend to become a part of their culture. . . .

"When I was in my mid-twenties I got into trouble with the Mexican authorities, and had to hide out in Nahá for six months. I lived here, in a small hut in Mateo's farthest *milpa,* and he and his wives took excellent care of me. He risked his neck for me more than once, lying to the *federales* to get them off my trail. I had no money at the time, and Chan K'in lent me three hundred pesos so I could get back to Mexico City and clear my name. Mateo went even further: He offered me Chan Nuk, who had been cooking for me and who was barely thirteen at the time. Well, I took a long walk in the forest to think it over, and realized that I could never be a full-time *hach winik,* as Carlos Frey had tried to be. There are patterns of upbringing in me — hangups if you will — that go very deep, and would always pull me back to the West. In other words, I really loved these people, and I owed them, and I did not want to screw up. When I returned to Nahá I brought Chan K'in a new .22 rifle and other gifts, and I had the opportunity to repay Mateo with a favor or two. . . .

"Mateo is no saint, I assure you. When you have something he wants, such as a rifle or a radio, he knows exactly how to go about removing it from you. But he is also a loyal and generous friend who gives as fully as he receives. This is a dimension that is missing from Young Mateo and his younger brother, Bol. To his credit, Old Mateo has never held it against me that I turned down his beautiful daughter, despite the serious temptation."

K'in Bor's Illness

I drop by K'in Bor's hut to give his son K'ayum a slingshot I had promised to bring him. K'in Bor is lying listlessly on his hammock. He is shivery and pale, and looks as if he's running a fever.

"I don't know what is happening to me," he says. "In the past three days, I feel suddenly weak, my legs go limp and my head burns. It goes away, I do my work, and it comes back and I feel faint, like a sick woman."

"Have you told Roberto?" I ask.

"Yes. Roberto gave me this medicine." He shows me some Aralen tablets.

K'in Bor has malaria.

Five-year-old K'ayum comes in from the kitchen, and I give him the ten-peso slingshot I'd bought for him in San Cristóbal. He leaps at it, flexes the rubber band experimentally, and grins with delight.

We go outside to test the slingshot. It is already dark. K'ayum places a large pebble on the leather pouch, bends his body into a bow and stretches the rubber band with all his strength. He releases it straight up into the night sky and listens for the pebble to crash through the tree branches and fall to the ground.

"*Xilal en!* — I am a man!" K'ayum shouts, and pats his chest.

I do not regret having brought him this fledgling weapon, with which he might kill a few bright-plumaged birds — as his older cousins already have. His days of freedom in the forest are numbered. In years to come his hunter's skill and other yardsticks by which he can measure his manhood will have become, at best, attenuated.

Journal

January 5, 1978. Hans and Fritz have made sturdy, grown-up slingshots by cutting rubber strips from the inner tube of an automobile tire, which Robert brought them from Mexico City.

"Chich in muk! — I am strong!" they shout, flexing the black rubber thongs to the fullest and releasing stones into the bush. They have already brought down two or three small birds. When not in use, the slingshots are carried around their necks.

"I am a hunter. I am a man. I am strong." Little Chan K'in boasts, over and over, and slaps his chest. He asks me if he should kill a bright small bird singing on a tree branch. "I am very strong," he repeats.

"Then kill an alligator," I say.

"Yes," he says.

"Or a paca."

"Yes — I will kill one."

"Or a tapir."

He considers. "That is too big."

"Well, the bird is too small."

"Ahhh." He looks at me with bulging eyes as he grapples with this new formula.

During lunch Chan K'in is telling little K'in that a cayuco will last ten years at the most. When it is old and begins to leak, he will have to make a new one. But if the white men come and chop down the large mahoganies, they will topple the smaller trees with them as they fall, and there will be nothing left. A cayuco requires a large tree, because of all that is lost around the edges when it is hollowed out. A good dugout cannot be made from a small mahogany. K'in keeps plying Chan K'in with sharp questions: "Can a cayuco be made with pine or cedar? Can it be made of the same material airplanes are made of?" Little K'in, like K'ayum, is in his father's tradition, but they have begun to construct frames of reference outside the forest.

Teresa

After lunch Robert and I paddle across to the north shore, where he has been invited to another *balché* session with Jorge and Young Mateo. I pass up the *balché* and pay a visit to Teresa Keane, an attractive young Englishwoman who flew in two days ago from San Cristóbal, and is staying a week at the Hotel Maya Caribe to do research on Lacandon symbols and nomenclature. She is an anthropology graduate student at the London School of Economics.

Teresa is slender and tall, about twenty-seven or twenty-eight, and a good friend of Geneviève's. Like most plucky travelers who make their way to Nahá from distant corners of the world, she says she had felt "compelled" to come. She has all the earmarks of a seeker, courageous and resourceful, with a misty air of irresolution about the eyes. Teresa's Spanish is excellent, and she speaks it with a refreshing English accent.

Our conversation opens with Lacandon nomenclature, in which Teresa has evidently done her research. "The men have only four names basically — Bol, K'in, K'ayum and Nuxi', which mean, respectively, Sustainer, Sun or Prophet, Lord of Music and Ancient One. The women have only two, Nuk and Koh: Large One and Tooth. They tack on the diminutive Chan — Little — for variation, and a number of women have adopted *ladino* names, like Margarita. But even they tend to choose the same ones again and again. And little kids are called Och — literally, 'Possum' — until they are four or five, when it appears they will survive."

I ask, "How do you explain this?"

"Well, it's the community, you see, and the *onen*. These people identify themselves according to their animal lineage. I agree with Robert that the *onen* must be a degenerate form of the *nahual* or animal double who embodies the qualities of one's soul and acts as a protector — you know, rather like the loyal hunting dog who swims his master's soul across the waters of the underworld. Now, the Lacandones don't need a patronymic and a 'Christian' name like John Smith to give themselves an identity. They call one another by kinship terms, like 'cousin' or 'brother-in-law.' We need our names and social security numbers and so on to have a bit of ground under our feet — our little purchase on the vast, anonymous universe. The Mayas do not see the universe as vast and anonymous; their world occupies a specific space and shape, and it is peopled with creatures very much like themselves. Traditional Mayas like Chan K'in still fulfill themselves within their community, and within the cosmology that has grown out of their interrelationship with the forest. It is only

169

when that bond starts to dissolve, as in Lacanjá, that they take on foreign names like Pancho Villa and Obregón."

I congratulate Teresa on this perception, and tell her I think it is shared, in a tacit way, by Old Chan K'in himself. "You could say the forest is the source of their physical community, and Chan K'in's storytelling is the glue of their spiritual one."

"A nifty balance," Teresa says. "But don't you think Chan K'in would lose his authority outside the forest?"

I ponder this hard question, and recall Trudi's prediction that Chan K'in would be "swallowed up" in the city. "Yes," I conclude sadly, "he would."

"In other words, no forest, no Chan K'in."

"That's right," I say. "And for all we know, the converse might also hold true."

Teresa asks if I've had any experience in Nahá with the phenomenon of "soul loss."

I say that Robert had written of the Lacandon belief that when someone is about to die, his or her soul leaves the body and wanders around, visiting places and people it has been familiar with. "When a shout is heard in the village, and it is not caused by a snake, Chan K'in might remark, 'Ah, that must be so-and-so's soul reentering his body.' So this also becomes a way for a villager to anticipate to the others that he will soon die." It strikes me suddenly that this could also explain some of José Güero's bizarre pranks. I let Teresa in on the idea that he might be letting the community know, in his own way, that he is not long for this world. I add, "But you can never be certain with José Güero. He's so crafty he might turn his death into another of his tricks."

We laugh, and once more I thank Teresa for leading me to an important insight. I admire her gumption and keen intelligence, and anticipate that she will soon gain acceptance in Nahá, as her friend Geneviève already has.

Teresa wonders what the equivalent of soul loss might be in the States, where even the mention of death is still a taboo. I suggest that the nearest parallel would be the crisis telephone lines in the big cities, where someone contemplating suicide can call in and talk to a therapist or a priest.

"That's kind of sad," Teresa says.

At this point in our absorbing conversation Young Mateo stumbles in, glassy-eyed, and asks if we are comfortable. We assure him we are.

"I'm very drunk," he says, redundantly. He is bringing a gourd of *balché* for Teresa to taste, which she does, gingerly.

"It is good for a cold," Mateo says, and giggles.

"I don't doubt it," Teresa says, but she nearly gags on the brandy-spiked *balché*. "Interesting," she says, politely.

Mateo's small daughter leads her future husband in by the hand. Juan José is roaring drunk once again, and sings Mexican songs off key. Chan K'in Chico comes in with his toy jet plane, and he and Juan José get down to play on the ground, like infants. It is time to go.

María Bonita

I pick up Robert at the god-house, and we paddle back to Nahá. The *balché* had been second-rate again, he assures me, but it was still better than nothing. And he emphasizes that he was also fulfilling a social obligation. "You should have been here three days ago. Old Chan K'in made a batch of *balché* with four quarts of honey I brought back from the city. It tasted something like old English mead. You would have been converted."

As we paddle, Robert tells me for the second time the story of María Bonita — how she had married a Lacandon named José, from Monte Líbano, who had moved to Mensäbäk after the invasion of the *ladinos*. María Bonita had given birth to a daugher and to a boy who was paralyzed from the waist down and mentally defective. She carried him around on her back for fifteen years, until he was bigger than she, and then he died. José also died soon after, and María Bonita, still young and extremely attractive, returned to Nahá and acquired the reputation of a loose woman who slept with Tzeltales and unattached Lacandon men. "I took a fancy to her myself," Robert says, with glowing cheeks. "She was a damned good-looking woman. I'm curious to know how she's held up."

We stop to pick up a bottle of Scotch, get directions from Chan K'in, and set out for María Bonita's house. We get lost on a side trail and double back to Old Mateo's backyard, so that one of his angelic young sons has to guide us the right way. We come to a large, sunny clearing, in the middle of which sits one of the largest and best-made structures I've seen in Nahá. It is about fifty feet long, and each end is rounded, like the apse of a cathedral. The hut belongs to María Bonita's father-in-law, Nuxi', who invites us in for a smoke. I remember Nuxi' from the first *balché* ceremony; he is a hearty, well-built gentleman of about fifty, who has recently resettled from El Censo with his entire family. (I learned afterward that Nuxi' is the father of Vicente, the impulsive firebrand who had shot Nuk in the face because her complexion did not suit him. Following Vicente's expulsion from Nahá, Nuxi' and his two wives and remaining children had discreetly relocated in El Censo. After Nuk's marriage to Paco, Chan K'in had welcomed Nuxi' back to Nahá.)

Robert opens the whisky bottle and pours each of the men in the hut a drink, using the four plastic cups we had brought from San Cristóbal. The two women sitting in the rounded stern of the hut are Nuxi's wives. From the liberty with which they laugh at Robert's jokes and ask him questions, I take this to be a "progressive" household, within a traditionalist setting. Robert and Nuxi' discuss firearms and harvests, and finally we inquire if we might visit his two sons and his daughter-in-law.

"Yes, yes. She and my sons live across the field."

He escorts us out and we approach a small hut surrounded by dry cornstalks. The sun feels warm, although it is late afternoon, and there is more blue sky overhead than I've seen anywhere in the village.

171

"*Tal in wilech* — I have come to see you," Robert calls out. A tall husky young man of about seventeen or eighteen greets us at the entrance, grins and nods approvingly when Robert holds up the whisky bottle. Apparently we've brought the right lubricant.

As we enter, a woman of about forty emerges from the hut with an infant in her arms and gives Robert a radiant smile that reveals she has no upper front teeth. She covers her mouth with one hand but her eyes go on sparkling gaily, and yet shyly, hinting that she and Robert shared unspoken memories.

"Come in," says the young man, with a formal, proprietary sweep of his arm. Inside sits another young man, a year or two younger, who is listening to Guatemalan marimba music on a green plastic transistor radio. A very fetching little girl of five or six sits next to him. When she sees us she runs to her mother and stays close to her skirts during the remainder of our stay.

"Welcome to our house," says María Bonita, smiling close-mouthed. "I am sorry that I have nothing to offer you. This is unexpected."

"It is not important," Robert says. "We brought our own refreshment." He sets down three plastic cups by the radio, fills them, and passes one to each of the young men and one to María Bonita. She waves her free hand, then giggles and covers her mouth. The older boy drinks his whisky straight down, but the younger one sniffs it and sips hesitantly before screwing up his courage. He seems a little disoriented by our presence.

"And whose little boy is that?" Robert asks, indicating the big-eyed, solemn infant in her arms.

"He has two fathers," she says, pointing to both boys. As yet, he does not much resemble either of them. She adds, "The girl has no father." She pats the head of the pretty mahogany-skinned girl, who peers at us with coal-black eyes from behind the folds of her mother's skirts.

Robert then pours drinks for me and for himself, leaving the half-full cup by the radio. "*Lechaim* — to life," he says in Hebrew, winking at me, and we tip up our plastic cups.

"Have you been in Mexico?" asks María Bonita, who still stands by the door.

"Yes, too long," says Robert. "*Ma' tsoy* Mexico. It is not good for me."

The two young men, Robert and I have another drink, as the third cup sits untouched by the radio. The youngest husband again makes a face, but the older one grins manfully. "Very tasty," he says, and his voice cracks.

My head and stomach warm, and I suddenly see María Bonita as she must have looked at eighteen or twenty, when she was the beauty of Monte Líbano and carried her invalid retarded son on her back. Her eyes are clear brown and her body sturdy and full, but the weight of the years and of childbearing have caused the coffee-toned skin of her face to sag, except when she smiles.

Robert again presents her the half-full cup of whisky, and this time she gulps it down, breathes deeply, coughs and spits on the ground. "Ne ki' — very tasty," she says, laughing. She shifts her little boy to her other hip, and wipes her hand on her skirt.

Nuxi' the father-in-law comes to the hut and jabbers excitedly until Robert fills one of the cups to the brim, so he can take it to his wives. He then ushers in a Tzeltal of twenty-five or so, who wears a wide-brimmed straw hat, *ladino* trousers and boots. He greets Robert warmly, in Spanish.

"I am Juan, Don Roberto, don't you remember me? I was a small boy when you and my father went hunting together."

Robert looks him up and down, warily. "Are you evangelist?"

"Oh no, Don Roberto," Juan says with a laugh. "Don't mistake me. My father and you used to drink *chucho con rabia* [rabid dog] — don't you remember? I take after my father."

"Then have some whisky, *amigo* Juan," Robert says, and pours him a half cup. Juan sits down and talks animatedly about Robert's exploits, including some I'd not read about in Robert's diaries. He recalls one episode when Robert had hidden from an aroused jaguar in a hollow tree trunk, and had waited there until dawn, shivering from cold and hunger.

"Don Roberto was not frightened," Juan says. "He had been lost in the forest three days, and was trying to think of a way to kill the tiger, so he could eat him."

"That's true," Robert says, flushing; we all gasp, and then laugh at his embarrassment.

Juan raises his cup in a toast: "Around here, Don Roberto, you have become a man of legend."

While they talk, I study María Bonita's husbands, who speak little Spanish and do not take part in the conversation. The younger one asks to look at my Swiss knife, whose blades he opens and closes repeatedly. He is just learning about his body, what it can do. The older brother sits with stiff, proprietary dignity as María Bonita stands by the door with her baby on one hip, looking from Juan to Robert and back in silent appraisal. I think of her grinding corn for the tortillas, rolling cigars, weaving and going about her sundry wifely chores. She is the counterpart of Koh II, another strong woman and the mother of two generations of sons and daughters; but María Bonita has chosen an unconventional life in this traditional community. She has borne her burdens and paid the price to remain herself: a "modern" woman in an ancient patriarchal culture. Even her name, María Bonita, bestowed on her by Trudi, speaks of independence and eccentricity. María Bonita, María Bonita. As a girl, she must have begun life as Nuk or Koh.

Although she stands shyly by the door, rocking her infant son while the men do all the talking, María Bonita's presence dominates this household. She walks barefoot like her contemporary Koh II, and wears a flower-print skirt under her working tunic; she has long, flashy earrings and several strands of bright red beads around her neck.

María Bonita switches her son from one hip to the other, and turns her body in a swift, sensual movement that takes my breath away. In the next instant I get a whiff of the fecund musk of her skirts. In her movements, her woman odors, María Bonita is a supple, still-beautiful woman. And now, after years of living on her own, sleeping with whomever she chose, she has returned to respectability by agreeing to marry these two adolescent brothers. The fact is that there is now a scarcity of childbearing women in Nahá. The younger ones tend to go crazy after the first or second birth, like K'in Bor's wife, or become thin and sickly, like Young Chan K'in's wife, or bossy and demanding, like Paco's, Atanasio's and Chan K'in Chico's wives — while María Bonita at forty-plus looks as if she will go on having healthy, contented-looking children for another decade.

I visualize the night both men entered her and their sperm converged on her egg cell in the same instant (as she insists), fusing together to form this sturdy, large-eyed little boy: two fathers, two brothers twinned in the same son. I see her squatting in the lonely birth hut as the two brothers pray in the god-house, each one certain that he alone is the father. I yearn to know what it is like to be María Bonita.

After a second drink and several more anecdotes, Juan finally takes his departure. Robert asks if we can take pictures of them all. María Bonita turns aside modestly; the older boy says yes, and they gather outside the hut for the family portrait. A litter of puppies tumble out of their box behind the hut and gather at María Bonita's bare feet, as Robert and I snap their pictures. The husbands stand stiff and self-conscious on either side of her, the little girl peers at us with one eye, demure behind her mother's skirts; the infant son stares uncomprehending. The full, sensuous smile fades from María Bonita's face, and returns the instant after our shutters click. The wider image seen through my inner lens throbs and sparkles; it will not show up in the photograph. The Guatemalan marimba music spills from the radio and the scent of María Bonita's skirts lingers in the air, taking me back to Chata, my Indian nursemaid, the beautiful Quiché-Mayan woman who had breast-fed me and looked after me until I was five — until the morning she had taken me to the kindergarten and moments after, only a short block away, had been knifed to death by her jealous Indian lover. It comes flooding back, this dark, secret memory of my childhood, which had taken place shortly after I saw the five Lacandones at Ubico's fair.

Robert asks them if they need anything. The older boy answers that he would like a Bic lighter, the younger one asks for alkaline batteries for his radio. María Bonita says nothing at first, then inquires if we have any medicine for the rash on her leg. She shows it to us. It looks too inflamed to have been caused by fleas or midges. When she looks up I see the exhaustion in her face, and I am reminded one more time of the private lives of these Lacandon women, to which I have no access. Can it be that María Bonita was pressured into marrying these two boys, in order to bear their children?

"Aloe vera!" I exclaim. "That should help her rash. We can bring some tomorrow — no, tonight, before sunset."

They thank us and we take our leave, after greeting Nuxi' briefly on the way out.

We are halfway back to our hut before the possibility occurs to either of us that Juan might be the father of María Bonita's little girl.

Late that night, after we have delivered the aloe jelly to María Bonita, Robert and I lie awake in our hammocks, heavy-lidded but unable to sleep.

"Well, Robert," I say, "her name still suits María Bonita to a T."

I hear a prolonged, raspy sigh. "Little brother, you should have seen her fifteen years ago . . ."

The Milpa

Little Chan K'in wakes us well before dawn for our excursion to the *milpa*. I have had restless dreams all night, of standing on a beach where a navy boat had sunk. Black oil fills the water, corpses and duffel bags bob up and down. When a coast guard boat appears, Robert and I get in it and watch the captain haul in bodies and bags, one after another, as the storm pitches us from side to side. We approach some cliffs, and Robert challenges the skipper to get us to shore intact. The captain, calm, keeps a taut line and guides the boat expertly, inches from the cliffs, until we dock safely. "It's just a job," he says, as I gaze at him in admiration.

I feel the dream is important, and that it involves Chan K'in.

A thick gray mist hugs the ground as we make our way to the landing. Chan K'in is already there, with Koh I and Koh II and little Chan K'in, who are bailing out one of the lighter *cayucos*. They all carry net bags with tumplines across their foreheads except for Chan K'in, who carries his lunch in his blue Lufthansa shoulder bag.

We bail out the heavy *cayuco* and set out behind Chan K'in's. The mist is starting to spread out and rise in dense, cottony rolls, permitting jagged glimpses of the opposite shore. I am excited at crossing the full width of the lake for the first time.

I paddle sitting crouched in the prow as Robert mans the heavy steering oar in the rear, with his legs braced against the sides. Diana sits in the middle with one of the hunting dogs, a brown-haired bitch who whimpers after her mate in Chan K'in's *cayuco*.

Although our *cayuco* is heavier, we manage to keep up with Chan K'in's by paddling steadily. Koh I is in the stern, Koh II in the prow, and Chan K'in sits in the middle with little Chan K'in and three dogs directly behind him. In my half-awake state, I feel that we are gliding above the water, which offers no resistance.

"Two strong men," Diana says, feeding my illusion.

"It's only mist," I say, but I know Robert's oar is doing the heavy work.

"I dreamed of a shipwreck," I say to Robert, to counterpoint the dreamlike scene. "You and I helped the skipper of the rescue boat to pick up corpses."

Robert grunts. "Sounds good. Save it for later."

I glance at my watch. It is six-fifteen. The mist is still rising, our strokes have become regular, and I have the impression that time has stopped and we will be on this shrouded lake forever, paddling behind Chan K'in.

"Robert!" I shout. "Is this what Metlán is like?"

"What is Metlán?" Diana asks.

He answers me first. "I don't know," he says. "I've not yet visited that particular hell."

"Oh Dadd-y," Diana reproaches him mildly, and asks again, "What is Metlán, Daddy?"

"Have patience, Chan Puk," he says, breathing heavily, and his tender rebuke calms me as well, as if I were his older son. "Metlán is the Lacandon hell, where the souls of evildoers are punished. It's pretty much like our hell, except that the punishments are more logical, and Kisin has ice water for the souls who are burned there —"

"You mean Kisin is good to them?" Diana interrupts.

"You think so? Wait until you hear the rest. The soul has to reach the underworld with the help of the soul of his best and most faithful hunting dog. If he was mean to his dog, then it is harder for him, because his dog won't want to help him across. So a man's dog is the first to judge him after death —"

"What about a woman? Does she have her own hunting dog's soul to guide her?"

"Well, Chan Puk . . ." — Robert rubs the back of his head, momentarily stumped. "In a woman's case, the dog has functioned as a watchdog — The process is essentially the same. If the man or woman has been good to the dog when he was alive, he will lead the soul to the house of Sukunkyum, in the beautiful forests of the underworld."

"Beautiful? Didn't you say Metlán is hell? Is hell beautiful?" Diana is always on the alert for logical inconsistencies.

"Not all of it, Chan Puk. Metlán is Kisin's part of the underworld. Sukunkyum's part has beautiful forests full of the souls of the animals that live and die on earth."

"What happens then?" Diana asks, in a softer voice.

"Well, it depends. If you've slept with a close relative Kisin takes hold of you and burns your urethra with hot irons. If you lied he puts a hot iron in your mouth, and if you stole he burns your hand. Your soul is then boiled down in a cauldron, and you return to earth demoted to a lower animal, such as a parrot or a coatimundi. It is all worked out with a certain logic. For instance, if you were a lazy man, you get turned into a dog; if you were selfish you come back as a pig, and if you were cruel or brutal you return as a mule. Now if you have murdered somebody Kisin will first freeze your soul in his ice chamber and then boil it down until it disappears altogether. You simply cease to exist."

"What about brave people?" Diana asks.

"Well, the valiant souls go up to Hachäkyum's heaven, where they consort with the souls of eagles, tigers and the big snakes. If you've been reasonably good, by Lacandon standards, you stay below as the guest of Sukunkyum, who is a very hospitable and decent fellow. But he has to approve you first, and Sukunkyum is no fool; nothing escapes his notice. When the dead man's soul comes to his house, Sukunkyum gives him a sharp look and he sees exactly what kind of person he has been, and what deeds he has committed." Robert grins gently. "I promise you, Chan Puk, compared to Old Sukunkyum, Saint Peter is just an amateur psychologist."

"Robert," I ask, "is there a special place for suicides?"

"Sukunkyum is in charge of those," he answers, with a half smile. "He ties them up and leaves them by his doorpost for a time, so they can reflect on their rashness. Periodically he will beat them with a stick and berate them: 'So you didn't want to live in the forest? You thought it would be better down here?' *Whack.* 'Now you know what it's like.' Eventually he will release them and relegate them to their fate, according to their previous merits or transgressions.

"If you look closely through the mist, Chan Puk," Robert counsels, "you might catch a glimpse of Sukunkyum carrying the sun on his back. He has kept it in his house all night, feeding it minnows and squash seeds and keeping it warm, and now it is nearly time to set it up again, up on that hilltop there — can you see, Chan Puk?" He points with his chin at a faint silhouette in the mist.

"What about Kisin?" I ask him. "What's he been up to?"

"Judging from your dreams," Robert laughs, "he's had a busy night. His time is up, though. Old T'uup is taking over now, to guide the sun through its daily course."

Minutes after, the first roseate wisps appear on the hilltop, through the thinning mist.

We reach the other shore and watch Chan K'in's canoe disappear into a narrow channel banked by tall reeds and sword grass. Robert maneuvers us into the mouth of the channel.

"You'll have to do some poling here," he says. "Push off against the roots of those reeds — and watch out for the sword grass. Their edges cut like a knife." We alternately paddle and pole along the winding channel, which is choked in places with lily pads. Once more, Robert does most of the work, guiding the boat from the stern while Diana and I push off against roots and clumps of grass. A single blade whisks my arm, and nicks the skin like a razor, drawing blood. I pull down my sweatshirt sleeves.

We emerge into a lovely small lake, which I recognize from K'ayum's painting in Na-Bolom.

"K'ayum really caught the feeling of this," I say, surveying the thick carpet of green, white and yellow lily pads, and the bands of color reflecting the shoreline.

"He missed the alligators," Robert says. "Used to be some big ones here. Now they're all hunted out."

Ahead of us, Chan K'in's canoe has entered a smaller channel and docked. Little Chan K'in is looking at us, while the elders wade through the marsh with their loads. The brown-haired bitch yelps from our prow, jumps in and swims after her mate.

I cannot shake off the sensation of dream.

We dock behind Chan K'in's *cayuco* and tie ours to a sturdy clump of reeds. I take off my boots, roll up my jeans, and wade in up to my knees. The bottom is soft and churns up silt. I worry about leeches, although Robert assures me they are not found at this altitude. After thirty yards or so we climb up on hard ground. The path leads through dense foliage and tall trees that form an intricate lacework above us. Suddenly there are huge butterflies everywhere, with brilliant, iridescent colors. I hear birdsong I've not heard in Nahá before.

"When you come to the clearing, keep a sharp eye out for game," cautions Robert, who has brought his .38 pistol.

I am enjoying the feel of hard soil under my toes, and the clusters of pink bromeliads and other bright flowers in the greenery; my watchful eye is keener for snakes than for deer or paca.

We turn right along the well-blazed trail and suddenly the sky opens overhead; we are in the *milpa* — an expanse of tall, yellowed cornstalks that is as wide around as the lily-pad lake, and no less breathtaking. Above the distant ridge the sun has just begun its ascent, a burnished wheel shooting spokes in all directions.

Chan K'in, little Chan K'in and the two Kohs await us by a large hut in the exact center of the cornfield. They have unloaded their gear in this storage shed, which is stacked high with row upon row of large, ripe corn; the husks cast a golden glow on little Chan K'in's face.

"Maize upon maize," I think at once, recalling the Third Creation in the *Popol Vuh.*

Chan K'in and the two Kohs set to work, without a word or wasted motion. The women pick the ripe corn from the stalks and toss them into a central pile. The dry, emptied stalks are uprooted and heaped on a separate pile, and then set on fire. Chan K'in clears the overgrown weeds and grass with his outsize machete.

"Chan K'in," I ask, "what will you do after you clear the field?"

"Plant tobacco," he says, without missing a stroke.

"And after that?"

"Plant corn again." The storyteller is a man of few words now; he is all business.

"And then tobacco again?"

He nods, without looking up.

"How many times?" I ask, following his crabwise movements.

"Three or four."

"And then?"

He pauses to wipe sweat from his forehead with his gnarled hand. It is astonishing that he can clutch the large machete at all with this twisted hand, much less swing it with such authority.

"After that we clear another *milpa*," he says, "and let this one recover."

"You mean you burn out a clearing in the forest?"

"*Eh hah*," he nods, "or we return to an old one that has recovered. After some years we'll come back to this one, when the new growth has replenished it." He bends down and picks up a handful of thin soil, speckled with limestone.

"See? This one is worn out." He rubs the dark moist earth in his hands until only the white granules and gray sediment remain. "We will have to let it rest a few years, and then it will be as good as new."

So this is slash and burn. Slash and burn. The abstraction reduced to a simple formula. For so many years I'd heard of slash and burn as the archenemy, devouring the pristine forest, turning it to stump and black, ashen soil. Here, it no longer seems so malevolent. It would take centuries of this practice, on the Lacandon scale, to significantly reduce the forest's hardwood trees — and by then, abandoned *milpas* would have had a chance to recover. A Lacandon family only needs three *milpa* sites, each of which is cultivated full-time only two years, and is then used one more year for harvesting root crops and tubers like onions and sweet potatoes. The full cultivation then shifts to a second site, and then to a third. By the seventh year, the first site is heavily overgrown with second-growth forest and the cycle may run again, and again, and again. No, slash and burn is not the enemy. It becomes destructive when inexperienced colonists move in by the thousands and raze the forest indiscriminately. Overpopulation is the enemy. Hunger is the enemy. Greed is the enemy. It is not the method that is at fault, but its uncontrolled abuse. The miracle is that the Lacandones can wrest corn at all from this thin forest soil, pitted with limestone. And what corn!

I return to the shed, drawn there by the golden reddish glow of its treasure. Once again I feel the warm radiation on my face, as if each ear of corn burned from within and cast a living corolla. They are stacked high but very neatly, to form a wide bed. And I remember that it is precisely in these sheds, on top of these beds of maize, that the men and women of Nahá couple and procreate. When Chan K'in wishes to have another child, he brings the wife of his choice to the *milpa* and in late morning, during a break in the work routine, they lie on the bed of maize to refresh themselves and make love.

The Lacandones believe that Hachäkyum and his consort made men and women of clay and sand, and that only their teeth are corn kernels. But the Quiché-Maya *Popol Vuh*, which draws from the fount of all Mayan creation legends, records three separate attempts by the Heart of Heaven to create men. First came the men of mud, who could not move properly to reproduce themselves or sing the praises of the Creator. The men of mud melted in front of their fires and were pulled apart by the heavy rains. Next came the men of wood, who were slender and tall, and looked much like the men of today. The men of wood were capable but soulless. They hunted with dogs and worked the fields, built sturdy huts and made utensils. But their wooden legs were stiff and would not allow them to kneel and offer incense to the gods. They did not pray to the gods

179

from their hearts because they had none. "They had sons and daughters, and soon were everywhere on the earth. But the men of wood did not have souls or minds, and they wandered aimlessly. When they spoke, their faces were blank, their hands and feet were weak. They were without blood's flower, with no moisture, no flesh, dry and yellow, and they no longer remembered Heart of Heaven."

The gods were displeased, and loosed a deluge on the men of wood. Eagles, jaguars, tapirs were sent to gouge out their eyes and mangle their bones. Black rain fell day and night. In the end, even their domestic animals and their pots and pans rebelled against the soulless men of wood. " 'You have eaten us, and now we shall eat you,' said the birds and the dogs that were kept to be eaten. The grinding stones spoke in rage: 'What torture you caused us! Crush, crush, dawn and dusk our faces went crush, crush!' " And now that they were not men any longer, the grinding stones crushed their faces. Even the faithful hunting dogs who had been ill fed and ill treated leaped on the wooden men and tore out their faces.

When the men of wood had been destroyed, the few survivors became the forest's monkeys.

The true men, the men of corn, came later, after the gods had played out their own dramas on the new-made earth, and after the immortal twins, Hunahpú and Ixbalanqué, rid the earth of impostors and evil giants; they challenged the lords of the underworld and outwitted them step by step, and then defeated them, thereby avenging the death of their father. The twins, who were the sun and the morning star, joined their four hundred companion stars in the heavens, where they were given the moon. Now there was light on earth for the first time, and the stage was set for the true men.

In preparation for the third creation the gods again consulted their divining beans and corn kernels. They elected four animals — the jaguar, coyote, parrot and crow — to gather the sacred maize. "Thus they discovered food, and this it was that entered into the flesh of man incarnate, of man made man. This was his blood. Of this was man's blood made."

In both the *Popul Vuh* and in Chan K'in's account, the first "true" men were intelligent and farsighted, and could contemplate all heaven and earth. They could even see the gods coupling and going about their affairs. They were thankful to their creators, and sang their praises.

This pleased the creators, but they were suspicious of their creatures' farsightedness and feared they might become arrogant with ambition one day and challenge their power. Hachäkyum took out his creatures' eyes and burned them in a hot earthen pan until they were opaque. Now the true men could no longer see the heavens and the gods making love, but the memory of their vision remained among those who continued to observe the rituals and give thank offerings to their creators.

Robert and Diana enter the shed where I sit with my notes and reveries; they carry netloads of corn, which they empty at the back door to prepare for sorting. The scrawny and worm-eaten ears will feed the animals, the rest will be stacked for future use. Little Chan K'in comes in with a huge load almost his own size, which he empties with masculine grunts and shoulder flexings.

"I am strong," he says softly, widening his eyes at me. It is a wholly different tone from the one he uses when flexing the slingshot at small birds. "I am a man."

"Why don't you help us, Uncle?" Diana calls. "It's good for you."

I spend the next hour helping the two Kohs pick the last of the ripe corn. We spread out in widening circles and toss the heavy ears into a common pile. The corn is so ready that most ears drop into my hand without my having to yank or twist. Of the three of us, Koh II is the fastest and most accurate. She has a pitcher's arm, and chucks one ear after another in a high looping arc, dead in the center of the pile.

Chan K'in interrupts his work to warn me against wandering from the cleared area.

"Many snakes in the underbrush," he says. "Here in the *milpa* is where they are most dangerous."

I take Chan K'in's warning to heart and lie down for a rest beside the bonfire pit, which is black with burned husks and stalks. The odor of corn ash is as pungent as the smell of fresh loam in the moist earth, still soaked from the rains. Scallion and cherry-tomato vines grow in a small orchard next to me, which is bordered with charred tree trunks. From farther off, the scents of mint, verdolaga and other herbs waft in and out on a passing breeze.

I take a deep breath. In this dream setting, I have never felt more awake. (And I know there will be a price to pay, in my other life, for this wakefulness, this fullness.)

A toucan flies overhead, its long beak sticking out like an ax handle: three strokes, glide; three strokes, glide. In the distant trees that ring the *milpa* I can see a gray hornbill hopping from branch to branch. A redheaded woodpecker beats its tattoo on a half-charred tree. The birdsong is continuous, an unbroken polyphony of calls, trills, whistles. Nowhere in the high forest, during my morning's hunt with K'in Bor, did I hear such an abundance of melodious sound. Fecundity permeates the very air here, as it fills María Bonita's small, crowded hut.

Here also I feel the extraordinary presence I've experienced in the godhouse and in Koh's kitchen: the sense of a place that is part of and yet transcends its physical space — the place where Chan K'in tells his stories; the place where he burns incense to his gods; the place where Koh weaves and makes tortillas.

This too is a place: a place of planting and harvesting, of procreation and sudden death, a place nurtured in the eternal cycles of birth, decay and renewal. All at once I know as certainly as I know anything in this life that this place has a bedrock, an invisible infrastructure which Chan K'in, the man of seeds and roots and dream-cores has always understood.

The forest, the *milpa,* even the stories, may be destroyed, for they are the transitory forms; but this infrastructure that Chan K'in has made manifest in his stories will withstand the ravages of time and of his fellowmen. He knows that our world provides the outer forms, the connecting links; the enduring home is elsewhere, in another heaven, whose reflection lives within us all.

Chan K'in, 1977
(V. P.)

Young Chan K'in and Old Mateo in the godhouse, 1978
(V. P.)

K'ayum carrying a balché pot to the god-house, 1978
(V. P.)

(left to right) Nuxi' (Old Mateo's son-in-law), Chan K'in and K'in García, 1978
(V. P.)

Geneviève Buot, "la doctora"
(V. P.)

Trudi Blom
(V. P.)

K'ayum, 1978
(V. P.)

K'ayum's front door, 1981
(V. P.)

María Bonita and her two young husbands, 1978
(V. P.)

Perera, a foreign laborer in the milpa
(DIANA LYNN BRUCE)

Little K'in ("Hans") at the Temple of the Cross, Palenque, 1979
(V. P.)

Young Bol by the roadside with felled mahogany, 1979
(V. P.)

Watching el tractor pass, 1979
(V. P.)

Domingo, his wife Nuk and Victor, 1979
(V. P.)

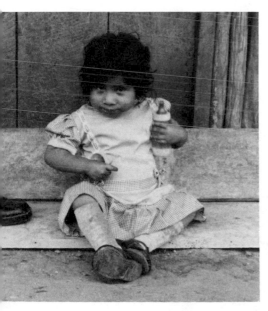

K'ayum's daughter Chankina, 1981
(V. P.)

Little Bol, deaf-mute son of Chan K'in and
Koh III, 1981
(V. P.)

Paco, Nuk of the twisted jaw and their daughter Chan Nuk, 1981
(V. P.)

K'ayum (right) and his son Mario (now also called K'ayum), 1981
(V. P.)

Juan José and his wife Margarita, the daughter of Young Mateo
(VIRGINIA RISSE)

Part 3.

Return to Nahá

My third visit to Nahá came as a direct result of a letter from Robert, dated December 14, 1978: "Bad news, the worst I fear. They have already cut the marked mahogany at Nahá leaving only 60 (according to Young Mateo) and 40 (according to Trudi) mahoganies for *cayucos*." The letter went on to say that the government logging road was now just five or six miles from Nahá, and would probably be completed by the New Year. Robert and Diana Lynn would visit Nahá over the Christmas holidays, to assess the damage, and Robert's wife, Alicia, planned to accompany them for the first time, despite her arachniphobia.

The following day I reached Trudi in San Cristóbal, and she confirmed the felling of the mahogany by the Mexican Forestry Department, even before the road had been completed. We had a poor connection, and I heard her say that Young Chan K'in had died of encephalitis at Na-Bolom, several days back.

"There was nothing to be done!" she shouted over the phone. "The government was determined to cut the mahogany, with or without Old Chan K'in's permission! . . . Yes, yes, your presence here will help in deciding the future for these people — but you'd better get here soon!" She added that she would soon leave for Switzerland, for a delicate operation on her eyes.

I had planned a brief visit to Nahá early in the year, in conjunction with a long-projected raft trip down the Usumacinta River. I canceled the raft trip and arrived in Mexico City on February 11.

Robert met me at the airport with the news that we would be able to drive all the way to Nahá in the VW Safari, as the road from Palenque and Chancalá had been completed.

Robert, who looked tired and cast down but not nearly as worn out as I'd feared, also informed me that it was not Young Chan K'in but his wife,

Koh, who had died of encephalitis, after developing an abscess in her right foot.

"Keep in mind, little brother, that the divination called for *all* of Chan K'in's sons to be present for the next *xu'tan* [end of the world], on or about 2008."

"How has he taken Koh's death?" I asked.

"Pretty well, apparently. Trudi says he has already taken up with Koh's younger sister Juanita, although they can't be formally married until a year after Koh's death." He paused. "A curious thing happened. Koh was of the Wild Boar lineage, and a band of one hundred or so collared peccary showed up in Nahá on the day she died, by the edge of the new airstrip. As you know, boar had not been seen around Nahá for at least ten years. They provided an unexpected if somewhat spooky bonanza, as K'in García and another hunter shot six of them. Some villagers seem to think it was Koh's parting gift to the community."

Pepe Pinto

The following morning Robert called me excitedly at the Polanco Hotel to say K'aýum was in Mexico City. He had arrived unexpectedly with a Lacandon delegation, to speak with President López Portillo about the felling of the mahogany.

"The Katzenjammer Kids came with him, along with Antonio's son, Chan K'in. K'in Yuk Bats' of Lacanjá also came with his family, to represent the southern group."

Amazed by their audacity, I asked, "Did they come on their own?"

"They were brought by Pepe Pinto, an anthropologist from Chiapas who has interceded for them in the past. He has government connections and a real flair for public relations. He brought little K'in and Chan K'in along to get some mileage out of the International Year of the Child."

Robert suggested I look up the morning newspaper *Universal*, and said he would call me again as soon as he heard from K'ayum.

The front page of the *Universal* carried K'ayum's request to speak with President López Portillo. Pepe Pinto, who was serving as spokesman for the group, claimed their forest was being despoiled, and they had received only crumbs in compensation for their mahogany. The story was well done, with an appealing human-interest angle, and suggested a good deal of support for the Lacandones by the press and the reading public of Mexico City.

In the afternoon Robert called again to say that a message from K'ayum had been sitting on his desk when he arrived at the museum. They were staying at the Hotel Gillow, near the Zócalo. He picked me up after work and we drove downtown through the choking commuter traffic.

"Who the hell *is* Pepe Pinto?" I asked, as we sat out a twenty-minute bottleneck on La Reforma.

"I don't really know. He's an enigmatic figure. He calls himself an anthropologist but seems to have no accreditation anywhere."

"How did he raise the cash to bring them here?"

"I think it's his own money. For as long as I can remember, the Pinto family was one of the wealthiest in Comitán. In Mexico, it is extremely bad taste to ask how wealthy families got that way."

"Are you suggesting he's acting on a guilty conscience?"

"Who can say? Let's just call him a philanthropist friend of the Lacandones and leave it at that, for now. I must say I admire his courage for bringing them here."

As we entered the main lobby of the hotel we saw them sitting in the rear of the dining room, watching us. K'ayum was the first to greet us, with a firm occidental handshake and a huge boyish grin. He did not seem particularly surprised to see us, or pretended not to be. Hans and Fritz smiled in unison, wan and a little dazed. They all seemed dwarfed by the huge dining room; the two boys were all but swallowed by their plush leather chairs.

"So, you have come!" Robert said in Maya, reversing the greeting he customarily receives in Nahá.

"As you can see," K'ayum said, simply. He added that his father is well, after recovering from a bad cold — but he is still sad over the death of Young Chan K'in's wife.

"And the trees?" I asked.

"Well, they've cut them, but they left some at the other side of the lake. I kept two big ones, for my new house."

"And the road?" Robert asked. "Is it true it's completed?"

"*Muchos tractores*," K'ayum said, switching to Spanish for my benefit. "Too many tractors, and trucks with Tzeltales. The road goes right past my new house, so I'll have to move it, I suppose." He shrugged, crossing his right hand over his left arm. "And it goes over the new airstrip on the other side."

Robert had told me of the new airstrip on the south shore, which had diverted most of the air traffic from Jorge's side of the lake. They had blazed it out of the forest and leveled it in jig time, using a "bulldozer" consisting of a thick mahogany board blade, powered by six or eight men pulling a rope guided by poles attached to the back. The pilots had told Robert it was the finest airstrip in the Lacandon jungle.

"And you, K'in, what brings you to Mexico City?" I asked K'in Yuk of Lacanjá, who had waited patiently while we greeted the Nahá contingent. He was the only one in western slacks and shirt, and his hair was cut at the nape, but his two sons wore tunics.

"I also want to speak with the President," he said, "because Carmelo and José Pepe are keeping all the money to themselves, and my family is hungry."

Robert and I nodded in sympathy with K'in Yuk's predicament: a southern Lacandon with no representation in Lacanjá.

"I only want a little justice for my family and myself," he added, in perfect Spanish, "and we plan to stay until we are heard out."

"We all met in Tenosique," K'ayum said. "Carmelo and José Pepe came to the airstrip and tried to prevent K'in Yuk from leaving with us. As we got on the bus Carmelo shouted, 'Do not come back, unless you bring one million pesos from the President.' "

"I'm not afraid of them," K'in Yuk said, shrugging one shoulder. "They talk big and make threats, but they are cowards at heart — especially Carmelo." He pointed to his temple and screwed up one eye. "I know them."

K'ayum sat between Robert and me and gave us the rest of the news. His Spanish was more fluent now, and he spoke with a new authority, although he still mixed up his genders and tenses. He was delighted when I asked him several questions in *hax t'an,* not suspecting that I had rehearsed them in the car.

He told us that he and Margarita had had a daughter, nicknamed Chankina, who looked exactly like her grandfather. Young Chan K'in's wife had also given birth — to a boy — several months before she died. "Her younger sister Juanita is looking after the baby," K'ayum said.

"You mean the *güera?*" Robert said, alluding to her ultralight pigmentation. Juanita is one of José Güero's two albino daughters.

"Yes, the older one," K'ayum said. "They will get married when the mourning period is over. I think it is good, it's a good thing so he won't be alone and sad — and she is already cooking for him, although they do not sleep together."

"How is K'in Bor?" I asked. Robert had mentioned that K'in Bor had moved to his father's side of the lake, after a heavy-drinking incident.

"*Ah, muy triste* — very sad," K'ayum said. The color drained from his face, and his eyes clouded. "K'in Bor is not the same since the loggers

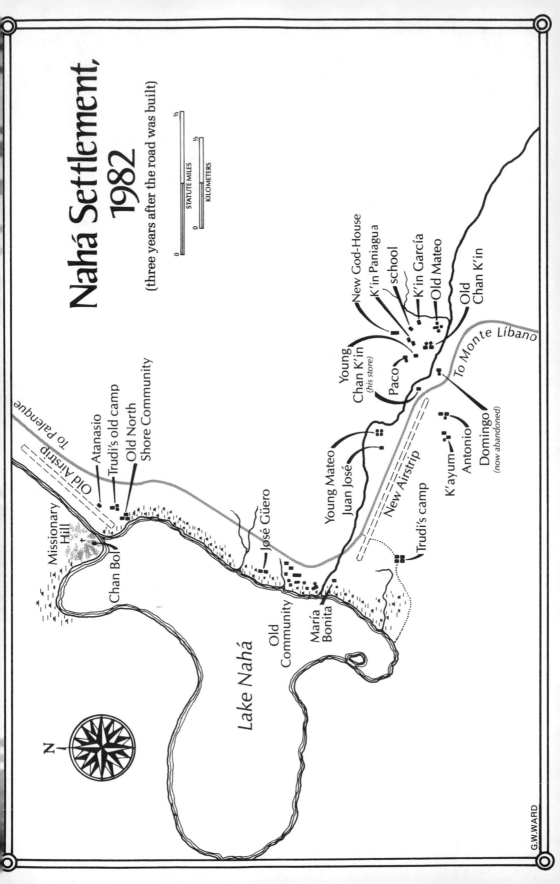

Nahá Settlement, 1982

(three years after the road was built)

STATUTE MILES

KILOMETERS

New God-House
K'in Paniagua
school
K'in García
Old Mateo
Old Chan K'in
Young Chan K'in
(his store)
Paco
To Monte Líbano

Atanasio
Trudi's old camp
Old North Shore Community

To Palenque
Old Airstrip

Missionary Hill

Chan Bol

Young Mateo
Juan José
New Airstrip
Trudi's camp
K'ayum
Antonio
Domingo
(now abandoned)

José Güero

Old Community

María Bonita

Lake Nahá

N

G.W. WARD

came. He drinks with them and gets into fights — even with machetes. One night he drank a lot of rum with the Tzeltal loggers. He got very drunk and beat up his wife, who is my sister Nuk. He threatened to kill us all with a gun, so Nuxi', Antonio and my brother Chan K'in had to tie him up to the doorpost of his house. We stayed up all night, watching K'in Bor so he would not hurt himself. He said terrible things, talking just like a *ladino.* It made me sad to hear him yell and shout profanities because I knew he was not himself — it is only the Tzeltal liquor that makes him that way. In the morning we untied him, but my brother as president fined him one thousand pesos for beating up his wife. That made K'in Bor angry, and the next day he moved to the other side, near his father, Jorge."

"And your sister Nuk?" I asked.

"She goes with him. She likes it there. Nuk and Chan K'in Chico's wife, Margarita, both had children this year, two boys almost the same age. They are together all the time."

"What a miracle, *amigo* Roberto!" A well-groomed, sturdy, middle-aged man walked in smartly from the lobby and gave Robert a Mexican bear hug.

Robert introduced me to Pepe Pinto, who ordered a round of drinks and invited us to dinner.

"How good to find you here," Pepe went on, addressing Robert as *"amigo,"* although they had met only casually. "Now we can work together to assure that these sons of the Mayan earth secure an audience with the President so they can present their just cause."

"Er — yes — of course," Robert said, taken aback.

"Working hand in hand, with your reputation and my humble persistence, we will triumph over all obstacles." Pepe lavished praise on Robert's "justly renowned" books and his "widely noted" contributions to the Lacandon cause. "And tomorrow morning you and your colleague will join us for an interview with *Excelsior,* and K'ayum, the princely heir of Nahá, and Professor K'in Yuk Bats' will air their grievances before the press."

"Most assuredly," Robert said, moving us from confusion to commitment.

The children retired to their room for a nap and the rest of us moved to the bar, where Pepe Pinto described the circumstances in which he received "the call" to shepherd the Lacandones to Mexico City, and how he overcame adversity and vanquished opponents. He is a mystical adventurer and a raconteur of a breed peculiar to Chiapas, where the Spanish colonial influence has lingered longer than in the rest of Mexico. Although he is of Spanish descent, Pepe called himself a "brother-Maya" to K'ayum and K'in Yuk.

Pepe turned to Robert and me and stage-whispered, "We will have to find some way to help K'in Yuk and his family. I fear that if he goes back, Carmelo's satraps may try to kill him."

This struck me as implausible and melodramatic, but no matter. I enjoyed Pepe's verbal play and quixotic flamboyance. As foreign nationals, neither Robert nor I had been in a position to bring off the Lacandones' urgent expedition to Mexico City. Now they were here, Robert and I determined to give them and Pepe all our support.

K'ayum, Antonio's son Chan K'in, K'in Yuk, Robert and I accompanied Don Pepe in second, third and fourth rounds of drinks, which he insisted on paying for. Every ten or fifteen minutes the headwaiter would bring Pepe the telephone, and a confidential but clearly audible conversation ensued with a government official or a well-placed acquaintance.

"By tomorrow morning," Pepe assured us, "we shall know if President López Portillo will grant us an audience, or whether we have to take our case to the people."

By "the people," I soon discovered, he meant more newspapers and the TV networks, where he also had connections.

At this juncture Chelena Traven, the widow of the German expatriate writer B. Traven, arrived. She was accompanied by a German TV reporter named Gerard Wenziner, who was doing a documentary on Traven's life. We introduced them to Pepe, who bowed from the waist and kissed Mrs. Traven's hand.

"It is a signal honor to meet the beautiful widow of the illustrious Traven," he said in Spanish, lisping his c's and z's like a Castilian courtier. "Although I did not know your husband personally, I have read his books, and consider him to have been a true friend of the Maya — and of Mexico. . . . Will you and your companion join us for a drink?"

"I'll be delighted to," Mrs. Traven said, smiling indulgently.

Pepe was somewhat cooler toward Gerard, who refused to go along with the protocol, but he consented to allow the children to be filmed in Mrs. Traven's house.

Chelena Traven is indeed a beautiful widow in her late fifties, and a jealous custodian of her late husband's literary estate. Traven was well advanced in years when they married, and she took over the management of his career, for he cared little about the business end of writing and courted anonymity to the very end of his life. The day I met her, with the prospect of collaborating on Traven's biography, she had confided, "Traven always insisted that he cared nothing for money, children or fame — and I'm afraid I conspired in providing him with all three."

She sat down between Robert and me and inquired aloud, "Who is this charming rake? I've not met his like in twenty years." Chelena had been brought up in Mérida, and was well acquainted with Pepe's courtly rhetoric, although they do not move in the same circles.

"José Pintado Meneses," Robert said. "He is an anthropologist and a friend of the Lacandones."

"Allow me to correct you, amigo Roberto." Pepe raised his glass stiffly. "A friend of the Lacandones, yes — for as long as I live — but call me rather an antropófago, a primitive savage disguised in these paltry contemporary rags."

K'ayum hooted aloud and we all laughed softly, except for Gerard, an Old Mexico Hand who does not mince words. "And may I ask how you funded this little expedition? Entirely by yourself?"

Pepe drew in his stomach and stuck out his chin, like a bantam cock. "Since you ask so forthrightly, my German friend, I will inform you that yes, I have provided the funds for this 'expedition' with some of the money that should rightly have been theirs, but had to be diverted through other channels." He stubbed out his cigarette, and squinted at Gerard. "Even stranger enterprises, I can assure you, have been financed by the cruelly despoiled wealth of our Lacandon forest. And that is all I wish to say on this matter," he concluded loftily, as the headwaiter brought him the telephone with a call from the President's secretary.

In the evening K'in Yuk and his family and the Katzenjammer Kids went off in Gerard's van to do some filming at Chelena's house. Robert and I accompanied K'ayum to buy some cloth for Margarita and provisions for the trip to Nahá. K'ayum, Chan K'in and the Kids had agreed to return with us, once their interviews were over.

K'ayum negotiated the crowded downtown streets far better than I had negotiated the forest trails. He pretended not to notice the passersby who stopped to gawk at him, and seemed more impressed by the zombielike mannequins in the store windows.

"I saw you in *Cascabel*," an older woman stopped to tell K'ayum. "May I have your autograph?"

K'ayum smiled and signed her scrap of paper as if he were a movie star.

"How do you like our city?" she asked him.

"*Muy bonita* — very pretty," he said diplomatically.

"Oh no, it's polluted and filthy. You should return to your home in the forest. This city is unfit for humans."

"Thank you kindly." K'ayum grinned affably, returning her scrap of paper.

During their stay dozens of people came up to K'ayum and the children to extend their good wishes, always with an undercurrent of personal loss and rueful envy. It seemed pointless to inform them that the Elysian forest they envisioned was being destroyed by their own government agencies.

After our shopping we took K'ayum to an excellent restaurant which specializes in traditional Mexican dishes.

"Yes, it is very good," K'ayum agreed with a sigh, after consuming a superb *mole poblano*. "But I long for roast parrot. When I return, the first thing I will do is take out my rifle and go hunt parrot, so Margarita can cook it with rice."

The following day we visited the offices of *Excelsior* and had our pictures taken with the group. It appeared in the next morning's edition under the caption: "Lacandon children visit Mexico City on the occasion of the International Year of the Child." An accompanying blurb quoted

Pepe's claim that the Forestry Department was continuing to remove hardwood trees from the Lacandon forest, and that the Nahá group was receiving only a fraction of the millions of pesos owed them.

When the interviewer asked K'ayum how he felt about the felling of the trees, he answered circumspectly, "We are thinking about the meaning of it," and pointed to his temple. Before he could elaborate, Pepe jumped in to finish K'ayum's reply, and then answered all of the interviewer's remaining questions.

In the afternoon they all appeared on the educational TV station, and the President's office called to arrange a brief audience with K'ayum for the following morning.

When I stopped by the hotel, Pepe was in an expansive mood, and we chatted and drank vodka-and-tonics late into the night. By midnight, K'ayum and Chan K'in had retired, and Pepe rambled on about the hidden mystical powers in the Mayan pyramids. He referred to all the great discoverers and geniuses of our time, including Albert Einstein, as "crypto-Mayas." To Pepe, the world is divided into Maya and anti-Maya, with all the arts and sciences marshaled on one side, and the industrial/military world on the other. He spoke of his mission with a messianic fervor:

"If one man can move a mountain and obtain an audience with the President for these neglected princes, two of us working together can change a country, and three can alter the face of the earth. Why, just look at Buddha, Christ and Mohammed!"

Pepe insisted on picking up all the tabs once again, hinting there was a good deal more in reserve. He spoke of his deceased wife, an Aries like himself, who belonged to a wealthy Comitán ranching family and had been extravagant in spending for worthy causes. "I am certain of her unreserved support for this adventure, from the other side of the grave."

When I finally got up to leave at around two A.M., he asked me a curious favor: Would I telephone K'ayum at dawn and say I was Colonel So-and-so of the Presidential Guard, calling to remind him of his appointment?

"A small favor, but it means a good deal to me," he said, squeezing my hand. "And I know K'ayum will appreciate it."

As I weaved home through the deserted streets, it dawned on me that I had consented to tell K'ayum a barefaced lie for the first time in our acquaintance.

"Colonel who?" K'ayum asked foggily, more asleep than awake.

"Colonel Garvas," I repeated into the telephone, which I'd muzzled with a towel.

"All right, Colonel Garvas, thank you — I'll be there on time."

I called again at noon, to verify that he had left for his appointment. Little K'in answered the phone.

"This is Victor," I said. "I am calling from far way, at the other end of the city."

"Yes, I know," K'in said. "K'ayum has not come back yet. He went to see the President." His voice was crisp and clear.

"All right, *bin in kah,*" I said, using the Lacandon formal parting.

"Xen!" he replied firmly, and hung up.

Only later, when I saw them accepting the images on the television screen with equal aplomb, did I stop to consider that little K'in's familiarity with the telephone had not been all that unusual after all; he quite likely regarded it as the occidental counterpart of a form of communication he took for granted in the forest. And like any imaginative child, K'in could go to the heart of a complicated gadget and figure out its operating principle.

What really impressed the children was the hotel elevator, which seemed to rise and fall with a will of its own, and a head-on collision they witnessed on La Reforma, between a van and a bus. "They went *puch'!*" — K'in said the phrase over and over, sending a fist into his palm — "and their noses went flat." Each retelling was accompanied by delirious giggling.

K'ayum obtained his audience with President López Portillo, who recognized him from the film *Cascabel.*

"I went through the corridor," K'ayum said, "pushing my way up and up. There were many people waiting but I pushed my way through and said to the President, 'I wish to speak to you.' The President embraced me and said he knew who I was. Then he took me into his office and shut the door. 'They are cutting our trees,' I said to the President, 'and we don't have any money. We are being robbed.' 'Yes,' he said, 'I have been told.' And then he said, 'I will do all I can to help you.' I liked the President," K'ayum concluded. "He has good eyes."

In private, Pepe, who looked worn and exhausted at last, confided that López Portillo had snapped at him after the interview, "I recognize the problem; don't make waves." The President left little doubt that by "waves" he meant the newspaper interviews and the appearance on TV.

With the presidential audience over there was no reason for K'ayum, Chan K'in and the Kids to stick around Mexico City, so we decided to leave the following day for Nahá. K'in Yuk and his family planned to stay on a few days longer, while Pepe set up an interview with the President's wife. Understandably, K'in Yuk was in no hurry to return to Lacanjá.

Pepe Pinto had shot his bolt, and his forward drive was apparently spent. The bantam-cock strut gave way to a muted, fat-cat aura of fulfillment.

Journey to Nahá

"I like Pepe Pinto," K'ayum said the following morning, as the six of us set out on the Puebla expressway, crammed snugly into Robert's Safari. "He is a good man, but he treats me like a small boy — and sometimes he says one thing and does another."

"Yes," I agreed, "and he asks others to do the same." I imitated my "Colonel Garvas" reveille from the "Presidential Palace."

K'ayum laughed. "I recognized your voice, but I didn't say anything. I knew it had to be Pepe who asked you to call me. In Mexico you are nobody unless you call yourself Colonel So-and-so or Licenciado So-and-so . . .

"But Colonel Garvas does not know how to lie," K'ayum added. "He is a bad liar, and President López Portillo will have to dismiss him and hire Licenciado K'ayum to make his calls."

"Professor K'in," said Hans, giggling and patting his own curly head. He liked the sound so much he repeated it off and on the rest of the day.

Tuxtepec

We stopped for the night at a hotel in Tuxtepec, a lowland outpost midway between Mexico City and Palenque. The drop in altitude and the balmy tropical air loosened us up. In an outdoor cafe, K'ayum told of his recent dreams, which abounded with heavy machinery, fallen trees and streams that dry up. The night before, he dreamed that a tractor had run over his son Mario, and he had become very sad. He interpreted this to mean that a spider monkey may have been killed by the loggers at Nahá. "I saw them shoot one just before I left," he said.

After supper we took them to see *Hell on Wheels* in the rundown cinema across the street. It was Hans and Fritz's first movie, and they became wholly engrossed in the cops-and-truckers chases that ended in spectacular pile-ups. They squealed loudest when the blond, blue-eyed hero rammed his two-ton rig into the retaining wall of the mob's headquarters and blew himself up in a splintering climax.

"Muy bonita," they concurred afterward, nodding their heads in unison.

After the Kids went to bed we sat in the hotel restaurant with K'ayum and Antonio's son and ordered pineapple screwdrivers. Chan K'in, a handsome and soft-spoken young man of sixteen who had recently celebrated his *meek'chäl,* livened up after two drinks and took part in the customary banter, sparked by K'ayum.

"When are you going to get married again, Victor?" he asked, in a half-serious, half-teasing tone.

"I don't know," I said. "Can you dream me up a bride?"

Chan K'in whispered into K'ayum's ear, and he nodded approvingly.

"Ah, of course! Chan K'in says you can marry his sister. She is just right for you."

"How old is she, Chan K'in?" I asked, feigning interest.

He shrugged. "Fourteen or fifteen, perhaps. But she is ready, and she will cook good food for you, real tortillas and beans, so you will be contented."

"I think he's looking for someone a little older," said Robert.

"Well, then ..." K'ayum scratched his head, gazing into my eyes. "Maybe María Bonita. Yes, she is ripe for you. Very good."

"But she already has two husbands," I protested, feeling the warmth rise to my cheeks. "And she seems to like them very tender."

"No, no. The older one, Pepe Camacho, has left her, and lives on Missionary Hill with Chan Bol's daughter."

"You mean the evangelist?" Roberto asked, mildly alarmed.

"That's right. Pepe wanted his own wife, so he married Chan Bol's younger daughter, and moved up on the hill. Now María Bonita only has José, and he is still too young for her. When we get to Nahá, you will ask María Bonita to be her second husband, and you will hunt game for her and work in the *milpa*." He raised his glass, and toasted our future engagement, like a father-in-law.

"I will teach you how to propose," K'ayum teased, with a roguish squint, as we gulped down our drinks. With his usual intuition, K'ayum had once again guessed and acted out one of my secret fantasies. During the past year I'd had periodic sensual dreams of María Bonita, which I'd confided to no one.

K'ayum and Chan K'in retired to their rooms slightly tipsy, and Robert and I had our first heart-to-heart talk in over a year. We were alone now in the dimly lit outdoor restaurant, as large insects circled the flickering light bulb overhead, and bats swooped and dove past the yellow street-lamp. Only an occasional howling dog or a bawling drunk disturbed the cricket song in the deserted streets. Tuxtepec is a kind of limbo, a halfway station between forest and city that asks for no aesthetic or emotional involvement. I would have even more reason to appreciate this way station on our return from Nahá.

We began with an argument over the right to bear firearms, which Robert wholeheartedly upholds and I wholeheartedly oppose. Our differences are familiar ones, aired every day in the media, but the intensity with which we defended our entrenched positions took us by surprise. After our *tsikbal* (soul session) we drank in silence, struck dumb by the gulf between us. Amazing that our love for the Lacandones, our strongest link, should be forged from such different metals. We had avoided political discussions because our views are so far apart there is hardly any common ground. I knew Robert regarded me as a romantic leftist, and I saw him more and more as a frontier anarchist with strong mystical underpinnings. We both rejected each other's categories as simplifications, while tacitly acknowledging that our differences on gun control were only the tip of the iceberg.

Where we did meet is in a bedrock belief in personal accountability for one's life, a philosophy that is also held by the Lacandones.

K'ayum woke us up at five-fifteen the next morning, in retaliation for my Colonel Garvas caper of two days before. He was in fine fettle and entertained us at breakfast with astute characterizations of mutual acquaintances.

Karen, a pretty American woman who works for Trudi, was "muy buena" (very good), but he was sad that she had a low opinion of herself — she thought herself too fat. "Inside she is very thin," K'ayum said, "and she has a big heart, but she thinks no one can see it. If I marry a second wife who is not *hach winik*, then I will choose Karen."

K'ayum said of K'in Bor that he is like two people. "When he hunts or plays guitar or goes fishing with his son he is very contented, and a very good friend. But when he drinks rum with the Tzeltales or the loggers he becomes crazy and talks just like them. The rum kills the good blood in him and he becomes full of shouting and violence. I am afraid of K'in Bor when he drinks and gets this way. I am afraid his blood will turn black, and he will kill my sister Nuk."

"And your blood, K'ayum?" I asked. "What happens when you drink too much vodka?"

"My blood stays red," he said, matter-of-factly. "I have very good blood from my father and mother. See?" He thrust his open palm next to mine and compared our veins. "See how yours are darker than mine?" Then he put his hand next to little K'in's. "See how ours are the same? My son Mario, his blood also has the same red color."

Robert asked, "Is that why you give away your blood to the white man's hospital?" K'ayum, he reminded me, had donated a pint of his O negative blood to the Red Cross in Mexico City.

"That's right! Now if a foreigner gets hurt in an accident and loses blood, they can give him two or three drops of my blood, and he will get well. But I told the nurse to give it only to good people," he added, with a smirk.

Robert and I shook our heads in disbelief, for there was a dead seriousness behind K'ayum's braggadocio, rooted in the Lacandones' sense of innate superiority. Small wonder the Chamulas and the Tzeltales fear and distrust them.

K'ayum admitted readily that he exploits Tzeltal laborers and even cheats them of their wages, on occasion. "They think they are smarter than we are because we live in the forest and wear tunics instead of shirts and trousers. But they do not know how to read or write or count money, so we pay them less than we should, when they are stupid enough to agree to it."

Robert quipped that K'ayum pretended to play Robin Hood, but in reality he was a kind of forest Bismarck who stole from the old rich to give to the nouveaux riches. We laughed, but recognized the logic of the Lacandones' taking advantage of people who encroach on their land, and who scorch and raze the forest indiscriminately.

We drove on another three hours until we arrived at the coastal port city of Coatzacoalcos, and headed straight for the beach.

In his eagerness to treat our charges to their first glimpse of the ocean, Robert drove through a red light. A traffic policewoman whistled us down, but when she looked in the back seat, her face lit up.

"Why, aren't you the Lacandones I saw on TV? But you're famous!" Her stern mask melted into a soft, mothering smile. "Why, you poor things. You're all perspired."

"We're taking them to the beach," Robert explained. "They have never seen the sea."

Mari-Carmen, as she introduced herself, not only let Robert off without a ticket or a bribe, but gave us directions to a seafood restaurant where we could get a generous discount. "Just imagine," she exclaimed, as she signaled us on our way, "and in the middle of the twentieth century."

We parked by the beach and they walked out barefoot on the sand, silently watching as the waves broke over their toes.

"The great water," K'ayum said, wide-eyed. I passed him a seashell and he turned it over and over in his hand.

"Who made this?" he asked, finally.

"It belongs to a small animal, called a clam," I explained. "It is similar to the conch you use to call the men to the *balché* ceremony."

"But these aren't like the clams in the streams around Nahá," he said.

"That's true," I said. "You can use it as an ashtray, for your cigars."

He stuck it into his shoulder bag, and listened raptly while Robert explained the tides that ebb and flow every twelve hours as they are tugged and released by the rhythms of Akna', the moon.

"That's good," he said, and nodded sternly, but I could not tell how much he had understood. ("Give him time," Robert said later. "Not even K'ayum can be expected to grasp Newtonian physics overnight.")

Chan K'in and the Kids, absorbed in their own silence, dug their toes into the sand, and knelt down to taste the salty water. A young man roared past on a dirt bike. His front wheel wobbled out of control, and he flipped over a sand dune.

Little K'in's eyes grew round. In Nahá, when anyone asked them about the sea, the Katzenjammer Kids would reenact the dirt biker's spill in graphic detail, with whoops of merriment.

What most impressed K'ayum were the great transatlantic tankers anchored in the channel. These were the *kaxtlan chem* he had always heard about from his father, the mighty vessels big enough to fit into their holds all the people and all the animals of this world, before the great flood covers it up.

After a hearty shrimp chowder at Mari-Carmen's cut-rate restaurant, we drove past mile after mile of pumping oil drills and open wellheads that shot fiery plumes into a bleached sky. We stopped to buy provisions in Villahermosa, capital of the state of Tabasco, which floats on a vast lake of petroleum.

In this boomtown, everything was nervous bustle and frenzied new construction, as Mexico's future is siphoned up from the ground.

Even here, where oil dominates all conversation, our charges were recognized and greeted amicably.

"Hey — Chan K'in — when are you making your next movie?" yelled a worker in a hard hat as we strolled down the street.

K'ayum stopped to buy guitar strings for his father, and Robert and I stocked up on tequila for the long, cold nights ahead.

A Strange Encounter

We turned south toward Palenque, where we planned to stop for the night. About fifteen miles from our destination, just before dusk, we passed a stalled truck by the roadside, surrounded by white-gowned figures, and K'ayum shouted, "It's my brother Chan K'in!"

Robert stopped and backed up the Safari as the truck's crew stared at us openmouthed. Young Chan K'in and his older brother, K'in García, appeared from the rear of the truck, where they had been pushing to get it started. Then I recognized José Pepe Chan Bol, of Lacanjá, who had visibly aged in the two years since I'd seen him last. Behind the huge horn-rimmed glasses his face looked yellowish and wizened.

"Do you have a wrench?" he asked Robert. Beside him stood a stocky man in slacks and shirt who gave the appearance of being in charge and who turned out to be Carmelo. Young Mateo's brother Bol stepped out of the truck, followed by Joaquín of Mensäbäk, then Alfonso, son of Obregón, who was the driver, and two other younger members of the Lacanjá "Mafia."

Robert's and my curiosity about how they all came to be together would have to await satisfaction until we found a way to get the truck moving. Apparently it had run out of gas, and when they put in a five-gallon reserve, the starter went dead.

After much bickering back and forth and several false starts, Robert tied a rope to his bumper and yanked the truck to get it going. We followed it four or five miles, until it ran out of gas once more. Robert decided to drive on with the extra cans and fill them at a gas station about ten miles down the road.

Young Chan K'in crowded in with us, and used the occasion to criticize Carmelo and his truck. "It is no good. They use dirty gas, the starter is broken, and they don't know how to repair it."

"What are you all doing together?" Robert asked, in a casual tone.

"We met in Villahermosa to order corrugated tin, for our roofs."

"I see," Robert said, not quite truthfully. But Lacandon courtesy required that you grant a respondent his own good time.

"It was Carmelo's plan," Young Chan K'in went on. "But he tells lies, so he can keep all the money to himself. He calls himself a Christian and will not eat meat, but he leaves his two wives behind and sleeps with prostitutes in Villahermosa."

Behind me, a low sigh from K'ayum. "Did you order the corrugated tin?" he asked.

"Yes, and I ordered provisions as well," he said, with a distinct tone of satisfaction.

"Carmelo is no good," Young Chan K'in persisted. "He cheats and lies."

K'ayum said, "José Pepe does not look well. He looks sick."

"Carmelo also is sick," Young Chan K'in said. "He coughs all the time."

"Like his truck," put in little K'in, and we all laughed.

K'ayum said, "Carmelo and his truck are the same. One lies, and the other uses dirty gasoline. The truck runs until it breaks down, and Carmelo lies until he gets sick."

Our laughter turned to fatuous giggling, as we were all punchy from the long drive. But the tone in Young Chan K'in's voice had given me a queasy feeling.

We filled the cans at the gas station and returned to get the truck started. From Carmelo and José Pepe, Robert got not a word of thanks. It was clear they had lost face by our having to help them, and it had made them resentful.

The Ruins

In Palenque, we found two rooms in La Cañada Hotel, which is owned by a friend of Robert's. The faltering truck arrived soon after us, and this time Carmelo stiffly offered Robert some money for the gasoline. But the offer was made with such an ill grace Robert turned it down and suggested that a couple of beers would suit him better.

Carmelo turned toward K'ayum and asked sharply if he had seen the President in Mexico City.

"Yes, I saw him," K'ayum said.

"What did he say?"

"He said he is going to help us."

"Did he give you the million pesos?"

K'ayum laughed, but Carmelo glared and asked sternly, "How much money did he give you?"

"Three hundred fifty thousand pesos only," K'ayum said, straight-faced, "and we will keep all of it, just as you have kept our portion of the money for the mahogany and for the film *Cascabel*." He pounced on the glowering Carmelo and pummeled him on the shoulder, hooting aloud. Although it was done in play, the startled Carmelo could not break K'ayum's grip before the laughter spread to most of the others.

Early next morning the truck was gone, and Young Chan K'in and his brother K'in left for Chancalá by bus, after assuring us the road was passable since the rains had stopped, and we should make it to Nahá in four hours.

Before leaving Palenque we stopped at the ruins to take pictures of K'ayum and his little brothers atop the Temple of the Inscriptions. None of them had been to Palenque before, and they stood at the foot of the

209

pyramid with a look of wonderment matched neither by the marvels of Mexico City nor by their first glimpse of the sea.

Little K'in and Chan K'in loved scurrying up the steps of the pyramid, which were too high for their short legs. Their hamstring muscles would ache for days afterward, and one or the other would groan, "Ay Palenque," when squatting down or rising from a crouch.

At the top of the pyramid we found the inner stairway that leads down to the Prince's tomb. K'ayum and the children stood unblinking before the huge sculpted tombstone. "That is very fine," he said finally. I could only guess how well he understood his ancestors' extraordinary achievement in carving such exquisite detail on such a massive slab of limestone.

"I will learn to make that," he said, with a new determination in his voice. "I will get the tools, and I will learn to work stone like my ancestors did. It is *very* fine."

We stocked up on cheese, deviled ham and honey at the town market, and set out for Nahá a little before noon. Five miles south of town we left the pavement and turned east on a gravel road, toward Chancalá and Nahá.

We reached the headquarters of the government lumber company, the Forestal, in less than an hour. The sawmill was strangely still and deserted, although we passed several trucks stacked with huge mahogany trunks.

We stopped for lunch at the town restaurant, where Robert bought his last six-pack of Tres Equis beer. We were approached by a *ladino* named Lucundo, in leather boots and a straw hat, who turned out to be the Forestal foreman. He told us he had been logging in the Lacandon forest for twenty years. He and K'ayum evidently knew each other: Lucundo hinted that favors had been exchanged between them.

When I questioned him about the fallen trees around Nahá, Lucundo voiced sympathy for the Lacandones' rights to their mahogany. He had intelligent, lively brown eyes, and surprised me by showing an informed sensitivity to the ecological issues.

"Look, I've been here twenty years. During that time I've seen nearly half of this forest destroyed, or close to one hundred and fifty thousand hectares. The topsoil of this forest is no more than ten centimeters deep, and below that is limestone and impenetrable gray sediment. The topsoil is used up in two or three years by the burning and razing of the Tzeltal farmers. What you must realize is that we are only one step ahead of the homesteaders who burn everything in their way. The directors feel they are rescuing the mahogany and other hardwoods that would otherwise go to waste."

"And how do you feel?" I asked.

Lucundo flinched and shook his head. "I feel the destruction of this forest as a personal loss. I come from the state of Tabasco, which used to be covered with trees until the loggers and the ranchers moved in, and now it is all flat denuded grazing land and oil drills." He dropped his voice. "To be frank, I feel what is happening here is not fate, but human failure.

The decisions are made by political technicians in Mexico City who care nothing about the forest and are interested only in profit. Perhaps, if the Lacandones had organized themselves and presented a united front, they might have prevented their mahogany from being felled. Isn't it so, K'ayum?"

"Perhaps," Kayum replied, with head lowered. "But I think it would happen anyway."

"But Chan K'in never gave permission to cut the trees," I interjected, "and yet you people moved in —"

"Ah, there you are mistaken. Young Chan K'in and his father both signed a release and a contract for the trees. We would not have proceeded without their authorization —"

Robert broke in, "But I myself delivered to the government Young Chan K'in's handwritten letter, in which he refused to authorize the felling of the mahogany around Nahá —"

"Well, that letter was rescinded," Lucundo said, with a shrug. "Apparently certain pressures were brought to bear, for they signed the release, last July."

"Is that true, K'ayum?" Robert asked, with hooded eyes.

"I am not sure," he said, hedging. "Perhaps yes."

Robert and I traded looks of dismay, but neither of us was entirely surprised. We had suspected the truth since our encounter with Young Chan K'in, but had been reluctant to ask K'ayum until we reached Nahá.

"To be frank, I was disappointed in them," Lucundo said. "But it was only a matter of time. If we hadn't cut the mahogany, another company would have — or the Tzeltales would have burned it down. "It's no use," he said, and shrugged in the classic Mexican gesture of resignation. "What one would wish and what is determined by others are two different things."

But Lucundo's rhetoric struck a false note, and a flash of guile in his eyes sparked my anger. "You say you have seen all the destruction and have studied the problems. Are you aware of the effect the felling of the trees will have on the rainfall in this hemisphere? Do you know what happens to the water table when the roots of the giant trees die? Do you know how much of the oxygen we breathe will be lost?"

"Yes," Lucundo said, meeting my gaze. "I have studied the problem, and I know that no one has definite answers to those questions. I have also read that the carbon dioxide released by the burning of the trees will poison our air in years to come, and could change the temperatures of the planet, with disastrous consequences. Have you seen the burning in April and May? The smoke is so thick in the forest that no airplanes can land or take off. And I know also that the cattle ranchers are behind a good deal of the burning by the farmers — just as they were in Tabasco. Your own cattle industry plays a part in this, for they pay our ranchers to raise beef cattle for export to your country, so you gringos can have steak on your tables."

"And you certainly play your part," I reminded him.

Again Lucundo flinched. "Logging is my work," he said, in a slow deliberate voice. "I am good at it, and see that only the marked trees are cut down. We account for every tree we log, not only the mahogany but the cedar and the *chicozapote* — and we pay full restitution for each one. Other loggers don't give a damn."

Lucundo's eyes were clear again, but something was wrong. I felt as if I were speaking to a gang of Lucundos with a single spokesman. Lucundo the student of ecology and Lucundo the lumberjack must make uneasy bedfellows.

"Our quarrel is not with you," Robert said to Lucundo, and I had to agree.

"You should speak with the engineer in charge," Lucundo said in a conciliatory tone. "The one here — Roberto Núñez — not the ones in Mexico City. They don't give a damn for the forest. But I think you'll find Don Roberto responsive to your concerns."

I checked with Robert, and we made an appointment to speak with the head engineer the following week.

The Ranches

The gravel road ended at El Diamante, one of the older cattle ranches that have become landmarks in the Lacandon forest. In the twenties and thirties, when the Spanish founders of El Diamante and El Real blazed their vast pasturelands out of the living forest, they had been intrepid pioneers, and their ranches became redoubts of European civility in the wild malarial bush. Colorful autocrats like Pepe Tárano, who presided at El Real, entertained adventurers and explorers, among them Frans and Trudi Blom, Charles Frey, B. Traven and the youthful Robert Bruce, who wrote of their sojourns with their witty, eccentric host, and contributed to a persisting frontier romance.

Today, these pioneer ranches are being replaced by a new breed of rancher, subsidized by the American cattle industry, who breed African cattle strictly for export, and who care nothing for the forest or the older rhythms.

In spite of his own collusion in the process, Lucundo knew what he was talking about: The lands these ranchers take over from the slash-and-burn farmers and reseed with forage grasses are soon overgrazed by huge herds of livestock, which rapidly deplete the new grassland and leave behind eroded hillsides and leached, barren plains.

We passed several of these ranches and saw the ugly pitted grassland that stretched for miles to the foot of distant hills. Several smaller ranches, already abandoned, looked like skeletons picked over by successive flocks of vultures. The hundreds of browsing gray zebu with dangling chest pleats and stunted horns, each with its own egret hovering nearby to feed on its ticks and leftovers, likened the scene even more strangely to a New World Serengeti.

The gravel ended abruptly and the new clay and dirt road rapidly deteriorated into sun-baked ruts and potholes. We passed Nueva Esperanza (New Hope) and several smaller Tzeltal settlements. They all looked the same: a simple plaster church and a greensward ringed with clusters of thatched huts. The treeline receded in a two-to-three-mile radius from the village centers, as the *milpas* were razed and abandoned, and then new ones were razed and abandoned, at the expense of the encircling forest.

About a mile past the turnoff to Mensäbäk we passed two white-robed figures, walking briskly north. Robert stopped when he recognized Pepe Valenzuela, a Mensäbäk patriarch who had recently turned Adventist. Pepe, a stocky man with a marked mustache, looked rattled by the encounter. He spoke guardedly and turned down the cigarette Robert offered him, as well as a swig of tequila.

The talk was polite, but strained. Did Robert plan to stop in Mensäbäk? "On the way back, perhaps," Robert said, and added pointedly, "to drink *balché* with old friends."

This ended all conversation. We said the obligatory farewells to Pepe and his nephew and drove on, as we had no room for them in the car.

And now the high tropical forest began, as the canopy of hardwoods soared to over one hundred feet. The ruts in the road grew deeper, and patches of mud and standing water slowed our progress. Overhead, screeching parrots made K'ayum's mouth water. "Roast parrot!" he shouted.

The Katzenjammer Kids perked up and turned garrulous, like the parrots.

"My father knows we are coming," K'ayum said suddenly.

"Of course," I said. "Young Chan K'in will have told him."

"He knows anyway," K'ayum insisted. "I have thought of him all day, and he knows. He sees us coming."

"Does he see Victor and me too?" Robert asked, in a half-teasing voice. "Does he see the car?"

"Yes — perhaps," K'ayum demurred.

"He sees the tequila," little K'in said, which broke us up without settling anything.

We passed Colonia Lacandon, the Tzeltal settlement closest to Nahá, and climbed the first of three steep hills. Near the old airstrip we spied Young Mateo in the distance, with his wife and son. K'ayum shouted and waved boisterously, knowing Young Mateo would be envious.

Another hill, and we caught a glimpse of Lake Nahá on the right, a gleam of mother-of-pearl in the late afternoon light. Immediately after, we came upon the first felled mahogany, piled in a bulldozed site by the roadside. There were at least forty of the long, massive reddish trunks, stacked hastily like giant cordwood, and numbered with white paint. Lucundo had said they were still taking out the mahogany from Colonia Lacandon, forty kilometers to the north. They would not get to these before April or May, at the earliest.

We rounded the next bend and came upon a welcoming reception of Nahá elders and children, squatting leisurely and smoking their evening cigars.

A Community in Mourning

The small children immediately ganged about the Safari, the first they had ever seen; we were the first "civilians" — neither loggers nor technicians — to reach Nahá by road.

"So you have come back!" Old Chan K'in welcomes me with a big smile and sparkling eyes, and takes my hand in both of his. He and Robert exchange the more traditional greeting, without touching.

Before unloading, Robert pulls one of the tequila bottles out of the car, to mark the occasion. As we pass it around I see a handsome woman standing down the road with a child in her arms and a small girl by her side. María Bonita smiles from afar. I gesture her to come join us, but she covers her mouth and slips away. The road goes right past her father-in-law's backyard, exposing the roof of their hut.

We sit by the shoulder to smoke a *hach k'uuts* (homegrown cigar), after the children and grownups finish gawking at the car. Robert promises Mateo's small children a ride later on, but their squeals sound subdued. Chan K'in's fourteen-year-old son Bol sits alone, watching Robert and me with a sad, reflective gaze. There has been a profound shift in Nahá, and the sadness is thick in the air.

K'ayum starts recounting his meeting with the President but stops, suddenly, as everyone's ears perk up.

After a few seconds I hear the faint growling sound, which grows into a rattling drone. All eyes turn east, toward Ocotal Chico, and then the yellow tractor appears around the bend. They all watch without a sound as it moves by us, trailing a heavy chain. The driver waves tentatively, but no one responds.

"Miguel." K'ayum whispers the driver's name, and says nothing more until the tractor disappears behind us.

Afterward I recall that in the Lacandon language there is no word for silence. *Hum* means noise. *Mäx hum* is the absence of noise. The silence they had taken for granted as part of their birthright has now disappeared forever from their forest.

Bol steps forward at last, shakes my hand, and offers to carry my duffel, just as he had on my last visit. I follow him along the jungle trail that passes Old Mateo's hut, and we soon come to Chan K'in's compound.

Once again we have the spacious storage hut next to Chan K'in's, which has been newly swept and cleared. Robert's hammock is already strung up, and K'ayum has gone to fetch my old jungle hammock. We have just enough time to unload and clean up before Bol appears to call us to supper.

Koh II's black beans and tortillas are already waiting for us on the kitchen table. She greets me with a faint smile and a nod, as if I had never been gone; as if, in fact, nothing at all had changed in the forest. One of Koh II's chief functions is to provide an aura of continuity, so that the rhythms of daily life continue unbroken. At this she succeeds superbly, but even Koh has not been unaffected by the changes.

At first glance her kitchen looks about the same, but I detect subtle alterations one by one. There is more enamel crockery on the table and on top of shelves, and a mirror hangs on the rear wall. The stack of arrows above the roof beams is gathering cobwebs. (I saw no one carving bows or fletching arrows during our stay.) The dogs still howl at my approach, but their barks have become almost perfunctory. As watchdogs, they have begun to lose their authority with so many outsiders coming in and out.

Chan K'in asks us about Mexico City, and about our adventures on the way back. Little K'in reenacts the accident he witnessed in the city, and the dirt biker's vivid flop on the beach.

"And what did you think of Palenque?" he asks, with a smile.

"Very high steps," little Chan K'in says, without hesitation. "It hurts when I bend."

"Ay Palenque," Robert groans, rising up and imitating a bent old man. Old Chan K'in roars louder than anyone, envisioning Robert as a decrepit spider monkey.

K'ayum comes in with the new guitar strings, and fits them deftly on his father's guitar. His pretty wife, Margarita, and little Mario stand by the door as she shows off her new red hairpins. In her arms she holds their eleven-month-old daughter, Chankina. Margarita's contented smile suggests that her reunion with K'ayum has been a happy one, free of the customary reproaches and charges of infidelity.

K'in Paniagua comes in to greet us. He is a handsome son-in-law of Chan K'in's, about twenty-five or twenty-six, who is staying in his brother K'in Bor's vacated hut. K'in tells us that his little son had died, shortly before the death of Young Chan K'in's wife.

In his storyteller's voice, Chan K'in repeats the story of the band of wild boar that had appeared by the new airstrip, the night Koh died. "K'in shot one," he says, pointing proudly at his son-in-law. "He will be a good hunter, just like his older brother K'in Bor."

When I ask how K'in Bor is, the old man's face darkens and he lowers his eyes. "He moved to the other side," he says, with a sharp gesture of his knobby hand. "K'in Bor does not like it here anymore. He makes friends with the *ladinos,* and drinks with them, and gets into fights. He is no longer your friend."

I cannot tell if Chan K'in speaks more in anger than sadness, and if he is hinting that I should not see K'in Bor. But I intend to visit him before I leave, and hear his side of the story.

K'ayum picks at his father's guitar to try out the new strings, and then sings a few bars of "La Mixteca." In the past year, both K'ayum's playing and his singing have improved dramatically. As he warms to "Guadala-jara" his voice stays on key:

Ay Jalisco, tu tienes tu novia
Que es Guadalaja——raaaa

His eyebrows arch studiedly as he draws out the syllable with a high mariachi vibrato, and he glances toward his father.

But Chan K'in disapproves of mariachi songs, and has turned his back on him. "Did you see the mahogany by the road?" he asks Robert aloud, over K'ayum's singing.

"Yes, we saw about forty," Robert says.

"The others are by the new airstrip. They cut four hundred altogether, but many of them were hollow ones, and we were glad to have them re-moved from our *milpas.*" He smiles wryly at the questionable brilliance of *ladino* technicians who waste their equipment on hollow trees. "They left forty standing on the other side of the lake, and there are at least thirty young ones they missed entirely. In twenty years, we will again have all we need."

I doubt the truth of this, but Robert and I both nod, impressed by the old *t'o'ohil's* determination to put a positive face on the situation.

Young Chan K'in appears at the door, and K'ayum stops singing.

"I have brought it for you," he says to his father, in a loud, unsteady voice. He slips a roll of bills from under his tunic, peels off twenty-five one-thousand-peso bills and lays them on the table. They add up to a lit-tle over one thousand dollars.

"I ordered thirty thousand pesos of provisions in Villahermosa, and ten thousand for the corrugated tin. I kept fifteen thousand for emergen-cies —"

"Fine," old Chan K'in says, and repeats in Spanish, "Fifteen thousand for emergencies."

"No, it is better I leave five thousand more with you —" He peels off five more bills and places them on the table. "That makes thirty thousand for you, and ten thousand for emergencies."

"That's fine," Old Chan K'in says. "Ten thousand for emergencies."

Young Chan K'in lifts his tunic to replace the depleted roll in his money belt, but changes his mind once more.

"No — I will leave you another five thousand —" He counts out five more bills slowly: "*Uno — dos — tres . . . ,*" and lays them on top of the pile. "Now you have thirty-five thousand pesos, and I keep only five thousand for emergencies."

"Fine," Old Chan K'in says, and nods — but he has turned his eyes in-ward, absenting himself from his elder son's clumsy bookkeeping, as he had turned his back on his younger son's singing. He passes the money to Koh II, who folds the bills briskly and sticks them into her apron pocket. Her eyes light up for an instant before she slips away to put the money in safekeeping.

While Koh is away, Young Chan K'in sits down heavily and groans aloud. "I don't know what to do," he says in Spanish, shaking his head. "Carmelo lies and steals from us — and the others are all the same. I don't know what will happen. Kisin knows, and the gods know. Only they know." Tears stream down Young Chan K'in's face as he groans and shakes his head.

None of us know what to do or say. Robert has taught me that the men of Nahá are not equipped to handle emotional scenes, and Young Chan K'in is apparently drunk.

Juanita, who has stood by the door with Young Chan K'in's baby, hands it over to Margarita and starts to yank Young Chan K'in from his chair.

"Ko'ox — let us go," she says firmly.

We all feel the weight on Young Chan K'in's shoulders, but we say nothing. It has struck us dumb.

"Ko'ox," Juanita repeats, yanking at Young Chan K'in with all her strength, until she gets him up.

He is still crying and shaking his head as Juanita half carries, half drags her brother-in-law and husband-to-be to his hut.

K'ayum is the first to speak. "My brother is still sad from the death of Koh," he says. "He will get over it soon, now that he has Juanita."

"That is so," Chan K'in and Robert agree. "He will get over it soon."

Peering in through the west window is Koh I, Young Chan K'in's seventy-five-year-old mother, who rocks her two-year-old granddaughter in her arms. She looks distracted as she puffs on a long Havana cigar that Alicia Bruce had sent her through Robert. Beside her stands Koh III, her face impassive as usual. She cradles a two- or three-month-old baby boy, whom I at first mistake for Young Chan K'in's; but on closer look he is a miniature replica of Old Chan K'in. In the middle of so many unusual circumstances, eighty-one-year-old Chan K'in's fifth son in six years has been almost taken for granted.

We finish the bottle, and then K'ayum and K'in Paniagua and I retire to our hammocks. Just as I drift into sleep Old Chan K'in breaks into song, and I regret I cannot make an effort to stay awake.

When Robert comes in he is drunk and rouses me from a deep slumber when he brushes against my hammock.

"Ehh little brother — in case I forget, remind me in the morning about the four birds —"

"Four birds?" My logy brain kicks over, casting in vain for a clue. "What four birds? What are you talking about, Robert?"

"Chan K'in just told me a great new story about four birds which sorcerers use to make witchcraft. They point to the four directions, and tie in with the felling of the trees. It's important, and I want to tape it in the morning."

Within seconds he is snoring loudly, and I am wide awake. Chan K'in sings in his hammock in a loud unfaltering voice. I cannot make out the words, but his voice eases the heavy lump in my chest. "He is casting his seed into the wind," I repeat to myself, until the tears come and I can return to sleep.

In the morning when I remind Robert of the four birds, the story has gone clear out of his head; but I remember a vivid dream of four twisters with tall, powerful cones that are bearing down on Nahá. The air in the dream has a smoky red tinge, the way it looks in April when the heavy burns begin. The twister on the far right is the largest and the closest, and I know for certain that it will strike Nahá before we can get away.

"Ah, ne tsoy — very good," Chan K'in remarks when I tell him my dream. "The red color means blood. Your dream will bring us game — all kinds of game — and they will last us long after you're gone."

Robert looks as puzzled as I am by Chan K'in's interpretation, for I know by now that any kind of wind in a dream foretells the arrival of many foreigners.

"It's possible," Robert whispers in my ear, "that he is applying a reversal I am not familiar with."

But to me the dream had felt ominous, and I cannot help but wonder if Chan K'in is persisting deliberately in a positive outlook on calamities he feels powerless to prevent.

To my knowledge, no game of any kind was caught in Nahá during our stay or immediately after.

Of the first batch of gifts we bring to breakfast, the one that delights Chan K'in the most is a large ear of blue corn. A New Mexican Indian woman had entrusted it to me to present to him as a goodwill gesture from her pueblo.

"It is larger and has a better color than our own," he says, turning it admiringly in his hands. "I will plant it in the milpa, next to our own blue corn."

But Koh II spirits the corn away with the rest of the gifts, her eyes bright with the familiar acquisitive glint.

This morning the eggs are not so dry as last year, the tortillas are fluffy and warm, and the beans are fully cooked. Koh's cooking has kept pace with the modern trends in Nahá.

Later on Chan K'in escorts us to the site of his new milpa across the road. K'ayum comes along too, so he and Robert can pick out the site for the school Robert plans to set up in Nahá. Chan K'in's three wives and a half-dozen children all accompany us as far as the bend in the road where Robert has parked his Safari. First the children set up a clamor for a ride, as the women gawk inside the car like star-struck teenagers.

"They want to ride in your car, Robert," Chan K'in says.

"Gladly." Robert opens the car door. "Who wants to go first?"

"Me! me! me!" shout Old Mateo's two small sons and Chan K'in's little ones by Koh III.

"No, no, the mothers first," Robert says. Old Chan K'in invites his number one wife to step in the back seat, but Koh I backs away.

"It makes too much noise!" she shouts, rolling her Havana in her mouth. "It jumps up and down and hurts my head! I'm not going!"

Neither Chan K'in nor the other wives can persuade Koh I to set foot in the car. After some fretting and wavering, Koh II and Koh III climb in the back seat and sit paralyzed, with their knees clamped shut and their hands inert on their laps. Chan K'in slips into the front seat with Robert, and five or six kids pile in on top of them, squealing and squirming.

Robert drives them half a mile up the road, and then back. First the kids jump out, jabbering noisily, and then the two Kohs, flushed and giggling. As we walk up the road I hear them behind us, berating Koh I and laughing at her skittishness.

Old Chan K'in smiles and shakes his head. "Soon they will be asking for a car of their own, like Young Mateo."

We cross the top of the new airstrip, which is wider than the old one and runs down to the lakeshore. Robert recalls watching the men blaze the runway out of heavy bush in a matter of days.

The road climbs up a steep hill, and turns right. Below us on our left is a fine *milpa,* in a corner of which sits a small, open-sided god-house.

"That belongs to Domingo," Chan K'in says.

"You mean the hermit?" I ask in surprise. I had thought he lived deeper in the forest. The road not only exposes his *milpa,* but its left bank hangs perilously above his home; the first heavy rains could send a mud slide crashing down on his roof. "Does Domingo plan to stay?" I ask, and Chan K'in shrugs his shoulders.

"He is too old and sick to move somewhere else."

Robert suggests we visit him later in the week and offer our services since there is no longer any question of violating his privacy.

We come to K'ayum's unfinished new house, which sits squarely on the intersection of the runway and the road. With its bright red tar-paper roof and half-finished siding, it resembles an abandoned airplane hangar.

"Margarita doesn't want a palm-leaf roof," K'ayum explains, before I have a chance to ask. "She says this one keeps away the cockroaches."

Just beyond is a second batch of felled and cut mahogany, stacked by two yellow bulldozers that sit mired in the mud. María Bonita, her daughter, and her young husband sit on one of the logs.

"When will you take us in your car, Roberto?" she calls out, as we approach.

"Soon," he promises.

"If you leave it with us, my husband can learn to drive it." She holds back laughter with one hand over her mouth.

"I'll take you in the car," I say impulsively. "How about this afternoon?"

María nods and says nothing, but her eyes sparkle. With the older husband gone, she can afford to indulge in a mild flirtation. José, who must be all of seventeen but has grown to look a year or two older, stretches to his full height.

A muffled chuckle from K'ayum, and José's stern face cracks, as he too joins in the general laughter.

"Don't look now, but your cheeks are burning," Robert whispers to me, in English.

Farther on we turn left into a bulldozed swath in the forest that ends at a clear, fast-running stream.

Old Chan K'in draws up his hem and wades into the stream in search of snails. After the flesh of the snails is eaten, the women burn the shells to white lime, which they use to scrape off the hard outer shell of the corn for the tortillas. The ground-up shells are their chief source of calcium.

"Ah, here are some small ones." Chan K'in bends down and scoops up two young black snails from the bottom. "They will be ready to eat by July. It is a good sign." He explains that the snails' presence indicates that the stream will not dry up after the rains.

Robert and K'ayum continue upstream in search of a site for the school's hydroelectric plant. The rest of us ford the stream, and soon come to a large clearing, strewn with felled trees.

"This will be the new *milpa*," Chan K'in says. "We have finished the cutting. In April we will burn, and by summer we can plant the first corn."

There are fallen trunks everywhere: *chicozapote*, ceiba, madrone and smaller trees — but no mahogany. At the far end, the new road is clearly visible.

"Chan K'in," I ask, "what will happen to the old *milpa?*"

"We will plant one more tobacco crop. Then it will lie fallow for a time, so it can recover."

This was sensible, traditional Mayan agriculture. The Lacandones return to second-growth forest again and again, so that the razing of primary forest is kept to a minimum. What I could not figure out is why he had chosen this exposed site for the new *milpa*. In the dry season, when the truck traffic increases, the clouds of dust lifted by passing vehicles will settle on the new crops and complicate their harvest.

"But Chan K'in, why here?" I ask. "The road is so near —"

"Yes," he breaks in, with a nod, and juts out his chin. "It is a good place for a *milpa*."

Once again I have difficulty keeping up with the twists and turns of Chan K'in's logic. It appears that he is pitting his *milpa* against the intruders' road-making machinery, in an open act of defiance.

On our way back, Chan K'in points out several young mahoganies the loggers had spared because their girth was below the legal diameter. The lower trunks are enveloped in gauzy fern and green moss, while bright bromeliads cluster farther up. The tops disappear into the forest canopy. These striplings, only forty to fifty feet tall, seem isolated and vulnerable, as if the fate of their larger and older kin had already been inscribed on their bark, and had communicated to their rising sap. Chan K'in has taught me that trees are sentient beings, and the roots of all living things are closely intertwined. As we walk among them I sense the hurt of this bruised grove of trees radiate outward into the forest.

The Germans Are Coming! The Germans . . .

Young Chan K'in meets us on the road with his pretty little daughter, who is dressed in a red pinafore like a *ladina*. Robert calls her the Princess of Palenque because of her proud bearing. Juanita follows behind, carrying the baby boy on her back. She also wears a red skirt under her shift and — with her flaxen hair — resembles a runaway from a hippie commune.

Young Chan K'in says he will leave for Villahermosa in the afternoon to pick up the provisions he had ordered. He calls them *mercancía* — merchandise. His eyes are clear, and his voice has lost its raw edge. We speak casually, as if last night's embarrassing scene had not taken place.

His little daughter calls out Robert's name and mine, which Young Chan K'in has been teaching her.

"She seems to like you," he says. "When she sees other outsiders, she runs away and hides." Young Chan K'in is constantly testing and evaluating, drawing comparisons, weighing whites against *ladinos* and his own people against the southern Lacandones.

As we speak, a familiar drone turns our eyes to the sky.

"It is Jaime, from San Cristóbal," Young Chan K'in says, squinting at the red and white Cessna as it banks over the new runway.

"The Germans!" I remind Robert. "Must be Gerard and his crew, coming to film the mahogany."

"The Germans! The Germans!" the Katzenjammer Kids shout, jumping excitedly.

We pile into the Safari and speed down the runway, as the Cessna dips and comes in behind us.

"*Avión!*" little Chan K'in shouts, jumping in his seat. And I too have the fleeting illusion that we are about to take off and go for a spin around the lake, without benefit of wings.

Robert swerves to the right, and the plane taxies toward the thatched shed that passes for a terminal.

Gerard stepped out of the plane and waved his arms. "There is another plane coming! Clear the runway!"

Within minutes a blue Cessna landed behind them and pulled up alongside. Gerard, looking tan and fit, introduced us to his crew of cameramen and technicians. In the second plane was the project director, a burly, mustachioed Berliner named Wolfgang, and a silver-haired man wearing a pith helmet and old-fashioned khaki jodhpurs.

I described to Gerard and the director where the stacks of mahogany were, and they nodded enthusiastically.

"Excellent!" said the director. "We shall go there immediately." He turned toward Robert. "I say, may we have the use of your vehicle? It would be a great help to us; as you can see, we have a good deal of equipment."

Robert agreed at once, and took the director and film crew to the large stack of mahogany by the old airstrip. He returned for Gerard and me, and picked up three children whom Wolfgang wanted to pose in front of the trees.

Gerard explained in excellent English that he hoped to sell the film of the felled mahogany to his network, separately from their current project.

I asked him, "Will you be able to push the ecological issue?"

"Certainly. There is a good deal of interest in the Lacandon forest, in Germany."

I reminded Gerard of Chan K'in's prophecy, and of the incalculable effects on our climate and water supply, once the rain forests are all gone.

"Yes, of course," he said, fiddling with his camera dials.

I told him of the "greenhouse effect" that scientists predict will be brought about by the excessive carbon dioxide that is being released into the atmosphere by the burning of tropical forests and the excessive use of fossil fuels. "There is a very real fear that the rising temperatures will cause melting of the polar ice cap and touch off disastrous flooding of coastal cities all over the world —"

"Yes, I've read about it," Gerard broke in, and squinted up at the sun, which was directly above the stacked mahogany. "Let us hope the light will not be too bright."

The director set up the cameras and stood the Katzenjammer Kids and one of Mateo's small sons on one of the largest logs. He shouted and the cameras rolled as the silver-haired man in jodhpurs sat in the shade of a madrone and fanned himself with his helmet.

The shooting was completed in minutes, and Wolfgang asked Robert and me if we could help round up old Chan K'in and some twenty Lacandones at a typical site — either by the lake, or next to a stream. "Can we get some canoes?"

"I suppose we can, but what for?" I asked, and Gerard stepped in to explain that it was to lend "human-interest background" to the mahogany story.

K'ayum went to check on his younger brother Chan K'in Chico, and found him and most of the north-shore males asleep in their hammocks after a night of heavy drinking.

The director herded together Chan K'in, K'ayum and K'in Garcia with a dozen children and other adults, and sat them by the bank of the stream.

"We need more canoes!" Wolfgang shouted, waving his arms.

Chan K'in Chico appeared belatedly, looking groggy, and volunteered to fetch his father-in-law's canoe.

And now the silver-haired man in the pith helmet and khaki jodhpurs sat facing the cameras, with his back to the Lacandones, and Wolfgang handed him a script.

"Well, Herr Traven, what do you think of your Lacandonen," he asked, in thick German, as the cameras rolled.

"Herr Traven" read a long discourse, which he fluffed repeatedly and had to begin over and over.

"My God, it's a farce!" whispered Robert, who has more German than I do, and picked up blatant inaccuracies in the opening paragraph of the "interview." "He's having 'Traven' speak in Yucatecan German. It's as phony as hell!"

The scene was retaken four or five times, as Old Chan K'in and the others sat patiently in the hot midday sun. I could hardly hold back my chagrin and embarrassment at having involved Chan K'in in this charade. But I still could not quite believe that Gerard might have been setting us up all along. When I met him at Chelena Traven's he had impressed us both with his grasp of southern Mexico and its native cultures, which he had been familiar with for over twenty years. He had know Traven personally, and we'd had lively discussions with Chelena about Traven's life and work. Gerard told us he inspired an intense admiration in Germany, particularly among the youth, because of the anti-Nazi activities that had forced him to flee Germany, and his antimaterialistic anarchist philosophy.

"What the hell is going on?" I asked him, when the shooting was finally done. "I thought you said this was not part of the Traven project?"

"Please understand, friend Victor," he said, in a patronizing tone, "there are two separate stories here. One is the mahogany, which we were not commissioned for; it is a free-lance project which I, personally, will do everything I can to see that it is shown in Germany."

Robert said, "Your Herr Traven got a number of things screwed up, I'm afraid — and his Mayan accent is atrocious."

"Oh really?" Gerard's sandy brows shot up above the rims of his Polaroid lenses. "I am sure the director will be most disposed to correct these errors. We are not shooting a film on Traven per se — we are doing a background story. Still, you are both authorities on the Lacandones, so any information you may have —"

"Gerard," I said impatiently, "Traven was never in Nahá. I asked Old Chan K'in, and he had never even heard of him. He met some southern Lacandones in San Quintín and Bonampak —"

"What is going on, please?" The director walked up briskly and Gerard told him of our objections.

"Come, come, my good fellows." He slapped Robert on the shoulder. "Do you seriously think the German television audience will know the difference?" Wolfgang actually twirled his thick mustachios, in unwitting parody of a Prussian officer. "Let us put aside these minor details, eh? We owe both of you fellows a real vote of thanks for your valuable and expert advice — as well as for the use of your vehicle. Now let us go drink and have a bite to eat together — what do you say, eh?" He slapped us both on the back.

"I suggest you first thank Old Chan K'in for his hospitality," I said coolly, "for he is the one you have inconvenienced."

"Oh my good fellow, I assure you he and the others will be amply recompensed for their services — eh, Sergio?" He turned to Sergio Castro, a fair-skinned *ladino* in a Panama hat. He was the same Sergio Castro who had introduced coffee trees to Nahá, and rendered other services as a friend to the community. Now he was here as a hired Lacandon "expert" and guide.

"Yes, yes, I have made all the arrangements," he said.

Robert returned with them, in the expectation of salvaging at least a cold beer or two from this misbegotten enterprise.

I left them by the road and suggested to Bol we go for a swim.

When Bol and I sat down to lunch in Koh's kitchen, I could hardly look into Chan K'in's eyes, although he seemed relaxed and genial over the whole affair. I explained the circumstances in which I'd met Gerard, and what a well-informed, conscientious person he had appeared to be.

"Lies, the Germans lie," Bol said, quietly. He had stayed away from the landing because he had not liked the Germans' harsh voices.

"Perhaps he is a good man," Chan K'in said. "But the other — with the boar whiskers — makes him say one thing, and do another."

We laughed at this astute description of institutionalized hypocrisy. However genuine Gerard's interest in the mahogany may have been, it was now obvious that Wolfgang had shot the trees only as a touch of local color.

Robert came back from his lunch looking crestfallen and surly.

"How was the cold beer?" I asked.

"What cold beer? Wolfgang treated me to a cup of warm apple juice."

"So much for those bastards." I smiled in spite of myself at Robert's aggrieved expression.

"What a pair of suckers we are," Robert said, shaking his head.

"But they took in Mrs. Traven too, Robert. When Chelena finds out what a travesty they've made of her husband's story, she'll hit the ceiling." Suddenly, I saw the humor in the situation.

"You know, Robert, if Traven were alive, he'd laugh his head off at all this bullshit."

"That's right. They are just the sort of people he came to Mexico to get away from."

"And now here they are, dogging his every footprint and picking over his bones. It's a sick joke."

"Well, you must admit they're disciplined," Robert said. "They did all the shooting in under three hours and got our services for nothing!"

I'd forgotten his admiration for German efficiency. "Well, anyway, you're still one warm apple juice ahead of two days ago, when you helped the Lacanjá evangelists with their truck."

"That's right! I'd forgotten." Robert lifted his fist and brought it down on the table. "Those bastards never did buy me that cold beer."

We dismissed the whole subject with a rousing rendition of "Lacanjá, Lacanjá über Alles," followed by a swig of warm tequila.

The German television crew flew back to San Cristóbal before dark, after Sergio distributed boxes of combs, mirrors, cigarettes and candy. Neither Wolfgang nor Gerard troubled to thank Chan K'in before departing.

Later we visited Old Mateo, who was confined to his hut with influenza. His younger wife, Nuk, sat half hidden in the shadows, but I could see that she wore bright ribbons on her skirt and colored hairpins, which were the new rage in Nahá. As we spoke with Mateo, their beautiful young sons entered the hut, chewing on the Germans' candy bars and bubble gum. They are Hans and Fritz's counterparts, both in age and mischief, their angelic faces notwithstanding.

Mateo said, "If my fever gets worse, my son Bol will drive me to San Cristóbal." He smiled, and I saw for the first time a hint of guile in his browless, sunken eyes. It gave his ravaged features a definition they lack in repose. Mateo's is the face of a would-be handsome and vital man who shows early signs of corruption. "Perhaps the road will be a good thing after all," he said, smiling and looking from one to the other of us. It occurred to me that his sons Bol and Mateo must have put constant pressure on him to accept the logging and the road, much as Young Chan K'in had persuaded his own father.

The skies clouded over from the north, and a heavy rain came down by nightfall.

"Norte," Chan K'in said. "Not good. Young Chan K'in will have difficulty getting back."

But to Robert and me it seemed a benison, as it washed away the sour aftertaste of the Germans' visit; and it meant that the road would be closed for at least two to three days. For a little while the appearance of wholeness would return to Nahá.

Antonio

"I saw your *onen* in Tenosique," Antonio calls from the door of our hut, starting us from our hammocks. "It was a long dolphin, almost the length of this room. It swam up the Usumacinta River, from the sea."

His hair is dripping wet and he is shivering in his tunic, which is soaked. Robert starts a fire, and opens our last bottle of tequila.

"Antonio," I ask him, "how do you know my *onen* is a dolphin?"

He gulps down a thimbleful of tequila and wipes his lips with the back of his hand. "I thought of you when I saw it," he says simply. "In Tenosique I also saw a whale, like the one you described in the god-house. It was all chopped up, but I could see its head and its big eyes. It had a fin this long." He spreads his arms as far as they will go.

I cannot tell if he "saw" the whale in a dream or in a waking visit to Tenosique. To Antonio, who is the least worldly of the Nahá elders, such fine distinctions have scant importance. He soon gets down to the object of his urgent visit: his wife is seven months pregnant, and is vomiting heavily and experiencing a good deal of pain.

Robert hands him a bottle of aspirin. "These may not be enough," he cautions. "Perhaps you should take her to San Cristóbal to see a doctor."

"Oh no," Antonio says. "She's had these before. The aspirins will do her good. But don't tell anyone, Roberto. She is ashamed in front of the other women."

Antonio sits down by the fire, and we join him in a second round of tequila.

"Now everything changes," he says, with a long sigh. "Many problems in Nahá."

"You mean the road?" I ask.

He nods slowly, with eyes shut. "Nothing will be the same. The Tzeltales will come and burn our lands, and then the cattle ranchers will follow and seed them with grass so that nothing will be left. Everyone knows it, but we do not talk about it. Instead, everyone is asking for gravel. Even my wife is starting to think the road is a good thing, because she can be driven to the hospital if she has a difficult delivery. *Ma' tsoy*, Roberto. It is no good. But I keep silent about it." He looks up. "Have you seen K'in Bor?"

I say we have not yet seen him, but expect to later in the week.

"K'in Bor was your friend, but he is no longer K'in Bor. Since the loggers came they drink rum together, and he becomes like one of them. K'in Bor can kill when he gets drunk."

"It's true," Robert says. "When a *hach winik* gives up his traditions, he becomes no different from the Tzeltales."

"Absolutely!" Antonio affirms this truth with a surge of his body, which lifts him off the ground. Just as abruptly he becomes drowsy from the tequila, and lies down for a doze.

When I remark to Robert on how the changes have affected Antonio, the elder opens his eyes and gives us a knowing wink.

"I know what you said. I understand English here —" he jabs at his temple with one finger. "You talk about how I have changed. True?"

We both nod, impressed.

"Don Felipe Baer talks about us in our presence, thinking we don't understand — but I always know what he says." To prove his contention Antonio repeats two phrases he has memorized, "apejil" and "kipat," which, after a good deal of guesswork we translate to "up the hill" and "keep out."

"See?" he says, grinning proudly. "What did I tell you?"

* * *

The winds howl through the slats and penetrate the fleece lining of my sleeping bag. The chill and rain do not deter the fleas, which are active all night, or the cockroaches, which infiltate the screen of my hammock and seek warmth under my earlobe. My sleep is troubled by visions of a fanged Kisin who looks like the masks of the demon Ravana in Sri Lanka and southern India. But these are small payments for the sense of restored order that the *norte* brings to the forest. I picture the clay churned up into impassable ruts and axle-deep muddy water, and my heart lightens, no matter how temporary the reprieve. One by one, I sink the Forestal's tractors and bulldozers into the rising ooze until I fall asleep. Eros dominates my fitful dreams, a sign that we will not run out of deviled ham and sausages during our stay.

The Jaguar Marries

In the morning we linger in the kitchen long past our breakfast, as the rain and wind continue unabated. Chan K'in listens avidly as the Katzenjammer Kids describe the elevators and buses in Mexico City, and K'ayum tells again of his visit with President López Portillo.

Hans and Fritz then blow up some zebra-striped balloons, which sail around the kitchen with a flatulent sound that breaks the boys up every time. When the rains stop, I will take out the yo-yos and marbles I brought, and the magic soap bubbles. I have never known boys to squeeze so much madcap glee from such scant materials.

Robert reminds Chan K'in and K'ayum that there will be a partial solar eclipse the following day, February 26.

Chan K'in's eyes widen. "*Ehh hah.* T'uup will have to be very watchful tomorrow, so that the celestial jaguars do not come out to devour us."

"Only a small part of the sun will be covered," Robert reassures him. "It will be only the eyebrows."

"Don't you mean a skullcap?" I whisper to Robert, raising a flush.

"Ah, true," says Chan K'in, "but an eyebrow is large enough to let a jaguar escape."

K'ayum says, knowledgeably, "If the sun turns red tomorow, we will know it is the blood of people killed by the jaguars. If it turns black, it will be a sign of their rotting flesh."

Little K'in turns to his father. "Tell us of the time when jaguars and men were friends."

"Ah yes," Chan K'in says, nodding agreeably. "Perhaps tomorrow, in the god-house."

"Tell us now," insists little Chan K'in. Since their trip to Mexico, the Katzenjammer Kids have grown more assertive.

"Well . . ." Chan K'in demurs, and all activity comes to a halt. K'ayum puts away his guitar; I slip my yellow pad under my seat. Koh II puts down the hen she is plucking for supper and sits down next to her husband. She rubs her shoulder against his, as if to warm and spark his storytelling cells. "Go on, tell us," she coaxes.

The circle of rapt, eager faces brings a smile to Chan K'in's face.

"In the old days," he begins, "the two daughters of an ancient found favor in a jaguar's eyes, and he followed them to the *milpa*. He would sit in hiding and watch them play and sing songs, and help their father gather his corn. They were not aware of their secret admirer.

"One day the sisters wandered close to the edge of the forest, and the jaguar leaped out and snatched them, and carried them back to his cave."

"Didn't he hurt them with his fangs?" asks little K'in.

"No, not at all," the storyteller replies, almost before the question is out of K'in's lips. "He carried them like a mother cat carries her kittens." (The light in the room has gathered about Chan K'in's eyes and lips, and his moving hands.)

"The farmer followed them, shouting and crying, until he lost track of the jaguar. When he returned to his home he and his wife mourned their daughters as if they were already dead.

"Ah — but the jaguar had not eaten them. He had made a bed for them of palm leaves — the soft kind — and after crying all day, the sisters fell asleep in each other's arms. The jaguar did not sleep; after night fell he left his cave, and when the sisters woke up, they found a freshly killed fawn by their feet.

" 'Aah, it's horrible.' The sisters recoiled from the bloody venison. The jaguar was puzzled, for he knew that people ate meat, but neither he nor the sisters knew how to start a fire and cook it.

" 'We're hungry!' the sisters wailed. 'If you are going to keep us here, you will have to feed us *posol* and tortillas, just like we eat at home.'

"Without a word, the jaguar left them, and crept unseen to his father-in-law's house —"

"Father-in-law?" interrupts little Chan K'in. "You mean they're already married?"

"Yes, certainly," Chan K'in replies. "According to the jaguar's customs, the sisters became his wives after they slept on the palm leaves he laid for them, and did not run away from his cave —"

"But they haven't cooked for him yet," Koh II points out, poking him with her elbow.

Chan K'in grins and nods. "It was different in those days. . . ."

The story continues, yet I am already full to bursting. The air around us is charged with the storyteller's presence. We are inside a magic circle, and no harm can befall us until the tale is done. Outside, the forest has closed over its wound, and spreads its sheltering canopy over Nahá. Perhaps, after all, Chan K'in's power to restore harmony is greater than the intruder's insistence on tearing it away . . .

Chan K'in goes on, switching tenses. "The jaguar steals a gourd of *posol* and some tortillas from his father-in-law's house, and leaves the fresh deer in its place. He brings the food to the sisters, who eat to their hearts' content. That night they sleep together, in the manner of husband and wives —"

A stern look checks little Chan K'in's snickers.

"When the father finds the deer at his door and some of their *posol* missing, he guesses the truth, and they rejoice that the jaguar has not eaten their daughters. The next day, the jaguar leaves a newly killed paca at their door, which has been left ajar so he can move freely in and out with the *posol* for their daughters.

"As time passes, the ancient and his wife become accustomed to having a jaguar for a son-in-law. They invite him to live in their house with his wives, so he can fulfill his term of service under one roof. He is an excellent hunter, and fresh game is seldom lacking from their table. When the daughters return, they bring with them their newborn offspring. They look just like human children, except that their tunics are covered with yellow spots.

"A relative who sees the jaguar bring fresh meat into his cousin's house becomes envious, and decides to kill the jaguar. One night the jaguar and his father-in-law stay up late drinking *balché*. After finishing his bowl, the jaguar thanks his father-in-law in a furry growl and asks formal permission to leave. After he falls asleep the cousin steals into the hut with his machete and kills the jaguar and his cubs.

"In the morning, he boasts to his cousin of his deed, expecting to be thanked for ridding the family of the beast. Instead they rail at him and shout, 'You have killed our grandchildren!' But the cousin argues that they were not human children, only jaguar cubs.

"From that day on, the two sisters refuse to eat their mother's food and waste away until they die."

The story ended, Chan K'in pauses before delivering the moral. He had acted out each of the personages in the tale, altering the tone and inflection of his voice. "From that time on the jaguars became the enemy of man, and attacked and killed him whenever they met in the forest — and it has remained so to this day . . ."

"*Muy triste* — very sad." I turn to find K'in Bor squatting on the ground, by the east door. Like a cat, he had slipped in unnoticed in the middle of Chan K'in's story.

"A very sad story," he says again, and turns on me his look of dark intensity. "How have you been, Victor? Chan K'in Chico told me you and Robert were here."

K'in Bor's appearance shatters the storyteller's spell, and sets the room into motion. K'ayum picks up his guitar, Koh II returns to stoking the fire with corn husks and to plucking the hen. The boys go back to their balloons and water pistols; even the dogs rise from their sleeping places and scratch noisily at their fleas.

I assure K'in Bor I had intended to visit him after the rains, and he nods his head.

"I've been sick with influenza," he says. "But I'm better now."

"I'll bring you some medicine," I promise, hearing the quaver in my voice. His abrupt appearance has shaken me.

Chan K'in rises and digs among the gift boxes left by the Germans. "For you —" He passes K'in Bor a mirror and two combs, and four or five packs of cigarettes.

K'in Bor accepts them, automatically. I accompany him to the door.

"They say there will be an eclipse tomorrow," he says, and a shadow darkens his face. Now I understand why he has walked through the rain to seek us out.

"It will be a small one," I reassure him. "And since it's raining, we probably won't see it."

"The jaguars won't come out of the ground?" he asks, his eyes large with fear.

"I'm sure they won't."

He nods, slips on the poncho I'd given him, and vanishes into the trees.

A Small Eclipse

By next morning the heavy rains have turned to light showers; the clouds clear for brief periods and allow glimpses of the sun.

Everyone has gathered at the god-house, but only Old Mateo lights incense pots, and prays to Hachäkyum. "It is not for us to die," he chants again and again, and asks for a speedy recovery from the flu. The boys bring pans of water, so they can watch the eclipse in reflection. Antonio and his son gaze into a thin puddle of water at the bottom of the incense canoe. When he sees me he smiles. "Did I make a good conversation last night?"

A little after ten, a smudge is visible on the sun's upper left corner. A rooster crows, and the dogs all start yowling at once. Then a silence settles over Nahá, except for Old Mateo's chanting, which rises in intensity.

As the smudge spreads, Robert explains the eclipse to the boys.

"That is Akna', the moon," he says, pointing his pipe stem at the sky. "She is passing over the sun's face, but will not cover all of it. She will only brush his forehead with her veil."

"Will they make love?" asks Mateo's youngest son, with a solemn look. Surprisingly, the Katzenjammer Kids do not giggle. They are intrigued by this novel way to view the eclipse.

"No, it's just a passing encounter," Robert says. "They will not be fully in each other's arms again for many years — not until the next century — and by then you'll be too old to appreciate it."

The boys squint up at the sun, but the clouds have covered it, and when they part once again, the eclipse is over.

Domingo

We approach the hermit Domingo's home from the rear of his *milpa,* which is the best tended and most productive in Nahá. Behind the tall, robust cornstalks we find clumps of grape and squash vines, and neat rows of sweet potatoes. In front of the god-house we find a small garden of mint and other savory herbs. Here Robert pauses to make a quail call and announce our presence. On the third call, a man's voice answers and invites us in.

I gaze up at the road looming over us, struck all over again at the precariousness of Domingo's situation. Another rain could start a disastrous mud slide and smother him inside his hut.

Domingo almost chokes on his reply of welcome when he spies me behind Robert. He looks younger than I expected, about sixty-five or -six, and wears a soiled, tattered tunic and a white cap. His deep brows and fine features are not at all typical Lacandon — they remind me of a medieval Spanish ascetic. He is so startled by our appearance he forgets to use his cane, which leans against the doorjamb.

"Ne *sis* — it is cold," he says, barely touching my fingertips. He waits for his wife to come out and invite us inside.

Koh is a round, blooming woman of about thirty-five, a daughter of José Güero's who has the ruddiest complexion I've seen on any woman in Nahá. The physical contrast between them is so striking I assume she must be pregnant, although Robert and Trudi have assured me that Domingo has had no children either with his first wife or with Koh, and is most likely impotent. As a small boy, Domingo had looked on helplessly as *ladino* raiders cut up his father with their machetes and threw him into the river.

Koh greets Robert warmly and invites us inside the hut, where we sit on flat mahogany planks. Domingo squats down in the half shadows, as if to shield the dark interior of his imperiled hermitage.

"It is cold," he says once more, drawing a shawl about his shoulders as his wife starts a small fire in the corner.

He and Robert go through the formalities while I take in the wealth of fruits and vegetables that fill Domingo's gourd bowls. Three varieties of corn hang from the eaves — white, red, and a blue specimen that is nearly as large and deep-toned as the sample I brought from New Mexico. Three enamel pots, a hand-worked brass jar and a Nestlé's container filled with ground coffee are the only visible marks of occidental culture. It is questionable how well Domingo can enjoy this abundance, for he has very few teeth: two uppers, a crooked brown lower and possibly a molar or two. Unlike Old Chan K'in and Mateo, who rotted their teeth out with sugar long ago, Domingo cannot afford dentures.

"The road is a bad thing," he tells Robert, in a voice so soft I can barely hear him. "It will bring many bad things" — he points a finger up at the ceiling — "and when the rains come . . . ." He shakes his head.

231

"At least, if he gets sick, he'll be able to go to a hospital," says Koh in a ringing voice. "Domingo would never get into an airplane —"

"Oh no, it is a bad thing," Domingo repeats, shaking his head. But his eyes are bright and steady. The deep stillness in the hut suggests that they communicate in an unspoken language most of their days, and welcome this opportunity to vent their feelings.

After Domingo's first wife died, childless, he had burned down his hut and moved away. Since then he stays close to home and tends his orchard with his second wife, only rarely consorting with his contemporaries, Mateo and Chan K'in, because his childlessness makes him feel ashamed in their presence. Now the completion of the road and the felling of the mahogany have substantiated his worst fears; but he has survived, and looks almost cheerful, like a man relieved of an oppressive burden.

Domingo is fascinated by Robert's briar pipe, and even more by his red and blue tam-o'-shanter.

"Good for the cold," he says, pointing to his own head. "How much does it cost?"

"I'll get you one," Robert offers, and Domingo hands him his white cap so we can take his measure.

"About six and a half," Robert calculates, after we each try it on.

"And for you?" I ask Koh. She wears false-coral earrings, and a red bead necklace strung with old coins and safety pins.

"Perhaps — earrings," she says, beaming, and then flushes, which makes her look sturdier than ever.

Domingo presents us each with a ripe, delicious squash to eat at once, and then places half a dozen more in Robert's shoulder bag. The promise of a new cap has improved his humor appreciably, and both he and Koh become almost voluble in their remarks about the road, the new airstrip, Young Chan K'in's excessive purchases. In his hushed, mournful voice Domingo recounts his recent colds and all his other undiagnosed illnesses and symptoms of the past two years, until Robert signals me that we really should be leaving.

"Did you see the eclipse yesterday?" Domingo asks, as we rise and start our leave-taking.

"Yes we did," Robert says. "It was rather faint."

"Ah, that makes no difference," Domingo replies, with shining eyes. "If you do not light a fire when the eclipse begins, then you freeze to death."

Montes Azules

In the afternoon the tractors and bulldozers set at once to repairing the road, which, as anticipated, had turned into a morass.

The first to arrive were Lucundo and a portly man in rimless glasses, who turned out to be the technical director, Roberto Núñez.

We made polite conversation, and I learned of China's invasion of Vietnam, which they had been following on the radio.

"Now, even the Communists turn against one another," the director said with a wry smile, and he added, "Lucundo tells me you have an objection to our logging mahogany." He spread wide his thick legs, and crossed his arms. Don Roberto is a university graduate of middle-class background who has lived most of his life in Mexico City.

"No, it is not the logging so much," Robert replied at once, in a soft, reasonable tone. "We are simply concerned that the people of Nahá get their proper share of the payments for the trees."

The director coolly explained that the payment of nineteen million pesos had been made in due and proper form to the presidents of the community, José Pepe Chan Bol and Carmelo, and proposed to show us the receipts.

"The difficulty is," Robert said, "that José Pepe and Carmelo represent only Lacanjá, not Nahá — and they keep all of the money to themselves."

"That may well be, but that is an internal matter that should be settled between the two communities."

Robert agreed, almost too hastily, and the director reminded him that Chan K'in and his son had signed the permission for logging in Nahá last July.

"Yes, they've admitted as much," Robert said, hanging his head.

"But tell me" — the director turned to Robert and rattled his keys, taking the offensive — "did I not see a photograph of the two of you in *Excelsior,* in which you appeared with a group of Lacandones and complained of our despoiling the forest? I don't mind telling you, that article has caused serious perturbation among my superiors."

I told the director that Pepe Pinto had been the spokesman for the Lacandones on that occasion, but that I personally shared his apprehension about the felling of the mahagony and its effect on the ecological balance of the forest and of our entire hemisphere.

The director asked me to elucidate, and I repeated the argument I'd made to Lucundo about the importance of the root systems to a stable water table, and of the forest canopy's role in generating rainfall and oxygen. I assumed he knew all of this, so I added some dark words about the "greenhouse effect" and ended with Chan K'in's parable about the interdependence of all living things. "But I'm sure you are well aware of all this," I said, "as Lucundo spoke knowledgeably on this subject when we last met."

"Yes, we have had many consultations with ecologists and scientists," the director said, in a more straightforward voice, "and we have calculated the quantity of trees it is safe to log without damaging the ecological balance, as you call it. But you have to understand that our hands are being pushed by the Tzeltal homesteaders, who burn down everything in their path. To us, the mahogany represents cash value; it is clear that if we don't cut the trees down now, the burns will waste them and other valuable timber in the very near future.

"Look," he went on, "I will take off my gloves and speak frankly with you, off the record. We calculate that the Tzeltales will burn the bulk of the forest in this area in the next eighteen months to two years. The Nahá community has some very hard and urgent decisions to make."

"That's right," rejoined Lucundo, looking faintly distressed, and brought up a government plan to relocate the Lacandones on a remote lake in the Sierra Miramar, one hundred kilometers to the southwest, where no logging roads would disrupt their way of life. The zone would be designated a protected national park, to be called Montes Azules.

"Is there mahogany there?" Robert asked.

"Not as much as here," Lucundo conceded, "but more than sufficient for their needs." Under further questioning, he granted that there were no streams or rivers in the area, which is two thousand feet higher than Nahá, and a good deal colder.

"Our company is prepared to provide warm clothing," the director said, magnanimously. "The Lacandones are a hardy people. I feel certain they could adjust to the higher elevation in a few months — eh, Chan K'in?" Don Roberto turned to the patriarch, who stood listening nearby, presiding over the discussion on his home soil.

"I have already explained to the *señor* director," Chan K'in said, addressing us in his slightly halting, deliberate Spanish. "So long as I am alive, we do not intend to leave Nahá. Our *milpas* and our god-house are here. My mother and uncles and others of our companions are buried in the surrounding forest, and these sites are sacred to us. After my death my sons can make their own decisions whether to stay or move away. Please explain that to the *señor* director."

Don Roberto and Lucundo, who had understood Chan K'in perfectly, shrugged their shoulders and returned to their pickup. Before driving off, Don Roberto reminded us to stop in Chancalá on our way out of the forest, so we could verify the mahogany payments to the Lacandones.

Robert sighed, and reminded me of Mexico's Ordinance 33, which calls for the deportation of any foreigner engaged in "pernicious political activity." "Well, little brother, we really stuck our necks out this time. We haven't heard the end of this affair. Not by a long shot."

I protested that the director had seemed a reasonable enough fellow, all in all. He had really listened.

"He may have seemed reasonable, but just keep in mind the agency he represents, and all the other government agencies lined up behind it. You've been living up north so long, you don't know what it's like here anymore."

I seek out Bol and we go for a swim, so I can reflect on our meeting with the loggers. After our swim Bol watches me silently as I soap my face and shave, balanced on the edge of the *cayuco*.

"Bol," I ask, "could you move out of Nahá and live somewhere else?"

"In San Cristóbal?"

"No, in some other part of the forest, far from here — far away from the Tzeltales, the loggers and the cattle ranchers."

He ponders this as he dries himself off. His towel displays a bikini-clad woman beneath an arched ACAPULCO in rainbow colors.

"Farther than Ocotal Chico?"

"Yes — farther than Ocotal Grande, too; it is in the Sierra Miramar, beside a beautiful lake."

"There is mahogany there?"

"Yes — and cedar and *chicozapote,* and all the other trees you have here. But it is cold there — colder than Nahá — and there are no rivers, only the lake. Could you live there?"

He slips on his tunic and sits on the oar to reflect. The sun is warm on our backs, with a sting from the lingering dampness. "Perhaps I could live there, yes, but I cannot leave my father. No, as long as my father is alive I will stay here with him." He throws up his hands and slaps his thighs, in a characteristic Bol gesture. "At night sometimes I can't sleep, and I think much about the road and the logging, and about the changes they are bringing to Nahá. But I still like it here."

The Vulture Wife

After lunch I walk over to K'ayum's house, to sound him out on Montes Azules.

K'ayum sits in his hammock, practicing on his guitar as Margarita grinds corn in a metal grinder. (Only the older women still use the stone metate.) Little Chankina, who is strapped to her back, bounces contentedly to her mother's movements.

"Come in, come in," K'ayum calls, before I announce my presence. One of the dogs snorts, sniffs at my jeans cuffs, and slinks away, growling. Two-year-old Mario points his finger at me and runs behind K'ayum. It has been over a year since I've seen him, and he does not recognize me.

"He thinks you're a *ladino,*" K'ayum jokes. "Give him a candy, and he'll remember who you are." Mario snatches the sweet I offer him and scurries back to his father. He pulls deftly at the paper wrapper and stuffs the sweet into his mouth, gazing at me with his large, appraising brown eyes.

When I offer a sweet to Margarita she accepts it avidly, and then blushes and starts to giggle so she cannot go on with her grinding.

"I did not mean to interrupt your work," I say, which causes her to giggle even more; she trots out of the hut, with a puzzled Chankina bouncing on her back.

"She seems to be in good spirits," I say to K'ayum.

"Yes, she likes the cloth and the tuna fish I brought her, so she does not scold me and beat me up, like last time."

On a sudden impulse, I ask K'ayum what he wants most out of life. "If you had three wishes, what would you ask for?"

K'ayum looks at me warily. The "make-believe" of three magical choices, which is so ingrained in our folklore, is altogether alien to K'ayum.

After I persuade him it is only a game, he chooses a good house first, then a Safari like Robert's. After long reflection on the third wish, he decides on more sons and daughters.

"How many more?"

"Many," he says, and laughs. "I like children."

I turn to Margarita, who has resumed her grinding, determined to keep a straight face. "Do you feel the same way?"

She does not understand, or pretends not to. When K'ayum translates my question, she smiles, and a ruby glow invades her face.

K'ayum asks me, "You are going to Palenque tomorrow, with Robert and my father?"

"What?" this is the first I've heard about a trip to Palenque.

"He didn't tell you? My father and Mateo have asked Robert to take them to Palenque, after the rains stop. Tomorrow will be a good day — I think they will go tomorrow."

"But the road will still be a mess," I say. "We hardly got through last week, when it had been dry for days."

"Perhaps by tomorrow the road will be all right — and Robert's Safari is very strong; it can go in the mud, like a tractor."

"And will you come?" I ask K'ayum. The trip seemed foolhardy to me, an unnecessary risk. Was it meant as a test of Robert's car and his skill as a driver?

"No, I have had enough travel for a time. I think I will stay home with Margarita, and my son Mario and my daughter Chankinita. But Margarita has asked me, if you go to Palenque tomorrow, to bring her some colored ribbon: red and green."

I promise, and then bring up the Montes Azules proposal.

"No, I will stay here with my father," he replies firmly. "Our dead are buried here, and now we are clearing out new *milpas*. It is good for us here ..." K'ayum's eyes grow distant. He has grappled with this question before, many times.

"But K'ayum, what if the Tzeltales come and burn down the trees and the *milpas,* and force you to move?"

He shrugs. "*Vamos a ver* — we shall see." He grins. "Perhaps I will go and live with you in San Francisco, and take my son Mario to school."

"That is fine with me," I say, "but what about the school you and Robert are starting? Won't Mario go to that?"

"Yes, yes ...," he says vaguely. "Of course." But I see that K'ayum already doubts whether there will be time enough to put up the school, much less conduct classes in it.

K'ayum plays and sings some *rancheras,* which I take down on my recorder. Then he decides to tell me a story about an ancient who marries a vulture woman:

This happened a very long time ago, when there were very few women in the world, and the ancient saw a vulture bathing in a stream. She had taken off her feather tunic, and from a distance she looked just like a naked woman, and so the ancient dived in, grabbed her ankle, and would not let her go.

"Now you have me," said the vulture woman, "will you marry me well?"

"Yes I will," said the ancient. "I will dress you in my mother's clothes."

So the ancient takes her home and dresses her in his mother's old clothes and she learns to cook *posol*, beans and tortillas for him, like a good wife. At night she is just like a woman, and they lie down together and make love. He goes about the forest, collecting copal for his incense burners, and sometimes he brings her a deer or a *tepeiscuinte* for her to cook. But at heart she is still a vulture, and she likes to leave the meat out in the sun until it spoils, so she can eat the little worms that gather in the cracks. She calls them chilis, and sometimes she spices his *posol* with them. The ancient vomits up his food and is so disgusted with the smell of the bad meat that he quarrels with his wife and goes off to the *milpa*, to sleep alone.

One night the vulture woman is raped by a red Xok, which is a large god like a fish who lives in the river. She becomes pregnant, and when her time comes she is so big she cannot move, and asks her husband to open her up with his machete. When he cuts her open, ten baby alligators fall out of her stomach. Then she asks him to cut her little finger at the third joint, and three calabash seeds spill out. She tells him, "These are our children. I will teach you how to plant them so they will grow well, and you will not go hungry after I die."

The ancient plants the seeds as she tells him, and after she dies two of the calabashes grow out of the ground. But he does not know how to cook them, so he leaves them by his doorpost. When he comes home from the forest that day, he finds warm tortillas and beans on his table.

"Ah," thinks the ancient, "the gods must feel sorry for me because I live all alone and I'm growing old." Every day, when he comes home from the forest he finds a stack of warm tortillas and beans or *posol* waiting for him.

One day he returns early, and when he is at the door of his hut he hears the sound of the grinding stone, crushing the corn for his tortillas. Inside he finds two pretty young women preparing his dinner. They are his daughters, which the vulture woman gave him so he will not be all alone.

"The daughters grew up and they married the sons of a neighbor," K'ayum concludes tersely, "and they had many children, who also married and had more children, and some of them are alive today."

"Eating maggots?"

"Yes" — K'ayum laughs — "and wearing black buzzard feathers in their braids."

"And what happened to the ancient?" I ask, wondering if he had suffered remorse.

"Oh, he married his neighbor's sister, but then he died a month later."

"Did he feel badly about the way he had treated the vulture woman?"

"Yes, I think so. Perhaps yes. The neighbor told him he had not been good to his wife."

I cannot tell if he suddenly remembered this, or if it is an embellishment to make the story acceptable to my occidental sensibilities. In a clear voice, K'ayum recites the moral: "That is why my father says that we must never kill vultures because at one time long ago they were our grandmothers."

"That is a beautiful story, K'ayum," I congratulate him. Later on I was to hear a fuller version from Didier Boremanse, a Belgian anthropologist and collector of Lacandon stories. K'ayum told the condensed version with bright, shifting eyes and quick-moving hands and an authority worthy of his father. He does not yet have his father's intense concentration or uncanny knack for getting inside the skin of each personage; his narrative is faster and more visual, so that the shifts and transformations appear to project outward, like images on a lighted screen. I could picture him making films one day, based on his father's stories.

"K'ayum, have you ever thought of tape-recording your father's stories, for safekeeping?"

"Yes — I've thought about it, but I know he doesn't like it. He tells me the tape recorder is for Mexican songs, and for the anthropologists. It is no good for the *hach winik*. I know that my father is unique, and after he dies there will be no one to tell the stories as he does. And he says to me, 'If you cannot remember the stories in your breast, then you will forget them even if you copy them on a recorder.' So I think he is right." Before I can digest this considered reply, K'ayum snatches the microphone from my hand.

"Now, I want you to tell me a story," he says. "I want to tape it so I can write a book about you in California. Speak: Is Los Angeles like Mexico?"

"Yes and no," I say. K'ayum often asks me to describe San Francisco and Los Angeles, where many of the friends of Nahá live. I had already told him about the cable cars, Chinatown, and the pink and blue houses that climb up and down the hills, all very much like one another and yet different. I had sketched for him the Golden Gate Bridge, the park and the beach and the seals basking on the rocks below Cliff House. I never know what he is visualizing; his questions and exclamations often turn around some detail of personal interest to him, such as the number of spider monkeys in the San Francisco Zoo: Are they the same as those in the forest? What do they eat? And so on.

Los Angeles is a bigger challenge. But K'ayum has now been to Mexico City twice, he is becoming well traveled, and I no longer have to translate the strangeness of the outside world into a forest context, as I still do for Bol and the small children.

Hollywood is too much to take on at the outset, so I begin with Santa Monica, where I had stayed with friends on my way down.

"There is a pier there," I say, "like a road that sticks out into the sea. People go there to swim, to catch fish and to play."

"How do they play?"

"There are games for them there, like wooden horses that you climb on and they go around and around to the sound of a music box; it is called a carousel, and sounds a little like your accordion."

"Ah yes. What else is there?"

"Well, this last time I was in Santa Monica there were many young people on roller skates."

"What's that?"

"These are shoes with four wheels each that you put on, and then you can skim along the boardwalk."

"You mean, like on a bicycle?"

"Not exactly. You wear them just like shoes; the wheels are small, but you can go fast, faster than running — almost as fast as a bicycle."

"And you? Did you put them on?"

"No, not this time. But there were many young people skating along the beach and on the pier. They wear funny clothes, carry radios strapped to their ears, and dance to the music —"

"What kind of music?"

"It's called disco — it's very loud."

"Ah yes, like in San Cristóbal!" He reminds me of the night he smoked pot with Young Mateo and they danced in the town discothèque.

"Yes, but this is out in the open, under the sun. Some of the skaters paint flowers on their faces, and the young women wear very tight, colorful clothes that show off their legs and breasts. I saw one woman skating with conch shells over her breasts —"

"And that's all?" His eyes bulge.

"She had a bikini bottom, like the girl on Bol's towel."

K'ayum whoops. "Victor, did you sleep with her?"

"I'd never seen her before, K'ayum. She was just skating along the boardwalk, with hundreds of others."

I describe the surfers in their wet suits, the old chess players and the body builders that work out on the beach, acquiring biceps and suntans. But I have no way of explaining to K'ayum why people would want deliberately to burn their skins brown in the sun, since it is his opinion that a light skin is one of the very few advantages occidentals have over the Lacandones.

He asks me what other games people play in Santa Monica, and I tell him about tennis, my own favorite. I describe the rules and the dynamics of the sport, which arouse only a faint interest.

And then I find myself telling him of Dr. Renée Richards, the transsexual tennis player I had watched in an L.A. tournament. This provokes a flood of incredulous questions.

"You mean they cut off his penis?"

"Yes, that's what he wanted."

K'ayum looks troubled, and I remember that the hermaphrodite is an object of fear among the Lacandones, as it still is among the highland Mayas.

"Why did he want his penis cut off? It would not get stiff?"

"I think it would," I say, "but he wasn't happy with it."

"Why not? Is he ugly? Couldn't he find a woman?"

"No, he's not ugly. He is tall and thin and strong, but he did not feel happy as a man. Inside, he felt more like a woman, and so the doctors cut off his penis, and gave him pills that made his breasts grow and his ass grow round, like a woman's —"

K'ayum's jaw drops. Then he shakes his head. "Lies. Victor tells lies."

"It's true, K'ayum — I promise. I saw her play. She is a good player. She has long, lean arms, and runs around the court like a vigorous young man, although she is over forty."

"He plays with the women?"

"Yes — she wins a lot too. Since he changed to a woman, she wins more games than he/she won as a man."

He squints at me and folds his arms over his chest, a dispassionate arbiter. "Tell me again what he looks like."

"She looks and walks like a tall, lean, athletic man who had two breasts stuck on his chest, and a woman's buttocks stuck on his behind."

K'ayum explodes with laughter, but his eyes remain skeptical. "When I visit you in California, you must introduce me to this person, and then we will make love so I can see if you have told me the truth."

"Gladly," I say, closing the subject and another chapter in K'ayum's occidental education.

"Next time I will tell you about another interesting place called Las Vegas."

To Palenque

Chan K'in appears for supper with his hair newly washed and his bangs trimmed, so they no longer hang over his brows. Koh II had also washed his best tunic, and hung it up to dry.

When we sit down to eat, the eggs are moist and lightly savored, the beans well cooked, and we find a newly opened tin of deviled ham on the table. All three Kohs are unusually friendly and garrulous, and drop continual hints about our journey to Palenque the following day, and the sorts of things they'd like us to get them.

After dinner Koh II shows Robert and me a fine wooden comb, for which she would like a mate; Koh I lets drop that she is running out of Havana cigars, and Koh III actually smiles as she gives us snippets of green and red ribbon. After Chan K'in Chico's last trip to San Cristóbal, his wife had sewn five bands of different colors on the hem of her skirt, and this had spurred on the other young wives.

"Robert, whose idea was this trip?" I ask, as we sip our citronella tea amid the excited chatter.

He shrugs. "Apparently it was Chan K'in's and Mateo's, with a good deal of encouragement from the wives. Old Chan K'in says he wants to visit the birthplace of Hachäkyum and make certain it has not been damaged by all the *turistas*."

Next morning I get up early, and walk on ahead to check on the condition of the road. The mud and clay stick to the heels of my boots, and the tire ruts are a foot deep in places. I do not see how we can make it to Palenque, but it is clear that Robert would lose face if he were to back down now, with anticipation running so high.

María Bonita stands quietly by the car, rocking her little son. "What happened to the ride you promised?" she asks in a lilting voice, lifting her clear brown eyes toward mine.

"Let's go now quickly," I suggest, half seriously, "before the others get here."

"The road is bad," she says. "We'll get stuck — and my little boy will be frightened."

"And you?" I tease her. "Will you be frightened?"

She grins, baring pink gums. "No, but I cannot go without José's permission, and he is in the *milpa*."

"María," I ask, "what happened with Pepe Camacho? Wasn't he happy with you?"

"He went away." She lifts one arm and points to the far side of the lake. "He is *muy bravo*, Pepe, and fights with his younger brother. Pepe wants his own woman, so he crossed to the other side and married the daughter of Chan Bol."

"Are you sad that he went?"

She rocks her little boy in silence, and shrugs one shoulder. "A little. But it is better like this. José is quieter, now that we are alone." She has been speaking in a mixture of Spanish and slurred Lacandon. Like the other women of Nahá, she tends to swallow her vowels and run consonants together in an unintelligible nasal stream. Whenever I don't understand a phrase or word she repeats it more slowly and gestures with her free arm.

I want to ask her how her marriage to the two brothers had come about, but I don't yet have the vocabulary, and I know she won't understand my Spanish. I ask instead, "Do you want more children?"

She shakes her head. "No, not now — I am not well."

"Why? Does José beat you?"

"No. Pepe, yes — he beat me."

"Does José take you places — to San Cristóbal?"

She shakes her head. "No San Cristóbal."

"Ocosingo?"

"No Ocosingo."

"Palenque?"

Again she shakes her head and says, "No Palenque," with a vigor that persuades me she has never been outside of the forest in her life. After her first husband died, a *ladino* liquor dealer had started her in prostitution, and she has been passed from one man to another ever since. The picture I had formed of María Bonita as a liberated woman who chose her way of life has little basis in reality. This most beautiful woman of Mensäbäk and Nahá has actually had very little say in the conduct of her life, or in her choice of husbands. If anything, her beauty has placed her at a disadvantage among the more traditional wives, who probably ostracize her.

"*Malo* Caribe," she says, after a long silence. "Bad Lacandon."

As Robert, Chan K'in and Mateo make their appearance I promise to take her on a ride when I return.

"Can I bring you anything from Palenque?"

She points to the rash on her calf. "It doesn't go away," she says.

I tell her I'll bring medicine, and she nods and disappears into her hut.

A delegation of wives and youngsters gather around the car to see us off. Young Bol shows up last, with his leather shoulder bag and a flushed look of excitement. His father has invited him along at the last moment, for his first venture into the civilized world. He climbs into the rear of the Safari, with Mateo and his father. They are all three wearing freshly laundered tunics and scrubbed, shining faces.

"Be careful!" Koh I shouts as we take off. The Katzenjammer Kids shriek and try to run behind us, but the mud holds them back. We skid perilously on the first of three hills.

"Looks like it's going to be a long day, little brother," Robert says, shooting me a worried glance. "We are expected back for supper."

"You like María Bonita?" Chan K'in asks softly, as we bounce along the deep ruts.

"Yes," I say. "I am worried about the rash on her leg. She's had it over a year."

Robert nods and says slowly, "Chan K'in thinks she may have tuberculosis."

"Oh no — that's just too much —" is all I can say.

The next two hours gave me little opportunity to reflect on María Bonita's travail. Robert navigated the remaining hills skillfully, and we made it past the first of several flooded sections. But the ruts were too deep in places, even for the high-beamed, high-axled Safari, and we bogged down just beyond Colonia Lacandon.

Bol and I jumped out to attach a rope to the bumper, and yanked the front tires clear as Robert rocked the car back and forth.

When we stopped on dry ground to remove the rope and survey the damage, Jorge trotted up by the side of the road, with his wife. They were bent almost double by the weight of bulging net bags on their backs.

"Going to Palenque?" Jorge asked, with a casual glance at the car from under his head strap.

"Yes, just for the day," Robert said. "What are you carrying there?"

"Crabs," Jorge said. "Fifty of them."

I asked where he got them.

"Below," he said, signaling vaguely down the road. "About two kilometers."

Jorge and his wife continued on their way, with their eyes to the ground. They did not exchange greetings with Chan K'in or Mateo.

"He didn't want to tell where he caught them," Mateo said, with a smile. "The river is only one kilometer from here."

"That's right," Chan K'in said. "There is only one place where you can catch crabs. We go there when game is scarce."

"I don't think he had fifty crabs," Mateo said. "The bag looked small to me."

"That's true," Chan K'in said, laughing aloud. "Perhaps they were only rocks."

"Pebbles. Jorge had fifty pebbles," said Mateo, laughing so hard he had difficulty catching his breath.

Chan K'in was rocking with mirth. "Tonight she will cook the pebbles, and Jorge will convince everyone they are crabs."

"They will have it with Presidente brandy," Robert joined in. "And he will tell everyone it is *balché* —"

"With honey," added Mateo, holding his sides.

Our optimism returned as Robert skillfully navigated several more marshy patches, and a spirit of adventure set in.

Near the turnoff to Mensäbäk we passed a Forestal pickup truck bogged down, and we gave a rousing cheer.

After the next hill we came to a muddy swamp that covered forty or fifty feet of road. This time the tires sank in the clay, all the way to the top of the bumpers.

Mateo and Bol cut branches swiftly as Robert and I dug around the tires with machetes and a small shovel. We jacked up the rear tires, freed the axles and placed branches back and front. When we all yanked on the rope together the car jerked forward and I fell on my butt. Old Chan K'in ran along the ruts and fell in the mud as he leaped out of Robert's way.

We stopped by a stream to wash off the clay and mud; but Chan K'in's tunic and my jeans were soiled beyond help.

"First Victor falls, and then I fall," Chan K'in said, with a big grin. He would repeat it like some cosmic riddle throughout the journey, and we laughed each time. There was a new warmth in his voice when he spoke my name.

We got to Palenque two hours later, and I proposed we spend the night at La Cañada Hotel. I told Robert I did not relish the prospect of spending the night stuck in some mudhole halfway to Nahá. Chan K'in and Mateo readily agreed.

As we entered the tiny supermarket on the main street, I was struck by how small and frail Mateo and Chan K'in looked. Bol, who had been so quick and sure-fingered cutting wood and helping to free the car from forest mud, now looked shrunken, dazed and helpless as he wandered up and down the aisles looking for cheese.

It was nearing sunset when we got to the ruins. A howler monkey was in full cry in the bush nearby, filling the plaza with his unearthly yells.

Bol and Mateo gazed in amazement at the Temple of the Inscriptions. The pyramid seemed to be just emerging from the grip of the forest, whose tallest trees rose fifty to a hundred feet above its crest.

Robert suggested we allow Chan K'in to be our guide. Chan K'in walked directly to the palace across the way and pointed up at the tower. "That is the House of T'uup, keeper of the sun. His father Hachäkyum's home is below."

As we walked among the temples I experienced once again the familiar rush of well-being. It was partly due to the small, almost companionable scale of Palenque. These majestic structures preserve undimmed the imprint of their architects, who built them with a sense of the pervading harmony in nature. Each of the structures refers to every other with geometric precision, and yet they form an altogether pleasing whole, with T'uup's Palace tower at the center, pointing up to the sun, and the Temple of the Inscriptions at right angles to it, inviting entry to the richness and dread of the Mayan underworld.

Touring this sacred site with Chan K'in provided an added boon, as one by one he assigned each of the buildings to one of the major or minor deities. The structure the Spanish named Temple of the Cross is the house of K'ayum, god of music, and the one next to it belonged to Bol, the god of wine. Appropriately, Bol's residence has the famous frieze of an elder smoking a cigar, or possibly a marijuana pipe. The abode of K'in was properly named the Temple of the Sun by the Spaniards, after they saw the solar symbols on its lintels.

We climbed the Temple of the Inscriptions, as Chan K'in continued to point out details of the gods' ancient residence. Robert recalled that Chan K'in had told him of the priests and lords who had been buried beneath their houses in Palenque, long before he knew of the famous "Prince's Tomb" discovered in 1954. He claims that another nobleman is buried under the palace.

Chan K'in reminded us that the gods had long since departed from Palenque. They had left after Kisin tried to kill Hachäkyum, and are now living in their separate heavens above ours.

"Only the brothers of T'uup remain," he said, pointing to two small connected structures to our right. "There live the Red Lords, older brothers of the keeper of the sun. They have to stay here because they tried to kill T'uup after he refused the niece they sent him for a wife. But it was only T'uup's *xiw* (stand-in) that they killed, who was made of palm leaf. T'uup is the favorite son of Hachäkyum, and his older brothers envied him."

Images of Joseph and his brothers invaded my brain. "You mean the Red Lords are still living here, even today?"

Chan K'in nodded. "That is their punishment. They have to stay here and see all the *turistas* walk in and out of their house, just as if no one was there. They will remain there until the end of the world."

A crowd had gathered and followed us around, curious to know if these were the same Mayas who had built the temples. A pair of Japanese tourists asked if they came from Lacanjá. When Robert corrected them they struck a formal pose, smiling their Japanese smiles as each snapped the other's picture next to a bemused Chan K'in.

Bol took everything in stride, with a look of breathless curiosity. "Ah, *muy bonito*," he said of each temple we explored. "Ah yes, very fine. I like the homes of the gods. I like them very much."

Don Moisés

On our return to La Cañada, Don Moisés, the owner of the hotel, invited us all to drinks in the open-air bar. On the way he introduced us to Petunia, a well-groomed female boar he had managed to domesticate, and who hung out by the restaurant, cadging beer and handouts from tourists.

Don Moisés Morales, a slender, silver-haired *ladino* of Asturian Spanish descent, is an old Palenque hand in his late fifties, who likes to guide favored visitors around the ruins in his spare time. He counts among his acquaintances Mayan archaeologists and anthropologists of repute from all over the world. Robert is one of the very few who have held on to his respect over the years.

"At least you write about the Mayas as a living people," he said. "Most others I know reduce them to footnotes in their Ph.D. theses or use them as clubs to hit each other over the head."

The last time we met, Don Moisés had spoken of his extraordinary encounters in El Granizo with an old Lacandon who recounted many of the same stories I would subsequently hear from Old Chan K'in.

"The limits are in us, not in them," he had said at the time. Now, with all the changes in Lacanjá and more recently in Nahá, Don Moisés felt torn and saddened by the corruption, and by what he regarded as a failure on the part of the Nahá elders to protect their vital interests.

"Oh, I've seen too much, I tell you," he said, waving an arm and affecting a world-weary, heavy-lidded look of disgust.

"So, you are becoming cynical, Don Moisés?" Robert twitted him.

"No, only a realist," Don Moisés replied. "For instance, here are two exceptional and noble gentlemen, living windows into the fabulous civilization of the ancient Maya." He pointed to Chan K'in and Mateo, who were quietly drinking beer across the table. "But even they are signing their patrimony over to the government, without putting up any resistance . . . And are they aware of what is happening to their sons? Young Chan K'in and Young Mateo will come here, swaggering like big spenders, and act as if they own the place. They want me to give them free room and board, advance them loans, indulge their taste in alcohol, and other things I won't mention. More and more they are behaving like their southern kin, Carmelo and José Pepe and the other so-called new

245

Christians. I used to lend them money and be a kind of father to them, but no more. Now I only extend them food and shelter, for which I expect full payment. The truth is, they are learning to cultivate us in the same measure in which we have cultivated them." He shakes his head. "Don Roberto, I tell you, when I think they are all that is left of the noble race that built Palenque and Yaxchilán, I want to close my eyes, let it pass over me like a bad dream, and just sit here every evening, enjoying my family and my beer."

Robert explained to Don Moisés the cyclical basis of Lacandon cosmology, which precluded their actively opposing the destroyers of their forest. "They now seem to favor the destruction, so they can begin anew. To the Nahá Lacandones the principle of xu'tan provides a kind of catharsis, as tragedy did for the Greeks."

Don Moisés agreed at first, but then argued that the Lacandones were given too much forest to begin with, and could have held on to their trees in a smaller reserve. "Much as I respect Doña Trudi, I fear she and some of her romantic cohorts were badly deluded when they persuaded the government to grant the Lacandones all those 614,000 hectares of primary forest. If they had settled for fourteen thousand, which is more than enough for their agricultural and hunting requirements, then a buffer zone could have been established, which would have allowed them to hold on to their mahogany and other precious hardwoods. . . . But that is all water under the bridge," he said, with a sigh, and waved his hand.

"You and I know, Don Moisés," Robert whispered huskily, "that the Forestal wanted that mahogany, and had the recourse to acquire it however and whenever they chose —"

The conversation was interrupted by the appearance of Ian Graham, the Harvard archaeologist and artist who was drafting the first detailed drawings — since Catherwood — of Yaxchilán and other important Mayan sites.

Don Moisés introduced them, and he and Robert were soon embroiled in a toe-to-toe dispute over Lacandon ancestry, with Graham arguing that no incense burners of the northern Lacandon type had been excavated in Palenque, whereas some had appeared in Yaxchilán and other sites along the Usumacinta.

I was well aware of the depth of Robert's emotional and intellectual commitment to Palenque as the ancestral seat of Chan K'in's Mayan forebears, and after witnessing Chan K'in's performance at the ruins that afternoon, I was more than ever disposed to support him. But I did not join the argument. The tequila had gone to my head, and I rather enjoyed the curious spectacle of these two tall, strapping Scotsmen going at one another while the parties in question sat quietly beside them, drinking Bavaria beer. Bol drank from a tequila bottle his father had bought, matching him drink for drink. His eyes were already glazed, as much from the unfamiliar ruckus around him, I surmised, as from the liquor he had consumed. In one way or another, Bol was having his second meek'chäl.

At that moment, Young Chan K'in and Mateo's son Bol burst noisily into the bar. Their unexpected appearance put an end to the anthropological discussion. In the excitement, no one noticed how inebriated they both were, especially Young Chan K'in.

Bol asked Don Moisés for a room, crudely waving in his face a roll of thousand-peso bills. He is wall-eyed, with none of his older or younger brothers' striking good looks — but he has more status than any of them. Bol is the *pícaro* of the family — the scamp who has made good in the world of the *ladinos* and the foreigners. And he drives a truck.

Don Moisés ordered beers for Young Chan K'in and Bol.

Young Chan K'in told his father they had been to Mensäbäk to borrow Joaquín's truck, which they would load up the next day with the purchases from Villahermosa. His slurred, unsteady speech suggested that they had drunk a good deal more than the couple of beers they admitted to.

"This is my son!" Mateo announced to Don Moisés, in his clarion voice. "He drives a truck! And I have seven other sons and daughters in Nahá."

"Yes," Don Moisés nodded. "I have had the pleasure of meeting your older son Mateo here, on a number of occasions."

"Is that so?" Mateo said, enthusiastically. "How many children do you have?"

"Eleven," Don Moisés answered, softly. "This young lady serving your drinks is one of my daughters, and the bartender is my oldest son."

"*Ehhh hah*," Mateo and Old Chan K'in remarked, approvingly, after looking over the two offspring.

"How many wives?" Mateo asked casually.

"Only one," Don Moisés answered. "That is the charm of it." He reached behind his waist for a flea, and cracked it between his nails.

"*Ne tsoy* — very nice," said Old Chan K'in.

By now Robert and young Bol had finished the tequila bottle between them. When Young Chan K'in asked if there was any more, Robert invited him to our room.

"We will go to my room first," Young Chan K'in said, "and leave my brother there. He is falling asleep."

"Not true," said Bol, but he had to be helped to his feet.

Young Chan K'in dropped off the two Bols and joined us in our room, where Robert had already opened his own bottle of tequila.

From this point on everything moved at an accelerated pace, with a momentum of its own.

We all drank straight from the bottle until it ran out — no one bothered with the salt or the six limes I had placed on the night table.

Young Chan K'in was the first to lose control. He removed the roll of bills from his money belt and started counting them out in a raucous voice. It was the same boastful litany he'd subjected us to in Nahá, except this time it was accompanied by a grotesque pantomime of what he intended to do if someone tried to rob him.

"They will try to rob me in Villahermosa!" he yelled in his father's face.

247

"I will have to buy a pistol, so they won't kill me." And then he counted out the fifteen bills once again.

Old Chan K'in sat at the edge of the bed and nodded absently as his son flashed his money and flailed about, aping a *ladino* with his pistol. The old man's lids and his mouth drooped and his eyes were far away. It was the first time I'd seen Old Chan K'in betray exhaustion.

From that night on, he would mention K'ayum's name more and more often when speaking of a successor.

Mateo could hardly keep his eyes open, but refused to go to bed before his elder kin.

I broke the impasse by rising and announcing we had a long day ahead of us. As I left the room Robert had his hand on Young Chan K'in's shoulder and was trying to calm him down, although his own eyes were almost as glassy and his speech was thick.

Before returning to my room, I decided to check on Young Bol. I found him propped up against the back wall of Young Chan K'in's room; Mateo's Bol had passed out on the bed. I lifted Bol by the shoulders and led him into the sultry night air. Palenque is lower than Nahá and does not cool down after dark.

Bol leaned his full weight on me. "Ah, now I am drunk," he said, unable to walk a straight line. "And you, Victor?"

"Yes," I said. "A little."

"Ah, but you knew when to stop," Bol said. "You are very intelligent."

This struck me as very funny, and I laughed out loud. *Inteligente* is used by the Lacandones to mean "you are good in my eyes."

"I like you too, Bol."

"Did I behave badly?" he asked, trying to meet my eyes.

"You behaved very intelligently, Bol," I assured him, "like a *hach winik*."

"Ah no," he said sadly. "Tonight I behaved more like a *ladino*."

We found that Chan K'in and Mateo had gone to bed at last, and their room was dark. Young Chan K'in and Robert were arguing outside.

"My brother Bol stays with me," Young Chan K'in called, on seeing us come up the porch steps.

"You have no room," I said, without turning around, and laid Bol down in bed, and then slipped into my own. Just before I passed out I heard the Safari start up, and assumed Robert was driving Young Chan K'in to his room.

I awoke at around three and looked out the window, but there was no sign of Robert or his car. At dawn, when I looked again, the car was still missing, but Robert was snoring in his bed.

A little while after there was a tapping at the window. Mateo and Old Chan K'in stood outside, silhouetted in the frosted glass.

"Roberto, are you awake?"

"I am awake," Robert answered, but did not open his eyes.

"Where is the car, Robert?" I asked.

"In a ditch," he said. "Young Chan K'in wanted to pick up some beer. I missed a turn at the intersection. We tried to pull it out, but the rope broke, and I seem to have snapped something in my leg."

In seconds he was snoring again, and I felt something snap within me as well.

"Wake up, Roberto," Mateo and Chan K'in called from the window. "The car is missing."

"I am awake." He rolled over and attempted to get up, but when he swung out his left leg, he groaned in pain.

More tapping on the window. I opened the door, and Mateo's Bol came in behind them to ask if Robert had a rope, so he could trying pulling the car out with his truck.

Very slowly and painfully, Robert rose and got dressed. He limped steadily enough to suggest he had no broken bones.

"I guess it's the calf muscle," he said. "I pulled it once before, under similar circumstances."

Mateo's Bol drove the truck around, and they went off to extricate the Safari from the ditch. Old Chan K'in went along to check on his belongings.

I roused the younger Bol, who had a hangover, and the three of us headed down to the restaurant for breakfast, where we were met by Young Chan K'in. I looked in his face for some sign of regret, but all I could tell was that he had weathered last night much better than Robert had.

"We couldn't find any place open," he said. "We tried to turn around, but he missed the road and drove into a ditch." He smiled faintly. "Robert had too much to drink."

"And you, Chan K'in?" I asked.

"Ah no, I drank, but not like Roberto. I can hold my liquor."

My opinion of Young Chan K'in hit rock bottom.

"It wasn't Roberto," Mateo said, loyally. "It was Kisin. Kisin was in Palenque last night, eh, Bol?"

"Yes, I think so," young Bol said, looking pale and small and contrite. "Maybe it was Kisin."

"Let us hope we left him behind in that ditch," I suggested, " — where he belongs." But my voice carried no conviction. Kisin or no Kisin, I had discovered in the past twelve hours that I could not live for very long by the stoical Lacandon standards of conduct. In a crunch, my inherited traditions reared up and took command.

Robert returned in the Safari, with Mateo's Bol right behind. A tow truck with a steel cable had stopped and pulled the car out of the ditch. As he limped in with his left foot bare and swollen, Robert chucked me the car keys. "You're driving, brother. I can barely lift my leg to press the clutch pedal."

The retrieval of the Safari seemed to break Kisin's spell; from that point on, our spirits rallied. But there had been a shift in the balance, and my relationship to Nahá would not be the same again.

Don Moisés did not appear to see us off. I pictured his rueful sigh and shake of the head when the gossip reached him. "More craziness," he would say.

Safe Return

I drove too fast, bent on putting Palenque behind us. Past El Diamante I finally got the hang of the steering and gained some control of the car. We reached Nahá after only one major delay, when we were stopped by a Caterpillar opening a new road around the swampy area that had trapped us the day before. The driver seemed amazed that we had gotten through in the first place.

K'ayum awaited us at the entrance to Nahá, his eyes bright from finding us safe and outwardly sound.

"My mother was very worried," he said, "when you didn't come yesterday." He tapped his temple. "But I dreamed you were all right."

"We had an appointment with Kisin last night," I said.

"Bol, you look sick!" K'ayum shouted to his brother. "You met with Kisin also?"

Bol rolled his eyes, and we all laughed. Farther down the road, María stood smiling and rocking her small son.

It was good to be back.

After unloading the car, Bol, K'ayum and I went for a long, cleansing swim. I returned to find Robert propped up in his hammock, hard at work on his manuscript. I had feared he would be flat on his back for the rest of our stay.

"You must come from one hell of a long line of hard-drinking Scotsmen," I said, and he broke into song:

> Oh, we're sick, sober and sorry,
> Broke, disgusted and sad . . .

"Must you *always* go through this before you get down to work?"

"I guess so, little brother, I guess so." He had never looked more chastened; he was puffy-eyed and scruffy, and yet an almost ascetic pallor shone in his face. Is the underside of the Scots boozer a Trappist monk? A mutual friend of Robert's and Malcolm Lowry's had suggested they had the same guardian angel. I could better understand now how Lowry had completed *Under the Volcano*.

At dinner, Robert asked, "What penance shall I do?"

"We'll leave that to the missionaries to decide," I kidded, not suspecting the encounter that awaited us two days later.

We passed out the gifts and medicines, which cheered the women up and helped restore harmony in Chan K'in's kitchen. The youngest Koh accepted her green and red ribbons with a rare, ungrudging smile, and wasted no time in sewing them on her skirt; the plastic comb Robert brought Koh II was whisked away as if it were mother-of-pearl. Only the elder Koh seemed disappointed with the machine-rolled cigars we found her.

"Alicia's are much better," Koh said, of the deluxe Havanas Alicia Bruce had sent her at no small expense. She lighted one of ours anyway with a stick of pitch pine, whose rosy flare gave her craggy features a spectral glow. "This is too bitter," she said, spitting the juice on the ground. "Not the real tobacco, like ours and Alicia's."

In the following days K'ayum, K'in Paniagua and the children riddled us with questions about the trip. Who got drunk first? How many tequilas did Bol have before he passed out? K'ayum wanted to know if I had drunk as much as Robert.

"No, I didn't," I confessed. "If I had we probably would still be in Palenque."

"Next time," K'ayum said, "you get drunk, and Robert not so much — and then everything will be equal."

"Right," I said. "And if we both get drunk the same night, and pass out?"

K'ayum laughed. "Xu'tan," he said.

Nuk the Traditionalist

When I brought the earrings I promised to Nuk of the twisted jaw, she and Paco were sitting outside as she combed his thick, new-washed hair. Since her second miscarriage Nuk pampered Paco constantly, and looked after the small infants of Nahá like a fond spinster aunt. She shared with Juanita the babysitting for Young Chan K'in's motherless boy.

I invited her to choose from the four sets of earrings and she unhesitantly picked out the imitation ruby, which was the most expensive. She turned them around on her palm, held them against the light, and then whisked them away with a gleam in her eye like her mother Koh's.

When she turned her back I glimpsed Bol over her shoulder, sitting in the dark corner of the hut.

"Still nursing your hangover?" I asked.

"I am telling Paco and Nuk about our trip." His voice was subdued.

"Too much drinking," I said to Nuk, and she batted her eyes in agreement, but said nothing. She finished combing out Paco's hair and started grinding corn flour. It occurred to me that the reason Nuk wouldn't converse with me in her fluent Spanish is that, with Paco always nearby, she did not wish to present even the slightest appearance of carrying on a flirtation with another man.

After helping to liberate many of the young women and introducing them to contraceptive pills and a taste for baubles and ribbons, happily married Nuk had turned around and now behaved like one of the reticent, traditional wives of Nahá.

Since her marriage to Paco — her third since the hotheaded Vicente shot her in the face because she was too dark-skinned — Nuk has lost two babies in childbirth. She lost her first one in a rural hospital, where they performed an emergency cesarean section. The cesarean had added shame to her loss, for Nuk felt she was incapable of bearing a child naturally, like a proper Lacandon woman.

Cynthia Wooley, Trudi Blom's former assistant, was with Nuk in May of 1978 in the San Cristóbal hospital where she lost her second child, a daughter. This time she had been led to believe she could have a normal delivery, but when her cervix proved to be too narrow, she refused to have a cesarean. Despite her wracking pains Nuk insisted on squatting to bear her child, as her mother, Koh II, had borne all ten of hers, grasping the crossbar all alone in the Nahá birth hut. But the baby was too large — Nuk is of the small-hipped Spider Monkey lineage, whereas Paco is a large-skulled Wild Boar — and Nuk's muffled screams convinced Cynthia and the nurses that she would die with the baby rather than submit to the knife a second time. Paco, who had stayed by her side throughout the ordeal, threatened to run in front of a car if Nuk should die.

After hours of agony, Nuk finally collapsed and her daughter emerged from her lacerated womb, dead of asphyxiation.

Cynthia reported that Nuk was on the mend by the following day, and when she visited the hospital found her and Paco joking and laughing and already planning her next pregnancy. After a lengthy discussion, Nuk reluctantly agreed to have a cesarean the next time. But there can be no certainty that she will not back out of her promise, for fear of shaming herself once again in her mother's eyes.

The Highway Hotel

After dinner I joined the younger men by the edge of the road, to await the return of Young Chan K'in and Old Mateo's Bol from Villahermosa.

It was a clear, star-filled night. We lay on our backs, and Bol pointed out the Boar, the Porcupine and other constellations his father had taught him. Then we remained still a long time, listening to the crickets and the occasional call of a night bird.

"I think about Palenque," Bol said softly, "and why my brother Chan K'in drinks so much. Perhaps it is because he does not have a woman."

"What about Juanita?"

"Oh, they are not husband and wife yet. She cooks and takes care of the baby, but they will not sleep together for another year."

"I'm glad you told me that," I said, trying to review my harsh opinion of Young Chan K'in in this extenuating light. But with all due allowance for the heavy weight on his shoulders, my throat still constricted at the manner in which he had lied to and manipulated his father.

K'ayum, K'in Paniagua and Antonio's Chan K'in arrived together, and we all huddled on top of one another and gazed up at the sky, like braves in a Sioux longhouse.

"This is a hotel," K'in Paniagua said. "The highway hotel."

This absurd idea touched off a round of giggling.

"Very cheap hotel," K'ayum said. "No rooms, no beds, no toilets — only a good view of the highway."

"No music either," Chan K'in put in.

Bol reminded him that José would be bringing his record player.

"Oh, then it will be a discothèque," K'ayum said. "The highway discothèque."

We squirmed in helpless laughter, lying in a tangle of arms, legs and heads.

"Better not tell Young Mateo about this," I warned. "He'll want to buy it."

José arrived with his record player, and soon a *ranchera* blared its quavering lament into the night, as fiddle and brass assaulted our ears. "You left me alone and desolate the night we meeeet," the *charro* sang, drawing out the syllabic pathos of his last broken romance. José and Chan K'in sang along in cracked pubescent voices.

"Anyone want to dance?" José joked.

I asked, "Where is María Bonita?"

"Asleep," José said, and all at once he started to pummel me and tickle my ribs. "You want to take my brother Pepe's place?" he shouted. "You want to make love with María?"

"Yes!" I yelled. "I want her child!"

K'ayum jumped on top of José, and we all ended up wrestling and pummeling one another, the way we used to on overnight hikes in Camp Hiawatha, in the Catskills, when I was fourteen.

Young Chan K'in arrived late, long after I'd retired to my hammock. In the morning, it took all the men over two hours to unload the truck of one hundred cartons of Fab detergent, Nescafé, Mazola oil, Carnation milk, Raleigh cigarettes, and other provisions and haul them into Young Chan K'in's store. He sat in his hammock with a ledger open at his lap, marking off each item as it came in.

K'in the Hunter

The grownups were not the only ones interested in blow-by-blow accounts of our Palenque expedition. The Katzenjammer Kids listened avidly to Bol's account of our visit to the ruins, our adventures on the road, and the drinking in the evening. The drinking engrossed them most of all. Little K'in — Hans — asked his older brother again and again if he really drank a half bottle of tequila by himself, and whether he enjoyed it.

"Yes, I like tequila," Bol said, affecting a grownup casualness. "It is better than beer, but not as good as *balché*. And if you drink too much, you get sick and dizzy, and your head hurts all of the next day. *Balché* is better."

Little Chan K'in — Fritz — poked gentle fun at Robert's limping around with a crutch, and both boys parroted tippling with their thumbs, just like their counterparts in *The Captain and the Kids*.

In the afternoon little K'in brought a small dead bird into the hut and threw it at our feet with a triumphant yelp.

"I killed it," he boasted, flexing his slingshot.

"Will you eat that little bird?" I asked him.

"No, I won't," K'in said. "Too many bones." He picked up the yellow and green corpse by the tail and tossed it at our feet once again, like a cat.

"If you won't eat it," Robert said, in a calm but stern voice, "Yum Chom will come for your soul, and turn you into an ugly black buzzard — a *zopilote*."

K'in burst into tears, and then remained quietly thoughtful while we returned to our books and journals. He took the bird outside and returned soon after with the yo-yo I'd given him.

"See, I can make it work," he said, flipping it in the air.

Little K'in did not kill another bird during our stay, but he and his brother continued to mock our foibles with as much zealous glee and accuracy as ever.

An Afternoon Outing

When I showed up at José and María Bonita's to take them on the promised ride, her in-laws were eating *tostadas* in the large house, munching noisily and staring out at us until María Bonita became flustered and turned her back.

In a formal tone that had no trace of last night's roughhousing, José informed me he was on his way to the *milpa,* and could not join us.

"You take María and the children," he said, with a hand on his hip.

Nuxi' and the other in-laws went on staring and chewing noisily as I handed María the medical cream I had brought for her rash. She hid it under her shift and took it inside.

"I'll be back," she yelled into the big hut, holding her chin high. Later on I learned that the in-laws had been appropriating most of the medicines and gifts we had given her.

As they climbed into the front seat of the Safari, six-year-old Nuk peered up at me, wary but game for adventure. The little boy, who was still called Och (Possum), clung to his mother, his face buried in her chest.

I started the engine and we lurched out of the muddy shoulder where the car was parked. The boy started to whimper at once.

"Is this your first time?" I asked María.

"Yes, the first time," she nodded, as we slid and bounced on the hardened ruts.

I turned to Nuk. "Are you afraid?"

She gazed at me with her coal-black eyes, and shook her head.

As I turned uphill, toward Ocotal Chico, the road surface deteriorated, causing the car to rattle and buck even more. Huge spreading cedars and smaller trees loomed up from either side, screening out the sunlight. I made a hairpin U at the top of the next hill, which had no shoulders, only a vertiginous slope.

María whispered in her son's ear, which stopped his whimpering. I made out the phrase *"sas wich"* and assumed it meant something favorable because seconds later, although the road was still rough, the little boy turned to me with a brave, trusting smile.

"Do you still think I'm a *ladino?*" I asked little Nuk, who had yelled the word *kah* at me when I approached their hut.

"*Ts'ul?*" she whispered.

"That's right." I placed a hand on her knee, and brushed María's fingers. "A friendly foreigner."

María flushed, and covered her mouth with one hand. She did not say another word, and did not meet my eyes when I left her by the hut.

"Did you enjoy the ride?" I asked, but she took her children and ran up the trail without turning and disappeared into her hut.

When I reported to Robert on our afternoon outing and asked what *sas wich* means, he lifted an eyebrow.

"Apparently María Bonita told her little boy you were clairvoyant."

"Clairvoyant!"

"Yes — and that, little brother, is a very high compliment in these parts. You may have to start looking at this little flirtation you're carrying on with María in a more responsible light."

I nodded. "I guess I wasn't thinking."

Lying in my hammock I brooded on María Bonita and her possible tuberculosis, and the way she had flushed when I brushed her fingers. I could not seem to untangle her from my arrested memories of my Quiché nursemaid. "Little flirtation" was hardly a fair description of the welter of emotions Maria evoked in me. But then it seemed I was not the only one with distorted perception. "Clairvoyant" indeed!

A New Cayuco

K'ayum invites me across the lake to the west shore, where José Güero's sons have felled a mahogany for a new *cayuco*. Robert is still hut-bound by his swollen calf, so K'ayum and I take off soon after breakfast in one of his father's small canoes.

It is a sparkling, windless day, and the lake surface is as smooth as silk.

As we near the water-lily lake a black duck rises from behind a bank of reeds and beats its wings to an unseen metronome, each feathery stroke a distinct note on an ascending scale. Once more I am drawn into the peculiar time spell of the lake — but I am inhibited by the changes in the forest, and a part of me remains outside. It is as if I am already experiencing this special place in hindsight, like a childhood landscape I can no longer afford to inhabit.

K'ayum slides the canoe into the far bank of the second lake, and we step out on the edge of a thickly forested hill. The climb is arduous and slow, for the trail is treacherously soft from the recent rains. Before we reach the first summit, my boots are dragging two leaden, soggy lumps of clay and mud.

The trail meets a wide rutted corridor made by a Caterpillar, and just ahead I see the first of the mahogany stumps.

"Here they took out about twenty trees," K'ayum says, pointing to the clean-shaven thick stumps on either side of the Caterpillar track.

I look up and see a hole of blue sky — and then one by one I make out the splintered trees around the base of each stump: madrone, *chicozapote*, chameadora palm. Each mahogany stump we pass has a blue hole in the canopy above it, and a semicircle of splintered and bruised vegetation. Some of the smaller trees were knocked over or broken by the mahoganies as they fell; the rest by the Caterpillar that hauled them out. And there are more gashed and splintered trees along the edges of the winding Caterpillar track.

I grope for words to articulate the ache in my chest, and picture a city through which a faceless army has passed unchallenged, seizing its strongest and bravest citizens and leaving the remainder maimed and dying.

The holes in the canopy call to mind inescapably Chan K'in's parable of the trees and the stars. And I remember an image from the *Popol Vuh*.

"K'ayum," I say, "did you know that in the old Mayan stories your ancients told of four hundred brothers who were killed by an evil giant? The Quiché called him Zipacná, and he was the ancestor of Kisin."

"Four hundred?" K'ayum exclaims, his interest aroused. "Then it's the same as the mahogany."

"And you know what happened to the four hundred brothers?"

"They went to live with Sukunkyum?" he suggests, reasonably.

"No — this was before the time of Sukunkyum. It was before the time of the sun and the moon, when it was dark everywhere on earth. In that time of the first creation the lords of the underworld played their rubber-ball game in the courtyards beneath the earth. The four hundred brothers were heroes, not men, and Zipacná the earthshaker tricked them into believing he was dead and then brought their house down around them, killing every last one."

K'ayum frowns and lifts his brows. "Then, where did they go?"

I point to the slice of sky visible through the rip in the treetops. "They became a constellation of stars, and brought the first light to the new-made earth."

"Ahhh." K'ayum rubs his chin thoughtfully. "Then the Forestal will kill them again, if they fly up in airplanes and cut down the trees in Hachäkyum's forest."

I nod and smile. "I don't think they're that powerful yet."

Suddenly K'ayum grins and slaps my shoulder in one of his abrupt shifts of mood. "No importa — it doesn't matter. My father says it is a good thing that this world dies soon, so that we get a new one. This world is too old already, by many years." His eyes sparkle as he grins from ear to ear. "Let it go, Victor. You take things too seriously," he says, and hoots aloud.

There is an answering hoot from the next hill, and then we hear the ax blows echoing in the forest.

On the next hilltop, beyond the edge of the ravaged grove, we come upon the crew of canoe builders, hacking away at a thick mahogany the loggers had overlooked. We arrive just in time to help roll over the hollowed-out trunk, and we then join K'in García, Young Chan K'in, Bol, Nuxi' and K'in Paniagua, who squat around the crackling campfire as José Güero's three grown sons shape the hull with axes and adzes. They work methodically, without missing an ax stroke or biting too far beneath the bark.

"Good tequila in Palenque?" K'in Paniagua asks, picking his teeth with a match.

"Yes," I answer for the sixth or seventh time since our return. "Tasty, but not as good as balché with honey."

"Tequila is better in Villahermosa," Young Chan K'in says, peremptorily. "And it costs ten pesos less."

The kibbitzing and gossip go on in leisurely fashion, against the steady hammering of the axes. Then it is Young Chan K'in's and Nuxi's turn to chop away at the hull, scattering chips in all directions. José Güero's sons have carved out the stern, and removed three flat slabs they will sand down and polish into stools for their father's god-house. The tree's shell already lies strewn on the ground, as the canoe emerges from its moist, russet core.

I squat on the ground, warm my fingers in the fire and settle into the rhythm of this event. The smoke curls slowly upward, escaping through the new vents in the forest ceiling. As it hits the slanting sunrays the smoke lights up in crosshatched silvery patterns, more luminous than the flames below. The forest floor is flecked with daubs of sunlight that dance here and there, like rain through a leaking roof. The smell of fresh resin blends with the pungent woodsmoke.

K'in García — Louis XIV — sits by the side, enveloped in gloom, and munches on black berries from a nearby tree as he cleans his .22 Winchester. Bol squats opposite him, smoking a cigar with his eyes to the ground. Since our return from Palenque he is often sunk in meditation, which he explains by jabbing his temple: "I am thinking."

"Did Victor get drunk?" K'in Paniagua asks of no one in particular, so that the question hangs in the air, between brackets of silence.

"Only a little," Young Chan K'in answers, between strokes of his ax. "Not like Roberto."

"How long did they sleep?"

The questions will be asked again and again, ritually, until reputations are redeemed and a rough parity is reestablished. (The day before, Old Mateo had asked me to repair his pocket flashlight, after first showing it to Robert. When I pointed to the wrong screw, Mateo shook his head and looked relieved. "Roberto knows which is the right screw," he said. Mateo is a whiz at repairing gadgets, so it seems likely he had loosened the screw deliberately, to test our mechanical skill.)

A half hour later the prow is nearly completed, and there is another shift as Bol and K'in Paniagua take up the axes.

K'ayum tells his brothers and José Güero's sons about Mexico City and his meeting with the President. What intrigues them most is his description of the television studio.

"Is it like the movie?" K'in asks.

"No," K'ayum says. "A movie is like a photograph; I saw how it's done in Mexico when they made *Cascabel*. It is many photographs that move very fast, and get thrown on a screen by a bright light. But in television it is happening at the same time. It is like a mirror with sound. You say something and you move your hand and you see it happening on the glass. But the picture can be thrown very far away, so many, many people see it at the same time. In Coatzacoalcos we were stopped by a police-woman who saw us on her television and we were far away in Mexico!"

For once, Young Chan K'in has nothing to say. He has never been inside a television studio. K'in García's eyes are hazel pools of concentration as he rubs his chin against the stock of his rifle. But K'ayum's imaginative vault across cultures has cost him, and I hear the weariness in his voice. He will not be traveling to Mexico City again very soon.

A quail calls twice, close by. At first I think it is someone signaling, but K'in quietly picks up his rifle and walks into the forest. Minutes later we hear two shots, and he returns empty-handed.

"K'in Bor told me they also have television in color," K'in says. "Is that true?" His preoccupation with this question had evidently spoiled his aim.

"Yes, they have," K'ayum says. "I saw my face on a color screen. It was yellow and red." He smiles. "I looked like one of our ancients, before Kisin turned us brown."

The lower hull of the canoe is now complete, as it lies half submerged in its bed of chips. The fine adz work on the interior is still ahead, but we take a break for lunch.

We roll the canoe upright and then start down the slope, joking and gossiping aloud, so that our laughter fans out in all directions. The sad spectacle of the mahogany stumps and the Caterpillar track is not so ap-

palling on second view. By salvaging the last of its trees, the canoe builders have in some measure reclaimed the entire grove.

Return to the Milpa

Bol leads the way, almost cheerful now, and suggests we visit the *milpa*
and check on the new tobacco crop. We get into the small *cayuco* and
paddle toward the channel, which is overgrown with sword grass and
water lilies; Chan K'in has not been to his *milpa* since the road was completed.

Bol leads us straight to the tobacco patch, and K'ayum withdraws to
take a nap in the shed. The sun is bright and warm, highlighting the dense
green color of the tobacco leaves.

"They are almost ready," Bol says, and teaches me to split off the small
top leaves, leaving only the full-grown, darkest ones for the harvest. If the
plant is allowed to flower, the tobacco leaves would lose their strength
and texture. "These are the real tobacco," Bol says, rubbing them for texture. "We will cut them and dry them in the shade, and during the rains
my stepmother, Koh, will roll them into cigars, in time for the next *balché*
ceremony."

"And when will that be?"

Bol shrugs. "Perhaps after we plant the first corn in the new *milpa*. Or
when we make the new incense burners."

My ears perk up. "You mean an incense-pot renewal? But there hasn't
been one in years."

"That is why," Bol says. "And now, with the road and all the changes,
my father is thinking of making a new god-house further up the hill. . . .
But don't tell anyone yet. It's a secret."

When I ask Bol if they grow blue corn, he leads me to a patch of thin,
dry stalks and bares open a small, pale-blue, snaggletoothed specimen.

"These are the last," he says. "We will not plant corn here anymore."

The whole *milpa* already feels fallow, its reproductive power spent.
But the new cycle has not yet begun. There is no birdsong today, no electric charge in the air, and even the sun feels wrong: too high and pitilessly
bright on the brown, papery stalks. Also missing is the bedrock sense of
place I had felt so powerfully here the year before. It has withdrawn, to
reemerge wherever the new cultivation will birth the next cosmic round.
But I had not felt that fertile presence in the new *milpa* either. Where
had it gone? And how long could the Lacandon community survive without it?

"Bol, why did your father cut his *milpa* so close to the road?"

"I think," he says, after pausing to reflect, "that he wants to show them
something."

It is true, then. Chan K'in is pitting his *milpa* against the intruders and
their gods. Like his ancestors before him he is trying to swallow the invaders, "Mayanize" them with Lacandon magic.

We rouse K'ayum from his siesta, and he smacks his lips and rubs his stomach. "I am hungry. I dreamed of eating sugarcane."

"Let's go then," Bol says. "I know where to get some."

We return to the lily-pad lake and cross to the opposite shore. While K'ayum and I wait by the bank Bol goes in with his machete and returns with three long stalks of ripe, red-skinned sugarcane. We cut them into segments and gorge on the sweet fibers, splintering them in our teeth to suck out the juice and spitting out the gristle.

"Ahh, now I am awake," K'ayum says, picking slivers from his teeth. We cut up another stalk and gorge again.

Evangelista!

We were on the third and last stalk, our mouths dripping with the sticky juice, when a blue Cessna buzzed the lake, its metal wings gleaming in the sun, and landed smoothly in the old airstrip.

"*Evangelista!*" K'ayum and Bol exclaimed at once. Only Phil Baer and his Wycliffe Bible Translators still used that runway.

On our return I found Robert outside our hut, speaking with a stocky, silver-haired occidental, while a pink-faced couple waited under the shade of the banana trees.

Robert introduced me to Philip Baer and his associates, Dr. and Mrs. Quackenbush from Kansas.

"So you're Bob's sidekick?" Phil Baer said, studying me intently. He has deep-blue eyes and a large square jaw set in a fixed smile. "Well, I was just telling Bob how heartsick I feel at seeing this road and the fallen trees. I'm sure that all of us here want to see these people hold on to their way of life." Baer spoke in a strong, sincere voice that matched the smile and the handshake. "But you know, they're going to have to take matters into their own hands."

"As in Lacanjá?" I suggested.

His eyes narrowed, but the smile remained in place. I did not doubt that he felt badly about the road and the trees, but his motives were a complete mystery.

"Exactly so," he said, pointing a finger for emphasis. "No one is going to run over those fellows, I can tell you. And you may have noticed" — he chuckled jovially — "no one pulls the wool over Carmelo's eyes."

"Yes, well that is one of the things I wished to talk over with you," Robert said.

"Of course, of course. . . . The leg any better, Bob?" He pointed to Robert's bare calf. "Perhaps Quackenbush here should have a look at it. He's a medic."

"I'd be delighted to," Quackenbush said, stepping forward, but Robert assured him he was recovering nicely on his own, thanks all the same. The Kansas missionary doctor was about sixty-five, wore a blue golf cap slightly askew and a loose blue polo shirt over his bulging stomach. His wife had on an ankle-length flower-print dress, nurse-white oxfords and a floppy, turn-of-the-century beach hat. Beneath its rim her eyes turned upward, wavering slightly, as if she were awaiting revelation or, more likely, sunstroke.

"About Carmelo —" Robert tried again, but Phil Baer cut him short with another hearty chuckle.

"Been having a little too much hootch out on the town, eh? Same old Bob. I want you to know that Jim and I were praying for you yesterday —"

"I think — I think I'm going to —" Mrs. Quackenbush suddenly called out from under the banana tree.

"No you're not, honey, it's all right," her husband said, rushing to her side. Her round cheeks were radiant, and her eyes rolled in her head.

"She'll be all right," Baer said. "Just a touch of the sun."

Quackenbush took his wife to a shaded hut, and laid her down on a hammock.

When Robert again brought up Carmelo and the mahogany payments, Phil Baer suggested they discuss it later in the evening, at his cabin.

"Jim and I are going to look in on Old Chan K'in," Baer said. "I understand there's been some influenza among the little ones. You are welcome to join us."

We followed Baer and his associate into Chan K'in's hut, where they examined Koh III's two littlest sons, who had been coughing in the night again. Baer speaks fluent Lacandon Maya with a Lacanjá accent. His conversation with Chan K'in was brief and to the point. After leaving some medicines, they went on to check Antonio, who had an abscess on his foot.

"Slippery fellow, isn't he?" I said to Robert, after we returned to the hut so he could lie down and rest his painful calf. Baer's visit seemed to have brought on a relapse.

"Phil Baer is no fool," Robert said, in a low, angry voice.

I shook my head. "I can't figure him out at all. Christ, he's been at this since 1943."

"Well, little brother," Robert sighed deeply, "neither can I. Sometimes I think he does it just for the perverse satisfaction of destroying a living culture that is older and finer than his own."

"I think perhaps Chan K'in said it best," I reminded him. "They are missing something, and want to complete themselves by making others the same as they are."

"Right," said Robert. "What I can't get over is Baer's bullheadedness. He's like a man obsessed."

After completing their medical rounds Baer and Quackenbush stopped by to let us know that Antonio's wife was all right and the swelling in Antonio's foot had gone down. Robert and Chan K'in had both been concerned about the abscess because the encephalitis that had killed Koh had begun the same way.

When I asked them if they had noticed that the Lacandones' blood clotted much faster than ours, Quackenbush raised an eyebrow.

"Oh, really?"

"Yes," I said, "it's been remarked on by a number of doctors. And do you have any explanation of why they have no gray hair?"

For just a moment, Baer's smile deserted him. "I guess they must use Grecian Formula Number Two — eh, Jim?" he said, and slapped his colleague on the shoulder, laughing boisterously.

"I meant that in all seriousness," I said, put off by his overreaction.

Baer came over to shake my hand, his smile firmly in place once more. "I am sorry, sir. I did not mean to be facetious. I guess questions like that just tickle my funny bone." He turned and walked on toward the canoe landing, with Quackenbush and his recuperated wife behind him.

The doctor returned alone seconds later to ask Robert if he could take a picture "of his pretty face."

"I want it right in front of me on my desk, Bob, so I can pray over it every day."

Before we could take in this bit of missionary presumption, Quackenbush snapped a photo of Robert's puffy, unshaven face; I then insisted that he pose for my camera.

"Be glad to," he said, and doffed his blue golf cap to reveal a shiny bald pate. "That a Retina?" he called, as I snapped his picture standing next to Robert. "Damn good piece of machinery."

He started to leave, and turned back once more. "Let me say, Bob, I think Phil has done wonderful things with these people. Last time I was here they had almost one hundred percent infant mortality. Hell, if it weren't for Phil, they probably wouldn't be here today."

"That's a very questionable figure," Robert said.

"One more thing, Bob" — Quackenbush rolled up the golf cap in his hand and jabbed it in our direction — "I think you'd be much better off sticking with Phil than going against him. He's got God on his side."

Robert managed to reply, "Well, you can't buck those odds. . ." But Quackenbush was gone.

As the afternoon wore on, Robert got angrier and angrier with himself for not having told Baer and his sidekick where to get off.

"Well, older brother, those two are beyond belief," I said to calm him, "but as you said yourself, they are not the enemy."

"The thing of it is, I was brought up as a Scottish Baptist and Baer knows it, the sonofabitch. He loves to rub salt in the wound."

When their plane took off I recorded it on my tape, and replayed it at full volume fifteen minutes later for the satisfaction of watching everybody look up at the sky. The best way to close this whole episode was with a Lacandon joke.

At dinner K'ayum did a telling impersonation of Phil Baer's cotside manner, and Chan K'in remarked with a big grin:

"K'ayum picks up everything quickly, like Victor's tape recorder picks up the evangelists' airplane."

In the next two days there were several more flights from Yaxoquintela, the missionary forest training center. Groups of four and five evangelists wandered through the settlement, checking pulses, distributing medicines and candy, and snapping their cameras. They were all midwesterners, tall, clean-cut and uniformly genial; they tactfully avoided comments on the poverty and dirt and the unsanitary conditions, remarking instead on the beauty of the lake and the purity of the air.

I stayed well out of their way. With all the evils coming down on Nahá all at once, it was hard to take these people too seriously.

Robert, however, still fumed. His quarrel with Baer had the overtones of an old family feud. At times I pictured them as rival coaches, each of whom strived to prove his team — the southern and the northern — superior to the other. The analogy broke down with the absurdity of Carmelo and Chan K'in as football captains; but nonetheless it was helpful in understanding the driving passions of the two men.

"Bunch of hypocrites," Robert muttered, when the first group of Bible Translators strolled through Nahá, disrupting its daily rhythm. "Now I know why Baer wants to preserve Nahá," he went on in his sarcastic voice. "So he can show it off to these greenhorn missionaries as Exhibit A: 'And now, gentlemen, let me take you to Lacanjá, where you can discover for yourselves the fruits of our missionary labor — note the new gas ovens and the tin roofs, the clean western dress, the absence of filthy cigars and heathen incense pots. This, gentlemen, is Exhibit B.' "

Robert informed me that Yaxoquintela is the missionaries' jungle training center for all of Latin America. The Wycliffe Bible Translators who train there will go on to evangelize in Central America and the Amazon forests of Brazil, Colombia and Peru.

"What gets me," Robert said, "is that they have almost unlimited funding to push their weight around and they are on excellent terms with the Mexican government. Goddamn, let's face it — it isn't only God Phil Baer has on his side."

K'in Bor in Shadow

Geneviève had returned to France, and the Mexican intern who spelled her in keeping up the forest clinic had gone on to some other work. Geneviève left the key to the dispensary with K'ayum, and next morning we paddled across to get some painkiller for Robert, and some other medicines. I also planned to pay K'in Bor a visit.

It was the third bright day in a row, and the lake was so crystalline I could see small fish and crustaceans swimming near the bottom. We

passed a canoe with three midwestern evangelists who waved good-naturedly and rhapsodized about the clarity of the water.

"No trace of pollution! Marvelous!" the younger man in the middle
shouted, trailing a leg in the water.

"Not yet!" I shouted back, "but watch out for the alligators!"

Atanasio, the hunter, who paddled their *cayuco*, laughed out loud
when the missionary nearly tipped them all into the water in his haste to
retrieve his leg. K'ayum joked that no self-respecting alligator would taste
missionary flesh, for fear of becoming converted.

We docked the canoe and visited the dispensary, which looked bare
and unkempt, as if it had been burglarized. The medicine boxes were covered with dust, and many were already dated. We did not find the pain-
killers or the Enterovioform we sought, and went on to the old store,
where Young Chan K'in was balancing his accounts.

"Soap, only thirty pesos — cheap," he called out to Vicente, one of
Jorge's sons-in-law, and ticked off all the other marked-down items: rice,
instant coffee, detergent, vegetable oils, which he was selling at half price
because he brought them by truck.

"Rice — cheap — forty pesos a kilo," he recited, like a television pitch-
man. "Instant coffee — cheap — seventy pesos a jar —" He dazzled and
mesmerized Vicente with figures, until Vicente bought a sack of rice, a jar
of Nescafé and more Fab than he was ever likely to use.

Young Mateo came in the store to buy a carton of cigarettes. He looked
pale and surprisingly frail. I asked him what had become of the Hotel
Maya Caribe.

"Finished," he said, with a shrug. "I don't like it anymore."

"But didn't the loggers stay there? K'ayum told me they pay you good
money — better than the *turistas*."

"Yes," he said, in a petulant voice, "but they complain too much, and
do not like Nuk's cooking."

"Mateo likes *turistas* better," K'ayum teased. "Especially the gringas."

Young Mateo flashed his lascivious grin. "That's right," he said; but his
eyes had lost their soulful luster. His features had turned slack and were
losing the angelic sensuality that made him so irresistible to gringas in
San Cristóbal. Like his father, young Mateo had not learned to disguise
corruption. It showed on his face like acid on litmus paper.

"Next week I close the hotel, and Carmelo and I are flying to Guatemala, in a Cessna."

"Who's flying it?" I asked, doubting his story.

"I am," he said, smiling wanly.

After he left the store, Young Chan K'in scoffed that Mateo was not
flying anywhere because he didn't have a license. "He can't read or write
like his brother Bol can."

"He needs no license to talk," K'ayum observed. "He can talk his way
to Guatemala, he and Carmelo." Almost unnoticed among the shifts and
changes in Nahá was K'ayum's break from his older brother-in-law's influence.

We were still laughing when Chan K'in Chico entered the store with Margarita, who straddled their baby boy on her hip. He is huge for his age, and lighter-skinned than either of his parents, which emboldened Chan K'in Chico to carry himself with exaggerated stiffness. He had aged four or five years since fathering the boy — an overnight patriarch of sixteen. Margarita still flirted with her eyes and would titter at anything, but she no longer made fun of her husband.

"K'in Bor is waiting for you," Chan K'in Chico declared, in a portentous tone.

As we walked toward K'in Bor's hut, Chan K'in Chico offered to teach me how to ask for a wife, in exchange for a bottle of Herradura tequila.

"I will teach you what gifts they like and what you say to the father. It has to be done properly."

I played along. "And what if she has no father?"

Chan K'in Chico squinted his good eye at me, and grinned. "Then you must ask her husband. I can teach you that, too."

I told him — firmly — that I was not interested in a woman from Nahá at present, and if I had been, I was accustomed to doing my own pleading on my own terms. I assumed this closed the subject, but on entering K'in Bor's hut Chan K'in Chico announced in a loud voice, "Victor likes María Bonita — he wants to marry her," which set off a fit of hysterics from Margarita and K'in Bor's Nuk, who was hidden behind the mosquito screen.

K'in Bor invited me to sit in his hammock, as he used to on the other side. His color was back, and he looked recovered from his last drinking bout. But his eyes were restless and distant.

"So you and Robert and my father-in-law had some good tequila in Palenque?" He flared his nostrils and widened his eyes at me.

"Yes, it was good," I said, "but we drank too much."

"And my father?" asked Chan K'in Chico, standing by the door.

"He and Mateo drank less."

Chan K'in Chico blurted out with sudden passion, "I want my father to return to Palenque and buy a hat and trousers. I want my father to look clean and pretty."

This startling remark triggered another giggling fit, in which we all joined. Sensing the relaxation, little K'ayum left his mother's side to place his three-month-old sibling on my lap. We joked about my inability to tell her sex right away.

"And you , Victor," Nuk asked, still hidden behind the screen. "Are you a boy or a girl?"

"Whatever you like," I replied, to a chorus of titters.

K'in Bor became serious. "I am not angry at my father-in-law," he said. "He is a good man. But Young Chan K'in hit me when I was drunk and charged me one thousand pesos."

I remarked that my impression was that he had struck first, and hit Young Chan K'in on the side of the face.

"Well, I don't remember everything," he admitted, with dimmed, sullen eyes. "Anyway, I like it here better. Yesterday I burned my new *milpa* by the lakeshore, behind Felipe Baer's house." He showed me some of his new treasures: a table he had carved from a thick burl of mahogany, and a stack of toucan feathers, which he would sell for five hundred pesos a set.

"Do you want one?" he asked, extending a set of feathers.

I held them in my hand, uncertain what to do with them.

"For your woman," K'in Bor said. "She can wear them in her braid."

From the back Nuk teased, "María Bonita doesn't wear feathers," and dissolved into muffled laughter. Since moving to the north shore Nuk is much freer with her tongue, but she still wouldn't show her face to outsiders. When she finally did peer out I was struck by her resemblance to her older brother, Young Chan K'in.

Juan José came in with Young Mateo's six-year-old daughter and asked if K'in Bor had any letters to dictate. Juan José, the sixteen-year-old son of evangelist Chan Bol, is one of the few literate Lacandones, and wrote K'in Bor's letters for him. K'ayum had been teaching K'in Bor to read and write before he moved away.

Although they are not yet officially married, Juan José and little Nuk were already living together in the new hut. She carried her one-year-old brother strapped to her back, and looked saucily pretty in a short skirt. K'in Bor signaled Juan José to come back later.

"I send letters to my friends in Mexico, but they do not answer," K'in Bor said, in an aggrieved tone. "I send them feathers to sell and ask them to send me a stereo set with speakers. I don't know why they don't answer."

"K'in Bor," I said, "do you have any idea how much a stereo set costs?"

"Yes. I priced one when I was in Mexico. They have one with batteries for seven thousand pesos."

"That's a lot of toucan feathers."

He nodded. "How much do they pay for a live toucan?"

I said I'd seen one in a Santa Cruz pet shop that sold for twenty thousand pesos (eight hundred dollars). "But that includes freight, import duty and a license, and other expenses. You'd probably have to sell it for one quarter of that."

K'in Bor calculated in his head, his eyes lightless. "And how about a live quetzal?" he asked, looking squarely at me.

"K'in Bor," I said coldly, "I have not the slightest idea."

We were interrupted once again — by a burly Tzeltal who walked in unannounced and greeted K'in Bor familiarly.

"This is my drinking companion," he said, winking in K'in Bor's direction.

My skin prickled at the man's intrusion, and I wished suddenly to be gone from the hut. K'in Bor drew inward and became silent.

"K'in Bor likes his rum," the Tzeltal said. "Two nights ago we tied on a good one — isn't that so, K'in Bor?" He slapped K'in Bor's shoulder, but K'in Bor had turned inert, like stone.

"Are you with the Forestal?" I asked, avoiding his red-stained reptilian eyes. His overbearing manner implied he had a position of some authority.

"*Sí, señor,* I am the assistant foreman on this side. K'in Bor here is one of our local recruits. How many mahoganies have you cut, K'in Bor? Was it twenty-five?"

"More or less," K'in Bor said, morosely.

"Yes, we paid him well," the assistant foreman said. "K'in Bor is a good worker, when sober. But if he tries to get violent again, we'll tie him up and throw him in the lake."

I told K'in Bor that I'd be back and walked out, leaving the toucan feathers behind.

"K'in Bor is crazy now," K'ayum said as we paddled back in late afternoon. The sun had just slipped behind the western ridge, and the lake surface had turned brackish green. "Chan K'in Chico told me that he is drinking DDT when he can't find rum, and he is always chasing after other women. Two nights ago he got in a machete fight with one of the Tzeltales, and afterward he tried to kill himself."

"Yes, he's gone," I said. I had started grieving for K'in Bor from the moment the Tzeltal walked in and the hunter's eyes went lifeless, dead. I saw — as well as felt on my skin — the shadow come over his body, and knew that the darkness had already claimed him. We would never go hunting together or looking for quetzal. He would never take me to the cave where the winds are born.

"K'ayum — we will have to say good-bye to K'in Bor. He is no longer here."

K'ayum nodded, paddling steadily. "My father did not know how to tell you."

For the second time since my arrival in Nahá tears welled up in my eyes. I did not conceal them from K'ayum, who knows my heart, and knew also that these unseemly tears were not for K'in Bor alone.

At José Güero's

In the evening Chan K'in asked for details of my visit with K'in Bor as is his custom when someone returns to his protection from a trip "to the other side."

When I came to the foreman's abrupt entrance, and the alteration it produced in K'in Bor, my voice broke; Chan K'in's expression became concerned as I struggled to hold back tears.

I could not tell why K'in Bor's defeat affected me so much more than that of Young Chan K'in, whose eyes often reflect the same lightless abdication. In Old Chan K'in's silence I sensed acknowledgment of my special kinship with K'in Bor — my dark half brother — and a stubborn reluctance to give up on his son.

"Poor K'in Bor," he said at last, in a whisper. "His heart is no longer among us."

In the morning Robert's leg was much improved. We decided to leave the following day, as we had originally planned, and drive to San Cristóbal via Ocosingo. On our way out we would stop in Chancalá to pick up the mahogany receipts from the Forestal, so Robert could present them to his old friend Horacio Acuña, who works for the governor of Chiapas.

"Acuña is the governor's right-hand man," Robert said. "He plays a key role in funneling funds for the Lacandones through the Agrarian Reform Agency. He can help assure that Chan K'in and company get their proper share for the mahogany that has already been cut here." He added with a smile, "Acuña and I are old drinking buddies. We'll have a couple of beers in a Tuxtla bar and talk things over. He may turn out to be a reasonable fellow."

Robert's hale, beer drinker's grin was a sure sign that his penitence was nearly over. As his leg healed his thirst returned, particularly with the prospect of a cold Dos Equis or two less than twenty-four hours away.

I had one more obligation to discharge, which I could no longer put off. After breakfast I set out alone for José Güero's house, with some lighters and batteries and the earrings I had promised his wife a year ago.

Twice before I had set out to visit him, and had been turned back by the mud and by my nagging apprehensions. Robert had hinted that José Güero had been drinking heavily since the death of his daughter Koh. And he confessed that he had not visited José since he had moved to Nahá from Mensäbäk, several years back. When I asked why not, Robert had shrugged. "The vibrations, I suppose."

The trail was pretty well chewed up, although it hadn't rained for three days, and I overshot the entrance to José's *caribal*. I was drawn back by an unusual birdcall, and came face to face with K'ayum, José Güero's walleyed young son, the top twirler, who gave me a twisted smile. Without a word he led me across the thin plank that fords the stream to the rear of his father's settlement. As we approached the main hut the roosters and dogs started up their yowling and crowing.

"Come in," K'ayum says, ushering me inside the hut, and then spins an imaginary yo-yo into the air, with the twisted grin on his face.

"I'll leave you one, K'ayum," I promise, patting his shoulder.

The first one I see is Young Chan K'in, who sits on a cot across from the door. His face and tunic are striped in light and dark by the sun streaming through the mahogany slats. Juanita stands in one corner, rocking the baby boy, and Jorge's son-in-law Vicente sits with his wife at the other end of the hut. Until that moment I had not realized that Vicente was one more of José Güero's innumerable progeny. I greet José, who sits on his pallet in the dark side of the hut, with his wasted leg drawn up beneath him. This impression of him has taken on a permanent cast in my mind's eye, like a sculpted sage on the frieze of an ancient temple. José's senior wife is lying down beside him, and the younger pale-skinned daughter sits sewing behind her.

I sit down on the cot beside Young Chan K'in, who goes on with his account of his travels and his plans to purchase fifty-five thousand pesos' worth of corrugated tin to roof Nahá huts.

"*Tsoy*," José Güero says, in a quavery voice. He is drinking from a rum bottle, which he grasps between his knees. It occurs to me that the slurred speech that had impaired our conversation last year may have owed more to alcohol than to senility.

Young Chan K'in seems in good spirits, and we strike up a conversation as José nods and half listens from his pallet.

"My father-in-law's mouth is bad," he explains; "he has difficulty speaking, and no longer plays the flute."

After yesterday's visit with K'in Bor my harsh feelings toward Young Chan K'in have subsided, but I have several forthright questions, and I begin with the matter of when and why he signed the agreement with the Forestal.

"It was last July," he says. "I talked it over with my father, and it was clear the Forestal was going to cut the mahogany with or without our signature. We did not want them to cut, and we did not want the road" — he shrugs — "but there was nothing to be done, and so we decided it was best to sign then, and make certain that we got some money for it."

"Do you know what is going to happen here now with the new road? Are you aware of all the changes it will bring?"

"Yes," he says, calmly. "I have given much thought to it. All of this land will eventually become grazing pasture for the cattle ranchers. None of us has the power to stop the changes. I have been to Villahermosa, to Mexico, more than the others; I have seen with my eyes what was coming before any of them. I have tried to prepare them. But it is hard. Not even my father knows how difficult my position is. Not even K'ayum knows."

"Yes," I concede. "Your position is difficult." I had mistaken his loud boasting and craziness for simple greed — but there is nothing simple about Young Chan K'in. I could see now that the struggle is still alive in him, that he has not yet given in to the darkness of K'in Bor's cave. Still, I am unmoved by his self-pity, which he exploits to excuse his numerous errors of judgment. I realize as we speak that Young Chan K'in had tried to take the brunt of the changes upon his own shoulders, so as to spare his father and younger brother. But it had proved too much for him —all of it: Graciela, the Forestal, Carmelo, Villahermosa — and so he drinks and brags to cover up his failure, and the pain of Koh's death.

Young Chan K'in admits that all the pressures had aggravated Koh's illness, and led to her early death. "I travel too much, and it made my wife sad, and then my little daughter got sick. It could not be helped . . ."

I choose this moment to let him know I had met Graciela in Canada. "Is there anything I should tell her?"

His eyes darken. "Just tell her what has happened — that is all." He says nothing more on the subject, so I mention my visit with K'in Bor, and the sorry condition I found him in.

"That is a pity," Young Chan K'in says, with a concern I have not heard in his voice up to now. "I had to fine K'in Bor after he threatened my sister's life. But he is not a bad man. He does not know how to drink; even a little rum makes him lose control, and he becomes crazy." He shakes his head and his features go soft, like his father's. When he speaks again his voice is thick with feeling. "My father will die here," he says, "and the rest of us will stay as long as we can. If the Tzeltales try to burn down our fields and our forest, we will fight them. We will live well as long as we can, but when the time comes to die" — his voice breaks — "one must accept it."

José Güero clears his throat and asks in a wavery voice, "When do you go?"

"Tomorrow," I reply, startled, and flush with embarrassment. I was so absorbed in conversation I'd forgotten about the gifts I'd brought for José and his wife.

I remove my shoulder bag and present him with the lighters and the batteries.

"Ne tsoy — very good," he says, placing them beside the rum bottle without bothering to test them.

"I brought earrings for your wife," I add, and she sits bolt upright on the cot. The pale-skinned albino daughter leans over my shoulder as I place a pair of glass earrings in José's palm. When he opens his hand, I see only one earring there.

"Why only one?" he asks, narrowing his eyes at me.

In confusion, I look down on the ground, but cannot find the missing earring.

"I must — have left it in the hut," I stammer, suddenly unable to recall if I had given him one or two. Is this another of José's pranks? I can tell nothing from his face, which is an inscrutable mask.

Defeated, I take out my last set of earrings, worth twice the first pair, which I was saving for María Bonita. I drop them in his hand. His wife snatches them away and examines them in a corner, while the daughter holds the single glass earring up to the light.

"When will you come back?" José Güero asks, in a garbled voice I can barely understand.

"Next year," I say.

"Well, you won't find me." He says it with such dramatic finality I do not know how to reply. "See? My left hand is cold — like my leg." He extends it toward me, but I do not take it. I am on to him now.

"You'll be here," I assure him. "And I will come to see you. But now I must go." I reach for his warm right hand and press it in both of mine.

"You may go," José Güero says, smiling.

The Parrot's Tail

That night, our last in Nahá, there is a spectacular sunset over the lake, as distant lightning flashes in the eastern sky. We all gather outside Chan K'in's hut and watch a large nimbus cloud above us pass through all the colors of the parrot's tail: yellow, orange, bright red, and finally a rich magenta that seems to linger forever.

Chan K'in reminds us of the ancients' belief that clouds were created by Mensäbäk, the god of rain, when he placed the copal soot from an incense pot on a macaw's tail and scattered it in all directions except the south, forming clouds of many colors which brought the first rains to earth.

"And the lightning you see over the ridge is the ancients banging rocks together."

"But there is no noise," little K'in points out.

"That is true," Chan K'in answers, before the words are out of his son's mouth. "This evening they only make sparks."

As the sun goes down behind the lake, Chan K'in describes Sukunkyum's task of placing it in his hammock and carrying it to his house beneath the earth, as a corpse is carried to its burial site.

"But the sun is not dead. He is only tired from his day's journey. Sukunkyum will feed him *posol,* squash seeds and minnows and lay him down to sleep. In the morning, he will be as good as new."

"What does the sun look like?" I ask Chan K'in, raising an indulgent smile to his lips.

"Well, to us he looks like a burning disk, but the ancients knew he is a tall man in a white tunic, with a ball of fire on top of his head. But there is more than one sun," he reminds us. "After an eclipse, the sun dies, and a new one must be made before the world can be renewed."

"Who made the first sun?" asks little Chan K'in, his interest aroused.

"Ah, that was K'akoch, the great father. He made the earth, the sea, the first sun and moon, and the celestial tuberose — *bäk-nikte'* — from which the other gods emerged and completed the world. But the earth was not firm in those times — oh no. It had no rock or forest trees to bind it and was very soft, like corn gruel. After his birth Hachäkyum remade the earth with lime and rock and sand, as it is today."

"That's right," K'ayum calls out, with a chuckle. "It was like the road which becomes soft after a rain, and must be made firm with gravel."

We laugh uneasily at the thought of *ladino* road builders preempting Hachäkyum's function. But this does help me to understand their clamor for gravel, and the near awe with which they regard tractors and earth movers.

After dark we go inside and sit around the kitchen table. Koh lights an extra kerosene lamp and sits down next to her husband. The sunset colors and the lightning have sparked Chan K'in's imagination, and he starts in again with a depiction of our world, which is round on top, like an overturned gourd. Hachäkyum's heaven is directly above ours, and above that are the four other heavens, with the home of the minor gods at the very crest, where it cannot be reached by the rays of the sun. In Lacandon cosmology, "Seventh Heaven" is a bleak, inhospitable place, steeped in perpetual darkness.

As Chan K'in finds his rhythm, we are drawn into the cadence of his voice. His body and soul resonate to the name of each god, to each new created substance. Language is the mold in which the Mayas have given shape to their gods, as the gods have given breath to them. Prayer and storytelling are one, and the obligations entailed carry equal weight.

As I hear it for the third time, I feel I am beginning to understand at last the parable of the trees and the stars. The seven heavens are all interconnected. When a star falls from our sky, a tree has fallen in Hachäkyum's heaven. The vault of Kisin's and Sukunkyum's netherworld is the floor of our own. The mahoganies are the linchpins of our forest biosphere, just as the stars are the linchpins of our firmamemt — which in turn holds Hachäkyum's forest in place. In the Lacandon world view, gods and men are as closely interdependent as are the trees and stars. As the root system of our own forest is destroyed, the sky of Sukunkyum's lower world will cave in and smother the sleeping sun. Put in contemporary terms, when you tamper with the roots of one life-supporting ecosystem, you endanger the existence of all the others.

"After Hachäkyum made the earth firm," Chan K'in goes on, "K'akoch gave our lord corn, and he and his wife learned to make tortillas and *posol*. And then our lord and his wife made the *hach winik* from clay and sand, one of each *onen* beginning with the Ma'ax or Spider Monkey. After the Ma'ax he made Lacandon of the Peccary, Jaguar, Pheasant, the Deer *onen* and all the others. But he did not create the *ladinos* and the *ts'ul*, ah no. Mensäbäk made the *ladinos* on his own, and Akyantho made the foreigners, whom he protects to this day by giving them cattle and money."

"And Kisin?" asks little K'in. "Who made Kisin?"

"Ah, Hachäkyum made Kisin, but that was before he made people. Kisin was not born of the tuberose with the other gods; Hachäkyum used earth and rotten wood to make Kisin, and he emerged five days later from a night flower, the *aak'alyoom*. Kisin eats tree mushrooms and nests of maggots, which he calls his beans. He dresses like a *ladino* in shirt and trousers, with a liana flower for a hat.

"After he made people Hachäkyum made the animals," Chan K'in goes on. "He made them with the same sand, earth and lime, but only the foreigners learned to domesticate the animals. The ones in the forest all fled and ran wild, and turned into the forest animals of today. From the excess clay in Hachäkyum's hands sprang the ants, scorpions, spiders, mosquitoes, fleas and other insects. But the ants were born first; they are man's helpers and were made from grains of dust."

"Tell about the snake," K'in says, squirming in anticipation.

"Ah yes, the snake was created by accident, when a long ribbon of clay

fell on the palm leaf, and came to life. Hachäkyum was going to mix it in
with the rest of the clay, but the snake was so pretty he allowed it to live.
Even Our Lord did not know the deadliness of what he had created, and
the fear and sorrow it would bring to the true people."

The stories go on long past our dinner and our second and third cups of
citronella tea. Cockroaches skitter over the scraps of food on the table,
moths circle the sputtering lamp and expire with a hiss; the fleas eat at
our ankles and calves, gorging on our ts'ul blood as if word had gone out
that we would be gone by daybreak. But all of this hardly matters. Chan
K'in's spell binds us closer with every new story, which flows from him
now as easily as the gods bloomed from the primordial tuberose.

He tells of Nuxi' the mole trapper, who fell in love with Kisin's daughter and became the Lacandon Odysseus, the first ancient to visit the underworld and return alive to share his adventures. Sukunkyum took him
under his protection and disguised him as a hummingbird so he could
enter Kisin's home undetected and pursue his courtship. When Kisin shot
him down with his bow the daughter claimed the hummingbird for her
own; at night the mole trapper reverted to human form and they lay
down together as man and wife. She prepared tortillas for his breakfast
and Kisin thereupon had no choice but to accept Nuxi' as his son-in-law.
The mole trapper and his wife soon returned to Sukunkyum's home,
however, as Nuxi' could not tolerate his father-in-law's diet of tree fungi
and carrion. But Kisin's daughter did not return to earth with Nuxi' because he neglected to sweep out a corner of his father-in-law's dwelling
as Sukunkyum had instructed him to, and Kisin was able to reclaim her
with a handful of dust. Had she returned to earth with the mole trapper,
Kisin's reign would have ended, and death would have been abolished
forever.

When Robert asks Chan K'in if K'akoch, the prime mover, had been
made of the same sand and lime as Hachäkyum and the other gods, Chan
K'in stops to reflect for the first time.

"Ah no — even the gods do not know the answer to that question," he
says. "K'akoch was, and K'akoch still is, but He is the supreme being, and
no one can see Him, not even Hachäkyum. Except when K'akoch chooses
to be seen."

By now the children are dropping off, and I too retire to my hammock,
bursting with images of the creation. But my dreams that night take me to
the land of my forefathers, Jerusalem, where I have to appear at the
mayor's office and establish my credentials. The mayor's aides, professor
types from Hebrew University, look over my files and conclude that I
write "too close to my hat"; but they may have to accept me anyway because of "excellent references." I awake before the issue is decided, and
do not know if I'll be allowed to stay.

In the morning we pack our gear, and on convening for breakfast discover that everyone has had vivid dreams, which they are eager to share.

"I dreamed of you and Robert," K'ayum says weightily, sitting by the
door. Before he can describe it Young Chan K'in peers in from the east

window and tells his father he dreamed of being all alone in a *cayuco*, on a fast-moving river.

"Ah, you will hunt *k'ek'en*," Chan K'in says confidently. Wild boar is the *onen* of his wives Koh and Juanita and of their father, José Güero.

Robert, in high spirits, reports his dream of being offered two women in marriage, one very beautiful and the other less pretty and more mature, but with a large inheritance.

"I chose the wealthy woman, because even if the marriage would not last, I knew that I could keep some of her money."

His eyes twinkling jovially, Chan K'in predicts that a large sum of money will fall into Robert's lap.

"Then I will get my grant," he says, exhilarated, "and we can start putting up the school in the fall."

I tell Chan K'in my dream, which he interprets as forecasting illness in my ancestral home, where my mother still lives. "High fevers, perhaps malaria," he says, and I smile inwardly, as there has been no malaria in the Holy Land for many years.

And then K'ayum tells us his rambling dream, which touches on all the recent calamities in Nahá: tractors and fallen trees, an ailing son, lakes with no fish, disappearing *cayucos*. He dreamed that K'in Bor beat up his wife and then wept uncontrollably. There was a thorn palm he could not make up his mind whether to cut down or spare.

"Then I awake, and when I fall asleep again I see we are climbing a hill, looking for a place to sleep. But there are stinging ants everywhere, and snakes. Suddenly, Victor disappears.

"I turn around and call, 'Victor, Victor' — but he does not answer . . . I look everywhere, but Victor is gone."

"You disappeared," he says, less in reproach than as a simple statement of fact.

"Sorry, K'ayum," I tease. "I had urgent business in Jerusalem."

"Then I dream of an old, old man who says Robert will have a lot of money, but there will be no school. I say to him, 'Yes, I think there will be,' but he says, 'No, there will be no school, it is a lie.'

"I do not know if he is right or not, but I am not sad, I say that is all right, and then I wake up . . ."

The whole settlement turned out to see us off, except for María Bonita. When I spied her daughter, Nuk, in the crowd, holding her brother in her arms, I called out, "Tell your mother not to forget: I'll be back next year." To make sure she remembered I jabbed at my temple and shouted, "*Sas in wich.*" Nuk flashed a full-faced smile before she turned around and skittered up the trail with her bouncing baby brother grinning over her shoulder. I knew María had sent Nuk as her spy.

"When do we see you again?" Chan K'in asked formally, and I reiterated my intention to return within a year. Robert said that if his U.S. grant came through he would be back in the summer to work on the school, for which K'ayum had already cut the beams.

Bol's parting words moved me most of all. "I shall be very sad," he said in a wistful voice, "to hear that you and Robert are dead."

We had lists of requests from the wives and the Katzenjammer Kids: ribbons, water pistols, cotton yarn, earrings, yo-yos. We folded them away in our shirt pockets like talismanic vouchers for our safe and prompt return.

"Be careful!" K'ayum's and Chan K'in's warning rang in our ears as Robert pulled out and I got a last glimpse of the silent, white-frocked true people in a pool of light at the edge of the trees.

Despite my promise to little Nuk and Chan K'in, I had no insight into the future of Nahá, or of my own. When I saw Nuk standing shyly to one side I remembered that her mother had been in my dreams the night before. I could recall only the scent of her skirts, so redolent of my nursemaid's musky *huipil* when I was an infant. In a sense, María had midwived my rebirth in the forest a year ago. Now I felt like an awkward adolescent who could fit neither his words nor his actions to his true feelings. I hoped to make it up by returning to Nahá as an adult.

The rest of the day slipped into nightmare. When we reached Chancalá the engineer and Lucundo were not in. A guard handed us an envelope with the receipts for the mahogany payments and escorted us to the office of the technical director, who had asked to speak with us.

A young man in horn-rimmed glasses and an older associate greeted us by announcing they had read the article in *Excelsior* with our photographs, and expressed their official displeasure at our "insinuations" against the "integrity of the Forestal."

"You will be able to verify by the receipts now in your possession that the Forestal pays full legal restitution for every single tree it has removed from the Lacandon forest. People like yourselves are not aware of the fact that the Forestal provides employment for a large number of farmers and laborers who live on the margin of starvation. Articles like yours create a negative atmosphere of adverse publicity that leads to work stoppages among the laborers, which seriously impair our operations. Do you realize that the sawmill has been shut down for two months because of work stoppages, the late rains and insurgent activity in the south? Even the eclipse played a part as it spread panic among some of the superstitious Chol and Tzeltal workers. And you people are no help, publishing articles that distort the facts. I must warn you that if this continues our entire operation will be imperiled, and there will be serious repercussions."

In one way or another I had heard this same speech from the mouths of state officials throughout my years in Latin America. At first I had no sense that it was addressed to us, but rather to some abstract cosmic conspiracy to subvert the established order.

Robert explained that our only concern was to see that the revenue from the trees is divided equally among both groups of Lacandones, and we were not interested in fomenting dissatisfaction or rebellion.

"We cannot solve your problems for you," I said, appalled by the man's lack of imagination. He seemed actually to expect from us an expression of sympathy or remorse. Far from feeling contrite, I was delighted the operation had snarled up and delayed for a while longer the cutting of more trees. But this bristling young technical director was so distraught it seemed futile even to mention the environmental issues or the matter of reforestation.

We left the office feeling frustrated as well as vaguely menaced by the director's repeated threat of "repercussions."

"Well, little brother, I hate to remind you I told you so. I knew we hadn't heard the last of it. We've now come up against the executive branch of the Forestal, which is based in Mexico City. They are concerned mostly with cost efficiency, profit and loss — and, of course, with security."

"Perhaps we should be thankful they didn't get the Gestapo after us."

"Well, we're not important enough for that. But keep in mind: Each of these government branches is tied to every other, and they reach all the way to the top."

What saddened and angered me most was that the dialogue we took pains to establish with Lucundo and Núñez had come to nothing; or more accurately, it had been trampled at the foot of the next bureaucratic wall.

Robert fared no better with Horacio Acuña, the Director of Agrarian Affairs, whom he visited the next day in Tuxtla Gutiérrez. Robert's old drinking buddy had him wait in the anteroom and then slipped out the back door on some private errand for the governor. Robert had to drink a consoling beer in a Tuxtla bar before returning to San Cristóbal.

Trudi was still in Switzerland, so we spent only one night in Na-Bolom and left for Tuxtepec and Mexico City the following day.

In Tuxtepec that night I sat by the swimming pool of El Rancho Hotel as a marimba played in the background, and the aftershock of our shakedown in Chancalá started to wear off. I sifted through my images of Nahá, pushing beyond the mahogany stumps, burned fields, bulldozers and grazing cattle. One of my treasured memories — although I did not witness it — was of K'ayum in the corridors of the Querétaro Palace, swimming like a salmon against the tide of petitioners, campesinos and security guards until he reached the President's side and tapped him on the shoulder.

"I wish to speak with you," I could hear him say in his clear voice, using the familiar tu. "There are many problems in our forest, and we need your help." And then the look of recognition on López Portillo's face as he embraced K'ayum and led him inside his office.

The rest was of secondary importance, including the President's pledge to help, hedged by the whispered aside to Pepe Pinto: "I recognize the problem; do not make waves."

The loveliness of this scene was in K'ayum's poised assurance that he addressed the President as a peer. This pride was his father's legacy, and to my mind more persuasive as proof of his royal lineage than a tombful of codices or a library shelf of scholarly works.

I pondered once again my attachment to Chan K'in, K'ayum, K'in Bor, Bol and María Bonita, and tried to understand why their lives affected me so deeply on planes — some of them symbolic and "parapsychologi-cal" — that I could scarcely apprehend. Do we all have "primitive" counterparts in some remote forest, desert or arctic waste, secret sharers whose lives in some ways complete the formulas of our own?

"The limits are in us, not in them," Don Moisés had rightly observed, and it is "they" who prescribe the limits of an outsider's involvement in their culture. Chan K'in had a number of ways of reminding me that I was not after all a *hach winik* because my blood was not the same substance as his, and my patron deity Akyantho has lesser status than Hachäkyum. K'ayum, Bol, even little K'in, also knew where to draw the line. In our most intimate moments an awkward gesture, something I said would give away my tainted *ts'ul* heritage, and an invisible veil would come down between us.

As a Sephardic Jew inculcated from childhood with the legend of the Chosen People, I felt at home with Chan K'in's sense of the *hach winik*'s innate superiority. It gave me one more mirror image to grapple with — perhaps the most humbling one of all.

At times, listening to a story of Chan K'in's, I longed to convert each of my cells into a vessel that could imbibe directly of his light and wisdom. The brain, after all, is a slippery and forgetful organ, and I have no doubt the stories and images will begin to slip away from me, as they have in the past, unless they are firmed up with the lime of consciousness. So far, I have not been able to acquire Chan K'in's and K'ayum's talent for letting go of the world, in the assured expectation that a new one will arise from its ashes. Like any other literate occidental's, my psyche is hostage to a numbing excess of ominous information. With each passing day I under-stand better Chan K'in's belief that the instruction to bring about the end of the world is inscribed in our cells, so that we have all become unwit-ting or purposeful agents of the *xu'tan*.

Each day I am away from the forest I have to dig a new hole in the gray wall that closes over my memories of Nahá. As time passes, the hole I am able to dig becomes each day smaller, from a large, unstained window to a misted porthole to a pinhole through which I can squint only dimly at the luminous days I lived with the Lacandones. There are moments when I think of those days as stars from a distant galaxy whose light will reach us only after they have become extinguished.

That night in Tuxtepec neither Robert nor I got any sleep. My dreams were so weighted with scenarios of impending disaster I kept waking up in a cold sweat, with the technical director's threats ringing in my ears. During one of these dark interludes I reflected again on Chan K'in's obsti-nacy in cutting his new *milpa* face to face with the road, as if to challenge its presence with his own. Unlike the highland Maya, who when threatened from outside shuts himself up within hard, impenetrable armor, the Lacandon opens himself wide to swallow the intruder: the protozoan versus the armadillo defense. The Chamulas will lie, steal, use every wile and deception to keep the intruder at a distance. They have learned in their history that the ts'ul and the ladino are not to be absorbed as easily as other Indian tribes. They have dynamite and other means to blast their way out.

Chan K'in chose to interpret the four twisters in my dream as a presage of game. That night in Tuxtepec I was once more beset by visions of the four blood-red funnels bearing down on the forest, and on my adopted family in Nahá. The one on the right, the northern loggers, has already struck. Ahead are the Tzeltal and Chol homesteaders, the cattle ranchers and the oil drillers. The screen of my dream was too narrow to include the package tours and the real estate developers, who will come later. Nor will they matter much to Chan K'in and Koh. By then, the issue between the hach winik and the rest of humankind will have been settled. The world as they know it will have ended, and a new one will or will not have been conceived.

"Yawat pixan," Robert mumbled with a sigh, after we both started awake from one of our nightmares . . . "Cry of the soul."

Epilogue

Postscript

Epilogue

Despite my promise to María Bonita and K'ayum, it would be another two years before I returned to Nahá. I had spent part of the intervening winter at an artist's residence in Jerusalem, as guest of Mayor Teddy Kollek. (The official invitation was sitting in my California post office on my return from Nahá.)

In Cuernavaca, where I stopped after leaving Nahá in March of 1979, I finally caught up with the leader of the band of adventurers who had abducted the southern Lacandones I saw at President Ubico's fair in 1938.

Mario Monteforte Toledo, a well-regarded scholar and novelist in his early seventies, is a dapper, still-slender cavalier with a passion for breeding racehorses. He has been a political exile from Guatemala since 1954. After we had dinner in his spacious colonial dining room we sat down to brandy in the library. Smoothing his mustache with a faraway gaze, Monteforte assured me that he recalled "as though it were yesterday" the morning they came upon the Lacandones in a lush forest glade near Agua Azul.

"It's hard to say which of us were the more astonished — ourselves, or the Lacandones. On catching sight of us they turned and fled into the forest like deer. I set up camp with my six companions, and after an hour or so several of the Lacandones approached us. Curiosity had overcome their terror. They were especially struck by our rifles, whose use we demonstrated by firing them into the air. Instead of recoiling in fear at the explosion and the acrid smoke, they immediately asked how to make the 'firesticks' work. They themselves traveled with primitive bows and arrows."

The leader of the Lacandon group, which had apparently left Lacanjá on an extended hunting expedition, was K'ayum Carranza, the same who was killed years later by his rival Obregón, the present-day "deacon" of Lacanjá. When Carranza asked Monteforte to sell them a rifle so he could use it against his enemy — presumably Obregón — Monteforte offered them the gift of a .22 if they would accompany him and his companions back to Guatemala.

After debating among themselves, four in the Lacandon party agreed to go: Carranza, a twelve-year-old named Ma'ax, Na Bor, who had the fine delicate features of a young woman, and an older man named K'ayum. Monteforte said a fifth Lacandon, whose name he could not remember, had gone part of the way with them before he changed his mind and returned home.

Monteforte's band and the Lacandones crossed the Usumacinta River and came to Sayaxché, near Tikal, where he telegraphed the mayor of Guatemala City to send a plane to transport them to the capital. It was Mayor Bickford, according to Monteforte, who hit on the idea of exhibiting the Lacandones at the national fair, with President Ubico's enthusiastic approval.

The rest of the story becomes a hazy string of anecdotes in Monteforte's retelling. The four Lacandones stayed seven nights in his house while they were on exhibition at the fair. The doctors who examined them found their blood had a clotting agent not found in occidentals; K'ayum had a full set of additional teeth and they were all infested with parasites and ticks. On one occasion Na Bor lifted his tunic and calmly defecated on Monteforte's living-room carpet as his mother was introducing them to distinguished guests. The Lacandones were mightily impressed with the elephant in the zoo, which they called "the beast with a snake," and they were allowed to enter the spider-monkey cages and "play with their kin."

Monteforte confessed that the four Lacandones had come down with colds and gastrointestinal disorders in Guatemala City, which has an altitude of five thousand feet. After the fair closed he insisted on returning them to the forest as he had promised — against the vehement protests of Mayor Bickford, who wanted to keep them in Guatemala on permanent exhibit. He flew them back to Sayaxché, loaded down with gifts. On emerging from the plane they threw away everything except the .22 and fled into the forest.

"Yes," he replied to my question. "My conscience did trouble me for some time after. At the time I was a young and intrepid romantic adventurer. If I had known they would get sick and be looked upon as freaks, I would have thought twice before taking them out of the forest. I have dealt with this personal conflict in my novel, *Anaïté*. You would do well to read it. But tell me" — he leaned forward, fixing me with his eyes — "what is the basis of *your* interest in these pathetic primitives?"

Several months later, when Paul Royer showed me photographs he had taken of the Lacandones in 1938, I verified that there had indeed been five of them at the fair, as I had remembered, and only four had made it back to their homes. The fifth, whose identity remains a mystery, had died of an apparent pulmonary infection in Guatemala.

I returned to Nahá with Robert in February 1981 on my way back from Guatemala, where I had traveled on a journalistic assignment. Robert had kept me informed by letter of the recent developments in Nahá, not all of which were discouraging. I knew that José Güero had died less than a year after my last visit, just as he had predicted. The family's reaction had been one of relief, for themselves and for a merciful end to José's infirmity, which had become a burden to everyone. The traditionalists assumed that José was happier now, hunting and playing music in the teeming forests of Sukunkyum's underworld.

Robert had written me of the departure of most of the north-shore splinter group for Lacanjá, including Jorge, K'in Bor, Chan K'in Chico and their wives and children. Although none of them had been formally converted by Phil Baer, they had come under the direct authority of José Pepe Chan Bol and Carmelo. K'in Bor, by all reports, is much happier at Lacanjá, where he can still hunt wild boar and puma — and he has even managed to kill two or three jaguars. On his one visit to Nahá he had brought gifts of wild-boar meat and hearts of palm to his father-in-law, Chan K'in.

When I stopped briefly in Na-Bolom after leaving Guatemala, Trudi had given me the excellent news that Nuk of the twisted jaw had finally submitted to a cesarean section — although she fought it to the very last — and had borne a healthy, large-headed girl by Paco. When they returned to Nahá, Nuk had told no one of her cesarean, and for several months she had rarely showed the little girl outside her hut for fear she might catch some disease.

As for Trudi, she had just returned from Switzerland, where she had undergone a cataract operation on one eye, and she was soon due to have another to restore her impaired vision. She complained loudly that she was going blind and senile, but she has started riding again, and she writes innumerable letters to the governor, President López Portillo, and anyone else she can think of to protest the continuing devastation of the forest. But her greatest concern was the spreading corruption in Nahá.

"The Lacandones are no better or worse than the rest of us!" she had shouted when I visited her study. "They kill and destroy, just as we do." She waved one hand in disgust. "I've gotten reports that Old Mateo's wife Nuk has set up one of her daughters in prostitution — and now the Tzeltales have brought syphilis to Nahá!"

Although she is as energetic as ever I found Trudi a good deal sadder, and Na-Bolom is becoming a rather somber place.

(In her most recent newsletter from Na-Bolom, sent out at the end of 1981, Trudi wrote, after referring to her impaired vision, "I seem unable to get old gracefully and to accept failures . . . My life is full of lost battles. Fighting against the Nazis, I had to see Hitler running all over Europe, and fascistic tendencies are reviving all over the planet today. . . . The trouble is, the spirit of fight is still in me. . . . Now fighting for the life of the tree — and to know by experts and my own empirical knowledge that the Lacandon forest has only ten years to live if we cannot stop what is happening there now. Destruction because of greed and stupidity combined.")

On our two-day drive from Mexico City to Nahá Robert informed me of another startling development. Phil Baer had been "invited" by the Mexican government to leave the country after a petition was presented to President López Portillo, signed by an impressive list of social scientists and influential public figures, alleging that the Summer Institute of Linguistics was corrupting Mexico's aboriginal cultures. The petition further accused the institute of fronting as an information-gathering agency for the CIA.

"I was given the petition to sign," Robert admitted, "but when it came right down to it, I couldn't do it." He shook his head. "God knows the harm Phil Baer has done to the Lacandon culture, but I did not for one moment believe he was CIA. He doesn't have the cast of mind — although he might have been an unwitting dupe."

I asked him, "What's become of the Nahá converts?"

"Well, Atanasio the hunter has relapsed, and is smoking and drinking like a normal person, as is Juan José, the teenaged husband of Young Mateo's seven-year-old daughter Nuk, who has renamed herself Margarita. Juan José's father, Chan Bol, the first evangelist of Nahá, has become more sociable since Phil Baer's departure, after he emptied out his cottage and put it up for sale. So far, there are no takers among the Lacandones."

Robert and Trudi had prepared me for the worst, so I was not unduly shocked by the concrete-block houses going up by Nahá's new airstrip, nor by the two trucks parked in hangars outside Young Chan K'in's and

Young Mateo's stores. I knew Old Chan K'in had moved his hut and his *milpa* to the other side of the newly graveled road, but I was surprised to see the settlement huddled so close together and exposed to the truck and tractor traffic. Only María Bonita and her in-laws and José Güero's family remained on the lakeshore. Otherwise, the lake was hardly visited, and the *cayucos* lay idly in their slips.

K'ayum's tin-roofed house still sat at the head of the new airstrip, visited almost daily by planeloads of French and German tourists. Far from being discomfited by the exposure, K'ayum and his father-in-law, Antonio, were erecting their new houses on the same site.

"We need a cement house for the *xu'tan*," Antonio explained, smiling, "so Akinchob can keep inside it all the trees and the flowers. The winds will knock down the thatched and tin-roofed houses."

"My house will be two stories," rejoined K'ayum. "The bottom for the animals, and the top for the *hach winik*."

In their own fashion, Antonio and K'ayum were constructing a Nahá version of Noah's Ark.

Old Chan K'in seemed in good spirits in spite of everything, and welcomed us with his customary warm reserve. In the past months Koh III had given birth to yet another child—their seventh—and Chan K'in was so embarrassed at having broken his word to have no more children that the infant was kept indoors with its face covered up, so that I was unable to determine its age or its sex.

Chan K'in voiced satisfaction that the new governor of Chiapas, Juan Sabines, was favorably disposed toward Nahá at the expense of the southern Lacandones, who had abused his generosity once too often.

"They don't know how to take care of their trucks," explained Young Chan K'in, who joined us in his father's kitchen. "They have crashed four of them, and the governor says he won't give them any more until they learn to drive better. We have two trucks. Young Mateo drives a pickup and I the three-ton rig. We are careful drivers, not like in Lacanjá, where K'in Yuk Bats' was killed when he and his companions got drunk and drove their truck off the road."

At Na-Bolom I had learned of K'in's senseless death, which had been another hard blow for Trudi. She had raised K'in as her own son. But I had not known that K'in García had lost a small daughter when a *ladino* doctor crashed one of the Nahá trucks into a ditch. The incident had caused bad feeling between K'in and his half brother Young Chan K'in, who seemed to have wiped the accident from his memory. A bout of tuberculosis complicated by pneumonia had temporarily checked Young Chan K'in's progressive alcoholism, but it had not slowed in the least his wheeling and dealing. He now ran two stores for the Tzeltales and the tourists, and he boasted frequently of the "improvements" (*mejoramientos*) he had helped bring to Nahá—among them the trucks, electricity and the cement houses.

* * *

On this visit there would be no *balché* ceremonies, no *cayuco* rides on the lake, and Chan K'in would not tell a story until the morning of our departure. But there were unexpected recompenses. I found a new freedom among the younger women, who displayed their proud sensuality openly, switching bright, beribboned skirts as they moved from place to place. The Lacandon children seemed to be adapting to the changes the best of anyone. The morning I arrived I was taken in hand by eight-year-old Chan K'in, oldest son of Koh III, and by his younger brother Bol, who is a deaf-mute. These two rowdy, irrepressible striplings were coming into their own, as their more refined, older half brothers became subdued and sad.

"Now we will play," Chan K'in said, gazing into my eyes, which were still glazed by the terrible violence I had witnessed in Guatemala. We spent the day playing with the toys I had brought them from a highland fair — wooden acrobats, papier-mâché noisemakers, clay duck whistles. I discovered that the Nahá children were incorporating trucks into their games the same way they had airplanes, and they got back at the tourists by mocking their incongruities. Lacandon children slip in and out of playing adult roles as naturally as they fall into slapstick and pantomime. When I would bend down to photograph their play, I entered their territory and became a landing strip for little K'ayum's new plastic helicopter, or the center post for the Nahá version of ring-around-a-rosy.

The adolescents were not faring as well. Young Bol, sixteen, had been drinking heavily since his occidental *meek'chäl* in Palenque, until a stomach ulcer forced him to reduce his consumption of Tzeltal liquor. The laughter had gone from Bol's reflective brown eyes, and he now traveled frequently to sell his arrows in Palenque and San Cristóbal. Little Chan K'in ("Fritz") had married José Güero's youngest albino daughter, who suffered from epileptic seizures, and he had moved into her father's house to perform his son-in-law service. The only time I saw him he had seemed somber and weighed down by his adult responsibilities, and he hardly even recognized me. ("My brother Chan K'in forgets everything," little K'in ["Hans"] explained afterward, with an impish grin. "He is not very smart, like I am.") Little K'in, now thirteen, slept in my old hammock and took me hunting with his father's .22 Winchester. He smoked and drank with the adults and frequently suggested, in a jousting pubescent voice, that we drive to Palenque to pick up some *chamacas* — chicks — and drink "killer cane." When on a trip to sell arrows in San Cristóbal, K'in had become infatuated with a fifteen-year-old *ladina* who works for Trudi. Apparently she had not discouraged his advances, but it was to be K'in's first and last fling as a bachelor. Arrangements were already under way for Bol and K'in to marry two of Antonio's daughters.

Perhaps the most cheering news was that María Bonita's scabies had dissipated without developing into tuberculosis, as Chan K'in had feared. I visited her in her home while José was in the *milpa,* and we had a leisurely chat, charged with the special chemistry that had marked all our previous encounters, but without the subjective distortions. She is a lovely, primal woman who is growing only slightly thick-waisted and matronly as her second generation of offspring come of age.

As we spoke under a ripe papaya tree, with her children beaming at either side of us, I realized that José could never give her the happiness that had eluded her all her life long; still, the events in Nahá had been in some measure liberating. The outside world had come to her doorstep and made some of its benefits accessible to her. She was no longer ostracized by the younger women, and she could now obtain medicines, ribbons, earrings and the other baubles as easily as they.

She told me about her parents, Jesús and María Cuahtehmoc, who had become Adventists in Mensäbäk and no longer ate meat. "I like meat, and my cigars," she said with a grin, as she sucked on a homegrown stogie. "I will never move to Mensäbäk and turn evangelist."

"Do you need anything, María?" I asked, out of habit. "Any medicines?"

"No, I am well now. And you? Are you contented?"

"A little saddened by the changes," I answered, half evasively. "Do they affect you?"

She shrugged. "Not so much. José takes me to Palenque now, and he is getting me new teeth." She evidently expected José to pick her dentures off the counter, the same way he had purchased her glass earrings. "But my children still don't have enough to eat. José has gone hunting for armadillo."

"What do you think of the *ladinos* and the *ts'ul* that arrive every day?"

"About as I expected," she said, with a shrug. "Only there are so many."

I asked her if she still wanted to travel to Mexico, and she smiled in the old flirtatious way, covering her mouth. "With you, perhaps."

We laughed easily. The sexual pull was still there; our laughter was in part a recognition that it would never be consummated, and that was all right, too. The world was taking us in opposite directions, at a quickening pace. In previous encounters we had functioned as catalysts for one another's unfulfilled longings. Now, we met as adult friends.

Nuk, Paco and their little daughter Koh are undoubtedly the happiest family in Nahá. They posed cheerfully for my camera, and Nuk spoke easily with me for the first time, in her excellent Spanish. When I told Nuk her daughter's birth was the best news I'd heard from Nahá in the past two years, she blushed and lowered her eyes, which gave her disfigured features an added poignancy.

"You and Roberto have been good friends to us," she said, softly stroking her daughter's curly brown hair.

Juan José and little Nuk, Nahá's most striking "child marriage," had moved into their own tin-roofed hut next to Young Mateo's, and they are clearly fond of one another. Like a proper "modern" Lacandon wife, seven-year-old Margarita, as she prefers to be called, wears long dresses, toucan feathers in her hair and a huge digital watch on her wrist. The afternoon I visited them she was sewing a new dress with the aid of her sister-in-law, Atanasio's Nuk, who diligently pedaled a Singer sewing machine. Margarita was nagging Atanasio for drinking with the Tzeltales, as Juan José lay sprawled on the floor, dead drunk on Tzeltal liquor. When I gazed at pretty Margarita, amazed by her ease with grown-up behavior, she gave me a salacious smile and turned her back to continue work on her dress. I was relieved next day to see her playing with children her own age, squealing, running and jumping like any seven-year-old.

On a later occasion I would find Juan José and Margarita rolling on their cot in preadolescent love play, and peering at an issue of *Penthouse* a visitor had left behind. The magazine was opened at the nude centerfold, but Margarita and Juan José were engrossed in a brimming bowl of fruit at her side. Trudi, who was less taken with Margarita's precocity than I am, referred to her as "the next whore of Nahá."

I had brought K'ayum a monkey mask from Chichicastenango, which provided some of our lighter moments together. When I first wore it to dinner, Chan K'in glanced at me edgily and went on speaking with Robert in a strained voice until I jumped up and down and peered out. "*Simio!*" I shouted, imitating K'ayum's ape yells, and then everyone leaped for the mask.

"Is it the one from *Planet of the Apes?*" K'ayum asked, as he slipped it on and flapped his arms wildly.

"No, it's used in the 'Dance of the Conquest' by highland Mayas in Guatemala."

"Chamula?" Bol asked, arching an eyebrow.

"No, no, Quichés. They are much better. They worship the corn gods and tell stories of the creation."

"How is it in Guatemala?" Young Chan K'in asked with a sudden intensity that shattered the playful mood. "The pilots told me there is much trouble there now."

"Yes, it's true," I said. "Twenty people are killed every day, and the army has picked out certain towns to wipe out, so their men won't join the guerrillas."

"Gorillas, gorillas!" shouted one of the little ones, with the mask dangling from his ears.

"No, these guerrillas are warriors who hide in the hills and the forest. They strike at the army and run, so they cannot be caught. Because of all the killing by the army, the guerrillas are gaining support among the *naturales* — as the highland Indians prefer to be called — but they have a long way to go. The Indians of Guatemala have a deep distrust of all *ladinos,* and with very good reason."

I turned to Young Chan K'in. "The army is very strong. Before, they used automatic rifles against the Indians. Now they have submachine guns and helicopters, so they kill many more. That is what *mejoramiento* means in Guatemala today — an improvement in the capacity to kill."

Old Chan K'in shook his head. "In Guatemala, the *xu'tan* has already arrived. Soon it will be everywhere."

Robert had told me that according to Chan K'in's calculations there would be a "little *xu'tan*" in 1982, when several key planets will be aligned, before the "real" World's End predicted for 2008.

There had been a shift in relations among Chan K'in's three wives, which I detected only gradually. Koh I now dressed more cleanly than I'd ever seen her, in a bright green apron above her soiled shift, although the half-smoked cigar was seldom missing from her lips. But Young Chan K'in's illness, the changes and the constant stream of visitors had disoriented her, and she seemed to be fading away in proportion as Koh III assumes greater prominence in the affairs of the household. The mainstay of Nahá is still Koh II, who works as hard as ever, day in and day out; she has even taken to hunting small animals in the *milpa* to supplement her children's diet now that big game has grown scarce.

In the *milpa* Koh II always sits next to Old Chan K'in, proudly erect as he sharpens his machete for the day's work. Koh III squats on the edge of the nuptial corn shed while Koh I hovers outside.

I was relieved to see a thriving crop of corn in the new *milpa*, most of it already harvested. But Chan K'in told me there would be no tobacco crop next year because the late, heavy rains had killed the seed. "A northeast wind brought them," he said. "That is a bad rain — it kills the seeds and roots."

A month later I learned that acid rain had fallen in Chiapas during December and January.

Throughout my stay I was constantly reminded of my conversations in San Cristóbal with James Nations, the forest ecologist who had already removed the Lacandon forest from his list of salvageable American rain forests. "If you blaze a trail into the forest from Chan K'in's *milpa*," he had pointed out, "whichever radius you take, you will come to a road or a Tzeltal *milpa* within a kilometer or two. That means the end of the forest."

In the afternoon I went for a walk around the abandoned settlement near the lakeshore and found that not only working utensils had been left in the huts — corn grinders, washboards, ceramic pots — but several boxes of moldering books, strung hammocks, assorted toys, a rusted tape recorder with some old tapes and a broken guitar. The old trails and the hut entrances were covered with creepers and spreading vines, and wild squash and cherry tomatoes clung to the sloping palmetto roofs. From the eaves of the old god-house hung nets heavy with *balché*-drinking gourds and other implements. A dozen hummingbirds fluttered around the blossoming orange trees. Far from resembling a ghost village, the abandoned settlement hummed and abounded with renewed life.

* * *

Domingo the hermit had moved once again, about two kilometers from the road, but still within hailing distance of the settlement. His thatched roof was visible from the trail to Chan K'in's *milpa;* his orchards, I was told, were as bountiful as ever. But he is a changed man. Since the road came his chosen isolation has been irreparably shattered, and he now makes occasional social visits to the *t'o'ohil,* Chan K'in.

Robert and I paid a visit to K'ayum. We took him a bottle of vodka and some pineapple juice, as he had acquired a taste for screwdrivers. He had hung the monkey mask I brought him on his front door, below a hand-lettered sign, "La casa de K'ayum," and next to several photographs of himself. On the rear wall young Bol had drawn a huge penis over the portrait of Norman Lippman, a mystical Jewish adventurer and friend of Nahá. "I like Norman," Bol had written in Lacandon Maya during one of their drinking bouts. "He is clairvoyant, and he has a big prick."

Robert remarked, "The *hach winik* have recently discovered mural painting. This is what thirty-five hundred years of Olmec–Maya civilization are coming to: Nahá's first subway graffito."

K'ayum had recently come back from a tour of Yucatán with a French filmmaker. Since then he had been carving a male figure in the late Classical Chichén Itzá style from a trunk of mahogany. He intended to present the sculpture to the governor of Chiapas, whose name he frequently mentioned as a personal friend.

"I am an artist," K'ayum said. "As long as they pay me for my art, I will continue to paint and make sculptures." It had now been three years since he had last made arrows and worked his own *milpa.*

After our first round of pineapple screwdrivers Margarita retired to the back room with little K'ayum (formerly Mario), "Chankina" and their newest child, a six-month-old daughter they still call Och.

I asked K'ayum if they planned to have more children, and he shook his head. "No, three is enough. Margarita feels the same way. We both wanted a large family but now there are too many outsiders, too many tractors and trucks to cut down trees. It is not a good time to have many children." K'ayum then gave us the most detailed description of the *xu'tan* I had heard to date.

"The world is going to die," he said, with the bright, obsessive gaze that overtakes the younger Lacandones when they speak of the world's end. "It is too old already. The flesh is also old. It is exhausted. The world will burn up soon. The sun will stop, not move in the sky, and it will burn everything down. It will burn everything until the world is naked. It will burn for three weeks. Then it will rain. It will rain for three weeks without stopping, until everything is flooded. Then, above, in the upper heaven of the minor gods all will be dark, and they will cut off the heads of the people and Ts'ibatnah will paint the houses with the blood of the good people. Their blood is bright red and smells very good, like the tuberose. But the celestial jaguars will eat the people with dark blood, which will be spilled on the ground. Then Akinchob will take the trees and the flowers out of his house. The sun and the moon will be made new by

Hachäkyum. Akinchob and Akyantho will plant the trees, and make the world new. Then there will be animals again, and foreigners — Japanese, Frenchmen, and also the *hach winik*. Akyantho, the god of foreigners, will make the Christians again. He is the father of Jesus, I think, and made love with the Virgin to give birth to him. Akyantho will make everything as it was before — machetes, airplanes, trucks and tractors — but the world will be new. The forest will be new. There will be no cares. Everyone will pray and give offerings; the people of Akyantho as well as those of our Lord Hachäkyum."

"K'ayum, how come Akyantho is so powerful now?" I asked, astounded.

"Because there are so many of his people now, so many foreigners, and so few *hach winik*. Akyantho has become the new owner of the sun. He took it away from T'uup and Hachäkyum, and he will be the one to make the next eclipse, and he will also bring on the *xu'tan.*"

Just as Kisin had risen in status after the arrival of the first chicle gatherers and the missionaries, now, with the arrival of the tourists from all over the globe Akyantho had been upgraded to a principal deity, nearly on a par with Hachäkyum. "Our end is now in the hands of Akyantho," K'ayum concluded. "It is in his hands alone."

When Robert suggested to K'ayum he play guitar for us, he shook his head sadly and confessed that on his return from Yucatán he had drunk a whole bottle of vodka and fallen down on top of his guitar.

"K'ayum has gone to Yucatán," he whispered with lowered eyes.

"And who is here, then?"

"I am his brother."

Robert spent his spare time repairing the turbine he had installed in the stream that runs through the new settlement, so that Chan K'in could have the electric light he had requested for Koh's kitchen, and the others could plug in their radios and record players without having to buy expensive batteries. Robert intended to use the remaining 300-watt voltage to light and provide refrigeration for the new school, the Hach Winik Cultural Center, whose thatched structure K'ayum had already erected. But news had come that the government intended to install their own school in Nahá, as well as a separate medical clinic on the north shore. Governor Sabines and the National Indian Institute were bent on dragging Nahá into the twentieth century, with the tacit consent of the *hach winik*.

Oil reserves had recently been uncovered in Pico de Oro, near the Guatemalan border, on a part of the 614,000 hectares originally set aside for the Lacandon communities. New stone bridges and culverts were going up on the road to Nahá, over which the heavy oil rigs would travel. Old Mateo's son Bol, who had become the new president of the Mensäbäk Adventist community after Joaquín departed for Lacanjá, had explained the governor's largesse in providing Nahá with trucks and the block houses as a buttering up for the expected "purchase" of the oil-rich lands in Pico de Oro, at a price comparable to the bargain the Forestal had struck for their mahogany.

"The governor knows where his interests lie," Bol remarked, "and so do we. We will get all we can from them, in exchange for the oil." Bol, who had trained in a government trade school in Ocosingo, had recently married a *ladina* from Huistán. Ahead of Young Chan K'in and of his older brother Mateo, whom he had taught to drive Nahá's trucks, clever Bol was setting the example for negotiating deals with the outside world.

But Bol did not speak for the traditionalists in Mensäbäk. Celestín, Gustavo and about thirty other *borrachos* (drunks) still clung to the old ways, and in Palenque Don Moisés had told me of another band which had migrated to El Granizo, where a fire had destroyed the remaining mahogany and the logging road had been abandoned. "They are the last real hope for perpetuating the Lacandon Maya traditions," Don Moisés had predicted.

Robert spent several hours each day caring for the fruit and nut trees he had planted on previous visits. The Chinese and black figs, the almond and plum were not doing too well, but pineapple and the mandarin orange saplings had caught on and were starting to bear fruit. On this trip he had brought forty stocks of table-wine grapes donated to Nahá by the Pedro Domecq winery, and I spent our last two afternoons helping Robert to plant the Exótica, Royal Thompson, Málaga, Bola Dulce and four other varieties in the clayey, limestone-pitted soil above the new godhouse. It was Robert's obsession to plant new seeds in Nahá, and he was undiscouraged by the soil's rejection of his first efforts. Although wild grapes grow abundantly in the forest, the frail taproots of the civilized wine grapes had difficulty penetrating the clay and large stones under the surface loam.

"Perhaps the tough wild-grape roots will mingle with these," Robert joked, grunting with exertion as he dug posthole after posthole with the aid of K'ayum and little K'in, "and give rise to a new hybrid — Nahá vintage, 1984."

A soaking northeast rain fell that night, out of season, and in the morning the leaves of the newly planted Exóticas and Ruby Reds looked wilted and a bit sad. But Robert went on clearing the brush and digging postholes until he had planted the last of the forty stocks.

"On my next visit," he said, rising to wipe his brow, "I'll have to put up some trellises."

That night Robert dreamed of a bitch giving birth and the next morning he immediately told Chan K'in, hoping it would be a good omen for his grapes.

"It means the birth of sickness," Chan K'in said, in a flat voice. Although he persists in interpreting developments in the forest in a positive light, and he still prays in the god-house with Old Mateo every morning before dawn, Chan K'in's sadness filters through his voice and gestures.

This year he has once more put off setting a date for the incense renewal, although the permissible span of eight years between ceremonies elapsed in 1978. Neither Robert nor I have dared to wonder aloud if he is waiting for the "little *xu'tan*" to pass, or if he has begun to lose faith in his gods. More and more Chan K'in approximates the prototype of the great leader in decline who clings stubbornly to his own panaceas and blinds himself to all contrary evidence. Even as his world disintegrates around him, he would never accept a comparison with King Lear, for no *hach winik* would ever lower himself to railing at the heavens.

After the rains a firefly flew onto the kitchen table, and Robert asked Chan K'in what it would portend to dream of a firefly.

"It would mean lightning," he replied. When Koh II accidentally brushed the firefly with her hand, it rose up and blinked its abdomen repeatedly.

Chan K'in extended a crooked finger and flicked it at the firefly to make it light up again, but the blow stunned it and it rolled belly up. "Ahh." Chan K'in laughed and shook his head, then flicked the firefly off the table. "The firefly is not as bright or as strong as the electric light."

K'in García brought a bottle of brandy when he visited our hut the evening before our departure. I soon discovered that the loss of his six-month-old girl in the truck accident had worked a change in his attitude toward occidental technology. He blamed his half brother Young Chan K'in for "having brought it all in," but his anger had turned to a generalized sadness that had deepened and softened his features as it had no one else's in Nahá. Against my expectations K'in had remained loyal to his father, who had passed him over for K'ayum as heir to the title of *t'o'ohil*. The sweetness in K'in's temperament that Robert had remarked on now shone through the shy reserve I (and others) had mistaken for spinelessness.

"You must return soon," he told us, "when the grapes will be ready to share and make into wine. There will always be a place here for you. In the past years we have learned who our real friends are, and which ones make use of us for their own benefit. K'ayum, Young Chan K'in, even my father, are pleased about the governor's favors to us. The governor wants to build a meeting hall in Nahá, to show his important visitors how well he treats the 'Caribe.' I don't think he is such a good man, the governor. He doesn't see the harm he does to us with his favors. He wants to be kind because the Forestal cut down our mahogany, but his favors do as much harm to our ways as the loggers do. I have given thought to this, and I think my father should ask the governor to leave us alone." He shrugged, poured each of us another brandy. "But now, I think it is too late. The mahogany cannot be restored, and my little daughter cannot be brought back to life. We can try to lead our lives as best we can, but things will never be the same again."

* * *

When we rose at three the following morning for the long drive back to Mexico City, Koh II was up and preparing our breakfast. Luckily, the stars were out after two days of rain, but there was a cutting chill in the damp, predawn air.

The twenty-watt bulb cast an eerie, greenish light on Koh's kitchen, as she kneaded the corn dough for the day's tortillas. She had already finished a stack for Robert to take to Alicia. As we sat down to our beans, rice and homegrown coffee, a cock crowed in the barnyard and was answered by another across the road, and then by a third in José Güero's compound by the lakeshore.

"Three-twenty," I remarked, consulting my watch. "This is an odd hour for the cocks to crow."

"Not true," replied Chan K'in, who had positioned himself between the fire heating our coffee and Koh's metate, so that his face was concealed by a house post. "This is the hour when it is darkest and coldest in the forest, and Kisin, the lord of darkness, feels his strength and comes up from the underworld to kill our Lord Hachäkyum.

" 'Ah, now I can kill the old man, while he is asleep,' Kisin thinks, 'and be rid of him once and for all. I hate him because he is so old.' " The light flickers momentarily on Chan K'in's cheeks as he turns toward the fire, then hides again behind the house post.

"And so Kisin kicks our Lord, and he kicks him again in his sleep.

" 'Now I have killed the old man,' Kisin thinks. 'Now I am rid of Hachäkyum forever, and I can take over this world and his creatures.'

"But it is not our Lord he has killed, only his *xiw*, his replacement made of guano leaves tied in a bundle. Hachäkyum was busy preparing the underworld and putting up the pillars of Metlán for Kisin to live in because of the mischief he did in our world. And so it is now, while it is still dark, that the cocks must crow. It is for this hour that T'uup made the rooster, so it will alert him when Kisin tries to kill his father Hachäkyum." Chan K'in's face gleams momentarily in the firelight.

" 'You have killed my father,' T'uup cries aloud, 'and now I will kill you.' And he raises his machete and smites Kisin, cutting off his head.

"But then Hachäkyum comes out and says to T'uup, 'Look, he did not kill me. It is only my *xiw* that Kisin killed. Poor fellow. He doesn't know what he is doing. Let him live. Put his head back on.'

"T'uup is happy to see his father alive, but refuses to put Kisin's head back on because he will only try to kill his father once more. But Hachäkyum says again, 'T'uup, put his head back on. There must be a Kisin. Poor fellow.' " So at last T'uup replaces Kisin's head on his body, and the lord of darkness is spared and sent down to Metlán.

"But he will try to kill Hachäkyum again, and next time T'uup will put on Kisin's head backward, so he cannot harm his father. But Hachäkyum will take pity on him and ask T'uup to put his head on the right way, and so the lord of darkness will be spared one more time and he will be sent down to Metlán. And our Lord too is alive one more time and once more

T'uup can make certain that the sun will rise in the morning from the depths of the underworld, where it is cared for by Sukunkyum. But if the cocks do not crow — ah, then some day Kisin may be strong enough and clever enough to kill not only Hachäkyum's replacement, but our Lord himself. And then the world will truly end, with no hope of its rebirth."

Chan K'in emerges from behind the shadow of the post, radiant with his storyteller's smile.

"*Ki' känänt a bäh* — take care of yourselves," he says, "and drive carefully so Kisin does not catch you on the road."

Postscript

On the afternoon of our arrival in Nahá in February 1982, we find the entire male population hacking away at the underbrush bordering the new airstrip.

"It is for the governor's helicopter," calls K'ayum. This was the first visit by the ruling party's new candidate for governor of Chiapas, and in a *helicopter*, no less, and so the Lacandones naturally assumed the runway would have to be widened for such an important dignitary arriving in such a substantial aircraft.

By the following afternoon the Lacandones of Nahá and Mensäbäk have been joined by several hundred Tzeltales from nearby settlements, who mill about the new government-built schoolhouse. The speaker's platform for the candidate's address has been erected alongside the community store and is papered over with posters of the smiling candidate.

As the official greeter, K'ayum has waited for hours outside his tin-roofed hut. (The cement-block house beside it is used mainly for storage.)

Shortly after noon the gold, white and black helicopter appears above Lake Nahá and begins its pinpoint descent onto the chalked landing site across from K'ayum's hut. For a few minutes, Lacandones and Tzeltales alike gaze upward with the awed expressions they formerly bestowed on mere Cessna Skywagons, loaded with tourists.

Just before landing the pilot revs up the propeller, and K'ayum turns to see the roof blown clear off the wooden supports of his house.

In the evening, following the candidate's departure, Old Chan K'in lights incense burners in the godhouse and makes copal offerings to restore harmony in the community. The candidate had made the usual promises and praised the Lacandones as hard-working heirs of the great Mayan lords before he flew off in his whirly-bird.

"He makes promises, like all the others," Old Chan K'in says, as we sit down to our tortillas and beans. "We'll wait to see if he keeps them."

The next morning we find K'ayum repairing the roof of his hut with reinforced sheets of corrugated tin and larger nails. By the weekend they expect a visit from the presidential candidate, Miguel de la Madrid Hurtado, who, it is rumored, will arrive escorted by *three* helicopters, each one larger than the gubernatorial candidate's. The Lacandones are becoming political kingmakers, even as their forest kingdom rapidly dwindles.

Although tourists have become scarce since the *hach winik* began driving their own trucks, candidates for office are not the only testers of Lacandon hospitality. In the past two years, highland Mayas fleeing persecution in Guatemala have set up camps nearer and nearer to Nahá, causing consternation among the younger and the elder Lacandones, whose distrust of the Chamula is legendary.

"For our Guatemalan kinsmen, the *xu'tan* has already arrived," Chan K'in had said in 1981, and now that evidence of their calamity is all around them, the Lacandones—in common with other Mayan communities settled closer to the border—have welcomed the refugees to their territory, a gesture they punctuate with a stoical shrug and the words: "Today is their turn, tomorrow ours."

Each of my three visits to Nahá since 1982 has met with palpable proof of the decline of Lacandon culture, in its haste to catch up with the twentieth century. In February of '82 I found that "little K'in" (Hans), fourteen, had broken off his courtship of Antonio's youngest daughter and had instead married a Catholic Tzeltal teenager from El Tumbo. Old Mateo's Adonis-like Chan K'in, fifteen, had also married a Tzeltal, and both couples had moved in with the groom's parents, in a further travesty of Lacandon tradition. Two years later, both wives were pregnant and had begun to speak a few words of *Hax t'an*. And this past June I was startled to see that the albino women have taken to dyeing their hair black and wearing mascara and lipstick, so they now look just like all the other made-up women of Nahá. On a more encouraging note, young Bol had married Antonio's second-youngest daughter, Nuk, who bore him a shy boy. When I ran into Bol selling arrows in Palenque last spring, he had quit drinking cheap *ladino* liquor and had recovered his gentle smile, if not his innocence.

Robert has been pleased to find his grape stock hanging on, month after month, in Nahá's inhospitable soil, but none of the plants have yielded enough fruit as yet to consider making wine. The schoolhouse begun by K'ayum for Robert's Lacandon education project still stands unfinished, beside the broken and idle turbine. Below, the government-built school is being used as a makeshift meeting hall and warehouse, since the volunteer teachers promised two years ago by the new governor have yet to arrive. Young Chan K'in, who has finally recovered from alcoholism and his other ailments, has turned over most ceremonial duties to K'ayum and devotes himself to his profitable storekeeping.

This year, once again, the incense renewal ceremony has been indefinitely postponed by Chan K'in, because Koh I is gravely ill. Her blood pressure is so weak that the new government doctor assigned to Nahá has warned Chan K'in she could die at any moment, and Chan K'in spends long hours praying in the godhouse for her recovery. Last January Koh III, who is now a thirty-two-year-old grandmother by her teenaged daughter, bore Chan K'in a son—his twenty-fourth or twenty-fifth child since the age of forty. No one any longer remarks on Koh's yearly deliveries, or on the extraordinary procreativity of this enduring and stricken patriarch, who has finally begun to show signs of his eighty-five-plus years of existence.

Last year the third child of K'ayum and Margarita, a one-year-old boy, died of asphyxiation as they were returning from a trip to Palenque, and Margarita sank into a prolonged bereavement from which she has begun to emerge, after becoming pregnant with her fourth child. Although K'ayum still enjoys playing practical jokes on outsiders, and the children of Nahá are as uninhibited and mischievous as ever, a new sense of foreboding hangs over the community since the phrase "bomba atómica" infiltrated the Lacandon vocabulary. In our most recent conversation, K'ayum referred to "la bomba atómica" as the instrument by which Akyantho will bring about the next xu'tan. "It was Akyantho who gave the white man the bomb," he asserts unequivocally.

With the eruption of the nuclear age upon their conscious lives, the Lacandones have truly entered the second half of the twentieth century. Even Chan K'in now accepts that Akyantho's xu'tan will destroy a world far larger than the rain forest that delineates the traditional Lacandon universe.

"The world wants to die," Chan K'in says, with a sad, faraway look in his eyes. When prodded he will add, after a glance at his newborn son, "When this world ends, there will be a new and better one . . . but not for us. When we die we will go to the dark heaven of the lesser gods— the Chembel K'uh—where there is no sun, no trees, no water. It is the punishment of Hachäkyum, because we have turned our backs on the gods and neglected our traditions."

Reflections

Glossary

Bibliography

Reflections

This section was intended as a summing up or afterword to Parts I and II, which originally concluded this book. It was composed on the assumption that Nahá still had five to ten years of comparative immunity from the encroachments of the loggers and the Tzeltal *agraristas*. In fact, the Forestal completed its logging road to Nahá within a few weeks of my completing this section, and the four hundred mahogany trees were felled immediately after.

The Women of Nahá

My first two visits to Nahá left a number of loose ends. My keenest regret by far was my inability to communicate adequately with the women. The fault lay not so much in my lack of vocabulary as in the traditional reticence of Lacandon women toward all outsiders, and particularly toward strange men, whether *ladinos* or foreigners like myself.

Chan K'in did not overtly interfere with our interviewing Koh II through Geneviève, but his disapproval hung in the air, and sometimes took the form of slights and snubs to which, as a privileged guest with an overactive imagination, I was perhaps unduly sensitive. Throughout my stay I was haunted by clues to and intimations of the secret lives led by Chan K'in's three wives, and by K'in Bor's Nuk, K'ayum's Margarita and María Bonita. I often sensed anger and frustration that were taken out on the village dogs or refined into sarcasm, usually at the expense of the husbands. I was also conscious of a substantial sphere of influence that is available to these women in their subservient roles as wives, mothers and daughters; but I was not there long enough to comprehend the dynamics of this influence or to assess its long-term effects.

In Lacanjá, nearly all acts of violence have traditionally involved disputes over women. In Nahá sexual conflicts are normally worked out in the privacy of their huts, although I have seen minor marital squabbles resolved through verbal sallies and horseplay; that is to say, in much the same way that all other dissensions are dealt with.

It is almost axiomatic in Nahá that fathers rejoice in the birth of a daughter, for it portends the eventual annexation of a son-in-law-in-service who will expand one's power and prestige in the community. Mores are staunchly patriarchal, and the women's public role in the affairs and ceremonies of the village is practically nil. Chan K'in has put it on record that on the day of judgment, when Hachäkyum cuts off the heads of his creatures to determine their worth, pregnant and menstruating women will be automatically disbarred because of their polluted blood. (During the incense-burner–renewal ceremony the husbands of pregnant women are not permitted to take part in the rituals, for they are also contaminated.)

It is hard to dismiss the possibility that newborn girls in Nahá may at one time have been slowly starved in favor of the boys, which has been a practice in Mensäbäk, and that this might have resulted in a generation of strong-willed women with physical and personality disorders. Too many of the younger wives suffer from wasting diseases or develop sudden behavioral aberrations; and the frequent miscarriages by K'in Bor's Nuk and other young wives present a sharp contrast to the continuing fecundity of Koh II, María Bonita and other sturdy, middle-aged mothers. Of course, the strains of involuntary communal living exact their own toll, whose long-term effects it is too early to estimate.

Graciela

In Nahá and San Cristóbal, no name generates more heat than that of Graciela, who had been the western "wife" of Young Chan K'in and lived with him in the forest for the better part of two years.

Graciela was trained by her mother-in-law, Koh I, to make tortillas and fulfill the basic functions of a Lacandon wife. In the process she learned a good deal about Nahá women's workaday lives and their intimate relations with their men. Although her attempt to introduce weaving as a profitable craft failed dismally — she blamed the women's apathy and their lack of a sense of design — Graciela did help to raise the hygienic standards of the community, at least temporarily, and she aided Young Chan K'in in his first efforts to read and write. Graciela came to know and respect her mother-in-law, and she acquired a special admiration for Koh II; but her frequent absences damaged her standing with her new family, and since her departure from Nahá her admitted self-absorption has colored her memories of her experience.

Robert and Trudi feel strongly that she betrayed a position of trust, and that she exploited Young Chan K'in scandalously when he visited her in Guanajuato and Mexico City, where he was treated as an amusing object of curiosity. (Young Chan K'in's impressions of his sojourn in the "civilized world" are in turn painful and hilarious.)

I met Graciela in Toronto through a string of coincidences, and we talked for two days about her experiences. She assured me she was still in love with Young Chan K'in and knew that she had hurt him deeply. In the five years since her departure from Nahá, she has had difficulty reestablishing herself in Canada, although she has an excellent reputation as a weaver.

Graciela, an intense and durable woman in her mid-forties, remains bitter about her expulsion from the forest, which she blames on the connivance of her two chief enemies, Trudi Blom and a Mexican photographer who accused her — falsely, she insists — of bribing Lacandon boys to set fire to his canoe when he was paddling in one of the channels of Lake Nahá.

Conjecture and controversy surround this Italian–Canadian artist like a magnetic field, so that there are as many versions of what actually took place between her and Young Chan K'in as there are participants in the drama. I found her a deeply conflicted woman, absorbed with her private demons and her singular projections of her universe. At our first meeting she told me, "I have a fantasy that when the world blows up, only three people will survive: Trudi, my mother, and me."

Graciela asked me to collaborate with her on a book about her years in the forest that would contribute to an understanding of Lacandon culture. She claimed to have come to know Nahá women better than anyone else, including Trudi, as she alone had "gotten inside their heads." I declined at once, partly through lack of time and partly because I sensed it would be most difficult to establish a fair and dispassionate account of her undoubtedly unique story.

Nahá and the Mayan Civilization

Among the many unanswered questions raised by these visits is the puzzle of how and why a sophisticated civilization descended to the primitive state of the present-day Lacandones. What happened to the Mayan obsession with chronology and astronomy? What became of their architectural and artistic skills? To the Lacandones a mountain rock face can be as venerable a shrine to the gods as the soaring man-made structures of Yaxchilán and Palenque.

Some of the Classical Mayas' sense of color and design lives on in the textiles of highland Chiapas and Guatemala, but the Lacandones have no glyphs or written alphabet, and they have forgotten to keep track of the passing days and years.

We did find evidence to support our suspicion that Chan K'in retains in vestigial form his ancestors' preoccupation with the stars, and it could be that he employs only that portion of his knowledge that is of practical use in the forest. It may also be that the plastic skills of the Classical Mayas atrophied in their descendants simply because the harshness of their existence denied them the leisure to build stone temples and monoliths. Trudi's claim that these skills have not been altogether extinguished — contrary to Tozzer's negative findings — may be tested in the graceful drawings by K'ayum and by other young sons of Chan K'in, and in the curiously oriental designs drawn by Chan K'in and the elder Mateo on their gourd shells and incense pots. (Robert has traced some of these ideogrammatic drawings and copied others in preparation for a study of Lacandon graphic symbolism.)

On the positive side, there is no question that the Lacandones have preserved their ancestors' skills as agriculturists, and they are consummate hunters. In place of the calendar they have upgraded the importance of dreams as instruments of prophecy. The ancient Mayas used calendrical computations and their understanding of zero to explore the remote past for events that would illuminate their own era. Through their grasp of the lunar cycles and the cycles of Venus they probed into the future and predicted solar eclipses and other stellar events. But life in the forest, far from the great Mayan ceremonial centers, might well have driven this spirit of exploration inward, into the internal heavens and hells, the hidden suns and moons, of Chan K'in's stories, and into the refinement of "extrasensory" means of communication, such as telepathy. Almost nothing is known of the oracular or necromantic skills of the ancient Mayas. In the absence of evidence it becomes possible to theorize that Chan K'in and his forebears, by emphasizing the importance of dreams, storytelling, myths and the parapsychological faculties, may have reverted to earlier, pre-Classical modes of perceiving the cosmos. A Palenque palace astronomer of the ninth century A.D. would most likely have found Chan K'in's creation stories overly simple and rather childish.

This assumption would help to explain the extraordinary blend of sophistication and primitivism that is a hallmark of the present-day Lacandones. *Idiots savants* abound in Nahá, among Lacandones of all ages.

The Storyteller

The longer I stayed in Nahá the less attention I paid to José Güero's psychic prowess (although his prankish witchery seemingly reached all the way to Peterborough, New Hampshire, when my brand-new Olivetti Lexikon 83 broke down irreparably just as I was describing the effects he'd had on our electronic equipment). I came to accept telepathic and even televisual communication between Lacandones as a matter of course, and I regarded my synchronous dreams with K'ayum as natural outgrowths not only of our particular kinship, but of the subconscious commonality that binds us all. And yet I have difficulty explaining to myself or others the sense of absolute fittingness I experienced whenever I had parallel or dovetailing dreams with K'ayum. I derived a profound reassurance from these dream-swaps, which, among other boons, have helped to rid me of my oldest fears of death and disability.

What most interested me, the longer I stayed in Nahá, was Chan K'in's ability to hold a community together through his skill as a storyteller, and his authority as the guardian of a cultural tradition descended from the earliest Olmecs and Mayas.

Chan K'in does not have to practice white or black magic to maintain this authority, as is true of most so-called "primitive" cultures where the witch doctor's (*curandero's* or *chiman's*, in Mesoamerican parlance) cachet in the supernatural realm determines his status within the tribe. Chan K'in does not regard himself as a medicine man or a shaman, although I witnessed more than once his ability to translate dream and vision into workaday realities. As a teacher Chan K'in has elected to instruct not by commandments or voodoo but by example, and by the use of parable, song and cautionary tale — the storyteller's unique catechism. There are no imperative forms in Lacandon grammar or religion, no thou-shalts and thou-shalt-nots. What you do in this life is a matter between yourself and the gods, to be settled after your death in the netherworld's halls of judgment, when Sukunkyum or Kisin will have the disposition of your soul.

At the heart of Chan K'in's vision is his ability to tell a story from the inside, so that the events and the characters shape the narrative and give it an independent life. We who have been nurtured on the classics, and have given up the oral tradition of storytelling for the printing press, have lost this capacity to tell a story directly from within ourselves. We begin and end with inherited structures that shut us off from the myths and images that informed our earliest perceptions of the world. (In dreams we can break free and return to this rugged, invigorating landscape.) A fabulist of the caliber of Aesop or Andersen takes the seed of a folktale and makes it flower, and in so doing reaches down into the same springs of our collective human experience from which Chan K'in begins each of his simple tales.

Chan K'in's power comes from a healthy spirit whose vitality radiates outward in the rhythms of his story. The cadence of his voice draws us into the rise and fall of his breathing, into his very pulse. At his best, as with Chan K'in, the storyteller has the power to heal when he uses paradox, metamorphosis, reversal and other devices to surprise and free our inmost faculties. Through the medium of his stories, Chan K'in empowers us to beat with his heartbeat, and to see with his eyes, which have retained their farsightedness even after Hachäkyum burned them in his earthen jar to diminish their range. Armed with this gift, and our enlarged vision, we can unmask the malignant encrustations on our lives which take the form of self-delusions, groundless fears, the whole spectrum of psychosomatic and mental ailments. And we can commence the task of exorcizing them.

But this healing can only take place in the storyteller's milieu, near the center of his power, where these regenerative forces are still alive.

The Fate of the Lacandones

There were times, sitting in the god-house at Nahá, when I could almost touch the frail thread that intertwines all living things in the forest, from the lowliest bed-louse to the noble jaguar. In the wake of these glimpses I began to understand how each synthetic object we admit into our lives nullifies a bit of our souls, and removes by that much our purchase in the natural order. In Nahá I saw this process at work in K'in Bor, K'in Garcia and Young Mateo. The weight of their freedom — however diminished — is becoming too great for them, and so they erect barricades of plastic gadgets that symbolize their passage from one way of life into another, and further their apprenticeship in the occidental laws of supply and demand. In a similar way, the toxic synthetic substances we breathe or swallow build a residue that eventually barricades our cells from the healing action of our bloodstream. Many of our rivers are being slowly asphyxiated by pesticides and industrial wastes which the beneficent bacteria in the water can no longer break down.

I learned in the forest that there is no essential difference between the sludge that is choking our seas and rivers, and the chemical sediment that accrues in the walls of our cells. And not only the process but the end result is similar, whether we call it death by poisoning or cancer.

Inevitably, both Lacanjá and the two northern communities of Mensäbäk and Nahá are being sucked into our technological vortex. The Lacandon forest sits on top of commodities too precious for an overcrowded industrial society to ignore; not only the chicle and mahogany, which will soon be gone, but the likelihood of petroleum exploitation lies ahead, and beyond that, perhaps the mining of uranium for nuclear plants.

With the destruction of the forest Chan K'in's power will slowly wither and die; it will die from sadness, and the internal wasting that overtakes an Indian cut off from his gods. Chan K'in knows full well what is going on around him as the bulldozers and the tractors move ever closer to Nahá. Chan K'in himself led me to the binding formula that governs their lives:

"Without its mahogany a forest dies into jungle, where only the snakes can live; without our traditions, the *hach winik* turn into drunken *ladinos*, no different from those who burn and destroy our forest."

Old Chan K'in, Mateo, José Güero, Antonio, one or two others in Mensäbäk, are the last true Lacandon elders. So long as they are alive, the inner forms of Lacandon culture and religion will continue to be upheld, even as the outer forms break down around them, one by one . . .

D. H. Lawrence wrote, in *Mornings in Mexico:*

> The Indian way of consciousness is different from and fatal to our own way of consciousness. Our way of consciousness is different from and fatal to the Indian. The two ways, the two streams are never to be united. They are not even to be reconciled. There is no bridge, no canal of connection. . . . The sooner we realize, and accept this, the better, and leave off trying, with fulsome sentimentalism, to render the Indian in our own terms.

This same sentiment has been voiced in more scholarly terms by a number of distinguished anthropologists, among them Claude Lévi-Strauss in *Tristes Tropiques:*

> The fact is that these primitive peoples . . . are all, in their different ways, enemies of our society, which pretends to itself that it is investing them with nobility at the very same time when it is completing their destruction, whereas it viewed them with terror and disgust when they were genuine adversaries.

He follows this with an outwardly modest disclaimer:

> Can it be that I, the elderly predecessor of these scourers of the jungle, am the only one to have brought back nothing but a handful of ashes? Is mine the only voice to bear witness to the impossibility of escapism? Like the Indian in the myth, I went as far as the earth allows one to go, and when I arrived at the world's end, I questioned the people, the creatures and things I found there and met with the same disappointment: "He stood still, weeping bitterly, praying and moaning. And yet no mysterious sound reached his ears, nor was he put to sleep in order to be transported, as he slept, to the temple of the magical animals. For him

there could no longer be the slightest doubt: No power, from anyone, had been granted him."

I have brooded on these passages often since my return from Nahá, and Lévi-Strauss's words have challenged my understanding of my experience in the rain forest. I have discussed these issues with Robert, who, since Charles Frey, has come closest to bridging the Lacandon and occidental ways of consciousness.

In his younger days, Robert was often compared to Charles Frey, the romantic American explorer who lived many years among the southern Lacandones of Lacanjá, until he drowned in a canoe accident on the Jataté River. (According to the Nahá version, he was macheted by a southern Lacandon following a quarrel over a woman.)

In Oaxaca one morning, during an intense discussion in a plaza café, Robert described Frey, himself and me as seekers who suffer from a neurotic longing to justify our lives with specific deeds, and who fail to realize that life itself is the primary value, and cannot be justified.

In Nahá I was to bump up against the limits of our "Lacandonization" again and again. During the *balché* ceremonies on the traditional side of the lake, Robert and I were allowed to remain in the god-house while K'ayum or Antonio lighted the incensories and conducted ritual prayers. But when Chan K'in had some important matter to take up with Hachäkyum, he hinted that it might be time for our dinner, and he did not begin chanting until we were well outside the range of his voice.

Robert has been adopted by Chan K'in as an occidental foster son, yet even he is excluded from the secret rituals. No doubt Chan K'in has good reason to safeguard from us — and particularly from me — his seminal tales and sacred ceremonies. I never lost the feeling that Chan K'in had the measure of us, and had carefully weighed our capacity to absorb information and reproduce it in our language within an acceptable margin of accuracy.

Chan K'in allowed us to take photographs because he considers these images to be merely shadows of the original, and not — as Moslems do — its living substance. There is some irony in my discovery that Chan K'in did not mind our tape recorders nearly as much as our notebooks, the presence of which often stopped him from finishing a story; but we could always play back the tape for his approval, and on at least one occasion he turned our own instrument back on ourselves, and insisted that Robert and I play guitar and sing for his private "tape library." The tape recorder was an equalizer, whereas our notebooks represented a part of our alien "*ts'ul*" culture that was beyond his supervision.

I am confident that Chan K'in and his companions, like their adaptable highland counterparts, took from us what was most instructive and useful, and gave us in return as much of their culture as they judged us capable of understanding. In this exchange, we came out immeasurably the richer, and with far more than "a handful of ashes."

It is true that in the first part of my stay in Nahá I often caught myself sentimentalizing the Lacandones, or ennobling them with my projections of their superiority to our decadent occidental culture. Admittedly, I went into the forest as a believer, and in the first weeks experienced Nahá as if I were an infatuated lover. The chief object of my infatuation was Chan K'in, and after the haze cleared and I was able to focus on him with some objectivity, he did not disappoint any of my expectations; on the contrary, he enlarged them.

But it was several weeks before I could perceive the deep rifts in K'in Bor's personality, which verge on a primitive schizophrenia — or the damaging indecisiveness in K'ayum, which makes him so susceptible to Young Mateo's bullying. K'ayum has an artist's soul, and his considerable talents are hedged with neurotic vacillations.

In time, however, these character failings only enhanced for me the extraordinary reality of these rude, sophisticated people. I was almost relieved to discover pettinesses in Chan K'in, such as his occasional secretiveness and his predilection for listening to gossip about his enemies, above all José Pepe Chan Bol. These shortcomings made him more readily accessible. In a real sense, they anchored him to this world.

Like the whales and dolphins, the Lacandones have much to teach us about our basic natures. They provide a mirror to our selves that will not be available much longer. And it is a mirror — like Alice's looking glass — that should be entered with optimism and faith, and a certain degree of innocence. Despite the considered caveats of Lawrence and Lévi-Strauss, I believe that any occidental with an open mind and a strong stomach can benefit from a brief immersion in Lacandon consciousness, if he is willing to pay the price in self-esteem or shattered illusions about sorcerer-shamans who can bestow personal power through the use of exotic drugs. The fact is that Chan K'in exists, and his teachings are accessible to anyone who will seek him out in his imperiled jungle fastness. I know that I will need Chan K'in's instruction within me on many a dark night to come, as we move into the Brave New World of the twenty-first century.

It is a tragedy that so many of us are awaking to the importance of protecting these last pockets of "primitive" culture, just as the destructiveness engendered by greed, overpopulation and centuries of missionary zeal attains its maximum acceleration. Even as our earth's resources dwindle, we are careful to preserve our Louvres and our Smithsonians, while we continue the extermination of living cultures that bear directly on our survival as a species. There appears to be an inbred perversity in our makeup that blinds us to the value of a life form that diverges from our own until our boot is on its neck and we are about to stamp it out. "Ah, so *that* is where this fits in," we say, as the bones snap underfoot.

We may well be witnessing the final stages of a campaign that dates back at least three thousand years, waged by cultures which have given up their formative myths and folk legends, against those few which persist in living theirs.

The parallels between the fate of the Lacandones and the disappearing whales is not as farfetched as it first seems. Both are essentially gentle, pacific beings who live in harmony with their environment. They both need silence and a minimal stability in their extensive habitats to keep up their forms of communication and to hold together their communal structures. Just as the heavily trafficked shipping lanes and the proliferating oil spills are disrupting the baleen whales' sonar contacts across deep-water channels hundreds of miles long, so the logging roads and the chain saws are destroying the forest silences Lacandones require to hunt for prey and to maintain their extrasensory "network." When a Lacandon slivers a leaf and imitates a wounded animal, the reverberations of his call fan outward into the forest, and the echoes can return to his senses from several miles' distance. It is similarly true of his telepathic signals, and of the untrammeled dreamspace he requires to keep in touch with his *onen*.

The blue whale ranges over thousands of miles to find a suitable mate, and once mated, they remain together for life. There is now a very real possibility that whaling ships with explosive harpoons are preventing blue whales in the Antarctic from mating in sufficient numbers to replace their losses. What will it take to discourage the younger Lacandones in the forest from mating and reproducing themselves? K'in Bor, K'in García and even K'ayum already show signs of a terminal sadness that is familiar to students of aboriginal peoples all over the world; none of the younger men in Nahá have more than one wife, and few have — or want — more than one or two children.

The plight of the Lacandones is not only for Mexico's conscience to grapple with, as it does in the film *Cascabel*. They are on the conscience of all of us, for their extinction will also seal the fate of the largest virgin rain forest north of the Amazon. The effect of this destruction on our climate, and on the ecological stability of our hemisphere, is incalculable. I choose to take Chan K'in at his word when he tells us that after the mighty trees are cut down, the rains will cease and not only the forest will dry up, but the highlands as well, "not only in this heaven, but in the higher heaven above." Chan K'in needs no scientist to explain to him the metamorphic process by which every cell of every leaf in each tree of the forest converts carbon dioxide into the oxygen we all breathe. On his own terms, he takes this for granted. And no scientist can accurately predict just how crippling will be the effect on our biosphere when the great American rain forests have been stripped bare and turned into pasture.

In a practical sense, these few hundred Lacandon Mayas may represent the last guardians of the forest, and not only through their intercession with the gods. Experience has taught me that Chan K'in is no idle prophet, and I do not take lightly his pledge that when the last Lacandon dies, the world will come to an end.

Glossary

The Pronunciation of Lacandon Maya

The six vowels are pronounced as follows: **a** sounds like the *a* in "father"; **ä**, like the *u* in "sun"; **e**, like the *e* in "men"; **i**, like the *ee* in "peek"; **o**, like the *o* in "bone"; and **u**, like the *oo* in "fool." Doubled vowels are longer than the single ones but they have the same sound.

An apostrophe indicates a glottal stop — the slight clearing of the vocal cords which in English occurs just before we pronounce a word beginning with a vowel (try saying "at, in, on," and the glottal stop will be obvious). In Lacandon the glottal stop often occurs in a double vowel. Example: *lu'um* (earth). The sound can be approximated by saying the English phrase "who oozes."

Lacandon consonants are very much the same as in English. There are two exceptions: *l* is pronounced *l* at the start of a word and *r* in the middle or at the end; **x** is pronounced *sh*. And there are glottalized consonants as well, which English does not have. To describe how to pronounce them would take us into technical linguistics far beyond the scope of this book. To pursue the study of Lacandon Maya further, consult Robert Bruce's *Gramática del Lacandon*.

aah: awake

aäk'alyoom: a night-blooming flower in which Kisin, the god of death, was born

Acantunes (Pagans; Maya wild Indians): an early Spanish name of the Lacandones

achiote (Spanish): red dye from the annato tree, used ceremonially to symbolize blood

agrarista (Spanish): a homesteader; a colonist who practices slash-and-burn agriculture

äh: the; they

Akinchob: the corn god; son-in-law of the Creator, Hachäkyum, and the protector of men and the *milpa*; builder of Yaxchilán

Akna' (Our Lady; Our Mother): the moon; any goddess

Akyantho: the god of commerce and foreigners (his importance has grown with the coming of tourists and other foreigners to the forest)

ba'ats':   the howler monkey; any ape (all primates except man and those classified as *ma'ax*, monkey)

bäh: self; oneself

bäho':   companion

bäk-nikte':   tuberose; the primary gods emerged from it

balché: an alcoholic ceremonial drink made from the bark of the *balché* tree

balum: any predatory feline (see also **hach balum**)

bay: okay; very well; yes

bin in kah: I go; I depart — a formal parting

Bol: the god of wine; one of the four commonest Lacandon male names

bolay: a small wildcat

Bonampak (Yucatec Maya):   the Classical Mayan site with the famous murals; sacred to the southern Lacandones

brujería (Spanish):   witchcraft; sorcery

brujo (Spanish):   a witch doctor; a sorcerer, especially one that practices black magic

cabrito (Spanish):   a species of small deer

caña brava (Spanish):   a wild cane used to make arrow shafts

caribal (Spanish):   a small Lacandon settlement, usually consisting of one or two families

Caribe: a Spanish name for Lacandon, still in use

cascabel (Spanish):   rattlesnake

cayuco (Spanish):   dugout canoe

Chaac (Yucatec Maya):   name for the rain god, Mensäbäk

Chamula: a group of highland Mayas who are traditional enemies of the Lacandones; a town of the same name

chan: little

Chan K'in (Little Sun; Little Prophet):   one of the four commonest Lacandon male names

chechem: the weeping tree (a poisonous tree of the rain forest)

chembel k'uh: minor god, a flexible term that can include a wide variety of supernatural beings we might call ghosts, goblins, banshees, and the like

chich: hard; intense

Chichén Itzá: an ancient Maya site in central Yucatán; its sacred well attracted countless pilgrims

chichin: a little; small amount

chico (Spanish):   small

chicozapote: the sapodilla tree

Chilam Balam of Chumayel: one of the Yucatec Maya *Books of Prophecies*

chiman (Spanish):   shaman

Chol: a group of Christianized Mayas who are moving into the Lacandon forest as colonists and agriculturists

chucho con rabia (Spanish) (rabid dog):   a cheap liquor, now more generally called *mata-caña* (killer cane)

chukuch nok' (long tunics): the southern Lacandones

compañero (Spanish):   companion

Copán: ancient Maya site in western Honduras, famous for its stelae and hieroglyphic stairway

corrido (Spanish):   a Mexican narrative song or ballad
curandero (Spanish):   witch doctor; healer

derecho de monte (Spanish):   forestry rights; monies paid by the government for logged trees

ech: you (cf. **tech,** to you)
eh hah: true; true indeed
ejido (Spanish):   common public land; homesteaders' settlement (originally conceived as a Mexican counterpart to the Israeli kibbutz)
en: I, me (cf. **ten,** to me)

guayacán: a lignum-vitae tree
güero (Mexican Spanish):   fair; light-skinned

Haab: the 365-day year, seldom used in the Olmec–Maya calendar
Haawo':   Lacandones of the Coatimundi and/or Raccoon *onen* (lineage), perhaps the most esoteric group of all, whose members are believed to have spoken directly with the gods
hach: true; real
hach balum: jaguar (*hach,* "real," distinguishes this from the generic *balum,* "predatory feline")
hach k'uuts (the true or real tobacco):   the Lacandon cigar
hach pixan (real soul):   a type of dream in which a soul, being or situation manifests itself directly to the dreamer without symbolic disguise
hach winik (the true or real people):   the Lacandon Mayas
Hachäkyum (Our True Lord):   the Creator; the principal deity of the Lacandones
hah: true
halach winik: the great lords of the Classic era in Mayan history (A.D. 300–900)
hax t'an (the true or real language):   Lacandon Maya
Hesuklisto: Jesus Christ (borrowed from the Spanish Jesucristo)
huipil (Mexican Spanish):   the blouse of the Highland Mayas
hum: noise; sound
Hunahpú: the Quiché–Maya equivalent of the Lacandon solar hero Nuxi'. Hunahpú (the sun) and Ixbalanqué (the morning star) were the immortal twins of the *Popol Vuh*

Itsanohk'uh: the lord of hail, cold, lakes and alligators; the lake of the same name
Ixbalanqué.   See **Hunahpú**

jobillo (Spanish):   a fine tropical hardwood used in making utensils

kah: *ladino* (a Spanish term used for all non-Lacandones who are not foreign Caucasians)
k'ak':   fire
K'ak', Ah ([He who is] Fire):   the god of hunters and archers
K'akoch or Ka'k'och (the Prime Mover):   the remote god who created the infirm earth and the first sun and moon, as well as the tuberose from which the primary gods emerged
k'ambul: curassow
Kanank'ax (Guardian of the Forest):   one of a class of forest deities
kaxtlan chem: a large canoe that will hold all the creatures of the world against the next flood; the Lacandon Noah's Ark

K'ayum or K'ayyum (Singing Lord; Lord of Song):   the Lacandon god of music; one of the four commonest Lacandon male names

k'ek'en: wild boar; peccary

ki' iba' a wilik (be careful what you see):   a formal parting before going to sleep

k'in: sun; day; prophecy; one of the four commonest Lacandon male names

K'in, Ah ([He of] the Sun; The Prophet):   the god of ceremonies; a priest; a prophet

k'inyah: divination

Kisin (He Who Causes Death):   the god of death; the devil; the earthquake

Koh (tooth; teeth):   the ceremonial name for the peccary; one of the two commonest Lacandon names for women

ko'ox: let us go

Kukulcán: the Yucatec Maya name for the Aztec god Quetzalcoatl

K'ulel, Ah (The Whirlwind):   one of a group of assistant gods at the service of the major solar deities

kuh: god; spirit; sacred; supernatural being

kun: the thorn palm

k'uuts: tobacco

Lacanjá Chan Sayab: the largest southern Lacandon settlement; the term Chan Sayab is a recent addition

Lacantún, El: a major river in the Lacandon forest; an early name for the Lacandones

ladino, ladina (Spanish):   a term generally used for all non-Indians except foreign Caucasians

lo'k'in: cannibal (surviror of the Mayan "Age of Wooden Men")

Luumkab: spirits of minor deities associated with the earth, stones and the rainbow (the rainbow is called Bel Luumkab — road of the Luumkab)

ma':   no; general negation

ma' tsoy: not good

ma'ax: monkey; spider; a member of the Monkey *onen* (lineage)

majaua (Mexican Spanish):   a forest tree whose bark is used for making hammocks, among other purposes

mäx hum: absence of noise

Mayapán: an ancient Maya site on the Yucatán Peninsula, near Mérida

meek'chäl: adolescent rites of passage; ceremonial initiation to adulthood

men: to make

Mensäbäk (Powder Maker): the rain god; the name of the largest northern Lacandon settlement; the lake of the same name

mestizo (Spanish):   of mixed blood; a half-breed

Metlán: hell; that part of the underworld in which Kisin punishes the souls of evildoers (a borrowing from Nahuatl Mic-tlan, "Death-place")

milpa (Mexican Spanish):   cornfield; any cultivated field

mole (Mexican Spanish):   a typical northern Mexican dish

morral (Mexican Spanish):   a net-cord shoulder bag

muk: strength

Nah Ts'ulu':   mythical jaguars of heaven and the underworld

Nahá (Great Water):   site of the most traditional northern Lacandon settlement; the lake of the same name

nauyaca (Mexican Spanish): a pit viper, the fer-de-lance (*Bothrops atrox*)

ne ki': very tasty

ne sis: cold

ne tsoy: good; very good

norte (Spanish): north; a rainstorm, typically lasting three days and accompanied by strong north winds and cold

Nuk (large): one of the two commonest names for Lacandon women

Nuxi' or **Nuxib** (old person; living being): the Mole Trapper, one of the legendary Lacandon ancients; a Lacandon male name

och: possum; used as the name for all children under three years of age, before they are given their own names

ocote (Mexican Spanish): pitch pine, used as torches and kindling

oken: come inside — a formal greeting

onen: animal name; family lineage

Palenque: a Classic Maya site in the Lacandon forest; one of the two sites most sacred to the northern Lacandones

paseo (Spanish): a stroll

p'enkach yaab: incomparably much or many; full to brimming

piñata (Mexican Spanish): a papier-mâché decorated pot filled with sweets, which is broken at weddings, birthdays, holiday celebrations

pom: ceremonial incense (the Mexican Spanish *copal*)

pooxah: leather pouch or purse

Popol Vuh (Book of Counsel): seminal Quiché-Maya account recorded in the eighteenth century

posada (Spanish): inn; lodging; a Christmas ritual and celebration commemorating the arrival of Joseph and Mary in Bethlehem sans reservation

posol (Mexican Spanish): the typical Indian gruel of ground hominy mixed with water; also used as a ceremonial offering

Quejaches: Spanish version of the Yucatec–Maya name (meaning "People of the Deer") for a coastal group of Indians believed by some to be the present-day Lacandones

quetzal: the royal bird of the Mayas

Quetzalcoatl: the major Aztec deity; the Mayan Kukulcán, associable with both Lacandon deities Ah K'ak' and Akyantho

rancheras (Spanish): Mexican songs, equivalent to "country-western" songs in the United States

sabak: soot

sak'al: army ant (the Spanish *marabunta*)

sas wich: clairvoyant

say: leaf-cutter ants (they have esoteric associations both with corn growing and ancient war societies)

solaw: policeman; soldier (loan word from the Spanish *soldado*)

suegro (Spanish): father-in-law

Sukunkyum (Elder Brother of Our Lord): lord of the underworld

ta': excrement; defecate

ta'k'in (shit of the sun): money; silver

tal in wilech: I have come to see you — a formal greeting

tech: to you

ten: to me

tepeiscuinte (Mexican Spanish): paca, a large rodent hunted by the Lacandones

tibil: enough (literally, "to there")

tibil chichin: just barely enough

Tikal: an ancient Maya city in northern Guatemala

t'o'ohil (the great one): a spiritual leader and guardian of the Maya tradition; a teacher

tostada (Spanish): toasted tortilla

Ts'ibatnah (Painter of Houses): the god of the graphic arts; the lake of the same name

tsikbal: talk; chat

ts'iktal: quarrel

ts'ok: finished

tsoy: good

tsoy y-ol: good person; of good spirit; in good spirits

ts'ul: a foreigner who is not an Indian

T'uub or T'uup (Little One): the lord of the sun, the favorite son of Hachákyum

turista (Spanish): tourist

Tzeltal: a group of Christianized Mayas who have moved in great and growing numbers into the Lacandon forest

Tzolkin: the complete calendric cycle, combining twenty day names with thirteen numerals; this 260-day cycle was the cosmic slide rule of the Mesoamerican calendar

Uaxactun: an important cycle in the ancient Mayan calendar: eight Tuns of 360 days each equals exactly twenty days more than eleven Tzolkins of 260 days each, and exactly forty days less than five formal Venus cycles of 584 days each; also the Mayan site of the same name in El Petén, Guatemala

uts: acceptable; okay

wilik: to see (as in the formal greeting *tal in wilik* — I have come to see)

winik: people; person; man; human

xämän or xaman: north; norther; *norte* (q.v.); the praying mantis

xen: go — a formal parting

xikul: shirt; dress; the traditional cotton tunic (a loan word from the Nahuatl *xicol-li*)

xilal: man, manchild

xiw: impersonator of the gods; a surrogate

Xok: mythical merman; a supernatural water being who is said to inhabit deep lakes and rivers and to carry away women who bathe in them

Xtabay: a class of minor goddesses or seductive nymphs (in Yucatán they are still regarded as evil female spirits who lure men to their deaths)

xu'tan (destroy the world): end of the world

yawat pixan: cry of the soul

Yaxchilán: a Classical Mayan site on the bank of the Usumacinta River, across from the Guatemalan border; sacred to both the southern and northern Lacandones

yuk: deer (a small species, called *cabrito* in Mexican Spanish, as opposed to the larger *keh* — stag or hind)

Yum Ah Say: lord of the leaf-cutter ants

Yum Ch'om: lord of the buzzards and vultures

Yum K'ax: lord of the forest, a dangerous and exacting supernatural forest being; in other Peninsular Maya groups, the title of the benevolent corn god

yumeh: lord; my lord — a term of respect used when addressing a Lacandon elder; also, a kinship term, reciprocal between parallel uncle-nephew, and the like

Zinacantán: the town of the highland Zinacantecos who, like the Chamulas, are traditional enemies of the Lacandones

zopilote (Mexican Spanish):   the common black buzzard

Annotated Bibliography

The proposition that this book should contain a convenient listing of other works available to the reader who wishes to know more about the Lacandon people and their culture would appear to be a simple, good idea, and nothing more. It entails several difficult problems, however, which we would like to explain.

First of all, the Lacandones of today are two ethnic groups—Northern and Southern Lacandones, as we have made clear in this book—the last two cultural survivors of a single people and culture, the Peninsular Mayas, often called simply "Mayas," though this latter term includes numerous other ethnic groups called "Highland Mayas" or "Mayense peoples." Obviously, the similarity of names reflects cultural affinities and shared ethnic origins among all these peoples, so in fact any separation of "Lacandon" from "Maya" literature is necessarily artificial and arbitrary. The more one knows of different Maya and Mayense cultures, the better one can understand Lacandon culture, and the more significant this understanding will be—but the field is simply too vast for us to attempt to deal with it all critically or systematically. One must draw the line somewhere, and the logical place to draw it is to include books specifically or primarily about the Lacandones, or books of a more ample cultural scope that include exceptionally important references to Lacandones among related cultures.

Even this basic rule runs into ambiguous exceptions: Landa's *Yucatan Before and After the Conquest* deals with the Mayas of Northern Yucatán, around Mérida, at the time of the Spanish conquest, so in basic theory it is "Maya in general" rather than "Lacandon." Still, this book is so important for any study of Peninsular Mayas, including the Lacandones, that we have included it for a double reason: on the one hand, some passages are of great value as representative of general Maya cultural traits that today are exclusively Lacandon (such as the renovation of the idols, or Lacandon incense burners), traits that have been eliminated among all other contemporary, Christianized Mayas; while on the other hand, certain prejudices and distortions make indiscriminate acceptance of this "classic" dangerous and misleading. Therefore we could not resist commenting on it.

In contrast, we have not included most works on the present-day Highland Mayas, though sometimes their exclusion was extremely dissatisfying. For example, we have reluctantly omitted Gary Gossen's works on the Chamulas, and Robert Laughlin's on Zinacantecos (two Highland Mayense groups), even though there are often striking parallel details with Lacandon culture; but widening our scope to include them would have obliged us to consider at least a dozen other valuable studies on the Highland groups. However, we have included the Highland Quiché *Popol Vuh*, which gives stories and traditions that parallel those of the Lacandones too closely and strikingly to be omitted.

And even within the narrower scope of publications dealing specifically (or at least nominally) with the Lacandones and the Lacandon jungle, some we have omitted for very good reasons: Dana and Ginger Lamb's *Quest of the Lost City* and Wolfgang Cordan's *Secret of the Forest* have certain merits if considered as adventure novels. But these books claim to be documentary, and we have chosen simply to avoid commenting on or evaluating them as nonfiction. We are also certain that other worthwhile and honest publications are omitted here simply due to oversight.

Although the *ideal* goal of this Annotated Bibliography originally was to comment on all the works that may be either valuable or misleading (or both) for further study of the Lacandones, we have not been able to do so, nor do we claim to. The following are simply some publications on the Lacandones, suggested for further reading.

Álvarez, Cristina
    1980   *Diccionario etnolingüístico del idioma maya yucateco colonial.* Centro de Estudios Mayas. Universidad Nacional Autónoma de México. México. (385 pp.)

This dictionary can be very useful for Lacandon ethnolinguistic studies. It combines the advantages of a coherent modern presentation by subject (1. Astronomy, Meteorology and Chronology; 2. Geography; 3. Botany; 4. Zoology) with a systematized presentation of the oldest Maya forms registered during colonial times. Though the material comes from the dialects of Peninsular Maya from the northern part of the Yucatán Peninsula, it is far closer to contemporary Lacandon dialects than to the Yucatec equivalents. This dictionary helps one to understand that the cultural, political, religious and economic domination by Spanish-speaking people caused far more rapid and drastic linguistic change than the centuries previous to the Spaniards' arrival, since all the peoples in question spoke very similar dialects of the same Peninsular Maya language.

Amram, David W.
1942   "The Lacandon, Last of the Mayas," in *México Antiguo*, vol. 6, pp. 15–30. México.

As its title indicates, this article was one of the first to anticipate the cultural importance of the Lacandones as heirs of the ancient Maya traditions. As important as this was for its time, the article was brief, and the Lacandones did not begin to receive the attention their traditional conservatism deserves for another two decades. It should also be noted that this work was written prior to the discovery of the ruins of Bonampak, which brought the Lacandones into the spotlight of public attention.

Baer, Phillip and Mary
1952   Lacandon Ethnographic Materials. *Microfilm Collection of Manuscripts on Middle American Cultural Anthropology*, no. 34. University of Chicago Library. Chicago.

This work on Northern Lacandon culture consists of 334 pages and is divided into nine chapters. At the time it was written, the Baers had spent quite a few years living among the Northern Lacandones, dedicated to efforts to Christianize them. The most interesting points of this work relate to the material culture and life cycle of the Lacandones, and the weakest points are those dealing with mythology, beliefs and religious practices, since the Baers were more interested in propagating their own than in learning those of the Lacandones.

Persons who do not respect a culture they study or observe are not likely to report much of interest about it. Still, this work was considered by Maya scholars of the time to be the most authoritative study since that of Tozzer (1907). Perhaps the principal value of this study today is that it provides us an indirect explanation of why so many conscientious Maya scholars, such as Eric Thompson, misjudged the importance of the Lacandones to Maya culture.

Fortunately, the positive contributions the discerning investigator might seek here are much better expressed in Baer and Merrifield (1971).

Baer, Phillip, and William R. Merrifield
1971   *Two Studies on the Lacandones of Mexico*. Summer Institute of Linguistics. México. (274 pp.; 5 charts; map; illustrations)

This book has much valuable information on the material culture of the Southern Lacandones (with only occasional, comparative references to the Northern Lacandones). Especially valuable is Part II of the study, "Lacandone

Subsistence." Although there are occasional interesting data in the rest of the book, everything appears to be overshadowed by the commitment to demonstrate that the Lacandones were murderous and degenerate brutes until Phil Baer arrived with the "Good News that Jesus Saves," from which point they became good, gentle and moral Christians . . . while the truth is that they were neither so evil before nor so good after. Although the incidence of violence among the Southerners has always been such as to horrify the Northern Lacandones (who considered such incidents among their own people as rare exceptions involving deviants), the study conveniently ignores or minimizes the cases of homicide, wife stealing, rape, and so forth, that occurred *after* their souls had been saved. Nor is there any mention of the new activities, which included political power plays, embezzlement, mismanagement of community funds, extortion and robbery of tourists, and drunken brawls and knife fights in the whorehouses of Palenque and Tenosique. It is our impression that no dishonesty is intended in the book; but when wishful thinking and self-delusion converge, dishonesty is not really necessary.

In order to separate the good and valuable contributions from the rest of the contents of the book, we recommend the following "rules of thumb": (1) Consider seriously only Part II, "Lacandone Subsistence"; and (2) Any paragraph in which there is an allusion to ". . . since Phil Baer arrived . . ." should be considered critically, if at all.

The kinship charts and the "Table of Vital Statistics," in which individuals are identified by arbitrarily assigned numbers, become unduly complex. Though the Lacandones' polygamous and quasi-incestuous social organization is partly to blame for the complexity, it is unfortunate that the authors did not register the patrilinear *Onen* (or lineage) name, which would have at least been a helpful indicator of genealogy, and which is (or at least was traditionally) important in the selection of marriage partners.

Blom, Frans and Gertrude Duby
1955   *La Selva Lacandona.* 2 vols. Editorial Cultura. México.

This book is a classic for any study of the Lacandones and their original rain forest. From the points of view of anthropology, history and ecology, it is significant and valuable, in that it was written at a time when demographic and ecological conditions that had remained relatively stable for several centuries were about to enter an era of rapid change. On Blom's map is an area marked "Unknown Jungle," though the Tzeltal population from Bachajón was beginning to spread into the vast jungle area originally inhabited by two small groups of Lacandones. The Lacandon jungle was a rich, green, ecologically stable entity stretching from the original Tzeltal territory (around Ocosingo, Bachajón, Oxchuc, etc.) to merge with the lowland jungle of the Guatemalan Petén. It had sealed its slight wounds, closing the trails and the open camps of the early mahogany cutters and chicle gatherers, just as it had covered the classic Mayas' ceremonial centers.

The discovery of the ruins of Bonampak less than a decade before had drawn the attention of the "civilized" world to this tropical rain forest, which had remained intact since classic Maya times. In this book, the authors describe the Lacandon jungle as it was when its destruction began. Now, a quarter of a century later, the destruction is near enough to completion to begin to alarm the ecologists.

Boremanse, Didier

   1981   "A Southern Lacandon Maya Account of the Moon Eclipse," in *Latin American Indian Literatures*, vol. 5, no. 1, pp. 1–6. University of Pittsburgh. Pittsburgh, Pennsylvania.

This article, though very brief, is of interest in view of the almost total lack of linguistic material from the Southern group of Lacandones. The text is presented in a phonemic transcription of the original, a lexeme-level translation, and a free translation, which permits the reevaluation of a few phonetic inconsistencies. This text is interesting when compared with the more abundant texts published from the Northern Lacandones. The phonemic system is basically the same as that used by Bruce, and the recognizable differences in the writing of cognate forms, as well as a few differences in lexical selection, correspond rather well to the dialect differences between Southern and Northern Lacandones.

Bruce S., Roberto D.

   1967   "Jerarquía Maya entre los dioses lacandones," in *Anales del I.N.A.H.*, vol. 28, pp. 93–108. S.E.P. México.

This article was one of the first presentations of Lacandon tradition as a continuation of classic Maya culture, identifying two classes of Lacandon "Assistant Gods" as representing the same hierarchy as the social classes or ceremonial functions found in the theocratic government of the classic Maya city-states at the time of the Spanish conquest. Since the basic structure of the aristocratic Maya solar theocracy would be most unlikely in an ethnic group descended from the peasants of classic times (as the "official view" supposes the origin of the present-day Lacandones to be), Thompson (1970) refers frequently to data presented in this article in his *Maya History and Religion*. He invariably searches for alternate explanations on the basis of previous studies, none of which recognized the Lacandon traditional conservatism. (Previous studies were almost always based on investigations conducted in Spanish, which the Lacandones spoke too poorly to convey the eloquence and sophistication of their traditions.)

Bruce's investigations, conducted in Lacandon Maya, produced results astonishingly and radically different from those of previous authors. A healthy suspicion of dramatic and radical conclusions (often the product of the author's imagination) is understandable, so Thompson's reluctance to accept at face value data not supported by other investigators is logically justifiable. (Additional evidence, though presented in 1968, was not available before *Maya History and Religion* had gone to press.)

Most of the positive contributions of this article are better expressed in later writings of the same author.

Bruce S., Roberto D.

   1968   *Gramática del Lacandón*. Departamento de Investigaciones Antropológicas, Pub. 21. I.N.A.H., S.E.P. México. (152 pp.; map; 6 figures; 6 plates)

This book (in Spanish) is a revised version of the author's master's thesis, presented to the *Escuela Nacional de Antropología e Historia* (México, 1965; reg. Library of Congress, Washington, D.C., no. A 805577). The most extensive and detailed study of the Northern Lacandon dialect of Peninsular Maya, it is most valuable (if not indispensable) for any serious study of Lacandon language and culture. It contains several appendices: Lacandon texts, the names and functions of Lacandon gods and supernatural beings, and traditional graphic representations (the "names of the gods" painted on the Lacandon incense burners, with the particular significance attributed to each of the various elements).

It is interesting to note that, when this book was written some fifteen years ago, the author frequently listed several potential linguistic analyses of ceremonial forms and titles, unable to decide which of the equally logical interpretations was the "correct" one. Despite ample evidence that Maya literary style plays with various simultaneous levels of meaning, somewhat in the manner of "punning" (though far more complex and sophisticated—see Bruce, 1974), many contemporary Maya scholars are still reluctant to recognize the existence of this practice which, in the Chilam Balam of Chumayel, is called "The Language of Zuyua."

This is the last work in which the author presents the Lacandon linguistic forms in i.p.a. (International Phonetic Alphabet). A semitraditional phonemic alphabet is used in his subsequent publications for reasons of economy for typesetters and facility for both the linotypist and the reader not specialized in linguistics.

Bruce S., Roberto D.
1974   *El Libro de Chan K'in.* Colección Científica (Lingüística), no. 12.
        I.N.A.H., S.E.P. México. (385 pp.; 11 appendices)

This book presents a selection of Lacandon stories regarding cosmology and mythology, according to the Lacandon oral tradition. The title recognizes Old Chan K'in of Nahá (the last Lacandon *T'o'ohil*, religious and civil authority of the Lacandones, and consequently of all the Peninsular Mayas) as the highest authority remaining in the Olmec-Maya-Lacandon cultural tradition. The material is presented in a format taken (with acknowledgment) from the linguistic magazine *Tlalocan*, which divides the pages into thirds: the upper third of each page contains the original Lacandon text, with morphemic cuts indicated by dashes; the middle third consists of a morpheme-level translation, according to the same arrangement of numbered lines of text, incorporating parenthetically lexeme-level interpretations and additional comments regarding semantic doubts or ambiguities; and the bottom third of each page registers a free translation (to Spanish) of the same numbered lines of text.

The content of the texts corresponds, sometimes strikingly, to the first part of the *Popol Vuh* of the Highland Quiché Mayas, which is to say it represents a stratum of Maya tradition, thought and values more basic than the cultural division into "Highland" and "Lowland (or Peninsular)" Maya cultures. Having two independent versions of the same mythological themes adds depth, clarity and understanding to both.

In the Introduction (pp. 7–14), examples are given of linguistic forms, especially ceremonial, which employ multiple levels of meaning to be understood simultaneously, a literary style of "punning" surviving in Maya cultures since classic times. The open format that confronts the Original Maya text with its morpheme-level linguistic analysis and free translation is designed to facilitate, among other things, further studies of the material.

The original Spanish edition is long since out of print, but it may still be found in libraries. An English version (*The Book of Chan K'in*) incorporating approximately 60 percent more material is now in preparation.

Bruce S., Roberto D.

1975–   *Lacandon Dream Symbolism.* 2 vols. Ediciones Euroamericanas
1979   Klaus Thiele. México. (363 pp.; 16 photographs—4 color and 12
        black and white)

Volume 1 (131 pp.) was published in 1975, and Volume 2 (240 pp.) in 1979, together with a clothbound edition of both volumes.

Every Mesoamerican culture with its traditions relatively intact—at least every one that we personally know of—preserves as part of its traditions a system of dream interpretation, usually considering dreams to be prophetic. This may be considered one of the universals of human cultures. For this reason, it is surprising that there are so few studies of this popular institution among the anthropological investigations of New World cultures. Robert Laughlin's publications (beginning in 1966) on dream interpretation in culturally nearby Zinacantán constitute almost the only other studies in this field to date. (Brief mentions of the interpretation of dreams sometimes appear in ethnographies and other studies in the area, but can usually be classified as anecdotes.)

Volume 1 presents a general description of the Lacandon beliefs regarding the interpretation of dreams, associated cultural values and philosophical concepts, and a list of specific dreams that were registered and interpreted, as well as the later events considered to be the confirmation of the prophecy in cases where such events occurred.

Volume 2 presents a dictionary-type listing (or traditional "Dream Book") of dream elements and their prophecies in original Lacandon text with English free translation. The English-Lacandon index immediately following this section can also be used as an English-Lacandon vocabulary for linguistic studies. In a series of six appendices, the material is rearranged to demonstrate some of the unique aspects of Lacandon Maya conceptual processes, as well as some mechanisms of association that would appear to be shared by most other cultures.

While this study could by no means be called "incomplete," it is intentionally "open," with numerous points at which the material itself invites continued treatment in more detailed studies or incorporation into the studies of related disciplines.

Bruce S., Roberto D.

1976   *Lacandon Texts and Drawings from Nahá.* Colección Científica
        (Lingüística), no. 45. I.N.A.H., S.E.P. México. (158 pp.; 6 photographs; 31 drawings; 16 facsimiles of handwritten text)

This book is bilingual (Spanish and English) and, in the first part, trilingual (Lacandon Maya, Spanish and English). The Spanish title, listed first, as is proper considering the publication of the book by an institution of the Mexican government, is *Textos y dibujos lacandones de Najá.* The first part of the book consists of sixteen Lacandon texts of traditional songs, chants and stories, translated in parallel texts, from the original Lacandon Maya into Spanish and English—and illustrated with drawings by young Lacandones of Nahá on the themes of the texts. This section of the book is directed to the reader with an interest in the aesthetic quality of the first written examples of the Lacandon oral tradition and of the spontaneous drawings they evoked.

The second part of the book consists of a facsimile of the original text, a peleography with phonemic analysis, and linguistic and ethnographic comments, some of which were considered too technical to interest the general reader but potentially too important to be omitted entirely. The book attempts a systematic compromise between one point of view, which would appreciate the "exotic" but lost contact with the reality of the culture to which it belongs, and the contrary point of view, which in the name of scientific objectivity would classify and quantify everything to the degree that all aesthetic quality is lost in the process.

Bruce, Robert D.

1978   "Figuras ceremoniales Lacandonas de hule," in *Boletín del I.N.A.H.*, pp. 25–34. I.N.A.H., S.E.P., México. (9 photos)

This ten-page article (in Spanish) deals with the various types of incense used in Lacandon Maya rituals, their ceremonial preparation, and the significance attributed to them. Special detail is given to the anthropomorphic figures made of natural latex (*k'ik'*), which are made with careful attention to detail and burned only in the most important ceremonies. The associations between rubber (*k'ik'*) and blood (*k'ik'-el*) are dealt with from the point of view of human sacrifice and its alternate practice, the autosacrifice of the worshippers' own blood, in Peninsular Maya culture.

The photographs, unfortunately, are of rather poor quality.

Bruce, Robert D.

1978   "The Popol Vuh and the Book of Chan K'in," in *Estudios de Cultura Maya*, vol. 10, pp. 173–209. México.

This article was written in answer to a challenge of the authenticity of the *Popol Vuh*. The comparison of the two narratives, the *Popol Vuh* of the Quiché and the *Book of Chan K'in* of the Lacandones, demonstrates that they deal with the same basic themes and employ the same symbolism and that the protagonists are the same ancient Maya deities.

This comparison permits a rather clear identification of the majority of the principal gods, their functions and their symbolic characteristics, and, in the case of the Quiché deities, permits one to associate the many alternate titles of the deities with their respective owners. Maya scholars have long recognized the value of the *Popol Vuh* as a guide to understanding Maya thought, even though this value was somewhat limited (in many cases) by our inability to distinguish clearly which of the deities may have been referred to by his or her many titles.

This study goes even a bit farther, progressing from individual identity to essential analysis of the deities in question. In a chart, the names of deities are placed on three major lines: Sun, Morning Star and Moon. A characteristic of the Peninsular cultures, not shared in the Highlands, is a class of Rain and Lightning deities, independent of the Sun and Morning Star prototypes. It appears to be an individual characteristic of Quiché culture that the Rain God (the Yucatec *Yum Chaak*, Lacandon *Mensäbäk* and Mexican *Tlaloc*) is simply another aspect or function of the principal solar deity, *Huracán* or *Heart of Heaven*.

Many of the ideas here synthesized and elaborated were first presented in Bruce, Robles y Ramos (1971). Any student of Maya cosmology who might feel doubt or skepticism regarding the identifications might prefer to consult the original documentation or the earlier publication.

Bruce S., Roberto D., Carlos Robles U., y Enriqueta Ramos Ch.

1971   *Los Lacandones 2—Cosmovisión Maya.* Departamento de Investigaciones Antropológicas, Pub. 26. I.N.A.H., S.E.P. México. (187 pp.)

This book is a comparative study of Maya traditions, based principally on the Lacandon *Libro de Chan K'in* (Bruce, 1974) and the *Popol Vuh*, the anonymous Quiché classic. A brief summary of both texts is presented, and conclusions difficult to draw from either text alone become rather clear, constituting a valuable contribution to our understanding of Maya thought and values.

While the positive contributions of this study are better expressed and elaborated in later studies (e.g., Bruce, 1978), this book is recommended for its basic methodology and logical progression to anyone who might entertain doubts regarding the validity of the often striking conclusions that may oblige the reader to reevaluate some of the views of the best-known authorities on Maya culture.

Cline, Howard

1944   "Lore and Deities of the Lacandon Indians, Chiapas, Mexico," in *Journal of American Folklore*, vol. 57, no. 224, pp. 107–115. New York.

This was one of the first studies of Lacandon tradition and mythology since the work of Tozzer (1907). From investigations in the Northern group of Lacandones, the author presents, among other things, the creation of the world and man by *Hachäkyum*; the eternal conflict between the Creator and *Kisin* (the Lord of Death); a list of the "nahuales" (*Onen*), or lineages, of the Lacandones; and a list of the names of the gods and their possible meanings.

Though well done, this work is primarily of historical value, identifying Cline as one of the discoverers of the rich tradition the Lacandones still preserve. Its limitations are due to the very brief period of field work (considerably less than a month) on which it was based and to the communication between the author and his informants in Spanish, which very few Lacandones spoke (and only poorly) at that time.

de Vos, Jan

1980   *La Paz de Dios y del Rey, La Conquista de la Selva Lacandona, 1525–1821.* Colección Ceiba, 10 Ensayo. Gobierno del Estado de Chiapas (Fonapas Chiapas). México. (524 pp.; 13 maps; photos; tables; glossary)

This conscientious and scholarly work (accessible to all Spanish readers) has many merits and only one major defect: its principal objective is to present "conclusively" the "Official Version of Maya History," which maintains that "the original Lacandones were a Chol-speaking people who were TOTALLY exterminated by 1769, so the present-day 'Lacandones' must be recent immigrants from Yucatán, as they speak 'Yucatec' (i.e., Peninsular Maya)." It should be remembered that this error, which has become the "official view," began with its formal proposal by Sir J. Eric S. Thompson in 1938. Thompson was neither a fool nor a careless scholar, and such an accusation would be nearly as unjust to many of the brilliant scholars who accept and follow his theory, as does de Vos. Recent material from contemporary Lacandon culture and tradition simply proves the theory erroneous.

The book begins (in the Prologue) by denouncing an ethnocide—the total extermination of the people originally called "Lacandones." The reconstruction of this criminal offense and the prolonged atrocity that was the Spanish conquest, presented in Chapter 9 (pp. 205–226), "La trágica historia del pueblo de los Dolores: Pacificación y exterminación de los Lacandones, 1695–1769," would appear to be possibly the best and most accurate account obtainable from the historical sources. The atrocity of this extermination is no less criminal and condemnable simply because there were a few survivors, the ancestors of the present-day Southern Lacandones.

The principal value of the book is the presentation of "new" (i.e., previously unpublished) material from the Archives of Sevilla and of the Government of Guatemala and, in the form of appendices, census lists from 1696 to 1712.

This valuable book is an excellent example of the ideal of honest and careful scholarship, in that it maintains the greater part of its value even when its initial argument and hence its conclusions are mistaken.

Duby, Gertrude
> 1944   *Los Lacandones. Su pasado y su presente.* Biblioteca Enciclo-
> pédica Popular, vol. 30. S.E.P. México.

This was one of the first works of Gertrude Duby's extensive production and is among the first of what could be called "modern writings" on the Lacandones, which began after Tozzer's work had stood as the unquestioned authority for nearly half a century. Duby's viewpoint is always ethnographic and is never excessively technical or esoteric. In recent years her interest has turned more to problems of ecology, still closely related to Lacandon culture; that is, over the centuries, Lacandon culture has become perfectly adapted to the jungle environment and would appear to be destined to perish with it.

Fisher, William Morrison
> 1973   *Towards the Reconstruction of Proto-Yucatec.* Ph.D. dissertation,
> Department of Linguistics, University of Chicago, T24462. (359
> pp.; 42 tables; 21 illustrations)

This is an extraordinarily thorough and well-done comparative study of the closely related Peninsular Maya dialects: Yucatec, Mopan, Itzá and Lacandon. It is one of the few studies that treat Northern and Southern Lacandon with the proper distinction. (This could have been done, but was not, with the various dialects of Yucatec, but the one presented may be considered representative.)

For a specialized linguistic study, the material is very clearly and simply presented (that is, without the intentional esoteric presentation that unfortunately characterizes some linguistic studies). Nonetheless, the attention and detail given to phonetics would probably not be of much interest to the general reader. Still, it should be noted that almost half the work consists of the presentation of 791 *cognate sets*, constituting a valuable source of comparative linguistic forms accessible to the specialist, beginning student, or the investigator of any other specialty who may have only an empirical knowledge of Peninsular Maya linguistic forms.

Gyles, Anna Benson, and Chloë Sayer
    1980   *Of Gods and Men: Mexico and the Mexican Indian.* British Broad-
                casting Corporation. London. (232 pp.; index; profusely illus-
                trated)

Though only a small portion of this accessible, nontechnical book is dedicated to the Lacandones, it does an admirable job of locating them historically
and culturally in the general panorama of Mesoamerica from the earliest times
to the present.

Unlike many books that attempt a scope so wide as to include "Mesoamerica,
past and present," the validity of the general view is not achieved here by
sacrificing veracity in specific cases. The Lacandones are presented in an interesting manner, as real people and without romantic distortion, in their proper
context in Mesoamerican culture and in the reality of present-day Mexico.

The book is also to be recommended for the wealth of excellent photographs
in both black-and-white and color that appropriately illustrate the text.

Landa, Fr. Diego de (1560)
    1864   *Relation des Choses de Yucatan.* Texte espagnol et traduction
                française en regard pour C. E. Brasseur de Bourbourg. Trübner &
                Co. London.
    1937   *Yucatan Before and After the Conquest.* Translation and notes by
                William Gates. Baltimore.
    1941   *Landa's Relación de las Cosas de Yucatán. A translation.* Edited
                with notes by Alfred M. Tozzer. Papers of the Peabody Museum.
                Vol. 18. Cambridge, Mass.
    1959   *Relación de las Cosas de Yucatán* (8a Ed.). Introdutión por Angel
                Ma. Garibay K. Editorial Porrua. México. (252 pp.)

Born in 1524, Landa arrived in Yucatán in 1549, became Bishop of Mérida in
1572, and died in 1579. He is best remembered for his *auto-da-fé* of July 1562,
when he burned an undetermined number of Maya codices (or traditional
books) in the plaza of Maní, as his colleague Fr. Juan de Zumarraga burned the
Mexican codices in the plaza of Texcoco. But Landa is also remembered for his
more than thirty years of missionary work, and especially for his methods of
persuading the heathen to embrace the doctrines of the gentle Jesus of Naza-
reth: hanging, burning, torture and mutilation. He was accused of atrocities
by his contemporaries and tried by the Spanish Inquisition. He was acquitted
of the charges, perhaps because his pious judges were themselves a bit less
squeamish than the French judges who imprisoned the Marquis de Sade.

It is not for us—but perhaps for the nine Lords of the Underworld—to judge
Landa's actions, but we should examine critically the person who continues to
speak to us from the pages of his *Relación*. Landa was a participant-observer in
the destruction of the classic Maya culture. His informants were classic Mayas,
including aristocrats who could read and write in the traditional Maya hieroglyphs. This valuable opportunity is a matter of historical record. The discipline of psychology is as respectable as history, however, and the textbook
characterizations of "manic-depressive" and "paranoid schizophrenic" keep
coming to mind when one reads Landa's text and attempts to visualize the man
who wrote it. There are passages of lucid, apparently valid descriptions of
traditional beliefs and practices. The description of the renewal of the idols in
the month of Pop, for example, is recognizably the same ceremony in which the

Northern Lacandones of today renew their sacred incense burners. Then suddenly, or imperceptibly, the viewpoint changes to that of a moralistic fanatic raving about the evils of idolatry. The intricate and fascinating picture beginning to take shape in the characterization of the deities that represent the values of the culture is suddenly lost when all become indiscriminately "the Devil, demons, the Malignant One." And then again, Landa will speak of the pagan priests' devotion, vigils, fasting—and weep crocodile tears for those who were his own victims. While sometimes it is all too obvious, at others it is most difficult to tell if Landa was in the manic or the depressive phase of his cycle when he wrote a given passage.

From a linguistic point of view, for example, even in the most lucid parts of his writing one can frequently find errors and deduce their cause. It is rather clear that though Landa knew a difference existed between the normal and glottalized consonants, he didn't master the pronunciation of the latter and therefore had difficulty in remembering them. We may also deduce that in at least one case, he was not certain of the distinction between his own Maya and his informant's Spanish, as the glyph he registers for Maya *ma'*, meaning "no," is really Maya *no(h)*, meaning "great."

Landa's work clearly demonstrates the principle that *one who does not respect the culture he is dealing with is not likely to recognize much of value in it*. Landa was eyewitness to things of such extraordinary value and significance that some information managed to seep through into his *Relación* despite his intentions—though usually he managed to distort the material to some degree. Interpretation is usually required.

For the student of Maya culture, to be unfamiliar with Landa's *Relación* would be as inexcusable as it would be to accept it all indiscriminately, taking it at face value.

Popol Vuh

Goetz, Delia, and Sylvanus G. Morley (from the translation of Adrián Recinos)
> 1950   *Popol Vuh, The Sacred Book of the Ancient Quiché Maya*. University of Oklahoma Press. Norman, Oklahoma. (267 pp.)

Burgess, Dora M., y Patricio Xec
> 1955   *Popol Wuj (Texto de R. P. F. Ximenez)*. Tipografía "El Noticiero Evangélico." Quetzaltenango. (320 pp.)

Edmonson, Munro
> 1971   *The Book of Counsel: The Popol Vuh of the Quiché Maya of Guatemala*. Middle American Research Institute. Tulane University. Pub. no. 35. New Orleans.

The *Popol Vuh* is a document written in the Quiché (Highland Maya) language in characters adapted from the Spanish alphabet (rather than in the hieroglyphs that were probably still in use by the Indian nobles at the time) in the middle of the sixteenth century. The names of the original Quiché author and the European who taught him the Spanish alphabet are unknown. In or about 1701, Fr. Francisco Ximenez discovered the century-and-a-half-old document in the church at Chichicastenango in Guatemala. The transcription made by Father Ximenez may have incorporated slight lexical and grammatical changes corresponding to 150 years of linguistic change in the Quiché language since the writing of the original, but an analysis of its content suggests that this original was respected most meticulously.

Besides being justly admired for its literary and poetic style, this book has been one of the most valuable sources of information regarding ancient Maya beliefs and traditions. It is as necessary and valuable for the study of Maya and Mayense cultures as would be the Old Testament for the study of European Christendom. Parts I and II of the *Popol Vuh* consist of basically the same stories, in only slightly different versions and with sometimes striking parallels, as the Lacandon traditions registered in *El Libro de Chan K'in* (Bruce, 1974). These beginning portions of the *Popol Vuh* are often referred to as "The Maya Genesis" and the allusion is quite valid. The latter portions merge with the specific history of the Highland Quiché and the genealogy of their noble families.

The parallels between the Lacandon traditions and the basic cosmology of the Quiché version are surprising, since one could reasonably expect to find greater individual divergence between Peninsular and Highland Maya groups, not to speak of the effects of over four centuries of temporal separation! The only conceivable explanation of the parallels is that both reach back to the most elemental and basic levels of the ancient Olmec-Maya traditions of cosmology and metaphysics. Obviously, having two versions of the same record is of extraordinary value, as each version provides additional possibilities for better understanding the other.

Robles Uribe, Carlos, et al.

1967   *Los Lacandones 1—Bibliografía y reseña crítica de materiales publicados.* Departamento de Investigaciones Antropológicas. I.N.A.H., S.E.P. México. (73 pp., 3 maps)

This work represents the conscientious effort of the authors to list and classify all the major works written on the Lacandones to 1966. Close to 250 titles are listed, and over 50 were selected for the section of *"Reseñas"* (annotation, description and criticism).

Though extensive, this bibliography was not as complete, even for its time, as it was intended to be. Regarding historical sources (i.e., principally colonial writings), comparison with the bibliography of de Vos (1980) will show how many important documents escaped the notice of Robles et al.

The annotations may be of interest to an in-depth study of the Lacandones, but for a more nearly complete bibliography, one should look to more recent works such as that of de Vos, the best known to us so far.

Romero Castillo, Moisés

1977   "La unidad lingüística del Maya peninsular," in *Anales del I.N.A.H.*, Epoca 8ª, Tomo 1, pp. 83–108. I.N.A.H., S.E.P. México.

We have frequently characterized the similarities and divergencies of the Peninsular Maya languages—or "dialects of the Peninsular Maya language"—by analogy to better-known linguistic groups. For example, to say that "the two Lacandon and the various Yucatecan dialects, Itzá, and Mopan are about as similar as the English dialects of Oxford, Alabama, Australia and Belize . . . or at least not quite as divergent as Spanish, Italian, Portugese and Church Latin" immediately gives the nonspecialist in linguistics a general idea of the grade of similarity and difference involved. We are aware, however, that readers with a more specialized interest in linguistics and with a greater familiarity with linguistic classification may want something far more specialized and formal.

This work is recommended for the linguist (or reader qualified to appreciate formal linguistic works) who is interested in linguistic data presented according to the methodology of modern linguistics. It should also be noted that, besides being a highly qualified academic specialist, the author is a native bilingual speaker of Spanish and the Peninsular Maya (Peto dialect) "Yucatec" languages. This obvious advantage is an additional recommendation for the scientific veracity and quality of the study.

The nonlinguist, however, might prefer something more general.

Schele, Linda
> 1982   *Maya Glyphs—The Verbs*. The University of Texas Press. Austin. (427 pp.)

This book is possibly the most valuable and interesting study on the Maya writings of classic times (i.e., "the Maya hieroglyphs") to the present. Presented with an admirable simplicity—though the Mayas themselves strove rather for the esoteric and the complex—this work affords contemporary scholars the highest level of understanding they can reach while still preserving their Occidental frame of reference. The responsible and intelligent linguistic methodology reduces the importance of which Maya dialect (Chol, in this case) is preferred as a point of departure. By analogy, if we didn't know whether the present-day descendants of the people for whom Geoffrey Chaucer wrote now spoke English, High- or Low-German, probably any one of these would present an equally valid point of departure for the study and analysis of the original linguistic form. It is far more important that the investigator's scholarship be as pertinent and thorough as is Schele's.

Schumann, Otto
> 1971   *Descripción estructural del Maya Itzá del Petén, Guatemala*. U.N.A.M., Centro de Estudios Mayas, cuaderno 6. México.
> 1973   *La lengua chol de Tila, Chiapas*. U.N.A.M., Centro de Estudios Mayas, cuaderno 8. México.

Although neither of these studies deals directly with the Lacandon dialect, they are indispensable for anyone attempting comparative studies of the Peninsular Maya dialects. In these studies the linguist can appreciate the proximity of Itzá to Southern and Northern Lacandon on the one hand, and on the other, the distinctive characteristics of Chol. Of the authors who argue that the classic Maya inscriptions of Palenque and other sites in the Central Maya Area were written in Chol, only a few such as Schele (1982) give proper consideration to the linguistic material now available for Chol; we consider Schumann the best.

Soustelle, Jacques
> 1935   "Le Totemisme des Lacandons," in *Maya Research*, vol. 2, pp. 325–344. Middle American Research Institute, Tulane University. New Orleans.

An incisive study, after Tozzer (1907), of the Lacandon *Onen*, or family lineages.

Thompson, J. Eric S.
> 1938   "Sixteenth and Seventeenth Century Reports on the Chol Mayas," in *American Anthropologist*, vol. 40, no. 9, pp. 584–603. Menasha.

In this article, Thompson presents his hypothesis that the Central Maya Lowland Area (the Usumacinta River basin) was originally inhabited by "Chol-speaking peoples." The hypothesis was firmly based on numerous historical references and affirmations by colonial Spanish writers, but it failed to evaluate the use by the Kekchí-speaking Highland Mayas who frequently served as guides for the Spanish *"Entradas"* of the word *Chol* to mean "heathen, savage." Many Peninsular Mayas also use the term *Ch'ol* with the meaning of "twisted," saying of neighbors, *"Ch'ol u t'an,"* "Twisted (is) their speech," or simply, "They are funny-talkin' varmints." This did not necessarily mean that the original inhabitants spoke the Maya dialect which today is called Chol and is spoken in Tila, Tumbalá and around Palenque. (The Chol-speaking community at Palenque was founded by Father Manuel José Calderón in the late 1700s, the inhabitants of his "pacified town" coming from the original populations of Tila and Tumbalá.)

Thompson's argument was logically sound and convincing in 1938—when little ethnolinguistic material on Lacandones was available—though it was revolutionary and presented innovations on the views of Alfred M. Tozzer, the accepted authority at that time. This article originated what is today the most widely accepted or "official" belief, that the original inhabitants of the Lacandon Jungle were Chol-speaking people, exterminated by the Spanish conquest, and that the present-day Lacandones descend from Yucatec-speaking immigrants. This idea was further elaborated by Villa Rojas, Hellmuth, de Vos, and others who, at a time when considerably more ethnolinguistic material was available, should have reexamined the premises, rather than considering (probably intuitively) that Thompson's well-earned fame as a scholar made proof of his hypothesis unnecessary.

Thompson, J. Eric S.

    1970   *Maya History and Religion.* University of Oklahoma Press. Norman, Oklahoma. (415 pp.; references; index; 17 plates; 10 figures; 3 maps)

    1975   *Historia y Religión de los Mayas.* (Spanish translation). Siglo Veintiuno Editores. México.

The book begins with a section on Maya history, Thompson's description of the total extermination of the hypothetical "original Chol-speaking Lacandones" of the Central Maya Area, followed by the repopulation of the area by apostate refugees from Yucatán, without considering (or, more fairly, without access to the knowledge) that the Lacandones who are supposed to descend from immigrants have no migration myths. The term *migration* does not appear in Thompson's index, and even the well-known migration myth (the people coming from Tula) in the *Popol Vuh* of the Highland Quiché Mayas may have been the contribution of the Toltec nobles whose ancestors infiltrated and rose to prominence in a culture from which they always remained aloof and separate.

Thompson then turns to myths, traditions and folklore from the whole Maya area, and sometimes to Highland Mexican (Aztec, Nahuatl, and other) cultures for principles valid for all Mesoamerican peoples. If his defense of a mistaken contention leaves him open to criticism, one should remember that there are very good reasons for his recognition as the foremost Maya scholar. The book contains a wealth of data from numerous Maya and Mayense ethnic groups, historic and contemporary. In this valuable contribution to the knowledge of Maya religion, which is practiced today—except for peasant agricultural cults—only by the Lacandones of the Northern group, paradoxically, the weakest part of the work is that which deals with the origin and culture of the Lacandones.

It should be remembered that the only modern work then available which represented the Lacandones' extraordinary traditional conservatism was "Jerarquía Maya entre los dioses lacandones," (Bruce, 1967). This revealed a Lacandon tradition so radically richer and more conservative than that shown in the writings of previous authors, such as Tozzer (1907), Amram (1942), Cline (1944), Baer and Baer (1952) and others, that Thompson frequently returns to these authors for alternate interpretations of the data, attempting always to minimize the cultural importance of the Lacandones. Despite his purpose, Thompson provides data from other Maya groups whose traditions more often than not show marked parallels with Lacandon traditions now available for study. This is an important contribution to Maya studies.

Tozzer, Alfred M.
   1907   *A Comparative Study of the Mayas and the Lacandones.* The Macmillan Company. London.

This book, based on studies conducted among the Northern Lacandones at the turn of the century, remained as the classic ethnography of Lacandon culture for over half a century. It was so well done for its time that it was considered "exhaustive," and its existence discouraged further studies of the Lacandones.

Though in terms of scientific anthropological methodology Tozzer's study was ahead of its time, by a half century later it was well behind the times. When Tozzer conducted his studies, it was still a time of "high adventure" for anthropological field work, and anthropologists then still had much in common with the great travelers of the century before. In romantic literature, authors were still frequently attempting to locate geographically and/or culturally the Garden of Eden, the Lost Continents of Atlantis and Mu, and the Lost Tribes of Israel; physical anthropologists were still looking for "the missing link." We should also remember that, if Tozzer's study corresponds to a time in which anthropological methodology was not as objective as it is today, Alfred M. Tozzer was one of the pioneers whose efforts produced the greater objectivity and the accumulation of working formulas and techniques that characterize the discipline today.

Tozzer's principal informant was the Lacandon *T'o'ohil* Enrique Bol García (*Kasyaho'*—*Ma'ax*—of the Spider Monkey *Onen*), the father of Old Chan K'in of Nahá. (The lake, "*pethá*," in question was nearby *Itsanohk'uh*, rather than *Nahá*.) In many cases, the differences between Tozzer's data and more recent data correspond to real changes in the cultural inventory in the years that have elapsed, as he often anticipated the requirements of an anthropological methodology that did not yet exist. In other cases, however, the disparities are due to differences in perspective that may make us feel a certain rueful envy of those less formal, adventurous days of the past.

A warning is in order. Of the linguistic forms registered in Tozzer's work, many are common to the Yucatec dialects of Peninsular Maya, but were probably not in common use among the Lacandones even at the time of the study. Today's Lacandones still obligingly try to use any Yucatec or even Tzeltal words a visitor may employ when they can understand them by context. This may please investigators at the moment, but it is often detrimental to their work.